Cross-Linguistic Studies of Imposters and Pronominal Agreement

Oxford Studies in Comparative Syntax
Richard Kayne, General Editor

The Syntax of Ellipsis: Evidence from Dutch Dialects
Jeroen Van Craenenbroeck

Mapping the Left Periphery: The Cartography of Syntactic Structures, Volume 5
Edited by Paola Benincà and Nicola Munaro

Mapping Spatial PPs: The Cartography of Syntactic Structures, Volume 6
Edited by Guglielmo Cinque and Luigi Rizzi

The Grammar of Q: Q-Particles, Wh-Movement, and Pied-Piping
Seth Cable

Comparisons and Contrasts
Richard S. Kayne

Discourse-Related Features and Functional Projections
Silvio Cruschina

Functional Heads: The Cartography of Syntactic Structures, Volume 7
Edited by Laura Brugé, Anna Cardinaletti, Giuliana Giusti, Nicola Munaro, Cecilia Poletto

Adverbial Clauses, Main Clause Phenomena and Composition of the Left Periphery: The Cartography of Syntactic Structures, Volume 8
Liliane Haegeman

Variation in Datives
Edited by Beatriz Fernández and Ricardo Etxepare

Locality
Edited by Ian Roberts and Enoch Aboh

Aspects of Split Ergativity
Jessica Coon

A Comparative Grammar of Borgomanerese
Christina Tortora

Cross-Linguistic Studies of Imposters and Pronominal Agreement
Edited by Chris Collins

Cross-Linguistic Studies of Imposters and Pronominal Agreement

EDITED BY CHRIS COLLINS

OXFORD
UNIVERSITY PRESS

OXFORD
UNIVERSITY PRESS

Oxford University Press is a department of the University of Oxford.
It furthers the University's objective of excellence in research, scholarship,
and education by publishing worldwide.

Oxford New York
Auckland Cape Town Dar es Salaam Hong Kong Karachi
Kuala Lumpur Madrid Melbourne Mexico City Nairobi
New Delhi Shanghai Taipei Toronto

With offices in
Argentina Austria Brazil Chile Czech Republic France Greece
Guatemala Hungary Italy Japan Poland Portugal Singapore
South Korea Switzerland Thailand Turkey Ukraine Vietnam

Oxford is a registered trade mark of Oxford University Press
in the UK and certain other countries.

Published in the United States of America by
Oxford University Press
198 Madison Avenue, New York, NY 10016

Library of Congress Cataloging-in-Publication Data
Cross-linguistic studies of imposters and pronominal agreement / edited by
Chris Collins.
p. cm. — (Oxford studies in comparative syntax)
ISBN 978-0-19-933686-9 (pbk. : alk. paper) — ISBN 978-0-19-933685-2
(hardcover : alk. paper) 1. Grammar, Comparative and general—Pronominals.
2. Grammar, Comparative and general—Syntax. 3. Grammar, Comparative and
general—Determiners. I. Collins, Chris, 1963- editor of compilation. II. Series:
Oxford studies in comparative syntax.
P279.C76 2014
415'.5—dc23
2013031896

9 8 7 6 5 4 3 2 1

Printed in the United States of America on acid-free paper

Contents

Acknowledgments

I would like to thank Paul Postal for reading over all the papers in this volume and providing valuable feedback to me and the authors.

I have benefited from presenting parts of the introduction to audiences at the Guangdong University of Foreign Studies (2011) and the Department of Linguistics, Harvard University (2012).

I thank Hallie Stebbins of OUP for ushering my project through the publication process.

Lastly, I am grateful to Eve Tauss for preparing the index.

Contributors

CHRIS COLLINS, Department of Linguistics, New York University

SATARUPA DAS, Department of Linguistics, Rutgers University

RACHEL DUDLEY, Department of Linguistics, University of Maryland

DALINA KALLULLI, Department of Linguistics, University of Vienna

DANIEL KAUFMAN, Endangered Language Alliance

VIOLETA VÁZQUEZ ROJAS, Centro de Estudios Lingüísticos y Literarios, El Colegio de México

EMILIO SERVIDIO, Dipartimento di Scienze Sociali, Politiche e Cognitive, Università degli Studi di Siena

EINAR FREYR SIGURÐSSON, Department of Linguistics, University of Pennsylvania

GABRIELA SOARE, Department of Linguistics, University of Geneva

CHYAN-AN ARTHUR WANG, Department of Applied Linguistics and Language Studies, Chung Yuan Christian University, Taiwan

JIM WOOD, Department of Linguistics, Yale University

Cross-Linguistic Studies of Imposters and Pronominal Agreement

1

Introduction

CHRIS COLLINS

1. Data

The primary data studied in Collins and Postal (2012) represent alternations in pronominal phi-feature values (person, number, gender) that do not correlate with any truth conditional differences. Some examples are given below:

(1) a. In this reply, [the present authors]$_1$ (= the writers of the reply) attempt to defend ourselves$_1$/themselves$_1$ against the scurrilous charges which have been made.
b. [This reporter$_1$ (= speaker) and his$_1$ son]$_2$ are proud of ourselves$_2$/themselves$_2$.
c. Your$_1$ Majesty should praise yourself$_1$/herself$_1$.
d. [Every one of us]$_1$ thinks we$_1$/they$_1$ are intelligent.
e. I am a teacher who$_1$ takes care of myself$_1$/himself$_1$.
f. Would [your$_1$/her$_1$ (= addressee) Majesty]$_1$ like her tea on the veranda?

In (1a), the reflexive can either be 3PL, agreeing in phi-feaure values with the antecedent *the present authors*, or 1PL. In (1b), the reflexive can be either 3PL, agreeing with the antecedent *[This reporter and his son]* or 1PL. In (1c), the reflexive can either be 3SG, agreeing in phi-feature values with the antecedent *Your Majesty*, or 2SG. In (1d), the pronominal subject of the embedded clause can be 1PL or 3PL (if there are only males in the domain of quantification, 3M.SG is also possible). In (1e), the reflexive can be either 3SG, agreeing with the relative pronoun antecedent *who*, or 1SG. In (1f), the possessive pronoun can be either 3SG or 2SG, in both cases denoting the addressee.

The remarkable property of these alternations is that they do not seem to correlate with differences in meaning. For example, the truth conditions of the two variants of (1a) are identical.

With the exception of Kratzer (2009), whose analysis of fake indexicals overlaps with the account that Collins and Postal (2012) give of examples like (1e), I know of no other linguistic work that treats the facts above. In particular, there is no existing semantic treatment of these facts that can be compared to the account given in Collins and Postal (2012).

Corbett (2006: 217) discusses a large amount of data that he classifies under the rubrics "syntactic agreement" and "semantic agreement". For example, consider the use of *committee* in British English:

(2) a. The committee has decided.
 b. The committee have decided.

Corbett (2006: 155) describes these data as follows:

> I shall use the well-established terms **syntactic** and **semantic** agreement. In the most straightforward cases syntactic agreement (sometimes called "agreement *ad formam*," "formal agreement" or "grammatical agreement") is agreement consistent with the form of the controller (*the committee* has *decided*). Semantic agreement (or "agreement *ad sensum*," "notional agreement," "logical agreement" or "synesis") is agreement consistent with the meaning (*the committee* have *decided*).

In the framework of Collins and Postal (2012), all the pronominal agreement options described in (1) are cases of syntactic agreement, as we shall see below. There is no semantic agreement distinct from syntactic agreement. In fact, a purely syntactic account of the data in (2) can also be given (see Dikken 2001).

2. Pronominal Agreement Condition

Syntacticians have recognized that pronouns agree with antecedents. Some quotes illustrating this are given below:

(3) a. Sag, Wasow, and Bender (2003: 208)
 The Pronominal Agreement Condition (PAC)
 Co-indexed NPs agree.
 b. Lasnik and Uriagereka (1988: 47)
 An anaphor must agree in syntactic features with its antecedent.
 c. Carnie (2007: 11)
 An anaphor must agree in person, gender, and number with its antecedent.
 d. Payne and Huddleston (2002: 486)
 Personal pronouns agree with their antecedent in person and number; in the third person singular, they also agree in gender.

None of these conditions can handle the facts in (1). For example, consider (1a). Carnie's formulation successfully predicts that the 3PL reflexive *themselves* should be acceptable, since its antecedent is 3PL. But without some further assumption, it is not clear how to allow the 1PL *ourselves.* Collins and Postal (2012) assume that there is a null DP called AUTHOR in the left periphery of the clause (see section 3). On this assumption, we can successfully capture the facts in (1a) if we assume that the reflexive has two different antecedents (*the present authors* and AUTHOR), and that the reflexive can agree with either one of them. Crucially, we must modify Carnie's formulation to allow agreement with one of several antecedents. So, instead of saying "with its antecedent," we need to say "with some antecedent."

Given this issue and many others that come up in the analysis of the sentences of (1), Collins and Postal (2012) propose the following condition to replace the conditions in (3):

(4) Pronominal Agreement Condition
If P is a non-expletive pronominal, then for all phi-features F of P for which P is not inherently valued, P agrees in F with some source.

This condition incorporates a number of innovations over earlier proposals. First, putting aside expletive pronouns and a few minor cases (singular-*they* and Nurse-*we*) where pronouns seem to have inherent feature values, all pronominal phi-feature values are due to agreement.

Second, pronouns can agree with any one of their antecedents, as in the example in (1a), or with some other source. A source is any DP that a pronoun can agree with in terms of phi-feature values. We give a full definition in section 5 below, where we show that there are a number of alternative (non-antecedent) sources from which a pronoun can obtain phi-feature values. To understand (3), it is crucial to note that all antecedents are sources, but not all sources are antecedents.

Third, a single pronoun can agree with several different sources. Hence, the NUM feature of a pronoun P can be valued by one source (a particular DP), and the PERSON feature of the same pronoun P can be valued by a different source (a different DP). In both cases, P agrees in F with some source, but there is not a single source which provides all the features that P agrees with. For reasons of space, I do not discuss this third innovation here (see Collins and Postal 2012, Chapter 14, for much more discussion of so-called split agreement).

3. Theoretical Preliminaries

Before showing how to account for the data in (1) in the system of Collins and Postal (2012), I will discuss a few background notions.

First, there is a relation of antecedence between DP nodes. Antecedence roughly corresponds to co-indexation in standard Principles and Parameters theory, the most important difference being that antecedence is asymmetric (X antecedes Y, but not vice versa). Antecedence does not require a c-command relation (just like co-indexing does not require a c-command relation), and hence antecedence is not the same relation as binding (c-command plus co-indexation).

When a pronoun has several antecedents, there are two that are of special importance: the immediate antecedent and the ultimate antecedent. For example, in the following sentence, the immediate antecedent of the reflexive is *he* and the ultimate antecedent is *John*.

(5) John_1 said that he_1 likes himself_1.

Second, all non-expletive pronouns have antecedents. The assumption that all pronouns have antecedents sharply distinguishes the system of Collins and Postal (2012) from all mainstream approaches in syntax and semantics which assume that some (non-expletive) pronouns do not have antecedents (as in Lasnik's famous example of an unpopular man leaving a party, and somebody saying "Well, he's left.").

Third, there are null DPs AUTHOR and ADDRESSEE in the left periphery of the clause encoding indexical information about the context in which the sentence is used. The relevant structure is illustrated below:

(6) $[[_{\text{DP}}\ \text{AUTHOR}]_1\ [_{\text{DP}}\ \text{ADDRESSEE}]_2$ [Mary hates me_1.]]

Note that even though there are no second person pronouns in (6), ADDRESSEE is still present, since ADDRESSEE is the syntactic way of encoding the fact that the sentence is addressed to someone.

AUTHOR is either 1SG or 1PL and ADDRESSEE is either 2SG or 2PL. Neither AUTHOR nor ADDRESSEE are pronouns, and hence do not obtain their phi-features values by agreement.

The structure in (6) is underspecified. There are two ways in principle that the details could be filled out: an approach based on an expanded left periphery, and an approach based on a null performative verb.

In the first approach, there would be special functional projections (Prt1 = AUTHOR participant, Prt2 = ADDRESSEE participant) in the left periphery of the clause containing AUTHOR and ADDRESSEE. The projection introducing AUTHOR is Prt1P, and the projection introducing ADDRESSEE is Prt2P. The hierarchical relation of these projections to ForceP, TopP, FocP, and FinP is unclear (on the expanded left periphery, see Rizzi 1997). In other words, it is unclear whether PrtP dominates ForceP, or vice versa. This approach is sketched below:

(7)

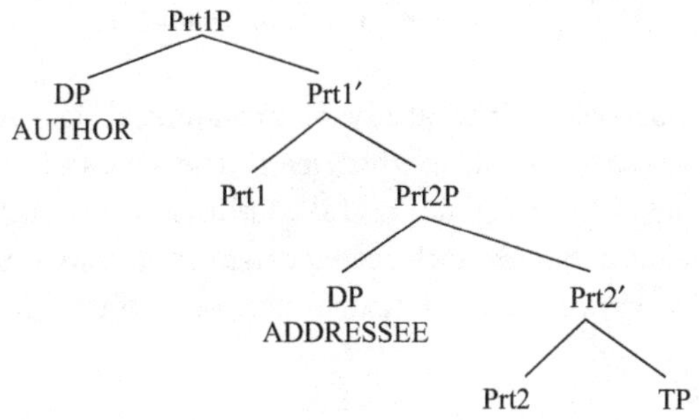

An alternative, based on Ross (1970), is that the DPs AUTHOR and ADDRESSEE are arguments of a covert performative clause. The main verb of such a clause is V_{PERF}. The ADDRESSEE argument is introduced by APPLP, and the AUTHOR argument is introduced by vP.

(8)

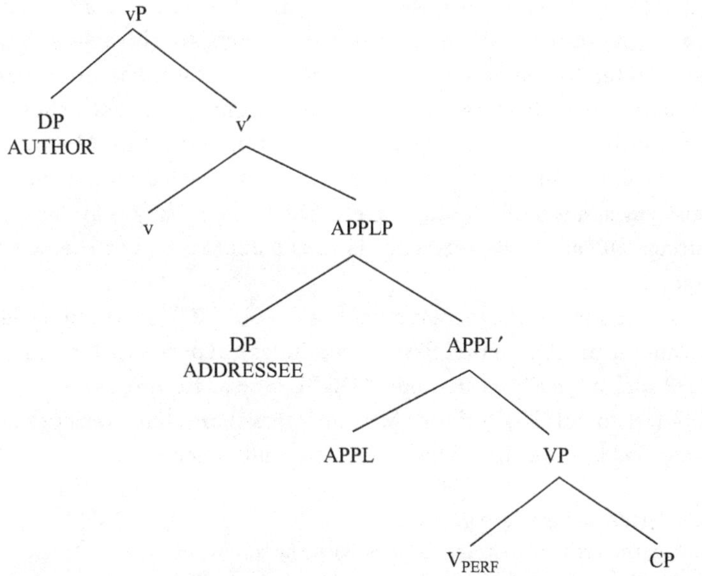

Many details of this structure remain unresolved. For example, what is the nature of the null verb in (8)? Should it be *say* or something more general? Also, are there functional projections dominating the performative vP (e.g., TP or CP)? I will not attempt to answer these questions here. I will adopt the approach based on the expanded left periphery for convenience below.

4. Imposters and Camouflage DPs

Some third person DPs, such as *Daddy, yours truly, the undersigned, the present authors, this reporter,* can be used to refer to the speaker. Similarly, some third person DPs, such as *Madam, the General, little Johnnie*, can be used to refer to the addressee. These DPs are referred to as imposters:

(9) An imposter is a notionally *n* person DP which is grammatically *m* person, $n \neq m$.

The importance of imposters for the study of pronominal agreement is that when they are antecedents they often give rise to the kinds of pronominal phi-feature alternations seen in (1) (as in (1a)). Collins and Postal (2012) propose that such ambivalent behavior with respect to pronominal agreement should be understood in terms of a null indexical pronoun contained within the imposter.

(10) An imposter contains a covert indexical pronoun.

So an imposter like *the present author* will have embedded within it a null 1SG pronoun (see (13) below).

Camouflage DPs are similar to imposters in terms of pronominal agreement, but are defined by the presence of an overt pronominal possessor. Camouflage DPs such as *your honor, your majesty, your grumpiness* are third person DPs that are used to refer to the addressee. Forms such as *my honor, my majesty,* and *my grumpiness* with a first person possessor are impossible with these camouflage DPs. The ACC (Ass-Camouflage Construction; see Collins, Moody, & Postal 2008) is possible with a wider range of possessors, including non-pronominal possessors: *my ass, your ass, Putin ass*, etc. The form *my lady* is an imposter, not a camouflage DP, since the reference is to the addressee, but the possessor is first person.

An imposter such as *the present author* takes AUTHOR as its antecedent, precisely because it contains a null first person indexical pronoun. Similarly, a camouflage DP such as *your majesty* takes ADDRESSEE as its antecedent.

Collins and Postal (2012) claim that imposters share characteristics with pronouns modified by appositive DPs, which they dub precursors:

(11) a. I, Nixon, am going to get even.
b. We, the present writers, disagree with the following points.
c. We, the undersigned, propose a number of improvements.
d. I, your faithful correspondent, should write more often.
e. You, Madam, should not try to deceive us.
f. You, my lord, can certainly win the tournament.

Such precursors are parallel in interpretation to imposters:

(12) a. Nixon is going to get even.
b. The present writers disagree with the following points.
c. The undersigned propose a number of improvements.
d. Your faithful correspondent will hereafter write more often.
e. Madam should not try to deceive us.
f. My lord can certainly win the tournament.

In general, precursor structures appear to provide the correct semantics for imposters. That is, imposters have non-third person denotations, and corresponding precursors have visible pronominal components with the right non-third person denotations. So each imposter in (12) is equivalent in denotation to its corresponding precursor in (11). Moreover, imposters have a third person lexical component that matches the predicate nominal of the corresponding precursor. And the nonrestrictive meaning provided by the precursor predicate nominal seems to represent as well the meaning of the third person component of an imposter.

Given the parallelism between imposters and precursors, Collins and Postal (2012) develop an account in which imposters are derived from underlying precursor structures. The analysis is shown below for the imposter *Nixon*, which is derived from the precursor *I, Nixon*:

(13)

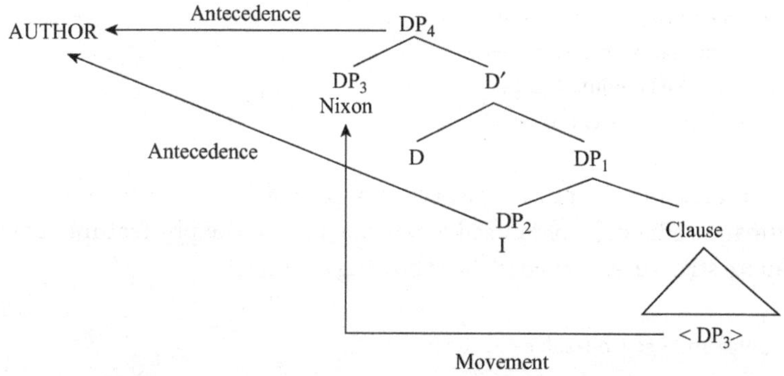

In this fully binary branching structure, the appositive DP_3 moves up to the specifier of a higher DP_4. A DP is moved up, and not just an NP, because possessed DPs like *my lady* can serve as imposters. From its raised position, the appositive DP_3 determines the phi-feature values of the whole imposter (DP_4). There are two ways that determination could work. First, via Spec-Head agreement, the moved secondary DP_3 agrees with the head D_4. Then, since D_4 is the head of DP_4, DP_4 inherits the phi-feature values of D_4. Second, it might simply be that since DP_3 is the highest DP in the structure with specified phi-feature values, the phi-features of DP_3 are the only ones available internal to DP_4.

In the remainder of this introduction, we will refer to DP_2 as the core or notional component of the imposter and DP_4 as the shell of the imposter.

5. Sources

As mentioned above, a pronoun can agree with an antecedent or some other source. A major claim of Collins and Postal (2012) is that in some cases a pronoun may agree with non-antecedent DPs. The list of sources argued for in Collins and

Postal (2012) (no doubt to be expanded in later work) is given below in (14) and (18). The role that these sources play in determining pronominal agreement will be discussed in detail in the next section.

In order to define the notion of *source*, we first define *primary source*, and then give a recursive definition of *source*. The recursive definition will allow us to account for the fact that there can be a long chain of source relations, where the pronoun agrees with any of the elements in that chain.

A primary source is a direct source of phi-feature values of a pronoun. For example, an immediate antecedent is a primary source. In the example in (5), the immediate antecedent of the reflexive is *he*, and the reflexive agrees directly with its immediate antecedent. The immediate antecedent is a primary source for the reflexive.

(14) Definition: *primary source*
A is a *primary source* for B if and only if:
a. A immediately antecedes B, or:
b. A is a key conjunct of B, or:
c. A shares a lexical basis with B.

(14a) represents the prototypical case of pronominal agreement with an immediate antecedent. (14b) is used when calculating the phi-feature values of a coordinate structure. Consider the following example:

(15) John and I saw ourselves in the mirror.

The 1SG pronoun *I* is the key conjunct of the coordinate structure, and hence the pronoun is a primary source for the coordinate structure. Intuitively, the key conjunct is the conjunct with the highest person feature value of all the conjuncts. Crucially, imposters such as *Daddy* and *yours truly* count as having 1SG feature values for the purpose of determining the key conjunct (see Collins and Postal 2012, Chapter 9, for precise definitions).

(14c) is used in the case of relative clauses and also to account for pronominal agreement with camouflage DPs (e.g., *your majesty*). Consider the following examples:

(16) a. The man who I saw
b. your majesty

In (16a), the DP headed by *the* and the relative pronoun *who* share a lexical basis (the noun *man*). In (16b), the pronoun *your* and the DP *your majesty* share a lexical basis (the noun part of the DP *your*; see Collins and Postal 2012: 85). The intuition in both cases is that there is a single noun that is being shared by two functional projections (see Collins and Postal 2012: 59 for a precise definition).

A secondary source is any kind of source that is not a primary source.

(17) Definition: *secondary source*
A is a *secondary source* of B if and only if A is a source of B and not a primary source of B.

A secondary source is an indirect source of phi-feature values of a pronoun, since secondary sources are defined in terms of primary sources. Secondary sources can transmit phi-features to a pronoun via an intermediate primary source. In the definition below, sources are defined recursively in terms of primary source (the base case (18a)) and the chaining together of the various source relations (the recursive case (18b)).

(18) Definition: *source*
A is a *source* for B if and only if:
a. A is a primary source for B, or:
b. there is a C which is a source for B, and:
   (i) A is a primary source for C, or:
   (ii) C is a predicate nominal and A is C's subject, or:
   (iii) C is a partitive DP and A is C's set DP.

(18bi) allows the chaining together of immediate antecedent relations. In example (5), *he* is the immediate antecedent of *himself*, and *John* is the immediate antecedent of *he*, so *John* is a (secondary) source for *himself*.

(18bii) says that if a predicate nominal is a source of a pronoun, the subject of the predicate nominal is also a source for the pronoun. Consider the following example from Collins and Postal (2012: 166):

(19) If you were a shirt, it/you wouldn't sell for very much.

The immediate antecedent of the main clause subject pronoun *it/you* is the DP *a shirt*. The pronoun can agree in phi-features with the immediate antecedent (3SG), or with the subject of the predicate nominal (2SG).

(18biii) says that if a partitive DP (such as *every one of us*) is a source of a pronoun, the set DP of the partitive (*us* in this case) is a source for the pronoun (see illustrations below).

6. Some Examples

In this section, I will show how the system applies to the examples in (1). Consider first (1a), shortened and repeated below:

(20) The present authors_1 (= the writers of the reply) attempt to defend ourselves_1/themselves_1.

A structural representation of this sentence is given in (21). I follow the expanded left periphery approach outlined in section 3 above. In the framework of Collins and Postal (2012), every sentence will have both AUTHOR and ADDRESSEE, but for the sake of brevity, I only include AUTHOR in the representation in (21). Also, for the sake of brevity, I do not include the vP/VP distinction, nor do I indicate vP internal subjects. In addition, the full structure of the imposter is not given (see (13)).

(21)

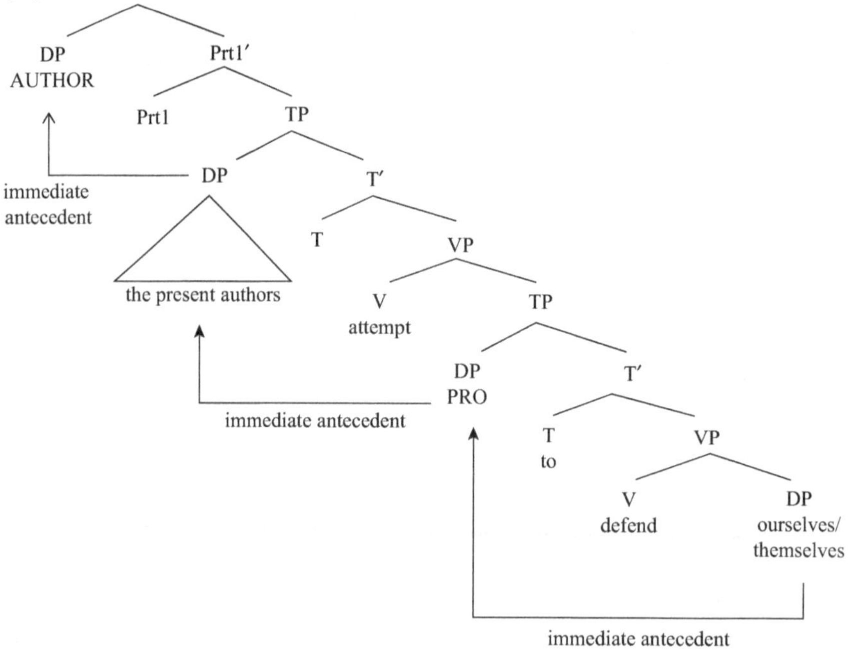

In this example, the immediate antecedent of the reflexive is PRO, and the immediate antecedent of PRO is *the present authors*. The immediate antecedent of the *present authors* is AUTHOR (which is plural). Therefore, there is a chain of DPs linked by antecedence relations: <AUTHOR, the present authors, PRO, ourselves/themselves>. Since AUTHOR itself has no antecedent, we call AUTHOR the ultimate antecedent of the reflexive. Note that the reflexive has three different antecedents, one of which is the immediate antecedent (PRO) and one of which is the ultimate antecedent (AUTHOR).

The immediate antecedent of the reflexive is a primary source by (14a). The ultimate antecedent is a source by the recursive clause in (18bi). Since both the immediate antecedent and ultimate antecedent are sources, the Pronominal Agreement Condition in (4) allows agreement with either, accounting for the pronominal agreement alternation in (20).

In the following example, repeated from (1b), the subject is a coordinate structure:

(22) [this reporter$_1$ (= speaker) and his$_1$ son]$_2$ are proud of ourselves$_2$/themselves$_2$.

The structure of (22) is given below in (23). I do not represent the internal structure of DP coordination.

(23)

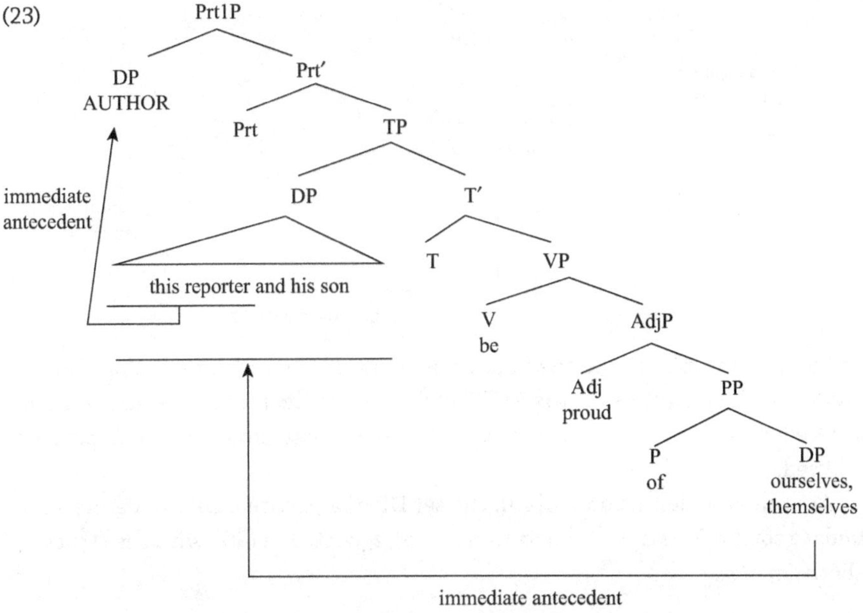

One important feature of this example is that *this reporter* simultaneously determines 3SG agreement on the possessor pronoun *his* and plays the role of a conjunct in a coordinate structure that is the immediate antecedent of a 1PL reflexive. So *this reporter* has truly ambivalent behavior, determining in the same sentence first person and third person pronominal agreement.

Since *this reporter* is the key conjunct of the coordinate structure, it is a primary source of the coordinate structure by (14b). Since AUTHOR is the immediate antecedent of *this reporter*, it is also a source for the coordinate structure. The coordinate structure is plural, but can agree in person with either *this reporter* (third person) or AUTHOR (first person). Therefore, the coordinate structure can either be 1PL or 3PL, determining the two possibilities for the reflexive.

Consider now (1c), repeated in (24), an example with a camouflage DP. The structure is given in (25). I do not represent the internal structure of the camouflage DP. Also, note that (24), like all sentences, will have both an AUTHOR and ADDRESSEE. Only ADDRESSEE is represented for brevity's sake.

(24) [Your$_1$ Majesty]$_1$ should praise yourself$_1$/herself$_1$.

(25)

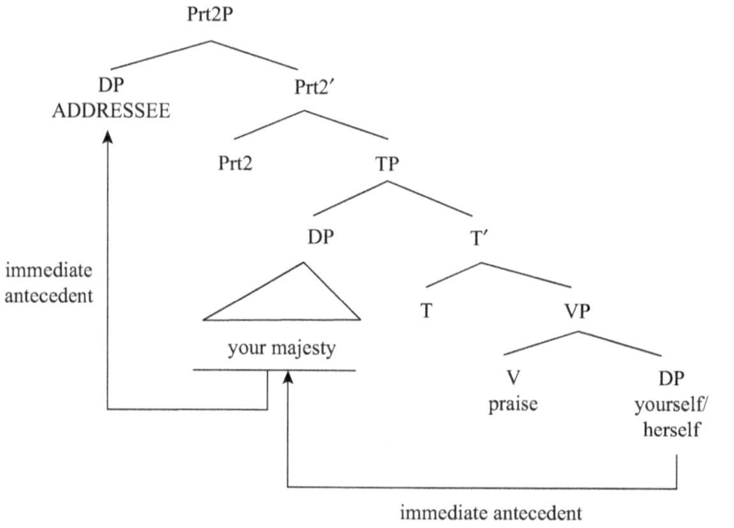

In this example, the immediate antecedent of the reflexive is *Your Majesty* and the ultimate antecedent is ADDRESSEE. Since the immediate and ultimate antecedent are sources, by condition (4), pronominal agreement with either is allowed.

According to definition (18biii), the set DP of a partitive DP can define a secondary source. This case is illustrated in (1d), repeated in (26), with the structure shown in (27).

(26) [Every one of us]$_1$ thinks we$_1$/they$_1$ are intelligent.

(27)

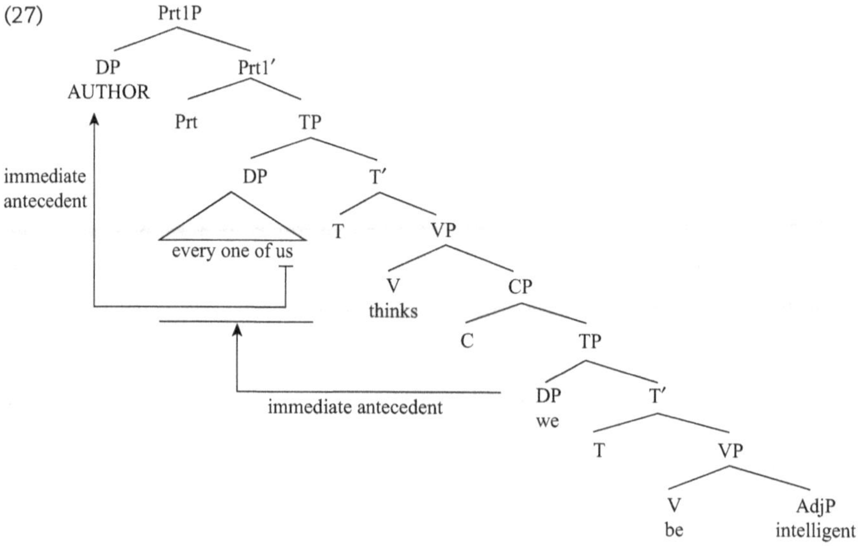

The DP *every one of us* is both the ultimate antecedent and immediate antecedent of the embedded clause subject pronoun *we/they*. In this case, AUTHOR is not the ultimate antecedent of the subject pronoun. If AUTHOR were the ultimate antecedent, then the pronoun would not have a bound variable interpretation; rather it would simply refer to the people that AUTHOR refers to. Similarly, the set DP *us* is not the antecedent of the embedded clause subject pronoun *we/they*. If the set DP were the antecedent, once again there would be no bound variable interpretation.

Crucially, even though the set DP *us* of the partitive DP is not an antecedent of the embedded clause subject pronoun, it counts as a source for the pronoun by (18biii) since the set DP is a source for any pronoun that the partitive DP is a source for. Therefore, the pronoun can agree with either *every one of us* (yielding *he*, if all the people in the denotation of *we* are male), or the set DP (yielding *we*). In the case of singular-*they*, the third person feature value comes from the DP *every one of us* and the plural feature value from the set DP *us* (a case of split agreement allowed by (4)).

In the relative clause case of (1e), repeated in (28), the immediate and ultimate antecedent of the reflexive is the relative pronoun *who*, which is 3SG (as shown by the form of the verb *takes*; compare to *I take*)

(28) I am a teacher who_1 takes care of $myself_1$/$himself_1$.

(29)

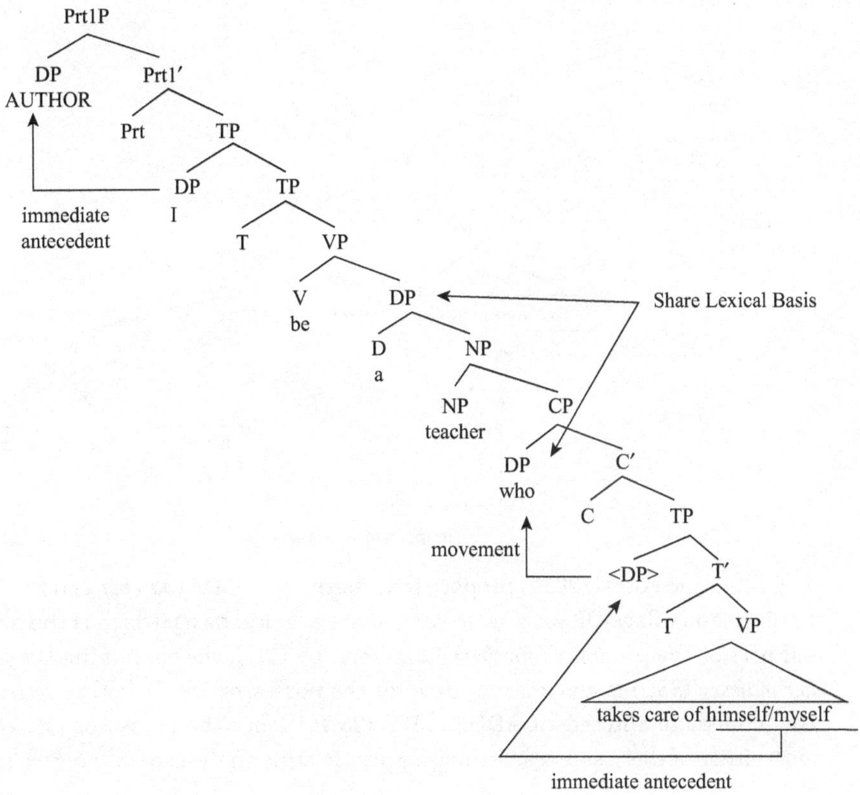

According to Collins and Postal (2012), *who* and *[a teacher who. . . .]* share a lexical basis, which makes *[a teacher who . . .]* a primary source for *who* (see Collins and Postal 2012 for specific analyses of relative clauses consistent with this assumption). Therefore, by (18bi), the DP *[a teacher who. . . .]* (3SG) is also a source for the reflexive. Lastly, the DP *I* is the subject of the predicate nominal. Hence by (18bii), *I* (1SG) is also a source for the reflexive. Therefore, by (4), the reflexive can agree with any of these sources (in addition to AUTHOR, which is the immediate antecedent of the subject *I*), accounting for the pronoun alternation.

Of these sources, only *who* is an antecedent of the reflexive. In particular, AUTHOR is not an antecedent of the reflexive. Semantically, the reflexive is a bound variable in a predicate modifying the head noun of the relative clause. There is no reason to think that there is an antecedence relation between the reflexive and AUTHOR.

In the last example (1f), repeated in (30), the immediate antecedent of *your/her* is ADDRESSEE, which is 2SG. So there is a real mystery as to why *her* is also possible.

(30) Would [your$_1$/her$_1$ (= addressee) Majesty]$_1$ like her tea on the veranda?

In the representation, I leave out inessential issues like subject-aux inversion.

(31)

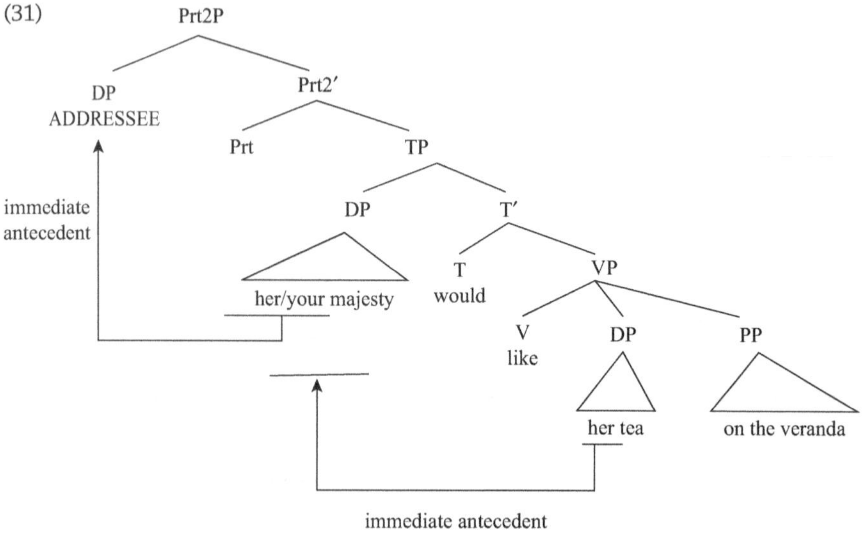

Collins and Postal (2012) propose that the possessor DP *your/her* and the containing camouflage DP *your/her majesty* share a lexical basis (which is the nominal part of the pronoun *your/her*). Therefore, by (14c), the containing DP *your/her majesty* (3SG) is a primary source for the possessor DP. The other source is the immediate antecedent ADDRESSEE (2SG). Hence the possessor can agree with either of these sources. Strong support for this analysis of (30) comes from systematic differences between different types of camouflage constructions (see Collins and Postal 2012, Chapter 17).

7. Summary

From these examples it is easy to see that the conditions in (3) are factually inadequate. The two biggest problems are that (a) they do not allow agreement with one of several different antecedents (when there is more than one antecedent and those antecedents differ in phi-feature values), (b) they only allow agreement with antecedents (and not other sources), and (c) they do not allow split agreement (not discussed here; see Collins and Postal 2012, Chapter 14). As the examples in (1) show, it is often possible for a pronoun to agree with one of several sources, and these sources do not necessarily have to be antecedents.

8. Summary of Chapters

The chapters of this volume provide a rich set of cross-linguistic data, illustrating how verbal and pronominal agreement works with imposters (and in the other constructions listed in (1) above). The chapters also provide insightful syntactic alternatives to the syntactic proposals of Collins and Postal (2012), paving the way for fruitful discussion and hypothesis testing in future years. In this section, I will highlight the empirical and/or theoretical contributions of each chapter. In later sections, I will show how the data described in these chapters fit into a cross-linguistic typology of pronomial agreement.

The chapters of this volume were written by my students and colleagues, who were for the most part New York University students or visitors to NYU. No attempt has been made to seek out a cross-linguistically balanced set of languages for this volume. For example, a contribution on Japanese or Korean, or on the agreement-rich Bantu languages would have been quite useful. There are also questions that arise about what would happen with pronominal agreement with imposters in a language with indexical shift (see Collins and Postal 2012: 256–257). All these studies must await the interest of future scholars.

In Chapter 2, Satarupa Das investigates imposters in Bangla. Her main conclusion is that both verbal and pronominal agreement are always determined by the third person imposter shell. She gives an explanation of this fact by appealing to the Homogeneity Principle of Collins and Postal (2012: 145). Her claim is that subject-verb agreement is subject to the Homogeneity Principle, just as pronouns are.

Rachel Dudley, in Chapter 3, investigates imposters in Spanish. She obtained her rich data set using a questionnaire with 68 sentences administered to five Spanish speakers from various dialects. Her main empirical conclusion is that plural imposters in Spanish freely allow 1PL subject-verb agreement. In this way, Spanish differs from Italian and Bellinzonese, which do not allow 1PL verbal agreement with plural imposter subjects.

Dalina Kallulli's contribution, Chapter 4, shows that in Albanian singular imposters can trigger 1SG subject-verb agreement. Albanian is the only language in our sample with this property. Kallulli's contribution is the only one to take up the interaction of imposters with epithets. As Collins and Postal (2012: 137) show, imposters cannot be the antecedents of epithets. Surprisingly, this constraint does not hold (under certain conditions) in Albanian.

Daniel Kaufman, in Chapter 5, discusses the syntax of imposters in Indonesian. He focuses on the parallelism between imposters and first and second person pronouns with respect to word order in the patient voice. As Kaufman notes, in the patient voice, first and second person pronouns are proclitics on the verb: 1/2=V. Surprisingly, imposters also appear preceding the verb in the patient voice. From this, Kaufman concludes that imposters provide a strong argument for the syntactic view of imposters over a notional view (for a discussion of the notional view, see Collins and Postal 2012, Chapter 2). If imposters were simply third person DPs that happened to refer to the speaker or addressee, it is unclear why they would pattern syntactically like first and second person pronouns with respect to word order in the patient voice.

In Chapter 6, Emilio Servidio gives an overview of verbal and pronominal agreement with imposters in Italian. One of his important conclusions is that the imposters *il sottoscritto* ("the undersigned") and *il qui presente* ("the here present") behave differently from the others in terms of verbal and pronominal agreement. A coordinate structure with one of these two imposters as a conjunct admits 1PL subject-verb agreement. He dubs these *deep imposters*, since "they display agreement with the most deeply embedded layer of the structure." The special behavior of "the undersigned" is a recurrent theme in this volume, showing up in Wood and Sigurðsson's contribution on Icelandic (Chapter 9) as well. Curiously, camouflage DPs ("your majesty") behave like deep imposters in Italian, a fact that Servidio explains here.

Gabriela Soare, in Chapter 7, gives a fine-grained comparison of French and Romanian. One of her discoveries is that while 1PL subject-verb agreement is generally impossible with a plural imposter in both French and Romanian, it becomes much better if the subject is modified by the expression "here present" ("The authors here present have decided to get together."). She also documents widespread matching effects between verbal agreement and pronominal agreement, operative in both languages.

In Chapter 8, Arthur Wang discusses pronominal agreement with imposters in Mandarin. His main empirical contribution is that ". . . the pronominal agreement is never third person with Mandarin imposters. In other words, the agreement is always in accordance with the notional person." Wang explains this difference from English in terms of the structure of imposters. In Mandarin, according to Wang, imposters are complex DPs where a first or second person pronoun occupies D, and the third person expression (e.g., "teacher") occupies Spec DP. This structure explains why Mandarin imposters can only antecede non-third person pronouns. Wang provides strong support for his analysis from the distribution of overt first and second person pronouns occurring (optionally) immediately to the right of expressions like "teacher" when they are used as imposters: [teacher I]. Wang points out that the variation that one finds between Mandarin and English is natural on the syntactic view of imposters. Different syntactic structures give rise to different patterns of pronominal agreement. On a notional view of imposters, where they are simply regular third person DPs with the semantic/pragmatic property of referring to the speaker or addressee, it is less clear what could account for such cross-linguistic variation.

Jim Wood and Einar Freyr Sigurðsson, in Chapter 9, discuss imposters in Icelandic. Given the rich system of subject-verb agreement in Icelandic, their primary goal ". . . is to refine our understanding of the role of verbal agreement in pronoun/reflexive antecedent relations." The authors give a careful summary of the interaction between subject-verb agreement and pronominal agreement, discussing pronominal agreement in ECM constructions and cases of syncretism in subject-verb agreement. One of their many empirical discoveries about Icelandic is that when subject-verb agreement is first person, then the subject can only antecede a first person pronoun. When subject-verb agreement is third person, then in certain cases, the subject can antecede either first or third person pronouns. We return to this discovery below.

In Chapter 10, Violeta Vázquez Rojas discusses a case of an indefinite imposter in Spanish. She then gives an account of why such indefinite imposters are exceptional. Imposters are almost always definite in form (e.g., having a definite article or demonstrative).

9. A Preliminary Typology of Imposters

The above discussion of (1) has revealed previously unexplored dimensions to the analysis of pronominal agreement in English. The ingredients of that analysis include the Pronominal Agreement Condition in (4), primary sources (immediate antecedents, key conjuncts, DPs with a shared lexical basis), secondary sources (subjects of predicate nominals, set DPs, ultimate antecedents), imposters, and camouflage DPs. A natural question is whether the Pronominal Agreement Condition stands up cross-linguistically. In other words, can the system of Collins and Postal (2012) shed light on interesting patterns of cross-linguistic variation? And conversely, can cross-linguistic variation in pronominal agreement support or lead us to modify the main assumptions of Collins and Postal (2012)? This volume is devoted to answering these questions.

In the remaining part of this chapter, I will summarize some results from the contributions to this volume. Based on these results, I will propose a tentative typology of pronominal agreement systems. I will also point out some recurrent issues that deserve further investigation.

In Arthur Wang's contribution on Mandarin, it is shown that pronominal agreement with an imposter is always with the notional component, no matter whether the imposter is singular, plural, or coordinated. Mandarin does not have subject-verb agreement.

(32) *Laoshi$_1$ kuai yao shiqu {*ta$_1$/wo$_1$} de naixing le*
teacher almost going.to lose s/he I POSS patience ASP
"Teacher$_1$ (= I) is going to lose {*his$_1$/ *her$_1$/my$_1$} patience."

Indonesian, as discussed by Daniel Kaufman, shows a similar pattern, where pronominal agreement is only with the notional component. Once again, Indonesian does not have subject-verb agreement.

(33) *bapak mau mem-baca buku-ku dulu*
father want AV-read book-1SG.GEN first
"Father wants to read his book first."

In Satarupa Das's contribution on Bengali (Chapter 2), it is shown that both subject-verb agreement and pronominal agreement with an imposter is always with the third person shell, no matter whether the imposter is singular, plural, or coordinated.

(34) *ei sharma tar/*amar dhoirjya hara-te cholech-e*
this guy his/my patience lose-INF go-3
"This guy is about to lose his patience."

These three languages are strict languages, where agreement (pronominal agreement or subject-verb agreement) does not alternate between the notional and grammatical features of the imposter. The rest of the languages have a more ambivalent behavior, in that both subject-verb agreement and pronominal agreement can vary. Hence we have the initial typology, first suggested in Collins and Postal (2012: 225):

(35) *The Pronominal Agreement Parameter*
If an imposter A immediately antecedes a pronominal P, then:
a. P agrees only with A.
(Bengali)
b. P agrees only with A's ultimate antecedent.
(Mandarin and Indonesian)

c. P agrees with A or A's ultimate antecedent.
(English, Spanish, French, Romanian, Albania, Italian, Icelandic, Bellinzonese, Brazilian Portuguese)

We will refine this typology in the next sections, showing that the class of languages in (35c) can be further subdivided. Data from both Das on Bangla and Kaufman on Indonesian show that the formulation in (35) is not sufficiently general, since it only refers to immediate/ultimate antecedents, and not secondary sources more generally. A possible generalization is given below:

(36) *The Pronominal Agreement Parameter*
If third person A immediately antecedes a pronominal P,
and P has a non-third person secondary source S, then:
a. P agrees only with A.
b. P agrees only with S.
c. P agrees with A or S.

Much more cross-linguistic data on a wide range of structures involving secondary sources will be needed to show whether (36) holds.

10. *The Undersigned*

A recurring theme in the papers of this volume is the status of imposters corresponding to the English imposter *the undersigned*. In other languages, *the undersigned* has special properties, often determining first person agreement where other imposters do not.

As pointed out by Emilio Servidio for Italian (Chapter 6), even though coordinate DPs with an imposter conjunct cannot generally give rise to first person subject-verb agreement, when the imposter is *the undersigned*, such first person subject-verb agreement is possible.

(37) ? *Maria e il sottoscritto cercheremo di difendere noi stessi*
Mari and the undersigned attempt FUT.1PL of defend our selves
"Maria and the undersigned will attempt to defend ourselves."

Servidio analyzes *the undersigned* as [the undersigned INDIVIDUAL], and proposes that imposters with a null head noun have a different syntax (with respect to pronominal agreement) than the other imposters.

The special status of *the undersigned* is also discussed in Chapter 9 by Wood and Sigurðsson, who note that in Icelandic there is a difference between coordinate DPs based on *the undersigned* and those based on other imposters. They analyze the unique behavior of *the undersigned* in terms of its participial nature.

A very interesting theoretical question is to resolve which of the two explanations is correct (Servidio's based on null head nouns, or Wood and Sigurðsson's based on participles).

Cattaneo (2009) for Bellinzonese and Lima (2010) for Brazilian Portuguese also find differences between *the undersigned* and other imposters.

11. Singular/Plural Asymmetry

While the typology in (35) classifies languages according to pronominal agreement with imposters, there are many other differences that emerge from the present volume. In particular, of all the languages in category (35c), only Albanian allows either 1SG or 3SG subject-verb agreement with a singular imposter (see Kallulli, Chapter 4, of this volume):

(38)	*Mami*	*shko-n/shko-j*	*tani*
	Mommy	go-3SG/go-1SG	now

"Mommy is going away now."

In none of the other languages is 1SG subject-verb agreement possible with a singular imposter. However, 1PL subject-verb agreement is often possible with a plural imposter and/or a coordinate DP with an imposter conjunct.

The clearest case is Spanish, as discussed by Rachel Dudley (Chapter 3). Dudley shows that a singular imposter can never give rise to first person subject-verb agreement, but a plural imposter can:

(39)	*los*	*abajo*	*firmantes*	*pensábamos*	*en*	*vender*	*la*	*casa*
	the.PL	under	signed.PL	thought.1PL	about	to.sell	the	house

"The undersigned were thinking about selling the house."

Of course, a plural imposter can also give rise to 3PL subject-verb agreement, and a coordinate DP with an imposter conjunct can give rise to either 1PL or 3PL subject-verb agreement.

A similar contrast exists in French and Romanian, as discussed by Gabriela Soare (Chapter 7). In French, as Soare shows, 1PL subject-verb agreement is possible with a coordinate DP that has an imposter conjunct. Furthermore, 1PL subject-verb agreement is possible with a plural imposter if modified by an indexical modifier, as shown below.

(40)	? *Les auteurs*	*ci-présents*	*sommes*	*fier-s*	*de*	*nous-mêmes*
	The authors	here present.M.PL	are.1PL	proud-PL	of	our-selves

"The authors here present are happy with ourselves."

Similarly, as discussed by Jim Wood and Einar Freyr Sigurðsson (Chapter 9), a singular imposter can never give rise to first person subject-verb agreement, but a plural imposter (as well as a coordinate DP with an imposter conjunct) can:

(41)	*Undirritaðir*	*{hafa/?höfum}*	*haldið*	*þessu*	*fram*
	undersigned.M.PL	{have.3PL/?1PL}	held	this	forth

"The undersigned (plural) have claimed this."

In Italian, as discussed by Emilio Servidio (Chapter 6), a singular imposter never gives rise to 1SG subject-verb agreement, nor can a plural imposter, but a coordinate DP with an imposter conjunct can (if the imposter is *the undersigned*).

(42)	*?Maria*	*e*	*il*	*sottoscritto*	*cercheremo*	*di difendere*	*noi stessi*
	Mari	and	the	undersigned	attempt.FUT.1PL	of defend	our selves

"Maria and the undersigned will attempt to defend ourselves."

Table 1.1 summarizes the data on subject-verb agreement across all the languages in group (35c).

So there is a robust asymmetry between singular and plural imposters. If a language has first person subject-verb agreement with a singular imposter, it will also have first person subject-verb agreement with a plural imposter (as in Albanian).

There is also a less robust asymmetry between plural imposters and coordinate DPs with an imposter conjunct (for a possible explanation, see Collins and Postal 2012: 127). If a language has first person subject-verb agreement with a plural imposter, it will also have first person subject-verb agreement with a coordinate DP with an imposter conjunct.

Table 1.1 **Subject-Verb Agreement**

	Singular	*Plural*	*Coordinate*
Albanian	3SG/1SG	3PL/1PL	3PL/1PL
Spanish	3SG/*1SG	3PL/1PL	3PL/1PL
Italian	3SG/*1SG	3PL/*1PL	3PL/1PL
Bellinzonese	3SG/*1SG	3PL/*1PL	3PL/1PL
Icelandic	3SG/*1SG	3PL/1PL	3PL/1PL
French	3SG/*1SG	3PL/1PL	3PL/1PL
Romanian	3SG/*1SG	3PL/1PL	3PL/1PL
Brazilian Portuguese	3SG/*1SG	3PL/1PL	3PL/1PL

Table 1.1 glosses over many relevant details concerning when 1PL subject-verb agreement is licensed (e.g., the role of "the undersigned," modification by "here present" and topicalization). Putting these details aside, we have the following preliminary cross-linguistic implicational universals, which need to be tested in many more languages:

(43) Hiearchy of DPs for First Person Subject-Verb Agreement
  a. Singular Imposter → Plural Imposter
  b. Plural Imposter → Coordinate Structure with Imposter Conjunct

The basic asymmetry between singular imposters and plural/coordinate imposters seen in Table 1.1 also shows up in English with respect to pronominal agreement (plural subject-verb agreement does not show person distinctions). Although a plural imposter can be the antecedent of a 1PL pronoun (see (1a)), a singular imposter generally cannot (singular camouflage DPs are not so constrained; see Collins and Postal 2012: 90):

(44) a. Daddy is enjoying himself/*myself.
  b. Yours truly will only vote for himself/*myself.
  c. This reporter sees himself/*myself as managing editor in the future.
  d. This reporter will never himself/*myself agree to that.
  e. This reporter has never perjured himself/*myself.
  f. The baroness should take better care of herself/*yourself.

Although Collins and Postal (2012: 94) note this asymmetry, they were unable to account for it. This singular/plural asymmetry may be related to other singular/plural asymmetries in pronominal agreement, represented in conditions (45) and (46) from Collins and Postal (2012, Chapter 14).

(45) Number Attraction
  If the ultimate antecedent of a pronominal P is singular and a plural DP A is a secondary source for P, then if P agrees with A in person or gender, P is plural.

(46) The Ultimate-Antecedent Plurality Condition
  If the ultimate antecedent of a pronominal P is plural, then P is plural.

These two conditions give a very asymmetric view of singular/plural. They say that if the ultimate antecedent of a pronoun is plural, the pronoun must be plural. But if the ultimate antecedent of the pronoun is singular, the pronoun does not necessarily have to be singular. It is as if the singular value of the NUM feaure is being ignored or overridden. An example illustrating (45) is given below:

(47) a. [Every one of us]$_1$ thinks we$_1$ are /*I$_1$ am a genius. (see (1d))

In (47), the ultimate antecedent of *we* is *every one of us*, which is singular (as shown by subject-verb agreement), but the bound pronoun *we* is plural (agreeing with the set DP of the partitive DP as a secondary source). In fact, the singular *I* is not even possible with a bound variable reading. Since the subject pronoun agrees with the set DP *us* in person (first person), it must also agree in number (plural). In effect, the singular value of the ultimate antecedent is being bypassed.

An example illustrating (46) is given below:

(48) AUTHOR [Daddy and Jerrome]$_1$ are enjoying ourselves$_1$/*myself$_1$ at the beach.

AUTHOR is a source of *ourselves* (in fact, *ourselves* agrees in person with AUTHOR). However, since the ultimate antecedent of the reflexive is [Daddy and Jerome] (a plural DP), the reflexive must be plural, not singular.

Based on facts such as this (and many others dicussed in Collins and Postal 2012, Chapter 14), I make the following claim:

(49) The singular feature value of number is unrepresented syntactically.

There are two ways to implement this analysis technically. Either the NUM feature could be wholly absent from singular DPs, or the NUM feature could lack a value in the case of singular DPs. For concreteness, I will assume the latter.

Nevins (2011: 944), based on certain person/number asymmetries, claims that "person values are always fully specified in the syntax using binary features [+/- participant] and [+/- author], but number features are privative, meaing that [plural] is syntactically specified but that singular arguments are not." Using this assumption, Nevins (2011) derives the fact that while some languages have a Person Case Constraint, no languages seem to have a Number Case Constraint. Also, while some languages have Omnivorous Number Effects, no languages seem to have Omnivorous Person Effects. I take Nevins' (2011) conclusions to support my claim that the singular feature value of number is unrepresented syntactically.

Returning to (49), Wood and Sigurðsson also claim that the singular value of the number feature is unrepresented syntactically. Using this assumption, they consider how finite T with unvalued phi-features probes for the features of the imposter. They show that under a certain set of assumptions, only the plural imposter *the undersigned* will allow both 1PL and 3PL subject-verb agreement. Basically, only for the plural imposter *the undersigned* will the uNUM (unvalued NUM feature) of T be able to probe the 1PL core of the imposter (giving rise to 1PL subject-verb agreement). All singular imposters, and all other plural imposters, will only allow third person subject-verb agreement.

Since their account is specific to the plural imposter *the undersigned* and its special properties as a participle with gender and number phi-features, it is unclear how their account could be used to account for the singular/plural distinction found in English between examples like (44) and examples with a plural imposter. Also, it is unclear how it would account for the general singular plural/ asymmetry illustrated in Table 1.1. So the singular/plural distinction with imposters remains a mystery, and accounting for it is one of the greatest challenges for future work.

12. Person Mismatches

As several contributors have noted (Das, Dudley, Soare), when an imposter is a subject and the antecedent of a pronoun, the subject-verb agreement and pronominal agreement must match. Both Das and Dudley give accounts of this restriction in terms of the Homogeneity Principle (Collins and Postal 2012, Chapter 12). A French example from Collins and Postal is given below:

(50) a. *Votre serviteur et quelques amis sommes fiers d'eux-mêmes
your servant and a.few friends are.1pl proud of themselves
"Your servant and a few friends are proud of themselves."

b. *Votre serviteur et quelques amis sont fiers de nous-mêmes
your servant and a.few friends are.3pl proud of ourselves
"Your servant and a few friends are proud of ourselves."

In (50a), the verb has 1PL agreement, but the pronoun is 3PL. In (50b), the verb has 3PL agreement, but the pronoun is 1PL. Both cases are ungrammatical.

However, several authors (Wood and Sigurðsson, Kallulli, Dudley) report exceptions to this generalization, and the exceptions are only found when the subject-verb agreement is third person, as in (51b):

(51) a. Verb-3 Pronoun-3
b. Verb-3 Pronoun-1
c. *Verb-1 Pronoun-3
d. Verb-1 Pronoun-1

Even in English, where subject-verb agreement is impoverished, it is possible to find some cases of mismatch, and they are always of the form in (51b). Two such cases are the following from Collins and Postal (2012: 212, 157):

(52) a. Your Lordship likes to enjoy yourself on the beach.
b. I am an experienced teacher who takes care of myself.

In (52a), there is 3SG subject-verb agreement, but the reflexive is 2SG. In (52b), there is 3SG subject-verb agreement on the verb in the relative clause, but the reflexive is 1SG. So in both cases, there is a mismatch between the subject-verb agreement and the phi-features of the pronoun.

Given these cases, I suggest the following generalization:

(53) For subject S and pronoun P which has S as an antecedent,
if subject-verb agreement with S is first person, then P is first person.

This asymmetry between third person and first person is reminiscent of the asymmetry between singular and plural. Just like singular can be ignored in certain cases, third person can also be ignored in certain cases. In particular, in languages that allow (51b), third person subject-verb agreement is ignored for the purposes of the Homogeneity Principle. The implications of such asymmetries for the syntactic representation of person have yet to be explored.

One fact about English that makes it harder to analyze than Icelandic is that 1PL subject-verb agreement is identical to 3PL subject-verb agreement.

(54) a. They attempt to defend themselves.
b. We attempt to defend ourselves.

There is no difference in morphological shape between the verbs in (54a) and (54b). So in an example like (1) above (repeated in (55)), one does not know if there is 1PL or 3Pl subject-verb agreement:

(55) [the present authors]$_1$ (= the writers of the reply) attempt to
defend ourselves$_1$/themselves$_1$.

Collins and Postal (2012: 127) assumed that the form of the subject-verb agreement in (55) is 3PL (and the imposter DP *the present authors* is 3PL). However, given that some of the languages in Table 1.1 freely allow 1PL subject-verb agreement with plural imposters, we need to reconsider this assumption. Consider the following four represesntations, where we assume that there is homophonous 1PL and 3PL subject-verb agreement:

(56) a. The present authors attempt-1PL to defend ourselves.
b. The present authors attempt-1PL to defend themselves.
c. The present authors attempt-3PL to defend ourselves.
d. The present authors attempt-3PL to defend themselves.

Assuming in each case that the subject is an imposter, only (56b) would be ruled out by the condition in (53). Therefore, in English, the presence of a 1PL reflexive would be consistent with both of the representations in (56a) and (56c).

The representations in (56) make the assumption that the imposter *the present authors* is 3PL. Another possibility is that (55) involves an appositive structure with a covert pronominal head, as in the following:

(57) a. [WE, the present authors,] attempt-1PL to defend ourselves.
b. The present authors attempt-3PL to defend ourselves.

On this approach, we still need to explain why singular imposters do not have a representation like that in (57a) (with a covert 1SG pronominal head). Moreover, Collins and Postal (2012: 97) present arguments against the representation of imposters as appositives involving a covert pronominal head, as in (57a). They show that an imposter DP such as *the present authors* can trigger both 1PL and 3PL pronominal agreement in the same sentence, which is not consistent with a representation like that in (57a).

13. Conclusion

The cross-linguistic work in this volume supports the basic framework of Collins and Postal (2012). Part of the cross-linguistic variation can be easily defined in terms of the different source types (immediate antecedent vs. ultimate antecedent). It remains to be seen if a semantic account (see discussion in Collins and Postal 2012, Chapter 20) would also be capable of accounting for this data.

The chapters of this volume give rise to a vast number of research questions, both of a theoretical and empirical nature. I hope the questions raised in this volume will trigger cross-linguistic research into the little studied areas of imposters and pronominal agreement.

References

Carnie, Andrew. 2007. *Syntax: A Generative Introduction*. Oxford, England: Blackwell Publishing.

Catteneo, Andrea. 2009. Imposters and Pseudo-Imposters in Bellinzonese and English. Unpublished manuscript, New York University.

Collins, Chris, Simanique Moody, and Paul Postal. 2008. An AAE camouflage construction. *Language* 84(1): 29–68.

Collins, Chris, and Paul Postal. 2012. *Imposters*. Cambridge, MA: MIT Press.

Corbett, Greville G. 2006. *Agreement*. Cambridge, England: Cambridge University Press.

Dikken, Marcel den. 2001. Pluringulars, pronouns and quirky agreement. *The Linguistic Review* 18: 19–41.

Kratzer, Angelika. 2009. Making a pronoun: Fake indexicals as windows into the properties of pronouns. *Linguistic Inquiry* 40.2: 187–237.

Lasnik, Howard, and Juan Uriagereka. 1988. *A Course in GB Syntax*. Cambridge, MA: MIT Press.

Lima, Ananda. 2010. Some Imposter Data in Brazilian Portuguese. Talk, New York University.

Nevins, Andrew. 2011. Multiple agree with clitics: Person complementarity vs. omnivorous number. *Natural Language and Linguistic Theory* 29: 939–971.

Payne, John, and Rodney Huddleston. 2002. Nouns and Noun Phrases. In *The Cambridge Grammar of the English Language*, eds. Rodney Huddleston and Geoffrey K. Pullum, 324–523. Cambridge, England: Cambridge University Press.
Rizzi, Luigi. 1997. The fine structure of the left periphery. In *Elements of Grammar*, ed. Liliane Haegeman, 281–337. Dordrecht: Kluwer Academic Publishers.
Ross, John Robert. 1970. On declarative sentences. In *Readings in English Transformational Grammar*, eds. Roderick A. Jacobs and Peter S. Rosenbaum, 222–272. Waltham, MD: Ginn.
Sag, Ivan A., Thomas Wasow, and Emily M. Bender. 2003. *Syntactic Theory*. Stanford, CA: CSLI.

2

(Il)-licit Pronoun-Antecedent Relations in Bangla

SATARUPA DAS

1. Background

Collins and Postal (2012) study a certain type of DP in English that they call *imposters*. The distinctive feature of this type of DP is that it gives rise to third person verbal agreement but has first or second person reference. Furthermore, as illustrated in (2), non-singular imposters can antecede both third person and non-third person pronominal forms.

(1) a. Daddy is/*am sick of your tantrums. (third person DP referring to the speaker)
    b. Is/*Are Madam having a good time? (third person DP referring to the addressee)

(2) a. The present authors consider themselves/ourselves to have been slandered.
    b. Mommy and Daddy are enjoying themselves/ourselves on the beach.

Based on a broad sample of pronominal agreement facts such as those in (2), Collins and Postal (2012) pursue the hypothesis that although imposters appear to be identical to non-imposter DPs, their syntactic structure differs considerably from non-imposter third person DPs. More specifically, they argue that unlike garden variety third person DPs, an imposter contains a silent pronoun that corresponds to the intended referent. For instance, a first person imposter contains a silent first person pronoun.

Before continuing, a brief note on terminology is in order. The syntax of an imposter DP is as follows: $[_{\text{DPShell}}\ [_{\text{DPSecondary}}$ Daddy$][_{\text{D'}}$ [D] $[_{\text{DPCore}}$ I]]]. The visible DP is referred to as the "secondary DP" and the null pronoun is referred to as the "notional core". Both of these DPs are argued to be embedded in a larger DP, which is dubbed the "shell DP". The shell DP is akin to an appositive, which involves two DPs in a predication relation that distribute like a single DP. Collins and Postal assume that both shell DP and the notional core have a covert DP antecedent with the relevant phi-feature values: AUTHOR (singular or plural) in the case of a first person imposter, ADDRESSEE (singular or plural) in the case of a second person imposter. Finally, the notions of immediate/ultimate antecedence are defined as follows. A node *a* is an *immediate antecedent* of a node *b* if and only if *a* antecedes *b* and there is no *c* such that *a* antecedes *c* and *c* antecedes *b*. Node *a* is the *ultimate antecedent* of a node *b* if and only if *a* antecedes *b* and there is no *c* that antecedes *a*.

(3) [AUTHOR] [ADDRESSEE] Have you been taking care of yourself?

In (3), for instance, *you* is the immediate antecedent of *yourself*. The opposite situation, in which the reflexive antecedes the subject pronoun, is ruled out by Principle A "of the Binding Theory", which requires reflexive pronominals to have c-commanding antecedents. Furthermore, ADDRESSEE is the immediate antecedent of *you*, and also the ultimate antecedent of both *you* and *yourself*.

Given the syntactic structure of imposter DPs, there are three logical possibilities for pronominal agreement with an imposter: First, the pronoun could only agree with the notional core of the imposter, as in Indonesian and Chinese (cf. Kaufman and Wang, respectively, this volume); second, the pronoun could agree with either the secondary DP or the notional core, as in English (cf. (2)); and third, the pronoun could agree with the secondary DP alone, as illustrated by the case of Bangla. This third variation is illustrated here with a comparative study of the relevant facts from English and Bangla.

This chapter has a twofold aim. First, I show that failure of pronominal agreement with the notional core in Bangla happens to be a special case of a systematic ban on agreement with secondary sources (to be elaborated on in section 3). Second, I argue that the verbal agreement system of a language is the crucial factor that determines pronoun-antecedent relations. The rest of the chapter is organized as follows: Pronominal agreement with imposter DPs is discussed in section 2; agreement with secondary sources is taken up in section 3; section 4 analyzes the Bangla facts, pointing out that the case of control involving imposter DPs is not amenable to the proposed analysis; section 5 concludes.

2. Bangla Imposters and Pronominal Agreement

Some examples of imposter DPs in Bangla are given in (4).

(4) Bangla imposters:

a. First person:
ei sharma, ei mokkel "this guy"; *ei sangbadik* "this reporter" *ei chatro brinda* "this group of students"; *nimna-sakkhorito* "the undersigned"; *Archana Das* "Proper Name"; *baba* "Daddy," etc.

b. Second person:
mahashoy/a "sir/madam"; *dharmabotar* "your honor"; *amar pathok* "my reader"; *amar lokkhiti* "my darling"; *Archana Das* "Proper Name," etc.

All these DPs can be used as third person referential expressions. For instance, *baba* in (5) and *Archana* in (6) are garden variety DPs, which do not denote either the speaker or the addressee.

(5)	*baba*	*rege*	*ach-e*
	father	angry	be-3
	"Daddy is angry."		

(6)	*Archana*	*hathte*	*gach-e*
	Archana	walk	go-3
	"Archana went for a walk."		

But the DP in (5) can be used by the speaker to refer to himself and the DP in (6) can be used to refer to the addressee. In other words, these DPs lend themselves to imposter readings, as shown in (7) and (8).

(7)	*baba*	*rege*	*ja-b-e/*ja-b-o*			
	father	angry	go-fut-3/go-fut-1			
	"Daddy will get angry."					
(8)	*Archana Das*	*ki*	*ekhon*	*cha*	*khete*	*cha-i/*cha-o*
	AD	Q	now	tea	drink	want-3/want-2
	"Would Archana Das like the tea now?"					

The foregoing examples show that Bangla imposters determine third person verbal agreement. This generalization holds for all kinds of imposters (singular, plural, and coordinate).

In the following text, I provide data concerning Bangla imposters with respect to bound pronouns, reflexives, and control. The small, informal survey that I conducted shows a dichotomy among speakers: For six speakers (including myself), pronominal agreement is strictly with the secondary DP; however, for one of my informants, pronominal agreement in certain cases is possible both with the secondary DP and the core.[1]

2.1 BOUND PRONOUNS: LOCAL AND LONG-DISTANCE

This section shows that bound pronouns can only agree with the secondary DP alone, never with its notional core. For the singular cases, pronominal agreement is permissible only with the secondary DP, in both English and Bangla, as shown in (9) and (12). I will have nothing to say about this similarity. However, with plural or coordinate imposters, pronominal agreement with the ultimate antecedent of the imposter seems fine in English, as shown in (10b) and (11b). These data clearly show that, for nearly all Bangla speakers I have consulted,

[1] As far as pronominal agreement facts are concerned, her dialect is different from those of all the other native speakers I consulted. So, for the purposes of this chapter, I do nothing more than note the judgments elicited from her. Perhaps interspeaker variations of this kind could be taken up as a subject for future research.

only third person agreement is allowed between the imposter DP and a bound pronoun.

(9) a. _ei sharma tar/*amar dhoirjya harate cholech-e_
this guy his/my patience lose go-3
"This guy is about to lose his patience."
(Agreement with core OK for one informant)

b. This reporter is about to lose his/*my patience.

(10) a. _ei chatrora tader/*amader dhoirjya harate cholech-e_
these students their/our patience lose go-3
"These students are about to lose their patience."

b. The present authors are about to lose their/our patience.

(11) a. _baba aar ma tader/*amader dhoirjya harate cholech-e_
Daddy and Mommy their/our patience lose go-3
"Daddy and Mommy are about to lose their patience."
(Agreement with core OK for one informant)

b. The present author and his collaborator are about to lose their/our patience.

(12) a. _ei sharma thik koreche je se bideshe ja-b-e na_
this guy has.decided COMP he abroad go-fut-3 NEG
"This guy has decided that he won't go abroad."

b. *[_ei sharma_]$_i$ _thik koreche je ami_$_i$ _bideshe ja-b-o na_
this guy has.decided COMP I abroad go-fut-1 NEG
Intended: "This guy has decided that he won't go abroad."
(OK for one informant)

c. This reporter has decided that he/*I won't go abroad

(13) a. _ei chatrora thik koreche je tara bideshe ja-b-e na_
these student have.decided COMP they abroad go-fut-3 NEG
"These students have decided that they won't go abroad."

b. *_ei chatrora thik koreche je amra bideshe ja-b-o na_
these students have.decided COMP we abroad go-fut-3 NEG
Intended: "These students have decided that they won't go abroad."
(OK for one informant)

(14) a. _baba aar ma thik koreche je tara bideshe ja-b-e na_
daddy and mommy have.decided COMP they abroad go-fut-3 NEG
"Daddy and Mommy have decided that they won't go abroad."

b. *_baba aar ma thik koreche je amra bideshe ja-b-o na_
daddy and mommy have.decided COMP we abroad go-fut-1 NEG
Intended: "Daddy and Mommy have decided that they won't go abroad."
(OK for one informant)

2.2 REFLEXIVES

Similar to bound pronouns, reflexives also show a sharp contrast between Bangla and English with respect to antecedence possibilities by non-singular imposters. More specifically, while English plural imposters can serve as antecedents for non-third person reflexives, plural imposters in Bangla may only antecede third person reflexives. A parallel contrast exists in the domain of coordinate structures, where one conjunct is an imposter.

The examples in (15) show that in both English and Bangla, a singular imposter can only antecede a third person reflexive.

(15) a.

ei	*sharma*	*shudhu*	*tar/*amar*	*nijer*	*jonnoi*	*ranna*	*kor-b-e*
this	guy	only	his/ my	self	for	cook	do-fut-3

"This guy will only cook for himself."

(Agreement with core OK for one informant)

b. Daddy will only cook for himself/*myself.

This parallelism does not hold when one considers non-singular imposters. The example in (16a) shows that a plural imposter in Bangla can only antecede a third person reflexive. This contrasts with the English example given in (16b), which shows that an English plural imposter may antecede both a third person and a non-third person reflexive.

(16) a.

ei	*chatro*	*shudhu*	*tader/*amader*	*nijer*	*jonnoi*	*ranna*	*kor-b-e*
these	students	only	their our	self	for	cook	do-fut-3

"These students will only cook for themselves."

b. In this reply, the present authors$_1$ attempt to defend ourselves$_1$/themselves$_1$ against the scurrilous charges which have been made.

Similarly, as illustrated in (17), a coordinate structure in English, where one conjunct is an imposter, has wider antecedence possibilities as compared to its analog in Bangla.

(17) a.

baba	*aar*	*ma*	*shudhu*	*tader/*amader*	*nijer*	*jonnoi*	*ranna*	*kor-b-e*
Daddy	and	Mommy	only	their/ our	self	for	cook	do-fut-3

"Daddy and Mommy will only cook for themselves."

b. In the reply, the author$_1$ and his$_1$ assistant$_2$ attempt to defend ourselves$_{1,2}$ /themselves$_{1,2}$ against the scurrilous charges which have been made.

2.3 CONTROL

This section provides further evidence for the observation that English and Bangla imposters differ in their antecedence possibilities. Drawing on data involving chains of antecedents mediated by backward control, this section shows that while English imposters can antecede both third person and non-third person bound pronouns, their Bangla counterparts can only function as antecedents for third person pronominals.

Collins and Postal (2012) report that while the example in (18a) is perfect, the one given in (18b) is somewhat dubious, according to one of the authors. The anonymous Internet survey of grammaticality judgments reported in Collins, Guitard, and Wood (2009) supports this intuition. For (18a), out of a total of 15 participants, eight people rated it marginal and seven people rated it good. On the other hand, (18b) received eight bad, six marginal, and one good rating. The corresponding Bangla examples given in (19) show that a singular imposter that refers to the speaker can only antecede a third person pronominal.

(18) a. To keep himself from getting sunburned, Daddy will put on suntan lotion.
b. ? To keep myself from getting sunburned, Daddy will put on suntan lotion.
[= C&P 2012: 96, ex. (13 b, d)]

(19) *tar/*amar shorir shustha rakhar jonno ei sharma rojdin beyam kor-e*
his/ my body healthy keeping for this guy everyday exercise do-3
"For keeping his body healthy, this guy exercises every day."

For English, the judgments involving non-singular imposters are less controversial. The examples in (20) show that non-singular imposters in English can serve as an antecedent for both third person and non-third person reflexives, while the corresponding Bangla examples in (21) show that only third person pronominals are permissible.

(20) a. To keep ourselves/themselves from getting sunburned, the present authors will put on suntan lotion. [= C&P 2012: 96, ex. (14 b)]
b. To keep ourselves$_{1,2}$/themselves$_{1,2}$ from getting sunburned, the present author$_1$ and his$_1$ assistant$_2$ will put on suntan lotion.

(21) a. *tader/*amader shorir shustha rakhar jonno ei chatrora rojdin*
their/ our body healthy keeping for these students every day
beyam kor-e
exercise do-3
"For keeping their bodies healthy, these students exercise every day."
b. *tader/*amader shorir shustha rakhar jonno Mr. aar Mrs. Ray rojdin*
their/ our body healthy keeping for Mr. & Mrs. Ray every day
beyam kor-e
exercise do-3
"For keeping their bodies healthy, Mr. and Mrs. Ray exercise every day."

At this point, we can make the following empirical generalization: For nearly all Bangla speakers, pronominal agreement is only possible with the shell of the imposter DP. In what follows, I show that this pattern of pronominal agreement with an imposter DP happens to be a special case of pronominal agreement with any secondary source.

3. Sources

In section 2, it was established that pronominal elements in Bangla—unlike in English—can only agree with the secondary DP, never with the covert antecedent. In this section, I show that Bangla systematically disallows pronominal agreement with any secondary source. To begin with, we state the definitions of a *primary source* (Collins and Postal 2012: 156). Secondary sources are discussed in sections 3.1 and 3.2.

(22) Definition: *primary source*
A is a primary source for B if and only if:
a. A immediately antecedes B or
b. A shares a lexical basis with B.[2]

3.1 SUBJECT OF A PREDICATE NOMINAL

In (23), since the relative pronoun, DP_2, is the immediate antecedent of *myself*, DP_2 is a primary source for DP_3. Also, DP_1 shares a lexical basis with DP_2, since both DP_1 and DP_2 dominate the noun *person*. Therefore, DP_1 is a primary source for DP_2, and—by transitivity—DP_1 is a source for DP_3. Since the predicate nominal is a source for DP_3, the subject of the predicate nominal is considered to be the secondary source for DP_3, which accounts for why the first person form of the reflexive is permissible in the relative clause.

(23) I am $[_{DP1}$ a $[_{NP1}$ $[_{NP2}$ person] $[_{CP}$ $[_{DP2}$ who [<NP2>]] takes care of $[_{DP3}$ myself]]]].

The Bangla sentence in (24) is in sharp contrast to the above example. Here the pronoun in the relative clause *must* agree in phi-features with the relative pronoun, which in turn agrees with the third person singular head of the relative clause. In other words, the phi-features associated with the secondary source are not accessible to the predicate nominal.

(24) *ami ekjon lok je tar/*amar nijer shasther jotno nei*
I a person REL his my own health care take.3
"I am a person who takes care of himself."

[2] Definition: *lexically based/lexical basis:* A DP Q is lexically based on a noun N (N is a lexical basis for Q) iff Q dominates N and there exists a path of nodes Q. . . N, where every node between Q and N is a nominal (i.e., bears one of the following labels: {DP, D', NP, N', N}), a non-conjunct and a non-specifier (adapted from Collins and Postal 2012: 58–59). Collins and Postal also assume that pronouns like *I* are DPs with a null determiner whose noun is *I*. It then follows that the shell DP and the notional core of an imposter share a lexical basis (cf. structure of imposter DP in section 1).

3.2 PARTITIVES

The sentence in (25) lends itself to a bound variable interpretation. This is because the so-called set DP *us* is a secondary source of phi-features for the bound pronoun *we*. The Bangla example in (26), however, does not have a bound variable reading with the pronoun *amra* in the embedded clause, which indicates that pronominal agreement with the set DP is disallowed in Bangla.

(25) [Every one of $us_j]_i$ thinks we_i are talented.

(26) *[amader modhye protyeke]$_i$ mone kor-e̲ je se$_i$/*amra$_i$ sob theke buddhiman*
our among each think-3 COMP he we cleverest
"Each one among us thinks that he is the cleverest."

Finally, an ultimate antecedent—AUTHOR or ADDRESSEE—is the primary source for an imposter DP (by (22a)). Since an ultimate antecedent is a potential source of phi-feature values for a pronominal element, it is also considered a secondary source.

4. Toward an Analysis

The empirical generalization that emerges from the discussion in the preceding sections is stated in (27). Unlike Bangla, in pronominal agreement in English, generally speaking, both primary and secondary sources may supply phi-feature values.

(27) In Bangla, pronominal agreement with all secondary sources is blocked.

The analysis is developed in two steps. First, I explain why the finite verb can never agree with a secondary source. With this result in place, I then appeal to the *Homogeneity Principle* (to be elaborated upon in section 4.2) to derive the generalization given in (27).

4.1 VERBAL AGREEMENT IN BANGLA

All verbal paradigms in Bangla have a distinct form for expressing person agreement; number and gender are not marked on the finite verb. Furthermore, second and third person forms are also marked for honorificity. Three degrees of honorificity are maintained in the second person (familiar, neutral, and honorific), and two in the third (neutral and honorific), as shown in (28).

(28) The paradigm for the verb *bola* "speak" in the present tense.

1st SG/PL	bol-i		
2nd SG/PL (familiar)	bol-ish		
2nd SG/PL (neutral)	bol-o	3rd SG/PL (neutral)	bol-e
2nd SG/PL (honorific)	bol-en	3rd SG/PL (honorific)	bol-en

Following Collins and Postal, I assume that imposter DPs are structurally complex. Specifically, within the imposter shell, the secondary DP is hierarchically superior to the notional core (cf. Chapter 1 of this volume for an illustration of the syntax of imposters). Therefore, it is the secondary DP that is closer to the probing head T, which provides a natural account of why T can value its phi-features against the secondary DP only, and not the notional core.[3] T likewise fails to enter into an Agree relation with the set DP, which is embedded within the partitive DP. Finally, in sentences with a predicate nominal, the T head in the relative clause can only Agree with the raised NP, not with the subject of the predicate nominal in the matrix clause.

4.2 HOMOGENEITY PRINCIPLE

I provide an overview of the *Homogeneity Principle*, as stated in Collins and Postal (2012: 142–145). To begin with, consider the following sentences.

(29) a. [$_A$ The present authors feel that [$_B$ they often defend themselves against scurrilous charges]].
b. [$_A$ The present authors feel that [$_B$ we often defend ourselves against scurrilous charges]].
c. *[$_A$ The present authors feel that [$_B$ we often defend themselves against scurrilous charges]].
d. *[$_A$ The present authors feel that [$_B$ they often defend ourselves against scurrilous charges]].

To explain these and other related facts concerning series of pronominal elements, Collins and Postal define domains in which all pronominals sharing a common ultimate antecedent must agree; however, pronominals in different domains may fail to agree.

(30) *Homogeneity Principle (HP)*
If A and B are pronominal members of some U-availability chain, A agrees with B.[4]

[3] Alternatively, one might say that an imposter DP fails to trigger non-third person agreement on the finite verb because the notional core, which is the locus of first or second person features, is not sufficiently local to the probing head. This formulation is reminiscent of the Structural Condition on Person Agreement given in Baker (2008), according to which a functional head F can agree with XP in +1 or +2 only if F merges with XP, and XP is bound by a special operator (S or A, referring to Speaker or Addressee, respectively). The exact version of Baker's proposal cannot be adopted, however, because according to his view, imposter DPs do not have a pronominal component, and as such, they cannot be bound by these special operators. However, the rich empirical landscape involving pronominal agreement with imposter DPs does indeed support the idea that imposters are structurally complex.

[4] Collins and Postal demonstrate that the notional core cannot antecede anything external to the DP. As such, the notional core of an imposter DP remains outside the purview of the HP.

(31) *U-availability Chain*

For any constituent C, the U-availability chain in C has the following properties:

a. It is the maximal set of DPs [DP_1, DP_2, . . ., DP_n] that have a common ultimate antecedent;
b. It is dominated by C;
c. For any *i*, DP_i is *available* in C. A DP is available in C if it does not have its immediate antecedent in a sub-constituent of C.

Before discussing how the HP accounts for the facts in (29), I illustrate how one constructs a *U-availability chain* with the aid of the example in (32).

(32) [$_A$ Katie$_j$ said that [$_B$ she$_j$ takes good care of herself$_j$]].

Following Colllins and Postal (2012), I assume that the relevant (sub)-constituents are clausal. In (32), at the level of constituent B, both *she* and *herself* are available, since neither pronominal element has its immediate antecedent in a *sub-constituent* of B. At the level of the matrix clause A, *herself* is no longer available, since it has its immediate antecedent, namely *she*, within a sub-constituent (B) of A. Here, *she* is taken to be the immediate antecedent of *herself*, since the opposite situation, where the reflexive is the antecedent, is precluded by Principle A, which requires reflexive pronominals to have c-commanding antecedents. Therefore, the U-availability chain at the matrix level is [Katie, she].[5] This chain trivially satisfies the HP, since it contains only one pronoun.

Returning to the examples in (29), we can show that the deviant sentences are correctly ruled out by the HP. In (29c), for example, the U-availability chain at the level of clause B is [we, themselves], since neither DP has its immediate antecedent in any sub-constituent of B. This U-availability chain clearly violates HP, which accounts for the unacceptability of (29c). The example in (29d) lends itself to a similar analysis. Before proceeding to a discussion of the Bangla facts, let us study another English example. Consider the sentence in (33).

(33) [$_A$ AUTHOR [$_B$ I announced that [$_C$ your faithful correspondent deserved his medal]]].

Although the sentence contains non-agreeing pronominals, it is rightly not ruled out by HP. Following Collins and Postal (2012), I assume that the covert antecedent of an imposter DP appears only once, at the matrix level. Here, at the level of C, the U-availability chain is [your faithful correspondent, his], since *his* does not have its immediate antecedent within a sub-constituent of C. But since this U-availability chain contains only one pronoun, HP is vacuously satisfied.

[5] Note that given the clause in (31a), a non-imposter third person DP such as *Katie* is taken to stand in the antecedence relation to itself.

At the level of B, the U-availability chain is [I, your faithful correspondent]. *His* is not included in this U-availability chain since it has its immediate antecedent, namely *your faithful correspondent*, in the sub-constituent (C) of B. This U-availability chain also trivially satisfies HP. Finally, at the level of A, HP is vacuously satisfied once again, since the U-availability chain [AUTHOR, I] contains a single pronoun.

4.2 ANALYSIS OF CASES

In the analysis that follows, I assume that in Bangla, inflection on the finite verb is akin to a pronoun, and as such, it is subject to the HP. Consider, for instance, the example in (14b), repeated below. At the level of constituent A, *1 person* inflection is no longer available, since it has its immediate antecedent *amra* within a sub-constituent (C) of A. The U-availability chain at this level contains *3 person* and *amra*. This is because neither of these pronominal elements has its immediate antecedent within a sub-constituent of A.[6] This chain clearly violates the HP, which accounts for the ungrammaticality of (34).

(34)	*[$_A$ *baba*	*aar*	*ma*	*thik korech-e*	*je*	[$_C$ <u>*amra*</u>	*bideshe*	*ja-b-<u>o</u>*	*na*]]
	Daddy	and	Mommy	decided.3	COMP	we	abroad	go-fut-1	NEG

Intended: "Daddy and Mommy have decided that they won't go abroad."

The pronominal agreement facts presented in section 3.2 and 3.3 are also accounted for in a similar manner. Consider the example in (26), repeated below as (35a). As noted earlier, the bound variable reading is only available with the pronoun *se* in the embedded clause. If *amra* is chosen as the subject of the embedded clause, then the U-availability chain at the matrix level contains *3 person, amra*, which violates HP.

(35) a. [$_A$[*amader modhye protyeke*]$_i$ *mone kor-<u>e</u> je* [$_C$ <u>*se*</u>$_i$/*<u>*amra*</u>$_i$ *sob theke buddhiman*]]]
our among each think-3 COMP he we cleverest
"Each one among us thinks that he is the cleverest."

b. [*amader modhye protyeke*]$_i$ *mone kor-<u>e</u> je* <u>*se*</u>$_k$/<u>*amra*</u>$_k$ *sobtheke buddhiman*
our among each think-3 COMP he we cleverest
"Each one among us thinks that he/we is/are the cleverest."

Notice that on the other reading of the sentence given in (35b), both *se* and *amra* are permissible in the embedded clause. Since, under this reading, the ultimate antecedent of the embedded clause pronoun is not co-referential with

[6] Either *3 person* could be taken to be the antecedent of *amra*, or vice versa. It is, however, important to note that the antecedence relation is asymmetric. In other words, if A antecedes B, then B does *not* antecede A. Since at level C *amra* was treated as the antecedent of *1 person*, at level A we cannot reverse this choice. Had this been possible, then *amra* would no longer be available, and hence not part of the U-availability chain, at level A.

the subject of the matrix clause, the U-availability chain in the matrix clause is [*amader modhye protyeke, 3 person*], which satisfies HP vacuously.

Finally, let us consider the example in (24), repeated below as (36). If the pronoun *tar* is chosen, then, at the level of the constituent B, the U-availability chain is either [*tar, 3 person*], which obeys to HP. However, if *amar*, is chosen instead, then we have an illicit U-availability chain, [*amar, 3 person*].

(36) *ami emon ekjon lok je* [$_B$ *tar/*amar nijer shasther jotno nei*]
I such a person REL his/ my own health care take.3
"I am the kind of person who takes care of his health."

In this section, I have discussed why the finite verb can never agree with a secondary source. Given this result, and the assumption that inflection on the finite verb is in some sense pronominal, I then appealed to the Homogeneity Principle to derive the generalization that Bangla disallows pronominal agreement with any secondary source.

4.3 CONTROL CASES

In this section, I discuss the case of control, for which the HP analysis fails to procure the desired results. Consider the examples in (37). The HP analysis predicts that both first person and third person pronouns should be admissible. In the absence of subject-verb agreement within the embedded or purpose clause, we can isolate direct pronominal agreement with the imposter. The data in (37) show that this prediction is not borne out. For instance, in (37a), at the level of the matrix clause, the U-availability chain is [this author, PRO], which satisfies HP vacuously. However, at the level of the embedded clause, the U-availability chain is given by [PRO, *tar*] or [PRO, *amar*]. To account for the unacceptability of *amar*, one would be forced to stipulate that PRO must be third singular. A similar conclusion holds for the subject control example in (37b).

(37) a. *sobai ei lekhok-ke* PRO *tar/*amar boi chapa-te bolech-e*
everyone this author-OBJ his/ my book print-INF told.3
"Everyone has told this author to publish his/*my book."

b. [$_A$ PRO$_{3,Pl}$ **amader/tader shorir shustha rakhar jonno*
our their body healthy keeping for
[$_C$ Mr. & Ms. M *roj beyam kor-e*]]
Mr. & Ms. M every day exercise do-3
"For keeping their bodies healthy, Mr. and Mrs. M exercise every day."

Unlike in Bangla, PRO in English may receive phi-feature values either from the imposter DP or its covert antecedent. In (38b), for instance, the first person reflexive is permissible in the embedded clause presumably because PRO is also first person, which in turn suggests that the covert antecedent must be the source of phi-feature values in this case. The same observation holds for object control, as shown in (39b).

(38) a. The present authors feel the need PRO to defend themselves.
b. The present authors feel the need PRO to defend ourselves.

(39) a. The editor persuaded the present authors PRO to substantially revise their paper.
b. The editor persuaded the present authors PRO to substantially revise our paper.

In Bangla, on the other hand, PRO can only receive phi-feature values from the imposter DP, not the covert antecedent. In summary, the contrast between English and Bangla with respect to pronoun-antecedent relation can be explained with an appeal to HP, and the assumption that—unlike in English—the inflection on the finite verb in Bangla is in some sense pronominal, and therefore also subject to HP. For the control cases, however, we would need to supplement this account with an explanation of the contrast between English and Bangla. I leave this task for future research.

5. Conclusion

In this chapter, I have presented a comparative study of English and Bangla, which shows a sharp contrast in pronominal agreement with secondary sources in these two languages. The facts presented here clearly show that pronominal elements in Bangla are systematically banned from agreeing with a secondary source. The probe T is precluded from entering into an Agree relation with the notional core of an imposter DP, since the secondary DP, which bears the relevant phi-features, is structurally closer to T. Similar locality considerations account for why other secondary sources do not control verbal agreement. To derive the generalization, I assumed that inflection on the finite verb is in some sense pronominal, and I showed that all illicit pronoun-antecedent relations fail to obey the Homogeneity Principle. Finally, I noted the systematic difference between English and Bangla with regard to control involving an imposter DP cannot be accounted for by the analysis presented here.

I am grateful to Chris Collins for his steady encouragement and guidance at every stage of this work. Thanks also to my father, Swapan Das, and other members of my family for their patience and good humor while I elicited grammaticality judgments; and an anonymous OUP reviewer for detailed comments and suggestions. Any errors or shortcomings are my own.

References

Baker, Mark. 2008. *The Syntax of Agreement and Concord*. Cambridge, UK: Cambridge University Press.

Collins, Chris, and Paul Postal. 2012. *Imposters: A Study in Pronominal Agreement*. Cambridge, MA: MIT Press.

Collins, Chris, Stephanie Guitard, and Jim Wood. 2009. Imposters: An Online Survey of Grammaticality Judgments. *NYU Working Paper in Linguistics* 2: 1–22. http://linguistics.as.nyu.edu/docs/CP/2345/collins_guitard_wood_imposters_online_09_nyuwpl2.pdf

3

Spanish Imposters and Verbal Agreement

RACHEL DUDLEY

1. Introduction

I provide evidence for a subject clitic doubling mechanism in Spanish by bringing together two different empirical observations.[1] The first observation comes from new research on agreement with Spanish imposters, namely, that singular imposters like *un servidor* "a servant" allow only third person verbal agreement and that plural imposters like *unos servidores* "some servants" optionally allow both first and third person agreement. The second observation comes from a fresh look at analyses of Spanish verbal morphology, which indicate that apparent inflectional morphemes on plural verb forms might actually be incorporated subject clitics. The argument is that observed singular/plural asymmetries in both domains (agreement with imposters and verbal paradigms) can be derived from the same underlying asymmetry in clitic doubling.

2. Spanish Imposters

The Spanish imposter data in this chapter come mainly from research I conducted while writing my bachelor's thesis, which examined the kinds of Determiner Phrases (DPs) that allow imposter readings in Spanish. Online corpora, as well as dictionaries and grammars, were used to catalogue the imposters that are standardly accepted across dialects of Spanish, given in (1). Further correspondence with informants confirmed that the DPs in (1) allow imposter readings in each one of the dialects that I examined.[2]

[1] This chapter started out as an undergraduate thesis at New York University. I would like to thank my thesis advisor, Christopher Collins, for extensive support and advice during that time. Additionally, I would like to thank Richard Kayne, also a member of my thesis committee, for valuable comments. Since then I have had fruitful discussions about this work with Stephanie Harves, Valentine Hacquard, and Tonia Bleam. All remaining errors and omissions are my own.

[2] More detail on the dialects investigated can be found in section 4.

(1) Spanish Imposters
- a. Definites: definite determiner ("the") + plural common noun denoting human
  - i. *las mujeres* "the women"
  - ii. *los escritores* "the writers"
  - iii. *los filósofos* "the philosophers"
- b. Demonstratives: proximal demonstrative ("this/these") + common noun denoting human
  - i. *este estudiante* "this student"
  - ii. *este doctor* "this doctor"
  - iii. *estos periodistas* "these reporters"
- c. Kinship: second person possessive ("your") + various kinship terms
  - i. *tu hijo* "your son"
  - ii. *tu abuelo* "your grandfather"
  - iii. *tu hija* "your daughter"
- d. Undersigned: definite determiner + "undersigned"
  - i. *el/la/los/las abajo firmante(s)* "the undersigned"
- e. Servidor: indefinite determiner + "servant"
  - i. *un/una servidor* "a servant"
  - ii. *unos/unas servidores* "some servants"
- f. Menda: various determiners + "guy/gal"
  - i. *el/la menda* "the guy/gal"
  - ii. *este/esta menda* "this guy/gal"
  - iii. *mi menda (lerenda)* "my guy/gal"

Menda "guy" is a type of imposter that I was not able to examine in great depth because I could not find an informant who accepted it as an imposter of his or her dialect. However, I did find mention of it in Beinhauer (1978) as a term related to *servidor* "servant." In my corpora search, I encountered different tokens of the *menda* type. I found the definites *el menda* and *la menda* and the demonstratives *este menda* and *esta menda*. Finally, *mi menda* seems to be a first person camouflage construction[3] with a meaning akin to the British English first person imposter *muggings (here)*. Although I was not able to find any informants who accepted *mi menda*, I have found examples of it online where it occurs as the object of a preposition, as in (2), and the subject of a clause, as in (3).

(2)

Una	*cervecita*	*para*	*mi*	*menda*[4]
a	beer	for	my	guy

"a beer for me"

(3)

Mi	*menda*	*piensa*	*tomarse*	*la*	*revancha*[5]
My	guy	think.3SG	to.take-REFL.3SG	the	revenge

"My guy thinks about taking revenge."

[3] For more information on camouflage constructions, I refer the reader to Collins, Moody, and Postal (2008).

[4] http://www.flickr.com/photos/53236182@N06/4914333209/

[5] http://www.religionenlibertad.com/articulo_imprimir.asp?idarticulo=9426

There are a couple of notable differences between the types of DPs that can have imposter readings in English and those that can have imposter readings in Spanish. As given in (1a), any plural definite DP that denotes a human can be a first or second person imposter in Spanish (which is not the case for English). This is captured with the generalization in (4).

(4) Any Spanish plural definite DP that denotes a maximal set of human beings (e.g., *los estudiantes* "the students," *las mujeres* "the women," *los médicos* "the doctors") that contains the speaker will be able to determine both third person and first person verbal agreement.

The generalization in (4) is often noted in the Spanish literature as part of the *unagreement phenomenon* (Mancini 2010; Ordóñez and Treviño 1999; Jelinek 1984; Bosque 2010). Another difference between English and Spanish, according to my consultants' judgments, is that diminutive kinship terms such as *Mamá* "Mommy" and *Papá* "Daddy" cannot have imposter readings, while their counterparts in other languages often do. Instead, the Spanish kinship imposters are formed by adding a second person possessive determiner to a kinship term.

3. Some Spanish Background

Due to cross-dialectal differences in second person verbal morphology, this chapter will only examine the first person imposters of Spanish, in an effort to catalogue the most general behavior across dialects. I leave the investigation of second person imposters and a closer examination of cross-dialectal variation for future research.

Before I proceed to discuss the Spanish imposter agreement data and arguments from verbal morphology, I should briefly mention the assumptions that I make about the Spanish verbal paradigm. Using *amar* "to love" as an example, I will discuss how verbs are segmented into morphemes, following Bosque (2010). According to Bosque (2010), there are four distinct parts of a verb: the root, the thematic vowel, tense-aspect-mood (TAM) inflection, and person/number (P/N) inflection. Table 3.1 demonstrates how a tense with "regular" morphology like conditionals is divided up into these four parts. For the complete paradigms from Bosque (2010), please see Appendix C.

The root of each regular verb will be constant across all persons, numbers, tenses, aspects, and moods. As demonstrated in Table 3.1, the root of *amar* is *am-*. The thematic vowel will be one of two options: it will either be null (ø) or take the form of the final vowel in the infinitival form of the verb. Table 3.1 demonstrates that, in the conditional, the thematic vowel of *amar* is *a*. See Appendix C for other tenses (e.g., subjunctive) where the thematic vowel can also take

Table 3.1

	Number	*Person*	*Root*	*Thematic vowel*	*TAM inflection*	*P/N marking*	*Surface form*
Conditional	sg	1st	am	a	ría	ø	amaría
		3rd	am	a	ría	ø	amaría
	pl	1st	am	a	ría	mos	amaríamos
		3rd	am	a	ría	n	amarían

the form *ø*. TAM inflection obviously depends on the tense, aspect, and mood; and Table 3.1 demonstrates that for the conditional, it takes the form of *ría*. By delimiting the set of possibilities for these three parts (root, thematic vowel, and TAM inflection) in this way, Bosque (2010) suggests that what remains is person and number inflection. This leaves us with the following P/N inflection: 1SG is *–ø*, 3SG is *–ø*, 1PL is *–mos*, 3PL is *–n*.[6] Although not all the tenses demonstrate the same regularity that the conditional exhibits, Bosque (2010) suggests that the verb root, the thematic vowel, and the person/number marking on the verb are regular, so any irregularity should be accounted for within the TAM inflection. This observation applies to the other paradigms discussed by Bosque (2010) as well, which are examined below.

The second two paradigms discussed in this section are past imperfective and present subjunctive. According to Bosque (2010), both of these tenses share the property that they are regular in everything but P/N inflection. The past imperfective forms of *amar* "to love" are given in Table 3.2, and the present subjunctive forms of the same verb are given in Table 3.3.

The verb forms given in Table 3.2 indicate that not only the verb root but also the thematic vowel and the TAM inflection are constant across each P/N. The verb root is *am-*, the thematic vowel is *a*, the TAM inflection for past imperfective is *ba*. This is demonstrated by the fact that each form (regardless of the P/N) shares as a common denominator the string *amaba-*. Based on the fact that every P/N shares *amaba-*, Bosque (2010) claims that any additional morphemes will be P/N inflection.

Table 3.2

	Number	*Person*	*Root*	*Thematic vowel*	*TAM inflection*	*P/N marking*	*Surface form*
Past imperfective	sg	1st	am	a	ba	ø	amaba
		3rd	am	a	ba	ø	amaba
	pl	1st	am	a	ba	mos	amábamos
		3rd	am	a	ba	n	amaban

[6] And, as discussed above, second person forms will vary by dialect.

Table 3.3

	Number	*Person*	*Root*	*Thematic vowel*	*TAM inflection*	*P/N marking*	*Surface form*
Present subjunctive	sg	1st	am	ø	e	ø	ame
		3rd	am	ø	e	ø	ame
	pl	1st	am	ø	e	mos	amemos
		3rd	am	ø	e	n	amen

The paradigm in Table 3.3 is parallel to the paradigms in Tables 3.1 and 3.2 in that each P/N combination shares a common string, in this case *ame-*. Accordingly, the differences in person/number marking are easy to see, and they have the same forms as in the paradigms in Tables 3.1 and 3.2. These three paradigms lead us to the generalization that there is one string that is common to 1PL and one that is common to 3PL but no such string that is common to their singular counterparts 1SG and 3SG. See Table 3.4 for the corresponding forms for each P/N combination.

Table 3.4 indicates that 1PL is marked by *–mos* and 3PL is marked by *–n*, while 1SG and 1PL are only marked by the zero string. The information in this table is also supported by the other verbal paradigms of Spanish, given in Appendix C.

That generalization—coupled with the claim made in Nevins (2010) that clitics, unlike agreement, are "tense-invariant"—points to the fact that there are subject clitics for 1PL and 3PL but not 1SG or 3SG. Based on the regularity in the paradigms in Tables 3.1, 3.2, and 3.3, my proposal is that the common strings, as given in Table 3.4, are actually incorporated subject clitics. The subject clitic for 1PL is *–mos* and the subject clitic for 3PL is *–n*, and there are no subject clitics for the 1SG and 3SG, leading to a singular/plural asymmetry in the presence of clitics. While these two strings could be construed to simply be examples of subject-verb agreement, it bears repeating that they are constant across all TAM, which is not a property of agreement. According to Nevins (2010), an important morphosyntactic criterion for distinguishing pronominal clitics from agreement affixes is that clitics—as pronominal elements—are not subject to variation between tenses, while agreement—which is properly part of the verbal complex—is subject to variation between tenses. Additionally, for some of the paradigms in Appendix C, it appears that the proposed subject clitics are not

Table 3.4

P/N marking	*1SG*	*3SG*	*1PL*	*3PL*
Common string	–ø	–ø	–mos	–n

the only markers of person and number; they are simply the P/N markers that are tense-invariant. For this reason, I do not advocate the rejection of the traditional notion of subject-verb agreement, but rather the adoption of an obligatory plural subject clitic.

4. Imposter Agreement Data

Some of the data in this chapter come from a questionnaire (provided in Appendix A) that invited native speakers of Spanish to provide grammaticality judgments (given in Appendix B) on sentences involving first person imposters.

Initially, I identified five informants who were trained linguists. Three of these informants are from Spain (speakers TS, HA, and VR), one is from Mexico (speaker VA), and one was born in Puerto Rico but spent time in Argentina as a child (speaker MS). While some of the informants are bilingual (Spanish/Catalan or Spanish/English), they all speak Spanish natively.

The initial questionnaire was composed of 17 sets of 4 sentences, and the directions were given in Spanish. I also took pains to ensure that informants were focusing on the imposter reading of the tested DPs. For more detail on the questionnaire, see the directions and test items provided in Appendix A. Each set of items on the questionnaire manipulated two of the conditions given in (5).

(5) Imposter questionnaire conditions
  a. first vs. third person verbal agreement
  b. first vs. third person pronominal agreement
  c. imposter DP vs. normal pronoun
  d. singular imposter vs. coordinate DP with imposter conjunct
  e. plural imposter vs. coordinate DP with imposter conjunct
  f. matrix-embedded clausal order vs. embedded-matrix clausal order

Speakers were asked to indicate the grammaticality of the questionnaire sentences with one of three options translated in Table 3.5.

While they were asked to give their judgments based on the three options in Table 3.5, all of the informants responded with five gradations of these judgments: OK, OK/?, ??, ?/*, *. The full spectrum of their judgments can be seen in Appendix B. A preliminary statistical analysis suggests that despite interspeaker variation in judgments, there is no evidence for interdialectal variation (p.c., Dennis Shasha).

In sections 4.1 and 4.2, I discuss some of the results from my questionnaire as well as some examples that I encountered online. All the sentences in those subsections can be assumed to have the imposter (reference to speaker) reading

Table 3.5

Judgment	*Description*	*Mark*
Grammatical	The sentence sounds completely natural in the daily speech or writing of your dialect.	OK
Marginal	The sentence sounds unusual or it might be difficult to understand in your dialect.	?
Ungrammatical	The sentence is completely anomalous or would never be used in your dialect.	*

as at least one of their readings. Though some of these examples were collected online, they come from the questionnaire unless otherwise noted.

4.1 VERBAL AGREEMENT DATA

Singular imposters consistently allow third person verbal agreement. This is reflected in the judgments given for the sentences in (6).

(6) Singular imposters, third person verbal agreement

a. *Un servidor vive al lado de la iglesia católica*
a servant live.3SG to.the side of the church catholic
"A servant lives beside the Catholic church."

b. *Tu hija ganó el partido ayer.*
your daughter won.3SG the game yesterday
"Your daughter won the game yesterday."

c. *Pues como no sabía que poner-se al final aquí una*
Well because NEG knew.1SG what dress-REFL.3SG in.the end here a
servidora lo combinó con una faldita y medias azul
servant it combined.3SG with a little.skirt and stockings blue
marino.[7]
marine
"Well, not knowing what to wear, a servant here combined it with a miniskirt and navy stockings."

d. *Y sí, el abajo firmante piensa que quitar la mili fue*
And yes, the under signed.SG think.3SG that to.remove the military was
una gran idea y que apoyar la Guerra de Irak no lo fue tanto.[8]
a great idea and that to.support the war of Iraq NEG it was much
"And yes, the undersigned thinks that getting the military out was a great idea and supporting the war in Iraq was not so much."

[7] http://melancora.blogspot.com/2012/01/pues-aqui-una-servidora.html

[8] http://blog.publips.com/tag/dia-c-club-de-creativos-cielo-infierno-aniversario-cdec/

In (6a), the singular *servidor* imposter *un servidor* determines third person agreement on the matrix verb *vive* "lives." In (6b), the singular *kinship* imposter *tu hija* determines third person agreement on the matrix verb *ganó* "won." In (6c), the singular *servidor* imposter *una servidora* determines third person agreement with the verb *combinó* "combined." Finally, in (6d), the singular *undersigned* imposter *el abajo firmante* determines third person agreement with the verb *piensa* "thinks."

However, that imposters allow third person verbal agreement is expected because their overt person marking is third. The more interesting question for imposters, since they seem to refer to the speaker, is whether they admit first person verbal agreement. The generalization from the data I collected is that first person verbal agreement is never acceptable with singular imposters.[9] Examples of the unacceptability of first person verbal agreement with singular imposters are given in the sentences in (7).

(7) Singular imposters, first person verbal agreement[10]

a. *_Un servidor le compré una flor la semana pasada._
   a servant CL.DAT.3SG bought.1SG a flower the week last

b. *_Tu hija gané el partido ayer._
   your daughter won.1SG the game yesterday

Based on the sentences in (6–7), we see that singular imposters in Spanish allow third person verbal agreement but do not seem to allow first person verbal agreement. This is a clear generalization that holds up across all dialects I have examined.[11]

The pattern of agreement that we see attested with singular imposters does not hold for plural imposters. Under the account in Collins and Postal (2012), plural imposters should only admit third person verbal agreement. Contrary to this prediction is the fact that Spanish plural imposters allow first person verbal agreement. For the judgments on first person verbal agreement with plural imposters, see the sentences in (8).

(8) Plural imposters, first person verbal agreement

a. _Los abajo firmantes pensábamos en vender la casa._
   the.PL under signed.PL thought.1PL about to.sell the house
   "The undersigned were thinking about selling the house."

[9] This generalization holds with the exception that one informant (speaker VR) found first person verbal agreement with singular imposters marginal (?) in two sentences.

[10] The sentences in (7) would be completely acceptable if the first person verb form was replaced with a third person form.

[11] This generalization is also corroborated by a quick online search. Searching for singular *servidor* type imposters with first person agreement returns about 3,000 results, most of which appear in cross-sentential contexts. But, a search for singular *servidor* type imposters with third person agreement returns approximately 81,000 results.

b. *Unos servidores quedamos en encontrar-nos a las siete al*
some servants decided.1PL on to.meet-ourselves at the.PL seven to.the
lado del cine.
side of.the theater
"Some servants decided to meet at 7 beside the theater."

c. *Y unos servidores pensamos que la mejor manera de darlo a*
and some servants think.1PL that the best way of to.make.it to
conocer era mediante una comunicación inteligente.[12]
to.know was.3SG through a communication intelligent
"And some servants think that the best way was to make it known through intelligent communication."

d. *Estos estudiantes somos los q(ue) estamos luchando*[13]
these students are.1PL the.PL who are.1PL fighting
"These students are the ones who are fighting."

In (8a), the plural *undersigned* imposter *los abajo firmantes* determines first person agreement with the verb *pensábamos* "were thinking." In (8b–c), the plural *servidor* imposter *unos servidores* determines first person agreement with the verbs *quedamos* "decided" and *pensamos* "thought," respectively. In (8d), the plural *demonstrative* imposter *estos estudiantes* determines first person agreement with the verb *somos* "are."

Alongside the sentences in (8) where first person verbal agreements are attested are the judgments that third person verbal agreement is also acceptable, as given in (9).

(9) Plural imposters, third person verbal agreement

a. *Los abajo firmantes pensaban en vender la casa.*
the.PL under signed.PL thought.3PL about to.sell the house
"The undersigned were thinking about selling the house."

b. *Unos servidores quedaron en encontrar-se a las siete al*
some servants decided.3PL on to.meet-themselves at the.PL seven to.the
lado del cine.
side of.the theater
"These guys decided to meet at 7 beside the theater."

In (9a), the plural *undersigned* imposter determines third person agreement with the matrix verb *pensaban* "were thinking," and in (9b), the plural *servidor* imposter *unos servidores* determines third person agreement with the matrix verb *quedaron* "decided."

The judgments in (9) demonstrate that plural imposters in Spanish admit third person verbal agreement. Contrary to the predictions for plural imposters,

[12] http://elblogdekliper.blogspot.com/2012/02/en-el-tintero-aquarama.html
[13] https://twitter.com/carlos_disarli/status/303880699973341185

the Spanish constructions seem to admit both first person and third person verbal agreement. Furthermore, according to my consultants, the plural Spanish imposters optionally determine either person agreement with no interpretive consequences, meaning that reference to the speaker obtains with either first person or third person verbal agreement.[14] Thus, we see that the generalization to be made for plural Spanish imposters is that they admit both first and third person agreement.

Coordinate DPs with imposter conjuncts are predicted under the system in Collins and Postal (2012) to admit both third person and first person verbal agreement, and this prediction holds up in Spanish. See the judgments in (10–11).

(10) Coordinate DPs with imposter conjuncts, third person verbal agreement

a. *Un servidor y Amelia viven al lado de la iglesia católica.*
a servant and Amelia live.3PL to.the side of the church catholic
"A servant and Amelia live beside the Catholic church."

b. *Tu hija y Isabel ganaron el partido ayer.*
your daughter and Isabel won.3PL the game yesterday
"Your daughter and Isabel won the game yesterday."

c. *Este servidor y Julio quieren quedar-se hasta las diez.*
this servant and Julio want.3PL to.remain-themselves until the.PL ten
"This servant and Julio want to stay until 10."

d. *Maria y el abajo firmante pensaban en vender la casa*
Maria and the under signed thought.3PL about to.sell the house
"Maria and the undersigned thought about selling the house."

e. *Un servidor y sus amigos quedaron en encontrar-se a las siete al lado del cine*
a servant and his friends decided.3PL on to.meet-themselves at the.PL seven to.the side of.the theater
"A servant and his friends decided to meet at 7 beside the theater."

The examples in (10) demonstrate the judgments that my consultants had for sentences where coordinate DPs with imposter conjuncts take third person agreement. In (10a), the imposter conjunct is the singular *servidor* imposter *un servidor* and the agreement on the matrix verb *viven* "live" is 3PL. In (10b), the conjunct is the singular *kinship* imposter *tu hija* and the verb *ganaron* "won" gets 3PL agreement. In (10c), the conjunct is the singular *servidor* imposter *este servidor* and the verb *quieren* "wanted" has 3PL agreement. In (10d), the singular *undersigned* imposter *el abajo firmante* is

[14] Apparently some speakers find interpretive differences between sentences with first person agreement and third person agreement (p.c., Carmen Gallar Sánchez), even on an imposter reading of the sentences with third person agreement.

the conjunct and the verb *pensaban* "were thinking" is a 3PL form. Finally, in (10e), the conjunct is the singular *servidor* imposter *un servidor* and the verb *quedaron* "decided" has a 3PL form. These examples allow us to generalize that coordinate DPs with imposter conjuncts can determine third person verbal agreement.

(11) Coordinate DPs with imposter conjuncts, first person verbal agreement

a. *Tu hija y Isabel ganamos el partido ayer.*
your daughter and Isabel won.1PL the game yesterday
"Your daughter and Isabel won the game yesterday."

b. *Maria y el abajo firmante pensábamos en vender la casa*
Maria and the under signed thought.1PL about to.sell the house
"Maria and the undersigned thought about selling the house."

c. *Un servidor y sus amigos quedamos en encontrar-nos a las*
a servant and his friends decided.1PL on to.meet-ourselves at the.PL
siete al lado del cine[15]
seven to.the side of.the theater
"Yours truly and his friends decided to meet at 7 beside the theater."

From the examples in (11), we can conclude that coordinate DPs with imposter conjuncts also optionally determine first person verbal agreement. In (11a), the conjunct is the singular *kinship* imposter *tu hija* and the verb *ganamos* "won" gets 1PL agreement. In (11b), the conjunct is the singular *undersigned* imposter *el abajo firmante* and the verb *pensábamos* "were thinking" takes a 1PL form. In (11c), the singular *servidor* imposter *un servidor* is the conjunct and the verb *quedamos* "decided" takes a 1PL form. Taken together, the examples in (10–11) demonstrate that coordinate DPs with imposter conjuncts can optionally determine either first or third person verbal agreement. According to my informants, there is no interpretive difference between the sentences with first person agreement and third person agreement.

Table 3.6 sums up the generalizations about the verbal agreement that is admitted by Spanish preverbal imposter subjects.

Further research is needed to determine what agreement obtains with post-verbal imposter subjects in Spanish, which could be interestingly different from preverbal subjects under some analyses of Spanish subjects (see Alexiadou and Anagnostopoulou 1998, Suñer 2001, and Zagona 2002, among others). Deeper discussion of those issues is outside the scope of this chapter.

[15] One informant (speaker VA) judged this sentence to be marginal (??) and said that *unos servidores* is awkward. This informant also finds *este servidor* odd as well.

Table 3.6

Verbal agreement	***Singular imposter***	***Plural imposter***	***Coordinate DP with imposter conjunct***
1st person	*	OK	OK
3rd person	OK	OK	OK

4.2 PRONOMINAL AGREEMENT DATA

The Spanish data also provide evidence for some generalizations about the pronominal agreement that is allowed with Spanish imposters. In order to examine pronominal agreement, the sentences I tested with my informants manipulate the person feature values on the anaphoric clitics *se, me,* and *nos* that are third person singular/plural, first person singular, and first person plural forms, respectively.

There is a clear generalization to be made about the pronominal agreement allowed by plural imposters in Spanish. The plural imposters I tested allow both *se* and *nos.* See the judgments given in (12).

(12) Plural imposters, pronominal agreement

a. *Unos servidores quedaron en encontrar-se a las siete al*
some servants decided.3PL on to.meet-themselves at the.PL seven at.the
lado del cine.
side of.the theater
"Some servants decided to meet each other at 7 by the theater."

b. *Unos servidores quedamos en encontrar-nos a las siete al*
some servants decided.1PL on to.meet-ourselves at the.PL seven at.the
lado del cine.
side of.the theater
"Some servants decided to meet each other at 7 by the theater."

In (12a), the plural *servidor* imposter *unos servidores* determines 3PL verbal agreement on the matrix verb *quedaron* "decided" and third person pronominal agreement on the anaphoric pronominal *se* that cliticizes to the embedded verb *encontrar* "to meet." In (12b), the same plural *servidor* imposter determines 1PL verbal agreement on the matrix verb *quedamos* "decided" and first person pronominal agreement on the anaphoric pronominal *nos* that cliticizes to the embedded verb *encontrar* "to meet."

The examples in (12) reflect the ability of plural imposters to allow both first person and third person pronominal agreement. While the plural imposters admit both types of pronominal agreement, it is important to note that the pronominal agreement must be identical to the verbal agreement as stated in (13).

(13) When an imposter subject binds a pronoun, the pronominal agreement must be identical in feature values to the verbal agreement determined by that imposter.

More precisely, if a pronominal has the subject imposter as its antecedent, it must agree with the verb. See the judgments in (14) for other cases where there is a match in verbal and pronominal agreement and (15) for cases of mismatch in verbal agreement and pronominal agreement.

(14) Plural imposters, verbal and pronominal agreement feature match

a. *Estas periodistas decidieron unir-se en promover esta causa.*
these reporters decided.3PL to.unite-themselves in to.promote this cause
"These reporters decided to join forces in promoting this cause."

b. *Unos servidores quedamos en encontrar-nos a las siete al*
some servants decided.1PL on to.meet-ourselves at the.PL seven to.the
lado del cine.
side of.the theater
"Some servants decided to meet each other at 7 beside the theater."

The sentences in (14a–b) are acceptable because the verbal agreement and pronominal agreement in each sentence have identical feature values. (14a) has a third person verb form *deciderion* and a third person pronominal form *se*. (14b) has a first person verb form *quedamos* and first person pronominal form *nos*.

(15) Plural imposters, verbal and pronominal agreement feature mismatch

a. **Estas periodistas decidieron unir-nos en promover esta causa.*
these reporters decided.3PL to.unite-ourselves in to.promote this cause

b. **Unos servidores quedamos en encontrar-se a las siete al*
some servants decided.1PL on to.meet-themselves at the.PL seven to.the
lado del cine.
side of.the theater

(15a–b) are ungrammatical because in both sentences the pronominal agreement is not identical in feature values to the verbal agreement. In (15a), the verb *decidieron* is third person but the pronominal *nos* is first person. In (15b), the verb *quedamos* is first person and the pronominal *se* is third person.

This phenomenon of harmony between verbal agreement and pronominal agreement also holds for coordinate DPs with an imposter conjunct. The sentences in (16) demonstrate that imposter coordinates admit both *se* and *nos*.

(16) Coordinate DPs with imposter conjuncts, verbal and pronominal agreement feature match

a. *Un servidor y sus amigos quedaron en encontrar-se a las*
a servant and his.PL friends decided.3PL on to.meet-themselves at the.pl
siete al lado del cine.
seven to.the side of.the theater
"A servant and his friends decided to meet each other at 7 beside the theater."

b. *Un servidor y sus amigos quedamos en encontrar-nos a las*
a servant and his.PL friends decided.1PL on to.meet-ourselves at the.PL
siete al lado del cine.
seven to.the side of.the theater
"A servant and his friends decided to meet each other at 7 beside the theater."

In (16a), the coordinate DP admits third person verbal agreement and third person pronominal agreement. In (16b), the same coordinate DP admits first person verbal agreement and first person pronominal agreement. In contrast to the examples in (16), the sentences in (17) show examples of mismatches in pronominal and verbal agreement with the DPs with imposter conjuncts.

(17) Coordinate DPs with imposter conjuncts, verbal and pronominal agreement feature mismatch
a. **Este servidor y Julio quieren quedar-nos hasta las diez.*
this servant and Julio want.3PL to.remain-ourselves until the.PL ten
b. **Un servidor y sus amigos quedaron en encontrar-nos a*
a servant and his.PL friends decided.3PL on to.meet-ourselves at
las siete al lado del cine.
the.PL seven to.the side of.the theater
c. **Un servidor y sus amigos quedamos en encontrar-se a*
a servant and his.PL friends decided.1PL on to.meet-themselves at
las siete al lado del cine.
the.PL seven to.the side of.the theater

In (17a–b), the verbal agreement is third person and the pronominal agreement is first person. In (17c), there is first person verbal agreement and third person pronominal agreement. So, in the sentences in (17), unlike the sentences in (16), a mismatch in verbal agreement and pronominal agreement seems to lead to ungrammaticality. From these judgments, we can conclude that pronominals anteceded by the imposter must agree in feature values with the verbal agreement.

Finally, singular Spanish imposters also seem to meet the pronominal agreement generalization in (13), with one caveat. Singular imposter sentences with the 3SG anaphoric clitic *se* are grammatical, but sentences with the 1SG anaphoric clitic *me* are ungrammatical. But this is as predicted under the generalization in (13) given that we have already seen in the previous section that first person verbal agreement is ungrammatical. See the judgments in (18–19).

(18) Singular imposters, verbal and pronominal agreement feature match: third person
a. *El abajo firmante quiere comprometer-se a luchar contra*
the under signed wants.3SG to.commit-himself to to.fight against
tales injusticias.
such.PL injustices
"The undersigned wants to commit himself to fighting against such injustices."

b. *Este abogado puede enojar-se cuando sus expedientes están*
this lawyer can.3SG to.get.mad-himself when his briefs are
perdidos.
lost
"This lawyer can get mad when his briefs are lost."

(19) Singular imposters, verbal and pronominal agreement feature match: first person
a. *El abajo firmante quiero comprometer-me a luchar contra*
the under signed wants.1SG to.commit-myself to to.fight against
tales injusticias.
such.PL injustices

(20) Singular imposters, verbal and pronominal agreement feature mismatch
a. *El abajo firmante quiero comprometer-se a luchar contra*
the under signed wants.1SG to.commit-himself to to.fight against
tales injusticias.
such.PL injustices
b. *El abajo afirmante quiere comprometer-me a luchar contra*
the under signed wants.3SG to.commit-myself to to.fight against
tales injusticias.
such.PL injustices
c. *Este servidor quiere quedar-me hasta las diez*
this servant want.3SG to.remain-myself until the.PL ten

The judgments in (18–20) appear to maintain the generalization about pronominal-verbal agreement. (18a–b) are grammatical because the agreement on the verb is third person and there is third person pronominal agreement. The sentence in (19) is unacceptable because the verbal agreement is first person, regardless of the fact that the pronominal agreement matches the feature values of the verbal agreement. (20a) is unacceptable either due to the first person verbal agreement or to a mismatch that violates the generalization in (13). But (19b–c) are unacceptable (despite the third person verbal agreement) because the verbal agreement and the pronominal agreement do not match in feature values: the verbal agreement in these examples is third person and the pronominal agreement is first person. The examples above allow us to make the generalization that singular Spanish imposters are subject to the verbal-pronominal agreement condition mentioned in (13).[16]

[16] However, there are some exceptions that do not hold across all dialects. A few speakers find some of the sentences in (20b–c) marginal. If these sentences with feature mismatch are acceptable, it is only the ones that have third person verb forms, which corresponds with generalizations for other languages like Icelandic and Albanian (Wood and Sigurðsson, Kallulli, this volume).

Table 3.7

	1st person pronominal agreement	***3rd person pronominal agreement***
first person verbal agreement	OK	*
third person verbal agreement	*(??)	OK

Table 3.7 summarizes the possibilities for pronominal agreement in Spanish based on the verbal agreement admitted with imposter DPs.[17]

Note that the verbal-pronominal agreement condition in (13) is very similar to the Homogeneity Principle, as formulated in Collins and Postal (2012), in that both require a pronominal to match another element in feature values. I leave it to future research to examine the Spanish data on singular and plural imposter objects as antecedents to pronouns, which could be informative about the status of the generalization in (13), because in those cases the imposter determines pronominal agreement without determining verbal agreement.

5. Toward an Explanation of the Spanish Data

The Spanish imposter data that I provided in the previous section demonstrate that there is an interesting singular/plural asymmetry in Spanish. Putting aside coordinate DPs with imposter conjuncts, which seem to freely determine whatever verbal agreement cross-linguistically, we see that singular imposters allow only third person verbal agreement and plural imposters optionally allow either first or third person verbal agreement. Unlike some other languages, first person verbal agreement with plural Spanish imposters is quite productive. It occurs with all of the types of plural imposters listed in (1), and, as demonstrated by the generalization in (4), the number of plural imposters is potentially infinite. Thus, unlike other languages, the first person verbal agreement that obtains with plural imposters in Spanish is not dependent on certain lexical items, as discussed by Lima (2010) for Brazilian Portuguese, nor on the presence of indexical elements like "here present," as discussed by Soare (this volume) for other Romance languages. As a result, this singular/plural asymmetry is most similar to the one found in Icelandic (Wood and Sigurðsson, this volume). Now, the question that

[17] Another exception to this generalization involves purpose clauses. Purpose clauses seem to marginally allow a mismatch in verbal agreement and pronominal agreement:

(1) *Tu hijo necesita un buen impermeable para no empapar-se/?me*
your son need.3SG a good raincoat in.order not to.soak-himself/?myself
hasta los huesos.
to the.pl bones
"Your son requires a good raincoat in order to not soak himself/myself to the bone."

remains: What underlies the singular/plural asymmetry in the verbal agreement that we see with Spanish imposters? In the next sections, I will describe a couple of unsuccessful analyses, before providing a more successful analysis that draws on the two singular/plural asymmetries discussed above in sections 3 and 4.

6. Some Unsuccessful Analyses: Co-occurrence with Little *pro*

Spanish is a null subject language, and there is already some argument about the status of overt preverbal lexical subjects in Spanish (cf. Suñer 2001, Alexiadou and Anagnostopoulou 1998, Zagona 2002). In light of this ongoing debate, and Collins and Postal's (2012) covert pronominal analysis, it could make sense to analyze the overt Spanish imposter DPs as co-occurring with a little *pro* that is the true subject and therefore true determinant of verbal and pronominal agreement. I will discuss two different conceptions of this: a left dislocation analysis and a covert appositive analysis.

6.1 LEFT DISLOCATION ANALYSIS

One potential analysis of imposters that might account for the optional first person agreement would utilize left dislocation. Since it has been proposed that overt preverbal subjects in null subject languages like Spanish and Greek can occur in left-dislocated structures (Suñer 2001, Alexiadou and Anagnostopoulou 1998), this analysis would have the imposter subjects occur somewhere in the left periphery, higher than the covert pronominal subject. As in some analyses of *pro*-drop languages, the verbal agreement in the sentence would not come directly from the left-dislocated imposter DP but rather from agreement relations with little *pro*, which might have the same ultimate antecedent (Collins and Postal 2012) as the imposter subject. In sentences where the verbal agreement is third person, little *pro* would have third person phi-features. Alternatively, in sentences where the verbal agreement is first person, little *pro* would have first person phi-features. Examples of what this left dislocation analysis would look like for plural imposters are given in (21) for both types of verbal agreement: third person in (21a) and first person in (21b).

(21) Left-dislocation analysis: plural imposters

a. [[*Los abajo firmantes*] [*pro* [*quedaron* [*en encontrar–se*]]]]
the under signed.PL 3PL decided.3PL on to. meet–REFL.3PL
"The undersigned decided to meet each other."

b. [[*Los abajo firmantes*] [*pro* [*quedamos* [*en encontrar–nos*]]]]
the under signed.PL 1PL decided.1PL on to.meet–REFL.1PL
"The undersigned decided to meet each other."

In the sentences in (21), the verbal agreement that is allowed is based on the phi–features of little *pro* and not the imposter DP, since the imposter DP is left-dislocated, potentially in a Topic Phrase. Since little *pro* can have either first person or third person phi-features, the verb can take either first person or third person forms.

However, if the left dislocation analysis were the appropriate account for the Spanish facts, then both of the sentences in (22) should also be possible. But, given the data presented above in sections 4.1 and 4.2, the one in (22b) is not possible in Spanish.

(22) Left-dislocation analysis: singular imposters

a. [[*El abajo firmante*] [*pro* [*quiere* [*casar–se* *con* *Elena*]]]]
the under signed 3SG wants.3SG to.marry–REFL.3SG with Elena
"The undersigned wants to marry Elena."

b. *[[*El abajo firmante*] [*pro* [*quiero* [*casar–me* *con* *Elena*]]]]
the under signed 1SG want.1SG to.marry–REFL.1SG with Elena
"The undersigned wants to marry Elena."

In (22a), the verbal agreement is third person because the phi-features on little *pro* are third person. In (22b), the verbal agreement is first person because the phi-features on little *pro* are first person. In Spanish, sentences like the ones in (21a–b) and (22a) are grammatical, but not ones like in (22b). As a result, the left dislocation analysis of imposters struggles to capture all the Spanish data because it cannot account for the singular/plural asymmetry in verbal agreement with imposters unless bolstered by some stipulation that blocks first person features on little *pro* with singular imposters.

6.2 COVERT APPOSITIVE ANALYSIS

Another similar analysis explains the acceptability of first person verbal agreement with a covert appositive. An appositive structure would look something like *we, the undersigned* or *I, yours truly* where the first person pronoun is covert. In sentences where there is first person verbal agreement, the agreement would come from the first person phi-features on the covert pronoun. In sentences where the verbal agreement is third person, the agreement would come from the third person phi-features on the covert pronoun.

This proposed appositive would look like the English appositive in (23), where the only difference is that the underlined first person pronominal is covert.

(23) I, yours truly, always make/*makes an effort to correspond more frequently.

In sentences like the one in (23), the reference to speaker associated with an imposter reading would come from the phi-features on the covert pronoun and would not be related to the imposter DP at all.

The covert appositive analysis is an attractive explanation for the first person verbal agreement in Spanish imposters because it takes advantage of an often proposed feature of Spanish, an unpronounced pronominal subject: little *pro*. However, it does not allow for any way to distinguish between the plural imposters and the singular imposters. In Spanish, little *pro* can be either singular, as in (24), or plural, as in (25).

(24)	*pro*	*Salgo*	*pronto*	*cada*	*manana.*
	1SG	leave.1SG	early	each	morning
	"I leave early each morning."				
(25)	*pro*	*Salimos*	*pronto*	*cada*	*manana.*
	1PL	leave.1PL	early	each	morning
	"We leave early each morning."				

If little *pro* can be either singular or plural, then the covert first person pronoun in the proposed appositive structure could also be either singular or plural, but we have seen that first person agreement is only allowed with plural imposters. Thus, under the appositive proposal provided in this section, the distinction between the Spanish plural imposters and singular imposters cannot be accounted for without some additional stipulation that blocks little *pro* (or rather 1SG little *pro*) but only in the presence of singular imposters. Such a stipulation would be extravagant in the absence of a motivation.

7. A Clitic Doubling Analysis

The analyses discussed in the previous section both take the form of stipulating that Spanish imposters have a different structure from imposters of other languages, but those analyses were unsuccessful. Might a successful analysis instead suggest a different mechanism of verbal agreement for Spanish? Under an analysis of this type, the distinction should not be accounted for as a parametric setting in the structure of imposters but instead as a parametric setting within verbal agreement. In this section, I argue for a reanalysis of Spanish subject-verb agreement.

Following Hale (1973), Jelinek (1984), and Ordóñez and Treviño (1999), I propose that the incorporated subject clitic is what is traditionally considered to be the P/N inflection on the end of plural verbs. This claim is supported by the parallelisms between subject-verb agreement and clitic doubling of objects, which for Suñer (1988) are the same mechanism. The evidence for this distinction in clitic doubling of singular subjects and plural subjects comes from the verbal paradigms of Spanish, discussed above in section 3 and given in Appendix C.

Under my proposal, plural subject DPs are obligatorily doubled by a clitic that incorporates into the verb. The plural subject DP can either be pronounced (as in 26a) or unpronounced (as in 26b). In addition, singular subject DPs are never doubled by a subject clitic, but they can still be pronounced (26c) or unpronounced (26d).

(26) Clitic doubling analysis

a. *Algunos estudiantes fuero-n a la biblioteca.*
Some students went.3PL-CL.3PL to the library

b. *pro Fuero-n a la biblioteca.*
3PL went.3PL-CL.3PL to the library

c. *Algun estudiante fue a la biblioteca.*
a student went.3SG to the library

d. *pro Fue a la biblioteca.*
3SG went.3SG to the library

Under this analysis of Spanish, the singular/plural distinction is captured by the fact that subject-verb agreement with singulars and subject-verb agreement with plurals are two different mechanisms. With singular imposters and normal singular Spanish DPs, the mechanism behind verbal agreement is traditional subject-verb agreement. Plural subjects, on the other hand, are obligatorily doubled by a subject clitic that either agrees with the phi-features on little *pro*, with the lexical subject DP, or with the ultimate antecedent of that lexical DP. In the case of plural imposter subjects, the difference is between agreeing with the third person imposter shell and the first person AUTHOR.

The clitic doubling structure that I adopt from Ordóñez and Treviño (1999) is given in (27).

(27)

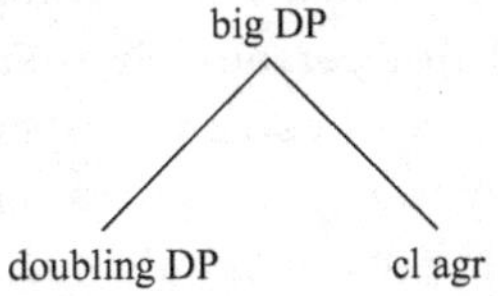

In (27), the subject clitic (cl agr) is the head of the big DP and the doubling DP in Spec big DP is either a plural imposter or a normal plural DP. A summary of my proposal is stated in (28).

(28) Plural subject DPs occur as part of the big DP, whose head is a subject clitic that either agrees with the plural subject DP or with the ultimate antecedent of the plural subject DP.

8. Open Question

While it is clear from the verbal paradigm data that there is no 1SG or 3SG subject clitic, I have not yet discussed any reason that clitic doubling of singular subjects would be blocked. In the literature, it is attested that the clitic doubling of objects is blocked by certain features (Schroten 2010) and that the doubling of different types of objects is restricted in different ways (Suñer 1988). But, as of yet, I have discovered no adequate reason that the feature [+SG] (or [-PL]) should block doubling of the subject. The lack of motivation for blocking of the singular is not an indication that the incorporated subject clitic proposal should be abandoned, however, because in languages that show robust clitic doubling of subjects like the Northern Italian Dialects (NIDs), there are often gaps in the paradigm. According to Rizzi (1986), "the largely predominant, and perhaps fully general pattern thus seems to be that for some choices of grammatical features the subject clitic is obligatory, for others it is optional or does not exist." I leave the identification of what blocks clitic doubling of singular subjects in Spanish for further research.

9. Conclusion

In this chapter, I have provided evidence for a subject clitic doubling mechanism that applies obligatorily to plural DPs in Spanish. Evidence for this mechanism came from new data on Spanish imposter DPs and the verbal agreement, patterns that are possible with those DPs, as well as recent analyses of regular verbal morphology. The generalization from the imposter agreement data included two components: (i) that sentences with plural imposters (third person DPs that are used to refer to a group that includes the speaker) optionally determine either first person or third person verbal agreement, and (ii) that sentences with singular imposters (third person DPs that are used to refer to the speaker) exclusively determine third person agreement. The generalization from Spanish verbal morphology was that regular person and number marking, which occurs only on plural verbs in Spanish, should be reanalyzed as incorporated subject clitics that occur obligatorily and exclusively on plural verb forms. Ultimately, the clitic doubling mechanism accounts for the singular/plural asymmetries in both domains because they should be derived from the singular/plural asymmetry in the clitic doubling mechanism.

Appendix A: Spanish Imposters Questionnaire

With this questionnaire, I'm looking for your opinions on the acceptability of certain sentences in the context of everyday or colloquial speech and writing.

Please read the sentences that begin on the next page and mark your judgments based on the following criteria:

- Mark the sentences with OK if they sound completely natural and you would expect them to be used in everyday speech and writing.
- Mark the sentences with ? if they sound unusual but you would understand them if others were to use them.
- Mark the sentences with * if they sound completely wrong and no one would ever use them.

If you see two or more words underlined, it means that the words all refer to the speaker or writer of the sentence. See the following examples:

Él tiene que bañarse antes de salir.
Ella siempre olvida sus gafas.

All of the following sentences contain expressions like "este estudiante," "un servidor," "el abajo afirmante," and "el menda." Please understand that they are not proper names.

If you have any doubts about a sentence feel free to give some comments or notes about it. I'd appreciate any information you can provide to increase my comprehension of this topic

Many thanks for your time.

- En este cuestionario, me interesa conocer sus juicios de gramaticalidad y/o aceptabilidad con respecto a ciertas frases en el contexto de discursos cotidianos o coloquiales (tantos verbales como escritos).
- Para completar este cuestionario, le ruego que lea las frases que empiezan en la pagina siguiente y las marque de acuerdo con las siguientes convenciones:
  - Use OK si la frase le suena completamente natural o si se imaginaría que se lo dice en el habla cotidiano de su dialecto.
  - Use ? si la frase le suena raro o si le parece que sería de difícil comprensión en su dialecto.
  - Use * si la frase le suena completamente anómala o si Ud. nunca lo usaría.
- Cuando una o más palabras aparezcan subrayadas en una frase, debe entenderse que esas palabras se refieren al hablante o escritor de la frase. Considere los siguientes ejemplos:

  Él tiene que bañarse antes de salir.
  Ella siempre olvida sus gafas.
- En cada frase del cuestionario encontrará expresiones como "este estudiante," "un servidor," "el menda," "tu hijo," y "el abajo firmante." Note que estas expresiones no son nombres propios.
- Si tiene dudas al respecto de cualquier frase o encuentra cualquier otra cosa digna de remarcar, le ruego que incluya su comentario o nota en el cuestionario. Cualquier información que pueda darme que contribuya a ampliar mi comprensión de este tema será del todo bienvenida.
- Le agradezco mucho su ayuda.

1. Un servidor le compró una flor la semana pasada.
2. Un servidor le compré una flor la semana pasada.
3. Yo le compró una flor la semana pasada.
4. Yo le compré una flor la semana pasada.
5. Este doctor y los otros tienen que curar a sus pacientes.
6. Este doctor y los otros tienen que curar a nuestros pacientes.
7. Este doctor tiene que curar a sus pacientes.
8. Este doctor tiene que curar a mis pacientes.
9. Tu hijo necesita un buen impermeable para no empaparse hasta los huesos.
10. Tu hijo necesita un buen impermeable para no empaparme hasta los huesos.
11. Para no empaparse hasta los huesos, tu hijo necesita un buen impermeable.
12. Para no empaparme hasta los huesos, tu hijo necesita un buen impermeable.
13. Este estudiante vive frugalmente para no gastar su dinero.
14. Para no gastar su dinero, este estudiante vive frugalmente.
15. Este estudiante vive frugalmente para no gastar mi dinero.
16. Para no gastar mi dinero, este estudiante vive frugalmente.
17. El abajo firmante afirma que sus solicitudes anteriores son de extrema importancia.
18. El abajo firmante afirmo que sus solicitudes anteriores son de extrema importancia.
19. El abajo firmante afirma que mis solicitudes anteriores son de extrema importancia.
20. El abajo firmante afirmo que mis solicitudes anteriores son de extrema importancia.
21. El abajo afirmante quiere comprometerse a luchar contra tales injusticias.
22. El abajo afirmante quiere comprometerme a luchar contra tales injusticias.
23. El abajo afirmante quiero comprometerse a luchar contra tales injusticias.
24. El abajo afirmante quiero comprometerme a luchar contra tales injusticias.
25. Un servidor y Amelia viven al lado de la iglesia católica.
26. Un servidor vive al lado de la iglesia católica.
27. Amelia y yo vivimos al lado de la iglesia católica.
28. Yo vivo al lado de la iglesia católica.
29. Este abogado puede enojarse cuando *sus* expedientes están perdidos.
30. Este abogado puede enojarme cuando sus expedientes están perdidos.
31. Este abogado puede enojarse cuando mis expedientes están perdidos.
32. Este abogado puede enojarme cuando mis expedientes están perdidos.
33. Tu hija e Isabel ganaron el partido ayer.
34. Tu hija e Isabel ganamos el partido ayer.
35. Tu hija ganó el partido ayer.
36. Tu hija gané el partido ayer.
37. Este estudiante solía sentarse detrás de Ana.
38. Este estudiante solía sentarme detrás de Ana.
39. Yo solía sentarse detrás de Ana.
40. Yo solía sentarme detrás de Ana.
41. Este servidor quiere quedarse hasta las diez.
42. Este servidor quiere quedarme hasta las diez.
43. Este servidor y Julio quieren quedarse hasta las diez.

44. Este servidor y Julio quieren quedarnos hasta las diez.
45. Este escritor siempre cena antes de pasear con su perro.
46. Este escritor siempre cena antes de pasear con mi perro.
47. Yo siempre ceno antes de pasear con su perro.
48. Yo siempre ceno antes de pasear con mi perro.
49. Aquí tu hijo opina que necesitas cuidarte mejor.
50. Aquí yo opino que necesitas cuidarte mejor.
51. Yo opino que necesitas cuidarte mejor.
52. Tu hijo opina que necesitas cuidarte mejor.
53. María y el abajo firmante pensaban en vender la casa.
54. María y el abajo firmante pensábamos en vender la casa.
55. Los abajo firmantes pensaban en vender la casa.
56. Los abajo firmantes pensábamos en vender la casa.
57. Unos servidores quedaron en encontrarse a las siete al lado del cine.
58. Unos servidores quedaron en encontrarnos a las siete al lado del cine.
59. Unos servidores quedamos en encontrarse a las siete al lado del cine.
60. Unos servidores quedamos en encontrarnos a las siete al lado del cine.
61. Un servidor y sus amigos quedaron en encontrarse a las siete al lado del cine.
62. Un servidor y sus amigos quedaron en encontrarnos a las siete al lado del cine.
63. Un servidor y sus amigos quedamos en encontrarnos a las siete al lado del cine.
64. Un servidor y sus amigos quedamos en encontrarse a las siete al lado del cine.
65. Estas periodistas decidieron unirse para promover esta causa.
66. Nosotras decidimos unirnos para promover esta causa.
67. Nosotras decidimos unirse para promover esta causa.
68. Estas periodistas decidieron unirnos para promover esta causa.

Appendix B: Results of Imposters Questionnaire

Table 3.8

Sentence #	*Speaker TS*	*Speaker HA*	*Speaker VR*	*Speaker MS*	*Speaker VA*
1	OK	OK	OK	OK	OK
2	*	*	?	*	*
3	*	*	*	*	*
4	OK	*	OK	OK	OK
5	?/OK	OK	OK	OK	?

(*Continued*)

Table 3.8 **(Continued)**

Sentence #	*Speaker TS*	*Speaker HA*	*Speaker VR*	*Speaker MS*	*Speaker VA*
6	*	*	*	?	*
7	OK	OK	OK	OK	OK
8	*	*	*	*	*
9	OK	OK	OK	OK	OK
10	*	?	?	*	?
11	OK	OK	OK	OK	OK
12	*	?	*	?	?
13	OK	OK	OK	OK	OK
14	OK	OK	OK	OK	OK
15	*	*	*	*	*
16	*	*	*	*	*
17	OK	OK	OK	OK	OK
18	*	*	*	*	*
19					
20	*	*	*	*	*
21	OK	OK	OK	OK	OK
22	*/?	*	*	*	*
23	**	*	*	*	*
24	*	*	?	*	*
25	OK	OK	OK	OK	OK
26	OK	OK	OK	OK	OK
27	OK	OK	OK	OK	OK
28	OK	OK	OK	OK	OK
29	OK	OK	OK	OK	OK
30	*/?	*	*	*	*
31	*/?	?	?	*	??
32	*/?	*	*	*	*
33	OK	OK	OK	OK	OK
34	OK/?	*	OK	?	??
35	OK	OK	OK	OK	OK
36	*	*	*	*	*

Sentence #	*Speaker TS*	*Speaker HA*	*Speaker VR*	*Speaker MS*	*Speaker VA*
37	OK	OK	OK	OK	OK
38	*	*	*	*	*
39	**	*	*	*	*
40	OK	OK	OK	OK	OK
41	OK	OK	OK	OK	OK
42	*	*	*	*	*
43	OK	?	OK	OK	OK
44	****	*	*	*	*
45	OK	OK	OK	OK	OK
46	*/?	?	*	*	OK
47	*	*	*	*	*
48	OK	OK	OK	OK	OK
49	OK	OK	OK	OK	OK
50	OK	?	OK	OK	OK
51	OK	OK	OK	OK	OK
52	OK	OK	OK	OK	OK
53	OK	OK	OK	OK	OK
54	OK	?	OK	?	OK
55	OK	OK	OK	OK	OK
56	OK	OK	OK	?	OK
57	OK	*	OK	OK	??
58	*	*	?	*	*
59	*	*	*	*	*
60	OK	OK	OK	*	??
61	OK		OK	OK	OK
62	*	*	?	?	*
63	OK	OK	OK	?	OK
64	*	*	*	*	*
65	OK	*	OK	OK	OK
66	OK	OK	OK	OK	OK
67	*	*	*	*	*
68	*	*	*	*	*

Appendix C: Verbal Paradigms from Bosque (2010)

Table 3.9

	Number	*Person*	*Root*	*Thematic vowel*	*TAM inflection*	*P/N inflection*	*Surface form*
Past Perfective	SG	1st	am	ø	e	ø	amé
		3rd	am	ø	o	ø	amó
	PL	1st	am	a	ø	mos	amamos
		3rd	am	a	ro	n	amaron

Table 3.10

	Number	*Person*	*Root*	*Thematic vowel*	*TAM inflection*	*P/N inflection*	*Surface form*
Present Indicative	Sg	1st	am	ø	o	ø	amo
		3rd	am	a	ø	ø	ama
	PL	1st	am	a	ø	mos	amamos
		3rd	am	a	ø	n	aman

Table 3.11

	Number	*Person*	*Root*	*Thematic vowel*	*TAM inflection*	*P/N inflection*	*Surface form*
Future	SG	1st	am	a	re	ø	amaré
		3rd	am	a	ra	ø	amará
	PL	1st	am	a	re	mos	amaremos
		3rd	am	a	ra	n	amarán

Table 3.12

	Number	*Person*	*Root*	*Thematic vowel*	*TAM inflection*	*P/N inflection*	*Surface form*
Past Imperfective	SG	1st	am	a	ba	ø	amaba
		3rd	am	a	ba	ø	amaba
	PL	1st	am	a	ba	mos	amábamos
		3rd	am	a	ba	n	amaban

Table 3.13

	Number	*Person*	*Root*	*Thematic vowel*	*TAM inflection*	*P/N inflection*	*Surface form*
Conditional	SG	1st	am	a	ria	ø	amaría
		3rd	am	a	ria	ø	amaría
	PL	1st	am	a	ria	mos	amaríamos
		3rd	am	a	ria	n	amarían

Table 3.14

	Number	*Person*	*Root*	*Thematic vowel*	*TAM inflection*	*P/N inflection*	*Surface form*
Present Subjunctive	SG	1st	am	ø	e	ø	ame
		3rd	am	ø	e	ø	ame
	PL	1st	am	ø	e	mos	amemos
		3rd	am	ø	e	n	amen

References

Alexiadou, Artemis, and Elena Anagnostopoulou. 1998. Parametrizing Agr: Word order, V-movement and EPP-checking. *Natural Language and Linguistic Theory* 16: 491–539.

Baker, Mark. 2008. *The Syntax of Agreement and Concord.* Cambridge, UK: Cambridge University Press.

Beinhauer, Werner. 1978. *El español coloquial.* Madrid, Spain: Editorial Gredos.

Bernstein, Judy. 2008. Reformulating the determiner phrase analysis. *Language and Linguistics Compass* 2(6): 1246–1270.

Bosque, Ignacio. 2010. *Nueva gramática de la lengua española.* Madrid, Spain: Espasa Libros.

Buring, Daniel. 2005. *Binding Theory.* Cambridge, UK: Cambridge University Press.

Carnie, Andrew. 2007. *Syntax: A Generative Introduction.* Oxford, UK: Blackwell Publishing.

Collins, Chris, and Paul Postal. 2012. *Imposters: A Study in Pronominal Agreement.* Cambridge, MA: MIT Press.

Collins, Chris, Stephanie Guitard, and Jim Wood. 2009. Imposters: An online survey of grammaticality judgments. *NYU Working Papers in Linguistics* 2: 1–22. http://linguistics.as.nyu.edu/docs/CP/2345/collins_guitard_wood_imposters_online_09_nyuwpl2.pdf

Collins, Chris, Simanique Moody, and Paul M. Postal. 2008. An AAE camouflage construction. *Language* 84: 29– 68.

Davies, Mark. 2002. Corpus del Español: 100 million words, 1200s–1900s. Available online at http://www.corpusdelespanol.org.

Dudley, Rachel. 2011. *Spanish imposters.* Undergraduate honors thesis, New York University.

Hale, Kenneth. 1973. Person marking in Walbiri. In *A Festschrift for Morris Halle*, eds. Stephen R. Anderson and Paul Kiparsky. New York: Holt, Rinehart and Winston.

Huddleston, Rodney, and Geoffrey K. Pullum. 2002. *The Cambridge Grammar of the English Language.* Cambridge, UK: Cambridge University Press.

Jelinek, Eloise. 1984. Empty categories, case and configurationality. *Natural Language and Linguistic Theory* 2: 39–76.

Jespersen, Otto. 1924. *The Philosophy of Grammar.* London: George Allen & Unwin.

Kayne, Richard S. 1994. *The Antisymmetry of Syntax*. Cambridge, MA: MIT Press.

Lima, Ananda. 2010. Some imposter data in Brazilian Portuguese. Paper presented at New York University.

Mancini, Simona, Nicola Molinaro, Luigi Rizzi, and Manuel Carreiras. 2010. When persons disagree: An ERP study of Unagreement in Spanish. Manuscript, BCBL, Basque Center on Cognition, Brain and Language, Donostia-San Sebastián, Spain.

Nevins, Andrew. 2010. Multiple Agree with Clitics: Person Complementarity vs. Omnivorous Number. Manuscript, University College London.

Ordóñez, Franciso, and Esthela Treviño. 1999. Left dislocated subjects and the pro-drop parameter: A case study of Spanish. *Lingua* 107: 39–68.

Postal, Paul M. 1966. On so-Called pronouns in English. In *Report of the 17th Annual Round Table Meeting on Languages and Linguistics*. ed. F. Dineen S. J. Washington, DC; Georgetown University Press. Reprinted in D. A. Reibel and S. A. Schane, eds., *Modern Studies in English: Readings in Transformational Grammar*. Englewood Cliffs, NJ: Prentice-Hall, 1969.

Rizzi, Luigi. 1986. On the status of subject clitics in Romance. In *Studies in Romance Linguistics*, 391–417. Dordrecht, Netherlands: Foris Publications.

Ross, John Robert. 1970. On declarative sentences. In *Readings in English Transformational Grammar*, eds. Roderick A. Jacobs and Peter S. Rosenbaum, 222–272. Boston: Ginn.

Schroten, Jan. 2010. Clitic doubling in Spanish: Agreement of the third kind. In *The Linguistics Enterprise: From Knowledge of Language to Knowledge in Linguistics*, eds. Martin Everaert, Tom Lentz, Hannah De Mulder, Øystein Nilsen, and Arjen Zondervan, 315–326. Amsterdam, Netherlands: John Benjamins Publishing.

Siewierska, Anna. 2004. *Person*. Cambridge, UK: Cambridge University Press.

Suñer, Margarita. 1988. The role of agreement in clitic-doubled constructions. *Natural Language and Linguistic Theory* 6: 391–434.

Suñer, Margarita. 2001. The lexical preverbal subject in Romance Null Subject Language: Where art thou? In *A Romance Perspective on Language Knowledge and Use*, eds. Rafael Núñez-Cedeño, Luis López, and Richard Cameron, 341–357. Amsterdam, Netherlands: John Benjamins Publishing.

Vázquez Rojas, Violeta. 2007. Indefinite imposters. Unpublished manuscript, New York University.

Zagona, Karen. 2002. *The Syntax of Spanish*. Cambridge, UK: Cambridge University Press.

4

Some Observations on Imposters in Albanian

DALINA KALLULLI

1. Introduction

This chapter sets out to describe some basic facts and observations concerning the morpho-syntactic behavior of so-called imposters in Standard Albanian, a pro-drop language with rich subject-verb agreement morphology, which makes it interesting testing ground for recent claims on their structure (see Collins and Postal 2012; henceforth C&P).[1] I will adopt Collins and Postal's (2012) definition of *imposter*, given in (1).

(1) An imposter is a notionally *n* person DP which is grammatically *m* person, $n \neq m$.

By this definition, *mommy* in (2) is an imposter since it refers to the speaker—it is thus notionally first person—but invariably exhibits third person subject-verb agreement in English.

(2) Mommy is/*am going to work now.

However, as shown in (2'), first person agreement is not ruled out in the Albanian counterpart of (2):

(2') *Mami* *shkon* / *shkoj* *tani.*[2]
mommy.the go.PR.3S go.PR.1S. now
"Mommy is going (away) now."

[1] There are two major dialectal varieties of Albanian, Gheg (spoken in the north) and Tosk (spoken in the south); Standard Albanian is based on Tosk.

[2] As in other Balkan languages (e.g., Bulgarian, Macedonian, Romanian), the definite article in Albanian is suffixed to the noun. It is a so-called portmanteau morpheme, in that it simultaneously marks case, gender, and number.

As shown in (2''), this pattern is also replicable with past tense (used here in a present sense, though):

(2'') *Mami* *shkoi* / ***shkova*** *tani.*
mommy.the go.P.3S / go.P.1S now
"Mommy is going (away) now."

The same contrast in terms of subject-verb agreement between English and Albanian also obtains for the so-called camouflage DP 'your ass' (Collins, Moody, and Postal 2008; C&P 2012), as shown in (3) versus (3').[3]

(3) Your ass is/*are in trouble.

(3') *Prapanica* *jote* *është* / *je* *në* *zjarr.*
behind.the yours is / are.2S in fire
"You are in trouble." (lit.: "Your behind is in trouble.")

Though these subject-verb agreement differences between English and Albanian are in need of explanation, they do not challenge the definition of imposters given in (1) since third person agreement is obviously also possible in Albanian.[4] In this context, note that even in English there is a sharp difference with respect to determining pronominal agreement between a singular imposter and a coordinate DP with an imposter conjunct, as pointed out by Collins and Postal. In English, for singular imposters, first person verbal and pronominal agreement is unacceptable, as in (4a). For plural imposters, while there is no difference between first person plural and third person plural subject-verb agreement, both first and third person plural pronominal agreement are possible, as in (4b).

(4) a. Daddy *am/is enjoying *myself/himself.
b. Daddy and Mommy are enjoying ourselves/themselves on the beach.

Given the fact that, unlike in English, first person subject-verb agreement is possible even with singular imposters in Albanian (as was illustrated in (2')), it

[3] The following abbreviations are used in the glosses: S (= singular), PL (= plural), PR (= present tense), P (= past tense), agr (= agreement morpheme), act (= active voice), nact (= non-active voice), CL (= clitic), NOM (= nominative case), ACC (= accusative case), DAT (= dative case), ABL (= ablative case), FEM (= feminine gender), SUBJ (= subjunctive mood), PROG (= progressive aspect).

[4] My intuition is that the difference in person agreement reflects a certain (emotive) difference in that the use of first person in (2) signals a higher degree of closeness to the addressee (and arguably more self-awareness) than that of third person. The same point seems to me to be valid for the use of second person as opposed to third person agreement with the second person camouflage DP in (3'). The Nurse-*we* examples discussed in C&P also seem to corroborate such a take on the matter. It seems, then, as if first and second person subject-verb agreement has an almost evidential flavor.

should come as no surprise that a coordinate DP with an imposter conjunct will allow for the same flexibility as its English counterpart; compare (5) and (4b).[5]

(5) *Mami dhe kuklla do (të) kënaqen / kënaqemi në plazh.*[6]
mommy.the and doll.the will enjoy.3PL / enjoy.1PL at beach
"Mommy and her doll will enjoy themselves/ourselves at the beach."

Likewise, plural imposter subjects as in (6a) exhibit both first and third person subject-verb agreement in Albanian, a fact that contrasts with the subject agreement pattern obtaining with run-of-the-mill (i.e., non-imposter) non-coordinate plural subjects, which only display third person agreement, as shown in (6b):

(6) a. *Të nënshkruarit **janë** / **jemi** të gatshëm për bisedime.*
agr undersigned.the are.**3PL** / are. **1PL** agr ready for negotiations
"The undersigned are ready for negotiations."

b. *Delet kullos**in** / *kullos**im** në. livadh.*
sheep.the graze.**3PL** / graze.**1PL** in pasture
"The sheep are grazing in the pasture."

Interestingly, third person singular verbal agreement is also possible in coordination contexts (in addition to third and first person plural agreement), irrespective of whether one of the coordinate DPs is an imposter, which contrasts with the pronominal agreement patterns obtaining in English—compare (7a) and (7b).[7] However, first person singular verbal agreement is out, as (7c) demonstrates.

[5] What is impossible, though, is second person plural verbal agreement even if "the doll" is referring to the addressee, a fact that matches pronominal agreement in English:

i. *Mommy and her doll will enjoy yourselves at the beach.

ii. * *Mami dhe kuklla do të kënaq**eni** në plazh.*
mommy.the and doll.the will enjoy.2PL at beach
"Mommy and her doll will enjoy themselves/ourselves at the beach."

[6] The future in Albanian is built by the combination of a specific particle, namely *do*, with subjunctive forms. Subjunctive in this language is always signaled by the particle *të*, which is, however, often (if not always) dropped in future constructions in spoken language, which is why I do not always gloss it and sometimes I drop it altogether in these contexts (see for instance (7b,c)), though I do gloss it as SUBJ in other contexts where it cannot be dropped (see for instance (23) and (24) in section 3).

[7] Singular agreement in (7b) seems to be due to some sort of VP-ellipsis in the relevant sense, i.e., the underlying structure must be able to derive something like "Mommy will enjoy herself and so will her doll."

(7) a. Both mommy and her doll will enjoy *herself/themselves/ourselves at the beach.

b. *Edhe mami edhe kuklla do kënaqet / kënaqen / kënaqemi në plazh.*
and mommy.the and doll.the will enjoy.**3S** / enjoy.**3PL** / enjoy.**1PL** at beach
"Both mommy and her doll will enjoy themselves/ourselves at the beach."

c. **Edhe mami edhe kuklla do kënaqem në plazh.*
and mommy.the and doll.the will enjoy.**1S** at beach

Already on the basis of the comparative data above between English and Albanian, an initial hypothesis is tempting: a language that allows first person agreement with singular imposters will also allow first person agreement with a coordinate DP with an imposter conjunct, but not vice versa. Of course it remains to be seen whether this statement has the value of a generalization, but if it does, the question that arises is why this should be so. While this chapter has little to offer on such theoretical questions, it contributes to a fuller picture of the morphosyntax of imposters cross-linguistically.

The rest of this chapter is organized as follows. In section 2, I present some preliminaries of Albanian morphosyntax that are important for understanding the way imposters behave in this language. Then, in section 3, I set out to describe the basic patterns of imposter and camouflage DPs in this language, paying special attention to highlighting the differences from their counterparts in English. I close with a programmatic agenda on a few novel observations, such as the interaction of imposter syntax with information structure and the role of the latter on antecedence and binding relations.

2. Preliminaries: Albanian Morphosyntax

In terms of morphological type, Albanian is an analytical language (Demiraj 1986). Adverbs, prepositions, conjunctions, and interjections are non-inflecting. Nouns, pronouns, articles, adjectives, and verbs are inflecting. There is also rich derivational morphology. A major category within the functional verbal domain of Albanian is that of voice, which is also crucial to understanding some of the agreement patterns exhibited by structures containing imposters. Similar to Latin and Modern Greek, Albanian has two distinct voice conjugational paradigms, namely *active* and *non-active* (Marantz 1984; Hubbard 1985; Massey 1991; Kallulli 2007; Kallulli and Trommer 2011).[8] In addition to voice, the finite verb forms are marked for mood, tense/aspect, person, and number. With the exception of the participle, the non-finite forms are marked only for voice.

[8] The non-active voice is similar in its syntactico-semantic scope to the passive conjugation in Latin, or the non-active conjugation in Modern Greek, in that it is used not only to build the passive, but also with reflexives, middles, and unaccusatives. In other words, while the active

Already in the example (5) above, repeated here with more detailed glosses, it can be seen that there is no distinct element corresponding to the anaphor "themselves/ourselves" in the English translation of this sentence. Instead, the verb *kënaqem* "I enjoy myself" is inflected for non-active voice.[9] It is precisely due to this morphological marking that the reflexive interpretation obtains, as can be seen through the comparison of (5) with (5'):[10]

(5) *Mami dhe kuklla do të kënaqen / kënaqemi në plazh.*
mommy.the and doll.the will enjoy.**nact**.3PL / enjoy.**nact**.1PL at beach
"Mommy and her doll will enjoy themselves/ourselves at the beach."

(5') *Jam e sigurt që do t'i kënaq**in** miqtë.*[11]
I am agr sure that will.them$_{\text{CL}}$ please.**act.3PL** guests.the
"I am sure they will please the/their guests."

As is obvious from the English translation, the difference with respect to voice marking between (5) and (5') affects the "meaning" of the verb in a way that is reminiscent of Belletti and Rizzi's (1988) discussion of psych verbs in Italian (see in particular their discussion of the "fear" versus "frighten" classes, which in Albanian would differ in terms of voice-marking, similar to "enjoy oneself" versus "please (someone)" in (5) and (5') above).

The feminine noun *vetja* and somewhat less frequently a reduplication version of it *vetvetja*, both meaning "self," serve as reflexive proforms in Albanian, as

form of a verb such as *thaj* "I dry" means "I dry (stuff)," its non-active form *thahem* may have several meanings, including "I dry (myself)," "I am being dried (by someone else)," "I am dry-able," "I am easy to dry," "I dry (e.g., in the sun)" (see, e.g., Embick 1997 and references therein for Latin and Greek, and Kallulli 2006, 2007 for Albanian). Such voice-related syncretisms are also familiar from better studied languages like German and Romance, which despite lacking full voice paradigms use a pronoun or clitic in (some of) the same syntactic contexts (Grewendorf 1989; Grimshaw 1982).

[9] The citation form of the Albanian verb is first person, singular number, indicative mood, present tense.

[10] The Albanian non-active voice conjugation displays a complex alternation employing three distinct linguistic means, namely affixation (as in (5)), cliticization, and auxiliary choice (specifically, the counterpart of the verb "to be"—versus "to have," which is used for the active conjugation). The distribution of these different means to realize non-active voice follows a complex default pattern discussed in detail in Kallulli and Trommer (2011).

[11] The example in (5'), as well as other examples later in this chapter, illustrate the phenomenon of "clitic doubling," whereby a clitic pronoun "doubles" a verbal argument inside the same clause, in the sense that the verbal argument and the clitic pronoun have the same referent, or are co-referent. This phenomenon will be looked at somewhat more closely in section 3, as it turns out to be relevant in the context of imposter morphosyntax as well.

shown in (8). These feminine singular definite forms may have as antecedent a DP of any person and number, as illustrated through the paradigm in (8).

(8) a. *E* *mblodha* ***veten*** / *vetveten*.[12]
$\text{CL}_{\text{ACC,3s}}$ gather.P,1S self.**the**$_{\text{ACC}}$ / selfself.**the**$_{\text{ACC}}$
"I pulled myself together."

b. *Mblidhe* *veten* / *vetveten!*
gather.$\text{CL}_{\text{ACC,3s}}$ self.the$_{\text{ACC}}$ / selfself.the$_{\text{ACC}}$
"Pull yourself together!"

c. *E* *mblodhi* *veten* / *vetveten*.
$\text{CL}_{\text{ACC,3s}}$ gather.P,3S self.the$_{\text{ACC}}$ / selfself.the$_{\text{ACC}}$
"S/he pulled herself/himself together."

d. *E* *mblodhëm* *veten* / *vetveten*.
$\text{CL}_{\text{ACC,3s}}$ gather.P,1PL self.the$_{\text{ACC}}$ / selfself.the$_{\text{ACC}}$
"We pulled ourselves together."

e. *Mblidheni* *veten* / *vetveten!*
gather.**CL**$_{\text{ACC,3s}}$.2PL self.the$_{\text{ACC}}$ / selfself.the$_{\text{ACC}}$
"Pull yourselves together!"

f. *E* *mblodhën* *veten* / *vetveten*.
$\text{CL}_{\text{ACC,3s}}$ gather.P,3PL self.the$_{\text{ACC}}$ / selfself.the$_{\text{ACC}}$
"They pulled themselves together."

In fact, a plural version of *(vet)vetja* yields ungrammaticality even when its antecedent is plural, as shown in (9a–c), which contrast with the grammatical (8d–f), respectively, where the anaphor is singular in spite of its plural antecedent.

(9) a. **I* *mblodhëm* *vetet* / *vetvetet*.
$\text{CL}_{\text{ACC,3PL}}$ gather.P,1PL selves.the$_{\text{ACC}}$ / selfselves.the$_{\text{ACC}}$
"We pulled ourselves together."

b. **Mblidhini* *vetet* / *vetvetet!*
gather.$\text{CL}_{\text{ACC,3PL}}$.2PL selves.the$_{\text{ACC}}$ / selfselves.the$_{\text{ACC}}$
"Pull yourselves together!"

c. **I* *mblodhën* *vetet* / *vetvetet*.
$\text{CL}_{\text{ACC,3PL}}$ gather.P,3PL selves.the$_{\text{ACC}}$ / selfselves.the$_{\text{ACC}}$
"They pulled themselves together."

The reflexive expression *(vet)vetja* may, however, optionally combine with pronominal adjectives, as illustrated in (10).[13] Such pronominal adjectives each consist of a so-called preposed adjectival article (such as *e* in *e tij* "his," *e saj* "her,"

[12] Clitics are mostly underspecified for gender in Albanian.

[13] Though judging by the data in (10c,d,g) this is a somewhat dispreferred option with third person pronominal adjectives.

e tyre "their" in (10c), (10d), and (10g), respectively) and a pronominal stem (such as *tij, saj, tyre* in (10c,d,g)), though for many first and second person forms these two components have become morpho-phonologically opaque (thus resulting in *vetja ime* "my (own) self" in (10a) instead of *vetja **e** ime*, which is quite marked). However, when the parts are distinguishable, as in (10c,d,g), the adjectival article reflects the case, gender, and number of the modified expression (i.e., of the anaphor *vetja* "the self"), whereas the stem of the adjective signals the number and person of its antecedent).[14]

(10)	a.	*Ma*	*ka*	*fajin*	*vetja*	*(ime).*	
		$\text{CL}_{\text{DAT,1S}}.\text{CL}_{\text{ACC,3S}}$	has.PR,3S	$\text{fault.the}_{\text{ACC}}$	$\text{self.the}_{\text{NOM,FEM}}$	my	
		"It's my own fault."					
	b.	*Ta*	*ka*	*fajin*	*vetja*	*(jote).*	
		$\text{CL}_{\text{DAT,2S}}.\text{CL}_{\text{ACC,3S}}$	has.PR,3S	$\text{fault.the}_{\text{ACC}}$	$\text{self.the}_{\text{NOM,FEM}}$	your.s	
		"It's your own fault."					
	c.	*Ia*	*ka*	*fajin*	*vetja*	*(?e*	*tij).*
		$\text{CL}_{\text{DAT,3S}}.\text{CL}_{\text{ACC,3S}}$	has.PR,3S	$\text{fault.the}_{\text{ACC}}$	$\text{self.the}_{\text{NOM,FEM}}$	agr	his
		"It's his own fault."					
	d.	*Ia*	*ka*	*fajin*	*vetja*	*(?e*	*saj).*
		$\text{CL}_{\text{DAT,3S}}.\text{CL}_{\text{ACC,3S}}$	has.PR,3S	$\text{fault.the}_{\text{ACC}}$	$\text{self.the}_{\text{NOM,FEM}}$	agr	her
		"It's her own fault."					
	e.	*Na e*	*ka*	*fajin*	*vetja*	*(jonë).*	
		$\text{CL}_{\text{DAT,1PL}}$ $\text{CL}_{\text{ACC,3S}}$	has.PR,3S	$\text{fault.the}_{\text{ACC}}$	$\text{self.the}_{\text{NOM,FEM}}$	our	
		"It's our own fault."					
	f.	*Jua*	*ka*	*fajin*	*vetja*	*(juaj).*	
		$\text{CL}_{\text{DAT,2PL}}.\text{CL}_{\text{ACC,3S}}$	has.PR,3S	$\text{fault.the}_{\text{ACC}}$	$\text{self.the}_{\text{NOM,FEM}}$	your.2PL	
		"It's your own fault."					
	g.	*Ua*	*ka*	*fajin*	*vetja*	*(?e*	*tyre).*
		$\text{CL}_{\text{DAT,3PL}}.\text{CL}_{\text{ACC,3S}}$	has.PR,3S	$\text{fault.the}_{\text{ACC}}$	$\text{self.the}_{\text{NOM,FEM}}$	agr	their
		"It's their (own) fault."					

Several additional things are noteworthy in this paradigm. First of all, while the combination of the anaphoric DP *vetja* with first and second person pronominal adjectives is possible, its combination with third person pronominal adjectives is somewhat marked, as already pointed out in note 13. But if the pronominal adjectives in these examples (i.e., (10c,d,g)) are replaced by the third person reflexive adjective *i/e vet* (roughly) "his/her (own)" as in (11a,b), then the examples lose their marked flavor.

[14] Datives and first and second person personal pronouns are invariably clitic doubled in Albanian (Kallulli 2000). As is obvious from the examples in (10), in a clitic cluster, the dative always precedes the accusative clitic.

(11) a.

Ia	*ka*	*fajin*	*vetja*	*(e*	*vet).*[15]
$\text{CL}_{\text{DAT,2S}}.\text{CL}_{\text{ACC,3S}}$	has.PR,3S	fault.the$_{\text{ACC}}$	self.the$_{\text{NOM}}$	agr.fem	3

"It's his/her own fault."

b.

Ua	*ka*	*fajin*	*vetja*	*(e*	*vet).*
$\text{CL}_{\text{DAT,3PL}}.\text{CL}_{\text{ACC,3S}}$	has.PR,3S	fault.the$_{\text{ACC}}$	self.the$_{\text{NOM}}$	agr	3

"It's their own fault."

Second, note that the anaphoric *vetja* "self" in (10) and (11) bears nominative case and is bound by the dative argument, which in these sentences is a non-overt DP (doubled by the clitic) in the Specifier of the CliticP.[16] This is borne out by the fact that in a sentence like (10a) no second or third person pronominal or reflexive adjective is possible, as shown in (12).

(12)

Ma	*ka*	*fajin*	*vetja*	*ime/*jote/*e tij/*e saj/*e vet.*
$\text{CL}_{\text{DAT,1S}}.\text{CL}_{\text{ACC,3S}}$	has.PR,3S	fault.the$_{\text{ACC}}$	self.the$_{\text{NOM}}$	my/your/ his / her / own

"It's my own fault."

Having described some aspects of Albanian morphosyntax that are important in order to understand the agreement patterns that arise with imposters in this language, in the next section, I present further data involving imposters, paying special attention to highlighting how they differ from their English counterparts.

3. Albanian Imposters and Camouflage DPs

3.1 A BIRD'S-EYE VIEW

To begin, the class of imposters in Albanian seems to be more restricted than in English. For instance, unlike in English, the set *this* + Common Noun denoting sentient beings is hardly possible in Albanian. The category of imposters in Albanian includes the following:

a. First person imposters:
   i. kinship terms either accompanied by personal names or on their own; for example, *mami (Dalina)* "mummy (Dalina)," *babi (Georg)* "daddy (Georg)," *daja (Gimi)* "uncle (Gimi)," *teta (Lili)* "aunt (Lili)," etc.
   ii. personal names (cf. (i) above)

[15] Recall that *vetja* is feminine, which is why the reflexive pronominal adjective shows feminine agreement (in the form of the agreement marker *e* preceding it).

[16] See Sportiche's (1996) analysis of clitic constructions, according to which clitics head their own maximal projections, which I adopt here as well as elsewhere (cf. Kallulli 2000).

iii. common nouns denoting sentient beings or various bodies; for example, *mësuesja* "the teacher," *autori* "the author" / *autorët* "the authors," *i nënshkurari/e nënshkruara* "the undersigned" / *të nënshkruarit* "the undersigned [plural]," *këshilltari/këshilltarët* "the counselor(s)," *gjykatësi(t)* "the juror(s)," *komisioni ligjor* "the legal commission," etc.
iv. *dora vetë* "yours truly," *lali* "yours truly," *motra* "sister" (used in the sense of "yours truly"), *shërbëtori yt/juaj (besnik)* "your (faithful) servant"

b. Second person imposters:
   i. *Zonjë/Zonja* "Madame," *Zotëri/Zotëria* "Sir," *Zonjushe* "Miss," *Im Zot* "my Lord," *bebi (im)* "(my) baby," *bebushi (im)* "(my) baby [diminutive]," *lepurushi (im)* "(my) little rabbit," etc.
   ii. the elements of (aii)
   iii. personal names (especially of little children, loved ones, pets, etc.)
   iv. *lal/lali* "[roughly] mine truly," *motër/motra* "sis," *motër e vëllait* "[literally] sister of the brother"[17]

In addition, Albanian also has so-called camouflage DPs (Collins et al. 2008, C&P 2012), which show similar syntactic behavior as imposters in that, like the latter, the former also take antecedents:

i. Social Hierarchy Camouflage (SHC) DPs; e.g., *Madhëria Juaj / e Saj / e Tij* "Your / Her / His Majesty," *Shkëlqesia Juaj / e Saj / e Tij* "Your / Her / His Excellency," etc.
ii. the ass-Camouflage Construction (ACC); for example, *prapanica jote* "your behind," *bytha jote* "your ass," *fytyra jote* "your face [pejorative]," *surrati yt* "your face [pejorative]," *turiri yt* "your face [pejorative]"

In spite of the fact that the class of imposters in Albanian seems more restricted than in English, the agreement patterns that they exhibit seem more complex, as was already seen in section 1. On top of the data discussed earlier, while the English *yours truly* cannot antecede a non-third person reflexive, its (probably closest) Albanian counterparts, *dora vetë* (literally: "hand-the self"), *lali* (literally: diminutive form of "brother") and *motra* (literally: "sister"), may do so, thus replicating the pattern discussed earlier with respect to verbal agreement (see the discussion of the examples in (2') and (3') in section 1). The difference between English and Albanian is shown in (13) versus (14).

(13) "Yours truly will vote for herself/*myself."

[17] Note that *lali* and *motër/motra* imposters are used both as first person and second person imposters.

(14) a. *Dora vetë do votojë për veten e vet / e saj / e tij / time.*
hand.the$_{\text{NOM}}$ self will vote.3S for self.the$_{\text{ACC}}$ agr self.3 / agr her / agr his / my

b. *Lali do votojë për veten e vet / e saj / e tij / time.*
hand.the$_{\text{NOM}}$ will vote.3s for self.the$_{\text{ACC}}$ agr self.3 / agr her / agr his / my

c. *Motra do votojë për veten e vet / e saj / e tij / time.*
hand.the$_{\text{NOM}}$ will vote.3S for self.the$_{\text{ACC}}$ agr self.3 / agr her / agr his / my
"Yours truly will vote for herself/himself."

Of course, the verbal agreement may also in this case be first person, yielding, however, incompatibility with a third person pronominal, as shown in (15).

(15) a. *Dora vetë do votoj për veten *e vet / *e saj / *e tij / time.*
hand.the$_{\text{NOM}}$ self will vote.1s for self.the$_{\text{ACC}}$ agr self.3 / agr her / agr his / my

b. *Lali do votoj për veten *e vet / *e saj / *e tij / time.*
hand.the$_{\text{NOM}}$ will vote.1s for self.the$_{\text{ACC}}$ agr self.3 / agr her / agr his / my

c. *Motra do votoj për veten *e vet / *e saj / *e tij / time.*
hand.the$_{\text{NOM}}$ will vote.1s for self.the$_{\text{ACC}}$ agr self.3 / agr her / agr his / my
"Yours truly will vote for herself/himself."

Note that the (obligatorily present) item *vetë* following *dora* in (14a) and (15a) is a non-inflected, hence particle-like element that functions in a way that is comparable to "self"-expressions in English in environments such as the one in (16), despite the fact that *myself* here has person features that *vetë* obviously lacks, as can be seen from the examples in (17).[18]

(16) I myself will vote for me.

(17) a. *Unë vetë ta dhashë atë këshillë.*
I self you$_{\text{CL,DAT}}$.CL$_{\text{ACC,3S}}$ gave.1s that advice
"I gave you that piece of advice myself."

b. *Ti vetë ma dhe atë këshillë.*
you self me$_{\text{CL,DAT}}$.CL$_{\text{ACC,3S}}$ gave.2s that advice
"You gave me that piece of advice yourself."

Similar to English, many common nouns denoting sentient beings can be used as imposters in Albanian, as seen for *mësuesja* "the teacher" in (18). Again, either third or first person verbal agreement is possible.

[18] Note also that *vetë* is not the indefinite of *vetja*; this would be *vete*. Incidentally, the word for the grammatical category of person in Albanian is *vetë* in the indefinite and *veta* in the definite.

(18) *Mjaft tani, mësuesja e humbi / humba durimin.*
enough now teacher.the CL$_{ACC,3S}$ lost.**3**s / lost.**1**s patience.the$_{ACC}$
"That's enough now, the teacher has lost her patience."

However, unlike the situation described in (14), when the verbal agreement with the imposter *mësuesja* "the teacher" is third person, a first person pronominal adjective is not licit, as shown in (19a).[19] That is, the two classes of imposters represented by *dora vetë* and *mësuesja*, respectively, behave differently. Similarly, when the verbal agreement is first person, the use of a third person reflexive adjective or of a third person pronominal adjective results in ungrammaticality, as shown in (19b). Recall, however, that in Albanian, a language in which, unlike in English, the definite determiner is not in complementary distribution with a pronominal, overt anaphoric pronouns are hardly ever used; at any rate, their use is at best optional. In other words, what I am suggesting is that due to the use of the definite determiner in sentences like the ones under scrutiny, the default "antecedent" of *durimin* "the patience" is the c-commanding sentient DP *mësuesja* "the teacher," just as *vetja* in previous examples is a c-commanding sentient antecedent DP.

(19) a. *Mësuesja e humbi durimin ?e vet / *tim.*
teacher.the$_i$ CL$_{ACC,3S}$ lost.**3**s patience.the$_{ACC}$ agr self.3 / my$_i$
"[That's enough now,] the teacher has lost her patience."

b. *Mësuesja e humba durimin tim /*e vet / *e saj.*
teacher.the CL$_{ACC,3S}$ lost.**1**s patience.the$_{ACC}$ my /agr self.3 / agr her
"[That's enough now,] the teacher has lost her patience."

That we are indeed dealing with two different classes of imposters is illustrated in the minimal pair in (19') below, which combines the facts discussed in (19) with those discussed in (14):[20]

(19') a. *Dora vetë do votojë për veten e vet / e saj / e tij / time.*
hand.the$_{NOM}$ self will vote.3S for self.the$_{ACC}$ agr self.3 / agr her / agr his / my
"Yours truly will vote for herself/himself."

[19] While the third person pronominal is also marked in this context (as indicated by the question mark in front of *e vet* "her"), the presence of a first person pronominal adjective yields a stronger contrast in terms of grammaticality.

[20] Note also that while the grammatically feminine imposter DP *dora vetë* "yours truly" in (19'a) is compatible with the third person masculine pronominal adjective *e tij* "his," the grammatically feminine imposter *mësuesja* "the teacher" in (19'b) is not.

b. *Mësuesja do votojë për veten e vet / e saj / *e tij / time.*
teacher.the$_{NOM}$ will vote.3s for self.the$_{ACC}$ agr self.3 / agr her / agr his / my
"The teacher will vote for herself."

The fact that different (types of) imposters in Albanian behave differently can also be illustrated through the behavior of kinship terms, which again show more flexible agreement patterns with anaphoric adjectives, as illustrated in (20) for the imposter *mami* "mummy," which parallels the behavior of *dora vetë* "yours truly" in (14).

(20) *Mami e ka shpirt bebushin tim / e vet / e saj.*
mommy.the CL$_{ACC,3S}$ has.3s soul little baby.the$_{ACC}$ my / agr self.3 / agr her
"Mummy loves her little baby."

However, just as for *dora vetë* "yours truly," when the subject-verb agreement is first person instead of third person, only a first person but not a third person pronominal adjective is licit, as shown in (21).

(21) *Mami e kam shpirt bebushin tim / *e vet / *e saj.*
mommy.the CL$_{ACC,3S}$ has.1s soul little baby.the$_{ACC}$ my / agr self.3 / agr her
"Mummy loves her little baby."

In other words, for several (singular) imposters, the relevant generalization seems to be the following:

(22) If verbal agreement is third person, a mismatch with the person feature value of pronominal agreement is possible.

However, as the examples in (23) and (24) show, if verbal agreement is second person, a mismatch with the person feature value of pronominal agreement is not possible.

(23) *Madhëria Juaj duhet të lavdërojë veten (tuaj) / (e saj).*
Majesty Your should SUBJ praise.act.3S self.the$_{ACC}$ your.2PL / agr her
"Your Majesty should praise herself/yourself."

(24) *Madhëria Juaj duhet të lavdëroni veten (tuaj) / (*e saj).*
Majesty Your should SUBJ praise.act.2PL self.the$_{ACC}$ your.2PL / agr her
"Your Majesty should praise your/*her own self."

Going back to the flexibility of the verbal agreement highlighted earlier, it is tempting to analyze cases such as (18) where the verbal agreement is first person as appositive-like structures with a non-overt pronoun on a par with (25) and (26) below, where the pronoun is overt.

(25) *Unë mami (po) shkoj / *shkon tani.*
I mommy.the PROG go.1s / go.3s now
"I, mommy, am leaving now."

(26) *Ne të nënshkruarit jemi / *janë dakort me vendimet.*
we, agr undersigned.the are.1PL / are.3PL accord with decisions.the
"We, the undersigned, agree with the decisions."

The same analysis would then also extend to the Albanian counterpart of "your loyal servant," which likewise exhibits both first and third person verbal agreement, as shown in (27).

(27) *Shërbëtori yt besnik e gjeti / gjeta librin që kërkoje.*
servant.the your loyal $\text{CL}_{\text{ACC,3S}}$ found.**3s** / found.**1s** book.the that searched
"Your faithful servant found the book you were looking for."

This, however, would not quite work for the accusative DP *prapanica jote* "your ass," discussed earlier and repeated below for ease of reference.

(3') *Prapanica jote është / je në zjarr.*
behind.the your_{s} is / are.2s in fire
"You are in trouble." (lit.: "Your behind is in trouble.")

(28) **Ti, prapanica jote je në zjarr.*
you_{SG}, behind.the your_{s} $\text{are}_{\text{2,s}}$ on fire

(29) *?Prapanica jote, ti je në zjarr.*
behind.the your_{s} you_{s} $\text{are}_{\text{2,s}}$ on fire
"Your ass, you are in trouble." (lit.: "Your behind is in trouble.")

These camouflage examples notwithstanding, even if a pure appositive analysis with a null head (see C&P 2012, Chapter 5) were the right one to account for the possibility of first and second person subject-verb agreement with imposter subjects, that would still mean that a language can have both genuine imposters and the pure precursor look-alike analysis, which as Paul Postal (personal communication) has pointed out to me, would be significant (and bizarre).

3.2 EPITHETS

Another aspect in which Albanian imposters differ from their English counterparts concerns so-called epithets, which Collins and Postal treat as *bona fide* imposters. To illustrate, compare the English sentences in (30) (from C&P 2012) with the analogous Albanian sentences in (31). Note, among other things, that even though epithets take antecedents (cf. 30a), the latter cannot be first (or second) person imposters in English (30b). In contrast, this asymmetry does not obtain in Albanian—cf. (31b)—which, unlike its English counterpart, is grammatical.

(30) a. When Jack's mother$_1$ came in, Jerome told the fool$_1$ not to be too hard on herself$_1$/*himself$_1$.
b. *When Daddy$_1$ entered the room, they criticized the fool$_1$.

(31) a. *Kur nëna$_i$ e Benit$_j$ hyri brenda, Eva i tha (idiotes$_i$/idiotit$_{*i/j/k}$)*
when mother agr Ben came in Eva CL$_{DAT,3S}$ said (idiot.the$_{FEM}$/$_{MASC}$)
të mbyllte gojën (idiotes$_i$/idiotit$_{*i/j/k}$).
to shut mouth (idiot.the$_{FEM}$/$_{MASC}$)
"When Ben's mother came in, Eva told the idiot to shut up."

b. *Kur mami$_1$ hyri brenda, ata e kritikuan budallaqen$_1$.*
when mommy.the$_{NOM}$ came.3s in they CL$_{ACC,3S}$ criticized fool.the$_{ACC}$
[lit.] "When mummy entered, they criticized the fool."

Note, however, that verbal agreement in (31b) is third person. And though, as mentioned earlier, first person imposters may exhibit first person verbal agreement in Albanian, as (32) shows, a different state of affairs obtains when the verbal agreement is first person (instead of third person) in contexts involving epithets:

(32) **Kur mami$_1$ hyra brenda, ata e$_1$ kritikuan budallaqen$_1$.*
when mommy.the entered.**1S** inside they CL$_{ACC,3S}$ criticized fool.the$_{ACC}$
[lit.] "When mommy entered, they criticized the fool."

The same facts obtain with second person pronoun imposters; Albanian contrasts with English here, too—cf. (33) and (34):

(33) a. *If Madam enters the room dressed that way, they are going to criticize the doll.
b. *If the Baron gives that speech, the members will sneer at the idiot.

(34) a. *Në qoftë se Zonja hyn në dhomë e veshur në këtë mënyrë,*
if be that madam enters in room agr dressed in this way
*ata do **ta** kritikojnë bukuroshen.*
they FUT SUBJ.**CL**$_{ACC,3S}$ criticize.3PL beauty.the$_{ACC}$
[lit.] "If Madam enters the room dressed this way, they will criticize the beauty."

b. *Në qoftë se Baroni mban këtë fjalim, ata do* ***ta*** *tallin idiotin.*
if be that Baron holds this speech they FUT SUBJ.**CL**$_{ACC,3S}$ sneer at idiot.the
[lit.] "If the Baron gives that speech, they will sneer at the idiot."

Analogous to the facts discussed above for (31b), when second person imposters exhibit second instead of third person verb agreement, which, as we saw in section 3.1, is possible in Albanian, a different state of affairs obtains in contexts involving epithets; the sentences are ungrammatical, as shown in (34'):[21]

(34') a. **Në qoftë se Zonja hyni në dhomë e veshur në këtë mënyrë,*
if be that madam enter.2PL in room agr dressed in this way
ata do ***t'a*** *kritikojnë bukuroshen.*[22]
they FUT SUBJ.**CL**$_{ACC,3S}$ criticize.3PL beauty.the$_{ACC}$
[lit.] "If Madam enters the room dressed this way, they will criticize the beauty."

b. **Në qoftë se Baroni mbani këtë fjalim, ata do* ***t'a*** *tallin idiotin.*
if be that Baron hold.2PL this speech they FUT SUBJ.**CL**$_{ACC,3S}$ sneerat idiot.the
[lit.] "If the Baron gives that speech, they will sneer at the idiot."

Interestingly, as shown in (35), all the relevant examples (i.e., (31b) and (34)) are as ungrammatical as their corresponding ones in English in the absence of the (third person) doubling clitic.[23]

(35) a. **Kur mami$_1$ hyri brenda, ata kritikuan budallaqen$_1$.*
when mommy.the came.3s inside they criticized fool.the$_{ACC}$
[lit.] "When mummy entered, they criticized the fool."

b. **Në qoftë se Zonja hyn në dhomë e veshur në këtë mënyrë,*
if be that madam enters in room agr dressed in this way
ata do të kritikojnë bukuroshen.
they will criticize.3PL beauty.the$_{ACC}$
[lit.] "If Madam enters the room dressed this way, they will criticize the beauty."

c. **Në qoftë se Baroni mban këtë fjalim, ata do të tallin idiotin.*
if be that Baron.the holds this speech they will sneer at idiot.the$_{ACC}$
[lit.] "If the Baron gives that speech, they will sneer at the idiot."

The asymmetry between the data in (31b) and (34), on the one hand, and (35), on the other, shows that (third person accusative) clitic doubling in Albanian seems to interact with binding relations. Indeed, in Kallulli (2012), I have shown that clitic doubling gives rise to both weak and strong crossover obviation effects. The

[21] Note that social hierarchy imposter DPs combine with second person plural rather than second person singular verb agreement, though.

[22] Clitics are mostly underspecified for gender in Albanian, which is also the case for the third person accusative clitic.

[23] The example in (31a) is still different, though, because datives are invariably clitic doubled in Albanian.

minimal pair examples in (36a) versus (36b) and (37a) versus (37b), respectively, illustrate this point.[24]

(36) a. **Cil-in djalë$_i$ pa nëna e tij$_i$?*
which-the$_{ACC}$ boy saw.3s mother agr his
"*Which boy$_i$ did his$_i$ mother see?"

b. *Cil-in djalë$_i$ e pa nëna e tij$_i$?*
which-the$_{ACC}$ boy CL$_{ACC,3S}$ saw.3s mother agr his

(37) a. **Cilën fotografi të Anës$_i$ pa (ajo)$_i$ në gazetë?*
which.the$_{ACC}$ picture agr Ana saw.3s she in newspaper
"*Which picture of Ana$_i$ did she$_i$ see in the newspaper?"

b. *Cilën fotografi të Anës$_i$ e pa (ajo)$_i$ në gazetë?*
which.the$_{ACC}$ picture agr Ana CL$_{ACC,3S}$ saw.3s (she) in newspaper

While the question of how exactly clitic doubling interacts with binding is an important one, it cannot be dealt with in detail in this chapter. It is, however, well-established that clitic doubling systematically produces information structure in that the "doubled" DP is necessarily interpreted as topical (in the sense [+given]), as is evident from the Albanian paradigm (38) to (41) below, in which all the B-sentences, irrespective of the presence/absence of the doubling clitic in them, mean "Anna read the book." That is, DPs that are (part of the) focus domain cannot be clitic doubled (see Kallulli 2000, 2008).

(38) A: What did Anna do? B: *Ana (*e) lexoi librin.*
Ana CL$_{ACC,3S}$ read book.the$_{ACC}$
"Anna read the book."

(40) A: What did Anna read? B: *Ana (*e) lexoi librin.*

(39) A: Who read the book? B: *Ana *(e) lexoi librin.*

(41) A: What did Anna do with the book? B: *Ana *(e) lexoi librin.*

In turn, it is obvious that—though not always straightforward how exactly—information structure interacts with binding relations. Consider the English paradigm in (42):

[24] Chris Collins (personal communication) suggests that the data in (37) should be described in terms of Condition C (rather than strong crossover), with the clitic in (37b) making reconstruction for Condition C not obligatory. However, I think this raises more questions than it solves, since in addition to the fact that the weak crossover (obviation) data in (36) still remain unaccounted for, we would still need an analysis of how exactly the clitic in (37b) blocks Condition C reconstruction (and does not just render it non-obligatory). While I do propose an analysis for the latter problem in Kallulli (2012), what I wish to highlight here is simply the fact relevant for the matter at hand, namely, that clitic doubling interferes with binding relations.

(42) a. *Which picture of $John_i$ did he_i see in the paper?
b. Which picture of $John_i$ did he_i himself see in the paper?

The contrast between the grammatical (42b) and the minimally different ungrammatical (42a) obviously bears on the presence of a so-called intensifying self-element in (42b) that seems to contribute to a different information structure relative to that of the ungrammatical (42a).

4. Conclusion

The goal of this chapter was to highlight some peculiar properties of imposters in Albanian, notably the fact that both singular and plural imposters in this language exhibit both first/second and third person verbal agreement, that different types of imposters behave differently, and that information structure interferes with antecedence/binding relations. Each of these facts raises a multitude of non-trivial questions that future research will need to tackle.

This chapter had its beginnings in a talk that I gave in Chris Collins' seminar on Person in the fall of 2010. For feedback I thank the participants in this seminar, Paul Postal, two anonymous reviewers, and especially Chris Collins for giving me the necessary push to write the chapter, in addition to providing detailed written comments and editorial guidance and assistance. I gratefully acknowledge the support of the Austrian Academy of Sciences for funding my research stay at New York University (APART fellowship 11283).

References

Collins, Chris, Simanique Moody, and Paul M. Postal. 2008. An AAE camouflage construction. *Language* 84: 29–68.

Collins, Chris, and Paul Postal. 2012. *Imposters: A Study of Pronominal Agreement*. Cambridge, MA: MIT Press.

Demiraj, Shaban. 1986. *Gramatika Historike e Gjuhës Shqipe* [The Historical Grammar of Albanian.] Tirana: Shtëpia Botuese "8 Nëntori."

Embick, David. 1997. Voice and the interfaces of syntax. Doctoral dissertation, University of Pennsylvania.

Grewendorf, Günther. 1989. *Ergativity in German*. Dordrecht: Foris Publications.

Grimshaw, Jane. 1982. On the lexical representation of romance reflexive clitics. In *The Mental Representation of Grammatical Relations*, ed. J. Bresnan, 87–148. Cambridge, MA: MIT Press.

Hubbard, Philip. 1985. *The Syntax of the Albanian Verb Complex*. New York: Garland.

Kallulli, Dalina. 2000. Direct object clitic doubling in Albanian and Greek. In *Clitic Phenomena in European Languages*, eds. F. Beukema and M. den Dikken, 209–248. Amsterdam: John Benjamins.

Kallulli, Dalina. 2006. Unaccusatives with dative causers and experiencers: A unified account. In *Datives and Other Cases*, eds. D. Hole, A. Meinunger, and W. Abraham, 271–301. Amsterdam: John Benjamins.

Kallulli, Dalina. 2007. Rethinking the passive/anticausative distinction. *Linguistic Inquiry* 38(4): 770–780.

Kallulli, Dalina. 2008. Clitic doubling, agreement, and information structure. In *Clitic Doubling in the Balkan Languages*, eds. D. Kallulli and L. Tasmowski, 227–255. [Linguistik Aktuell/ Linguistics Today 130]. Amsterdam and Philadelphia: John Benjamins.

Kallulli, Dalina. 2012. Local modelling of allegedly local but really non-local phenomena: Lack of superiority effects revisited. In *Local Modelling of Non-Local Dependencies in Syntax*, eds. A. Alexiadou, T. Kiss, and G. Müller, 501–524. [Linguistische Arbeiten 547]. Berlin, New York: De Gruyter.

Kallulli, Dalina, and Jochen Trommer. 2011. Closest c-command, Agree and Impoverishment: The morphosyntax of non-active voice in Albanian. *Acta Linguistica Hungarica* 58(3): 277–296.

Marantz, Alec. 1984. *On the Nature of Grammatical Relations*. Cambridge, MA: MIT Press.

Massey, Victoria. 1991. Compositionality and constituency in Albanian. Doctoral dissertation, University of North Carolina at Chapel Hill.

Sportiche, Dominique. 1996. Clitic constructions. In *Phrase Structure and the Lexicon*, eds. J. Rooryck and L. Zaring, 213–276. Dordrecht: Kluwer.

5

The Syntax of Indonesian Imposters

DANIEL KAUFMAN

1. Introduction

1.1 IMPOSTERS: REFERENTIAL EXPRESSIONS WITH PRONOMINAL FUNCTIONS

Referential expressions are commonly used in place of first and second person pronominals in a wide range of languages. Collins and Postal (2012) argue that referential expressions in this function, e.g., "You won't have *Nixon* to kick around anymore" (as spoken by Nixon), possess a radically different syntactic representation from their plain noun phrase counterparts. The variety we are concerned with here involves a name or other referential expression not containing any overt first or second person features but which nonetheless refers to the speaker or hearer. These kinds of expressions are termed by Collins and Postal "imposters" (alluding to the covert pronominal work that they carry out) and are defined as follows:

(1) An imposter is a notionally X person DP that is grammatically Y person, X ≠ Y (Collins and Postal 2012: 5)

Imposters display a mixed behavior with regard to binding facts and agreement that had not been previously well documented. For instance, in the context of (2), *Mommy*, an imposter referring to the speaker, can only antecede a third singular pronoun.[1]

(2) $\text{Mommy}_i^{[1]}$ needs her_i/*my_i quiet time now.

Based on this evidence alone, we could imagine a purely notional theory of imposters that treated them as a phenomenon of interpretation rather than syntax. On such an analysis, imposters would not differ from regular (third person) phrasal

[1] Subscripted indices are employed here in the traditional manner to indicate coreference. Superscripted [1] and [2] are used to indicate the first and second person features associated with imposters.

arguments but would be interpreted as referring to the speaker based on real-world, extra-grammatical inferences. Such a theory runs into immediate trouble, however, when confronted with other English facts, such as the optionality shown in (3). Unlike (2), we find that the imposter can antecede both a third person anaphor as well as a first person anaphor, unexpected if imposters were a purely pragmatic phenomenon.

(3) In this reply, the present authors$_i$[1] attempt to defend ourselves$_i$/themselves$_i$ against the scurrilous charges which have been made.

More troubling for the purely notional approach to imposters is the discovery that there exists principled variation in their distribution across languages (as amply documented in the present volume). Variation of this type is traditionally modeled as part of the grammar and not the pragmatics.

The crux of the imposter problem is that they must sometimes be treated according to their overt NP form, that is, as third person, other times according to their covert reference, that is, as first or second person, and yet other times may be treated as either. The structure Collins and Postal (2012) posit to account for this and other attendant facts contains both an indexical (first or second person) pronoun and an ascriptive noun phrase. This stands in contrast to notional approaches to imposter phenomena, which see the referential expression as a plain noun phrase with a non-canonical interpretation. Unfortunately, differentiating between notional and syntactic accounts of imposters and related phenomena is rarely straightforward. First, the vast majority of the evidence for the syntactic differences come from complex binding facts, which themselves straddle the domains of syntax and semantics. Second, English and other familiar languages are rarely found to linearize imposter and non-imposter phrases differently (but see the chapters of Wood & Sigurðsson and Vázquez Rojas in this volume for unique distributional patterns of indefinite imposters). In this chapter, I show that Indonesian[2] holds a special

[2] Malay, the national language of Malaysia, and Indonesian, the national language of Indonesia, are best understood as two dialects of the same language. Confusingly, there exist other languages also referred to as Malay varieties, in both Indonesia and Malaysia, which are best treated as separate languages. The variety I focus on here is "Standard Indonesian." It is occasionally claimed (typically by foreign scholars) that Standard Indonesian is a purely engineered language only existing within textbooks, news broadcasts and other official media. This is an exaggeration. While there does exist strong diglossia, the situation is not far removed from other well-known cases described extensively for Greece and the Arab world, among many others. This point is important here because the central syntactic feature here, proclisis of referring expressions, is something which has been lost in many colloquial varieties. Nonetheless, speakers, especially those more familiar with the formal language, have strong intuitions about proclisis, even if they typically speak varieties that do not employ it regularly. The data in this chapter not attributed to other sources were obtained primarily from native speakers Amalia Suryani (Jakarta) and Lutfi Kurniawan (Yogyakarta). Citations of Classical Malay (labeled by text: Bayan Budiman, SAB, Bangka, S) were obtained from the Malay Concordance Project (http://mcp.anu.edu.au/).

place in differentiating the two approaches, as the referential features of imposters actually determine their surface position, forcefully ruling out a notional account.

1.2 INDONESIAN PRONOMINALS AND VOICE

In what we can consider the default case, person features in the input are spelled out by standard pronominals in Indonesian as expected. The unmarked pronouns of the standard language are shown in Table 5.1.

However, under a wide variety of common situations, often involving the need to be polite, imposters are employed instead. What makes Indonesian particularly interesting in this regard is that one type of argument is positioned differently in the overt syntax when functioning as a imposter. Specifically, imposters as patient voice agents (henceforth PV-agents) follow the same pattern as pronominals; they both procliticize to the verb when referring to "local" (i.e., first or second person) features, seemingly replacing the patient voice prefix *di-*, but follow the verb when referring to third person, as shown schematically in (4).[3]

(4) The Patient Voice (PV) Paradigm
  a. Local person: 1/2=V
  b. Non-local person: *di*-V-3

Table 5.1 **Standard Indonesian person-markers**

Feature	*Nominative*	*Genitive/Accusative*	*Proclitic*
[+1, -2, -PL] (1sg)	*aku, sayaaku, saya*	*-ku*	*ku=*
[-1, +2, -PL] (2sg)	*engkau/kamu*	*-mu*	*kau=*
[-1, -2, -PL] (3sg)	*dia*	*-nya*	*(dia=)*
[+1, -2, +PL] (1pl, excl)	*kami*	*kami*	*kami=*
[+1, +2, +PL] (1pl, incl)	*kita*	*kita*	*kita=*
[-1, +2, +PL] (2pl)	*kalian*	*kalian*	*kalian=*
[-1, -2, +PL] (3pl)	*mereka*	*mereka*	*(mereka=)*

[3] What is termed "patient voice" here has gone under a wide variety of names in the linguistic literature, usually involving the term "passive." The verb form with pronominal proclitics which we focus upon here is typically analyzed as a sub-type of the *di-* form, and has gone under the name of "Type II Passive" (Dardjowidjojo 1976; Sneddon 1996; Cole and Hermon 2005b), "Subjective Passive" (Sie 1989; Guilfoyle et al. 1992), "objective voice" (Arka and Manning 1998), "object preposing" (Chung 1976) and "patient voice" (Aldridge 2008). In the data discussed here, verbs in the actor voice are consistently prefixed with the actor voice prefix *meng-* and thus always glossed AV. Patient voice verbs, on the other hand, can either be prefixed with the dedicated patient voice prefix *di-*, glossed PV, or procliticized to by pronominals or imposters. In the latter case, the verbs are not explicitly glossed as patient voice, but this should be understood from the presence of the proclitic.

This can be seen more concretely in (5), where we find the basic case of a first person versus a third person pronominal PV-agent.

(5) Local versus Non-local Pronominals as PV-Agents

a. ini yang **ku**=pilih
this RELT 1SG=choose
"This is what I choose."

b. ini yang di-pilih-**nya**
this RELT PV-choose-3SG.GEN
"This is what s/he chooses."

The sentences in (6) and (7) show how two common types of imposters, proper names and kin terms, follow precisely the same pattern.

(6) Local versus Non-local Proper Names as PV-Agents

a. ini yang **Lia**[1/2]=pilih
this RELT Lia=choose
"This is what Lia (I/you) chooses."

b. ini yang di-pilih (oleh) **Lia**
this RELT PV-choose by Lia
"This is what Lia (she) chooses."

(7) Local versus Non-local Kin Terms as PV-Agents

a. ini yang **ibu**[1/2]=pilih
this RELT mother=choose
"This is what mother (I/you) chooses."

b. ini yang di-pilih (oleh) **ibu**
this RELT PV-choose by mother
"This is what mother (she) chooses."

This syntactic parity between imposters and pronouns offers a striking confirmation of the syntactic relevance of person features, even when they are not overtly spelled out by dedicated pronouns. The difference between imposters and regular noun phrases can thus not be one of mere pragmatic construal. That is, imposters do not merely allude to first and second person pronouns in Indonesian but rather contain their syntactic features. Given that imposters must contain local person features, the question arises of precisely where in the structure these features are found. I argue here that the radically syntactic implementation of Collins and Postal (2012), who posit the existence of null first and second person pronouns within an expanded DP structure, cannot be easily adapted to Indonesian. Rather, it appears more appropriate to maintain the standard phrase structure of the referential expression while allowing it to contain the appropriate person features morphologically.[4]

After locating this phenomenon within its proper historical and geographical context, I introduce the morphology of the morphological paradigms relevant to imposter phenomena and the anaphora and agreement facts in section 2. I consider the consequences of the Indonesian facts for Collins and Postal's (2012) theory of imposter phenomena in section 3.1. An alternative approach to the phenomena is briefly sketched out in section 4, and I conclude in section 5.

2. Titles and Agreement in West Indonesia

The key features of Indonesian imposters as described above were borne of a fortuitous coincidence of a partially developed agreement system and the ubiquitous use of titles with respected addressees to refer both to first and second persons. By way of background, both of these independent phenomena are described in the following.

2.1 TITLES AND POLITENESS

The use of titles and kinship terms as terms of address is one of the most common politeness strategies cross-linguistically. In the more stringent systems, this strategy has been extended to strictly exclude the use of regular pronouns when referring to respected referents. Instead, a stock set of titles and kin terms are used in these cases, with or without the addition of a name. This is, of course, not completely alien to English, where one could not felicitously address the Queen of England, judges, and other dignitaries using the second singular pronoun "you." Conventionalized titles, such as *her majesty*, *the queen*, or *your honor*, must be used here instead, as in (8).

(8) Would *her majesty*[2] like another cup of tea?

While the use of imposters for purposes of politeness is quite restricted in English, it is the norm in everyday speech in most parts of East and Southeast Asia. Pronouns in most languages of mainland East and Southeast Asia vary

[4] One of Collins and Postal's arguments in favor of covert pronouns in imposter constructions is the presence of overt referential pronouns in what they term "camouflage" constructions: "your majesty," "your highness," etc. Indonesian does not have such constructions, neither for the sake of politeness, as might be predicted by the strong avoidance of second person pronouns, nor of the jocular sort, e.g., "your ass." As Marsden (1812) notes, earlier stages of Malay did employ overt second person pronouns in imposters with first person reference, e.g., *amba-mu tāu* servant-2SG.GEN know "I (your servant) know" (Marsden 1812: 44).

according to social position, level of intimacy, age, and other factors. Names and kin terms are commonly used as substitutes for first and second person pronouns, which generally have a very circumscribed usage in the languages of this region.

In Indonesian, the focus of this chapter, there exists a plethora of kin terms that are used both to refer to real kin as well as to those who are simply of commensurate age with those kin. In Jakarta, the most common of these include *bapak/pak* "father," *ibu/bu* "mother," *om* "uncle," *tante* "aunt." Typically, each dialect area has other terms which are also added to the mix, such as *mas* "elder brother" and *mbak* "elder sister" in Java, or *uda* "elder brother" and *uni* "elder sister" in Minangkabau-speaking areas, among many others. These terms function both as titles (e.g., *Mas Joko* "elder brother Joko") as well as vocatives, (e.g., *Jangan, mas!* "Don't, brother!") and imposters (e.g., *Mas sudah makan?* "Did elder brother already eat?").

The use of these titles is ubiquitous in Indonesian. They are described briefly by Sneddon (1996: 163) in his descriptive grammar of Indonesian:

> As pronoun substitutes, *bapak* and *ibu* can also mean "I." Here they are restricted to use by older people to younger people, whether their own children or not:
>
> Ibu mau ke pasar
> mother want to market
> "I'm going to the market." (Said by a woman to someone younger)
>
> Kasi pada bapak!
> give to father
> "Give it to me!" (Said by a man to someone younger)
>
> Personal names are also commonly used as substitutes for "I" and "you." This is particularly common among children, as a substitute for *aku* and *kamu*:
>
> Dinah mau ikut
> Dinah want follow
> "I want to come along." (Said by a girl named Dinah)
>
> Ini untuk Dinah
> this for Dinah
> "This is for you." (Said to a girl named Dinah)

The extent to which imposter use has affected Indonesian can be seen clearly in its large repertoire of pronominals. Although pronouns are often cited as one

Table 5.2 **Borrowed pronouns in Indonesian**

Feature	*Inherited*	*Sanskrit*	*Arabic*	*Chinese*	*Dutch*	*English*
+1	*aku* (SG)	*sa(ha)ya* (SG)	*ane* (SG)	*gue* (SG)	*ik* (SG)	*mi* (SG)
+2	*engkau/kamu* (SG)	*kalian* (PL)	*ante* (SG)	*elo/lu* (SG)	*jij* (SG)	*yu* (SG/PL)

of the linguistic categories most impervious to borrowing, Indonesian/Malay appears to have quite a long tradition of creating new pronouns through borrowing from all the languages it has come into prolonged contact with (Donohue and Smith 1998; Tadmor 2007).[5] All of the borrowed pronouns in Table 5.2 can be heard in Jakartan Indonesian depending on the context and ethnic background of the speaker and hearer. For instance, the pronoun *yu* (you) will often be employed when speaking to Western foreigners, the Arabic pronouns are commonly used by Indonesians of Arab ancestry, and the Dutch pronouns were commonly employed until recently in certain social circles.[6]

In sum, the pronominal system of Indonesian and other Malay varieties has been historically volatile and is far more synchronically dynamic than more familiar pronominal systems. The relevance of this here is that choice of pronoun is significant on several social dimensions: the status, age, and ethnic origin of both speaker and hearer are typically taken into account. The socially loaded content of even the inherited pronouns within a strict politeness system has led to a situation in which these pronouns must always be replaced by respectful titles when addressing social superiors.

Based on the heavy use of titles and kin terms as pronominals, Mahdi (2001) has argued that there is no category of "pronoun" in Indonesian. Rather, there are only nouns that can be used in a pronominal function. Some evidence in favor of treating pronouns as plain nouns in Indonesian is that they can be modified by demonstratives and the definite marking *-nya*, for example, *kamu itu* (2SG that), *aku-nya* (1SG-DEF), a cross-linguistically unusual state of affairs. However, unlike plain nouns in Indonesian, putative pronouns cannot be reduplicated to indicate plurality, for example, *sapi~sapi* (cow~PL) "cows" but **aku~aku* (1SG~PL),

[5] Although, see Thomason and Everett (2001) for evidence that pronominal borrowing may not be all that rare.

[6] On the other hand, the relation between the etymology and the context is not always so clear. The pronouns *lu* (2SG), and *gue* (1SG), although originating from Chinese, are used colloquially by native Jakartans of all ethnicities. Uri Tadmor (p.c.) takes this as one piece of evidence that the Betawi ethnicity, which employs the Chinese pronouns most regularly, developed through intermarriages between Balinese women and Chinese men in Jakarta during the colonial period.

**kamu~kamu* (2SG~PL).[7] This is not the case with imposters, whose morphological behavior is identical to plain nouns including the possibility of plural marking via reduplication, as in (9).

(9)	Bapak~bapak[2]	sudah	siap	pergi?
	father~PL	already	ready	go

"Are fathers (you pl.) ready to go already?"

Real pronouns also resist modification by possessors. While no forms such as **engkau-ku* (2SG-1SG.GEN), **kamu-ku* (2PL-1SG.GEN), or **dia-ku* (3SG-1SG.GEN) exist or have ever been attested, we do encounter imposters with possessor modification, as in (10), from a Classical Malay text.

(10)	Ya,	Tuan-ku!	Jikalau	Tuan-ku	hendak	be-layar . . .
	EXCL	master-1SG.GEN	if	master-1SG.GEN	want	AV-sail

"Oh my master! If my master (you) wants to sail . . ."
(Bayan Budiman 319: 3)

Taking the above two facts as diagnostic, we find that none of the forms in Table 5.2 behave like a plain noun; they all resist plural marking and possessors. Thus, the position taken here is that there does exist a category of real pronominals in Indonesian, including borrowed forms, which belong to a distinct morphosyntactic class. The use of titles and other descriptors as pronominals is therefore comparable to the phenomena subsumed under imposter and camouflage constructions by Collins and Postal (2012), albeit subject to far more frequent use.

2.2 PERSON MARKING IN INDONESIAN

In the most common Indonesian agreement pattern, person markers from the genitive set are prefixed or procliticized to the verb. The accretion of proclisis across the Austronesian languages of Indonesia follows the person hierarchy quite strictly. With very few exceptions, second person only enters the agreement

[7] Mahdi (2001: 167) claims that "The personal pro-names do however have a reduplicated form resembling that of the plural of the nonpersonal nominals, which one could call the emphatic plural. . . ."

(i)	saya~saya	lagi=lah	yang	di-salah-kan
	1SG~EMPH	again=EMPH	RELT	PV-wrong-APPL

"And it's me again who gets the blame."

This, however, clearly has a different function, as there is no question about the singular interpretation of *saya* (1SG).

Table 5.3 **Person marking in the patient voice**

	Old Malay	*Karo Batak*	*Gayo*	*Clas. Malay*	*Minangkabau*
1SG.	ni-V-(ŋ)**ku**	**ku**-V	**ku**-V	**ku**-V	**den**-V
2SG.	(ni-V-**māmu**)	i-V-**əŋkō**	i-V-**kō**	**kau**-V	**aŋ**-V
3SG.	ni-V-**ña**	i-V-**na**	i-V-**é**	di-V-**ña**	**iño**-V
1PL.EXCL	?	i-V-**kami**	**kami**-V	**kami**-V	**kami**-V
1PL.INCL	ni-V-**(n)ta**	**si**-V	**kitö**-V	**kita**-V	**kito**-V
2PL.	ni-V-**māmu**	i-V-**kam**	i-V-**kam**	**kamu**-V	**kau**-V
3PL.	ni-V-**(n)da**	i-V-**na**	i-V-**é**	di-V-**mereka**	**iño**-V

system if first person has, and third person only enters if both first and second have. Many partial systems exist in which verbs only inflect for first person or first and second person. These developments, first documented by Haaksma (1933) for Western Indonesia and discussed by Wolff (1996), can be shown to have occurred independently in Sumatra and Sulawesi. The evidence for step-by-step accretion in Sumatran languages is shown in Table 5.3. The markers *ni-*, *i-*, and *di-* are cognate to Indonesian *di-*, and all mark the patient voice.

The pattern in which all pronominals encliticize almost certainly represents the original state of affairs. Accretion of only first person singular and inclusive plural markers in Karo Batak represents the first step toward full proclitic/prefixal agreement. In the next step, represented by Gayo, first person inclusive and exclusive are procliticized. In Classical Malay, all first and second persons are procliticized, while in the final stage, represented by Minangkabau, all PV-agents' pronominal arguments are procliticized. The pattern of pronominal proclisis shown above is a relatively recent development in Malay. We can see in (11) that both first person and third person were treated alike during the earliest documented stages of Old Malay; both *-ku* and *-ña* are suffixed to the verb.

(11) *Old Malay*

a. ni-galar-ku
   PV-title-1SG.GEN
   "I titled (him)." (Karang Brahi r. 9, 14–15, Kota Kapur r. 4,8)

b. ni-minuŋ-ña
   PV-drink-3SG.GEN
   "He drank (it)." (Talang Tuwo r. 5)

However, it was the intermediate stage of Indonesian as found in Classical Malay and represented above in Table 5.3 that gave rise to the modern pattern found with imposter pronouns. In Classical Malay, we almost only find elements with [+1] or [+2] features procliticizing to the verb, as illustrated schematically in (12).[8]

(12) *Classical Malay Paradigm*

a. Apa yang **ku**=ingin?
what RELT 1SG=want
"What would I like?"

b. Apa yang **kita**=ingin?
what RELT 1PL.INCL=want
"What would we (incl.) like?"

c. Apa yang **kami**=ingin?
what RELT 1PL.EXCL=want
"What would we (excl.) like?"

d. Apa yang **kau**=ingin?
what RELT 2SG=want
"What would you like?"

e. Apa yang **kamu**=ingin?
what RELT 2PL/SG=want
"What would you (pl.) like?"

[8] A careful empirical study of the development of proclisis in Malay has yet to be done. Needless to say, the historical record is not perfectly neat in this regard. Texts from several periods occasionally show third person PV-agents in pre-verbal position. This could have been due to influence from Minangkabau, whose speakers played an important role in the development of the national language. However, sentences such as (ii) and (iii) indicate that this might also be another construction altogether, as the pronoun is probably not proclitic. It precedes the adverb in (ii) and is modified by a demonstrative in (iii), apparently impossible in earlier stages of Classical Malay.

(i) ber-jalan pasiar senang-kan hati, ber-bagei macam jang **dia lihat-i**
AV-walk wander happy-APPL liver AV-various kinds RELT 3SG see-APPL
"Strolling gladdens the heart, the various things he sees" (SAB 111: 3b)

(ii) tiada tahu apa yang **dia sudah buat** di tanah Bangka
NEG know what RELT 3SG already do OBL land Bangka
". . . didn't know what he did in the land of Bangka." (Bangka 115: 19)

(iii) hal kehinaan dan kekejian yang **mereka itu per-laku-kan** itu
thing insult and cruelty RELT 3PL that CAUS-do-APPL that
"the insult and cruelty that they did" (S 3Oct31: 6)

An alternative structure for examples of these types is posited and discussed at length by Cole and Hermon (2005b) and below in section 4.1. See also Nomoto (2006: 110), who rejects the complementarity of local and non-local persons in the proclitic and post-verbal position, respectively, as "no more than an ideal." I believe that complementarity will emerge once variety and time-period are controlled for. Nomoto, for instance, cites the Old Malay data in (11) as evidence that first person PV-agents could always appear post-verbally, but this misses the point. Proclisis of local persons had not yet begun to develop at all in Old Malay but rather only begins to appear in Classical Malay.

f. *Apa yang **dia**=ingin?
what RELT 3SG=want
("What would s/he like?")

g. *Apa yang **mereka**=ingin?
what RELT 3PL=want
("What would they like?")

Crucially, imposter pronouns in the contemporary language still tend strongly to follow the more conservative pronominal syntax of Classical Malay, an intuition shared by the majority of Jakartan speakers interviewed and also corroborated by descriptive grammars (e.g., Sneddon et al. 2010). The imposter paradigm thus appears as in (13), parallel to (12).

(13) Imposter Proclisis Paradigm

a. Mana yang akan bapak[2]=pilih?
which RELT FUTURE father=choose
"What will sir/father (you) choose?"

b. Mana yang akan bapak[1]=pilih?
which RELT FUTURE father=choose
"What will sir/father (I) choose?"

c. Mana yang akan di-pilih bapak?
which RELT FUTURE PV-choose father
"What will sir/father (he) choose?"

d. *Mana yang akan bapak=pilih?
which RELT FUTURE father=choose

The robustness of the imposter proclisis pattern in Classical Malay can be seen in the following unambiguous examples drawn from Bayan Budiman, the earliest Classical Malay text in the Malay Concordance Project. The most common procliticized imposters in this text are *tuan* "master," with second person reference, *hamba* "slave," with first person reference, and the combination *tuan hamba* "slave's master," an imposter embedded in an imposter ultimately referring to second person. The use of these three in proclitic position can be seen in examples (14)–(16).[9]

[9] There are rare instances of non-procliticized patient voice agents in Bayan Budiman, as in the following two examples:

(i) tuan hamba hendak belayar, seyogianya hamba di-bawa oléh **tuan hamba**
master slave want sail fitting slave PV-bring by master slave
"As slave's master (you) wants to sail, it is only fitting that slave (I) be brought by master (you)."
(Bayan Budiman 4: 28)

(14) a. ... apa=kah nama Tuan Puteri yang **Tuan-ku**[2]=mimpi-kan itu ...
what=QM name master princess RELT MASTER-1SG.GEN=dream-APPL that
"What is the name of that princess that my master (you) dreamt of?"
(Bayan Budiman 97: 20)

b. Telah ku=ampun-i=lah barang dosa tuan yang tiada
already 1SG=forgive-APPL=EMPH thing sin master RELT NEG
tuan[2]=ketahu-i dan sengaja
master=know-APPL and intention
"I've already forgiven all of master's (your) sins that master (you) did not know of and did not intend."
(Bayan Budiman 172: 4)

(15) telah **hamba**[1]=ampun-i=lah dosa dan ke-salah-an meréka itu
already slave=forgive-APPL=EMPH sin and NMLZ-wrong-NMLZ 3PL that
"Slave (I) has already forgiven their sins and errors."
(Bayan Budiman 214: 27)

(16) Hamba[1]=lah bayan yang **tuan hamba**[2]=pelihara-kan dahulu itu
slave=EMPH parrot RELT master slave=care.for-APPL earlier that
"It was slave (I) who was the parrot slave's master (you) cared for at the time."
(Bayan Budiman 14: 26)

There should be no question as to the robustness of this pattern within certain historical periods and contemporary variants. In the following sections we explore certain grammatical properties of imposters in contemporary formal Jakartan usage.[10]

2.3 PRONOMINAL COREFERENCE

Collins and Postal (2012) discuss at length the patterns of pronominal coreference with English imposters. In many contexts in English, coreference is possible with either what is termed there the "ultimate antecedent," the actual local person reference of the imposter, or the "immediate antecedent," the formally

(ii) mem-be-lajar ilmu me-mindah-kan nyawa seperti di-ajar oléh **tuan hamba** kepada
AV-AV-learn science AV-move-APPL spirit like PV-teach by master slave to
hamba ini.
slave this
"to learn the science of switching the spirit as taught by master (you) to this slave (I)."
(Bayan Budiman 160: 19)

Most of these examples involve imperatives, as may be the case in (i), but further research is needed to determine if there exists a pattern to the exceptions or if proclisis was already in flux at the earliest attested stages of Classical Malay. Chris Collins (p.c.) notes that the postposition of complex PV-agents in examples like (43) below may be relevant here as well.

[10] I have attempted to bypass the above-mentioned complications in modern Jakartan speech by eliciting judgments in the more formal variant. Although separating distinct grammatical patterns within a diglossic situation is fraught with difficulty, a particular register can be targeted

third person noun phrase that directly antecedes the anaphor or pronoun. A simple case of optionality is shown in (17) (Collins and Postal 2012: 97).

(17) The present authors are proud of ourselves/themselves.

Unlike English, Indonesian imposters cannot be referred back to by third person pronouns, as shown in (18a). Either the entire imposter pronominal must be repeated, as in (18b), or the actual first or second person pronoun must be used, as in (18c). This third option, not entirely acceptable to all speakers, would only be felicitous at all when the social context permits the familiarity associated with pronouns.

(18) a. *Bapak$_i$[1] mau tidur dulu sebelum dia$_i$ pergi
father want sleep first before 3SG go
"Father (I) wants to sleep before he leaves."
b. Bapak$_i$[1] mau tidur dulu sebelum bapak$_i$[1] pergi
father want sleep first before father go
"Father (I) wants to sleep before father leaves."
c. %Bapak$_i$[1] mau tidur dulu sebelum saya$_i$ pergi
father want sleep first before 1SG go
"Father (I) wants to sleep before I leave."

The same pattern can be seen in the slightly different context of pronominal agreement between the possessor of an object and the subject of the clause. This is shown in (19).[11]

(19) a. *Bapak$_i$[1] mau mem-baca buku-nya dia$_i$ dulu.
father want AV-read book-3SG.GEN 3SG first
b. Bapak[1] mau mem-baca buku bapak[1] dulu.
father want AV-read book father first
"Father (I) wants to read father's book first."

by creating stimuli that employ forms only appropriate in that register. An example of this is the use of the affixes common in formal speech (e.g., *me-nemu-kan* AV-find-APPL) in places where other affixes (or lack thereof) would be employed in colloquial speech (e.g., *n-emu-in* AV-find-APPL). It bears repeating here that modern colloquial varieties have almost completely lost the local person restriction on proclisis and allow PV constructions with fronted third person pronouns, e.g., *Mana yang dia pilih?* (which RELT 3SG choose) "Which did he choose?" I claim such proclisis was ungrammatical in earlier stages, a state of affairs still reflected by imposter patterns in formal usage.

[11] One complication should be mentioned first, which is that the third singular genitive pronoun *-nya* also has a non-anaphoric, definite determiner-like function as well as being an optional possessor marker. It is thus acceptable in many contexts where an anaphoric dependency with an imposter cannot in fact be established. We can, however, force the anaphoric reading by using *-nya* in its genitive function followed by the desired pronoun, e.g., X-*nya dia* X-3SG.GEN 3SG, where the second occurrence of the third person pronominal can only have an anaphoric referent (as in (19)).

c. %Bapak$_i$[1] mau mem-baca buku-ku$_i$ dulu.
father want AV-read book-1S.GEN first
(For, "Father (I) wants to read his book first.")

2.3.1 *Reflexives*

Reflexives again behave in the same way, disallowing coreference between a third person reflexive and a local person imposter antecedent, as seen in (20).[12] The preferred means of expressing the proposition in (20) is as in (20a), with the imposter being repeated in object position.[13] The sentence in (20b) is perfectly acceptable as well, and that in (c) can be accommodated in a hybrid situation where both *bapak* and *Anda* are socially acceptable terms of address for the hearer. The (d) sentence, however, is unacceptable, as coreference between the imposter and the third person reflexive cannot be obtained.

(20) a. Hanya bapak[2] bisa meng-erti bapak[2]
only father can AV-understand father
"Only father (you) can understand father (you)."
b. Hanya bapak[2] bisa meng-erti diri bapak[2]
only father can AV-understand self father
"Only father (you) can understand father's self."
c. Hanya bapak[2] bisa meng-erti diri anda
only father can AV-understand self 2SG
"Only father (you) can understand yourself."
d. *Hanya bapak[2] bisa meng-erti diri-nya dia
only father can AV-understand self-1SG.GEN 3SG
"Only father (you) can understand himself."

[12] As discussed by Cole and Hermon (2005a), not everything that looks like a reflexive in Indonesian is a true reflexive. The conclusions reached in that work were that the *diri*+pron forms were ambiguous between reflexive and pronominal, whereas the *diri*+pron *sendiri* form was a true reflexive. For our purposes, the locality issues involved are not critical and I will thus use the ambiguous form.

[13] Note that, as in English *Daddy votes for Daddy*, there is no Principle C violation here. This is not the case with plain R-expressions in either language, as shown by (i).

(i) a. Aisha$_i$ me-lihat diri-nya/*Aisha$_i$ di koran
Aisha AV-see self-3SG.GEN/Aisha PREP newspaper
"Aisha saw herself in the newspaper."

In English, the lack of Principle C effects may be due to the possibility of imposters having inherently reflexive (homophonous) counterparts and the lack of a distinct reflexive type of the form **Daddy's self* (although Chris Collins (p.c.) points out that some Condition C effects do hold, e.g., *He$_i$ voted for Daddy$_i$). There do, however, exist overtly reflexive constructions built off imposters in Indonesian, e.g., *diri-nya bapak* (self-3SG.GEN father). It is possible that the lack of Principle C effects in (20) could be due to focus induced by *hanya* "only," but this possibility cannot be addressed fully here.

2.3.2 *Coordinate Imposters*

Coordinate imposters show a priori unexpected behavior in English and other languages. They license anaphora with first person plural pronouns in cases where a non-coordinate NP would not allow anaphora with a first person singular pronoun. Coordinate imposters in Indonesian, however, behave consistently with non-coordinate imposters in disallowing third person anaphora, as shown in (21).

(21)	[Mama dan Papa][1]	tak	bisa	menemu-kan	paspor	kami[1]/*mereka[1]
	mother and father	NEG	can	AV.find-APPL	passport	1PL.EXCL/3PL

"Mama and Papa can't find their passport."

(22)	Papa[1]	sama	Dahlia[2]	harus	habis-in	makanan	kita[1+2]/*mereka[1]	dulu!
	father	and	Dahlia	must	finish-APPL	food	1PL/3PL	first

"Papa and Dahlia have to finish our food first!"

2.3.3 *Nominal Predicates*

Collins and Postal (2012) discuss similar patterns of optional agreement with first or second person versus third person in nominal predication. Specifically, we find two possibilities for anaphora in structures like (23) (from Collins and Postal 2012: 159).

(23) You are an experienced teacher who takes care of himself/yourself.

Consistent with the facts outlined above, Indonesian does not countenance optionality with nominal predication. As shown in (24), a reflexive anaphor of the *diri*+pron *sendiri* form must be bound by a local pronoun (Cole and Hermon 2005a).

(24)	Saya	tahu	men-jaga	diri-ku/*-nya	sendiri
	1SG	know	AV-guard	self-1SG.GEN/3SG.GEN	self

"I know how to guard myself."

In the case of nominal predicates, consultants tended to reject third person anaphora with a local first person subject, as in (25) and (26).

(25) a.	Saya	tipe	orang	yang	bisa	men-jaga	diri(-ku/*?-nya)	sendiri
	1SG	type	person	RELT	know	AV-guard	self-1SG.GEN/3SG.GEN	self

"I am the type of person who knows how to guard myself."

b.	Kita	para	tipe	orang	yang	tahu	men-jaga	diri	(kita/*?mereka) sendiri
	1PL	PL	type	person	RELT	know	AV-guard	self	1PL/3PL

"We are the type of people who know how to guard ourselves."

Web searches for both patterns using *aku tipe orang yang* (1SG type person RELT) yielded strong confirmation of the judgments received through elicitation. Several examples, given in (26)–(29), were found with a first person anaphor but none with third person *diri-nya* (self-3SG.GEN).

(26) Aku tipe orang yang banyak me-nyetir diri-ku sendiri.
1SG type person RELT much AV-drive self-1SG.GEN self
"I'm the type of person who often drives myself."
(www.kpopluperz.wordpress.com/page/11/)

(27) Ya aku tipe orang yang gak me-nunju-kan kerapuhan diri-ku.
yeah 1SG type person RELT NEG AV-point-APPL weakness self-1SG.GEN
"I'm the type of person who doesn't like to point out my own weakness."
(http://www.facebook.com/topic.php?uid=190425082025&topic=13432.)

(28) aku se-orang ber-dosa yang tidak bisa me-nyelamat-kan diri-ku sendiri.
1SG one-person AV-sin RELT NEG can AV-save-APPL self-1SG.GEN self
"I'm a sinner who can't save myself."
(http://jawaban.com/news/spiritual/detail.php?id_news=071213100441&next=1&total=6)

(29) Aku tipe orang yang suka ber-senang-senang dengan diri-ku.
1SG type person RELT like AV-happy-happy with self-1SG.GEN
"I'm the type of person who likes to have fun by myself."
(http://celebrity.okezone.com/read/2010/10/04/34/378734/enrique-iglesias-senang-telanjang-bareng-teman)

2.3.4 *Summary of Agreement Patterns*

Seen together, the patterns above all show the impossibility of what Collins and Postal (2012) analyze as agreement with an immediate antecedent. In Indonesian, as in Chinese, according to Wang (2009), the only agreement possibilities are those determined by the ultimate antecedent, that is, the first or second person notional reference. Collins and Postal (2012, Chap. 19) ask what underlies the difference between languages like Indonesian and Chinese on the one hand and English on the other. One possibility that is suggested for further research is that the difference may boil down to differences in the internal structure of the imposters themselves. The fact that the same pattern holds in cases of nominal predication discussed above in 2.3.3 militates against the idea that the structure of imposters can be held to account for this. This is because there is no imposter proper in the case of nominal predication. Rather it is the relative pronoun (the immediate antecedent) that appears to lose out in competition with the notional referent (the ultimate antecedent).

Wang (this volume) argues that similar phenomena in Chinese suggest that putative imposters should be treated as appositives. Chinese disallows anaphoric relations with the immediate antecedent, as shown by Wang in (30), where only the first person pronoun *wo* can refer back to the imposter *laoshi* "teacher."

(30) Laoshi$_i$ kuai yao shiqu *ta$_i$/wo$_i$ de naixing le
teacher almost going.to lose 3SG/1SG POSS patience INCHO
"Teacher$_i$ (I) is going to lose [*his$_i$/*her$_i$/my$_i$] patience."

Interestingly, Wang shows that Chinese allows the appearance of an indexical pronoun alongside the imposter, as in (31). He offers convincing evidence that this is not the result of a topic construction but rather that the imposter and the corresponding pronoun to its right form a constituent.

(31) Laoshi$_i$ wo$_i$ kuai yao shiqu wo$_i$ de naixing le
teacher 1SG almost going.to lose 1SG POSS patience INCHO
"Teacher$_i$ I$_i$ is going to lose my$_i$ patience."

Given both the ungrammaticality of agreement with the immediate antecedent as well as the possibility of an overt indexical, Wang posits the structure in (32) to account for Chinese imposters. This structure contains the indexical pronoun adjoined to on the left by the referential expression. The resultant structure is an appositive, conceived of here as a complex DP.

(32)

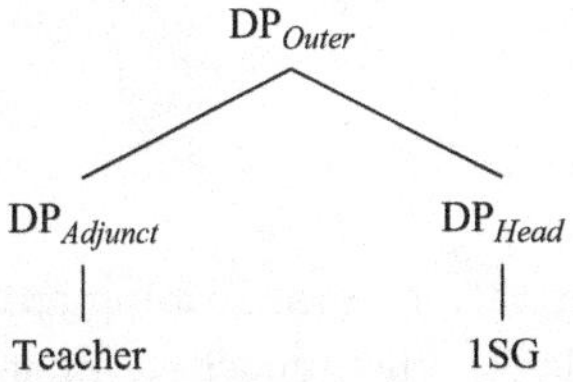

Although Indonesian shows a similar anaphoric pattern with Chinese, it differs in two crucial respects. First of all, there is no possibility of including an indexical pronoun together with an imposter in Indonesian. Second, there is strong evidence that imposters can appear where appositives cannot. The complex DP approach, while seemingly appropriate for Chinese, is thus at odds in accounting for the full set of Indonesian data. In the following section, I explore an analysis that treats Indonesian imposters as syntactically unremarkable DPs with non-canonical morphological features.

3. Accounting for Indonesian Imposters

3.1 COLLINS AND POSTAL 2012: A SYNTACTIC APPROACH TO IMPOSTER PHENOMENA

Collins and Postal (2012) propose a radically syntactic theory of imposters in which both the referential expression (e.g., *daddy, this reporter, yours truly*, etc.) as well as the true indexical reference (e.g., ME, YOU, etc.) have their own independent positions in the phrase structure. Abstracting away from the details, their proposal posits a structure shown schematically in (33) for an imposter pronoun like *the present authors*. Crucially, every imposter is made up of two full DPs, termed "shells," an inner one which contains an indexical, that is, the intended reference of the imposter, and an outer one containing the expected (third person) feature makeup of a regular noun phrase. It is the interplay between these two shells that is argued by Collins and Postal (2012) to account for the mixed behavior of imposters in terms of agreement and coreference.

(33)

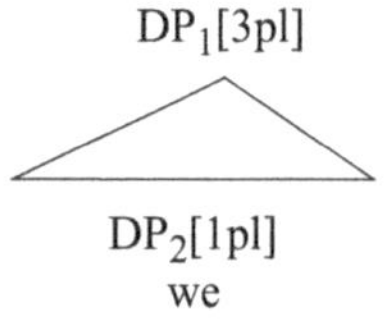

Crucial to their analysis are certain parallels between imposters and appositives, termed "precursors." The relation between the two DPs referring to the subject, "I" and "Nixon," in (34) mirrors the relation between the overt DP and hidden indexical (e.g., YOU, ME) found with imposters.

(34) I, Nixon, am going to get even.

Collins and Postal (2012) offer the following derivation transforming appositives into imposters. From the nonrestrictive clause, the appositive raises to an outer DP shell where it is spelled out as the only overt portion of the entire DP structure. The two possibilities for anaphora are derived from the option of agreeing with the third person features of the raised predicate or with the indexical pronoun in the inner shell.

(35)

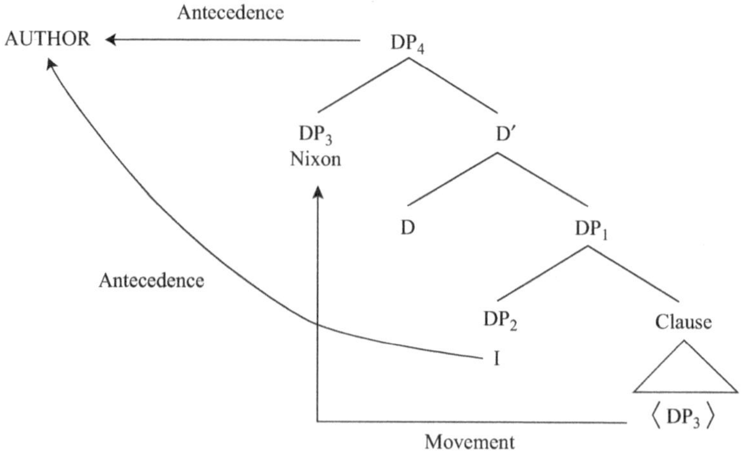

Collins and Postal (2012: 63–64) note certain discrepancies between precursor structures and imposters which are difficult to account for under this view. For instance, unlike imposters, precursor structures do not allow anaphoric relations or agreement with the third person appositive, as they show with the examples in (36) and (37).

(36) Anaphora with Precursors versus Imposters
 a. *I, Nixon$_i$, support him$_i$/himself$_i$.
 b. Nixon supports himself.

(37) Agreement with Precursors versus Imposters
 a. Are/*Is you, Madam, unhappy with that outcome?
 b. Is/*Are Madam unhappy with that outcome?

To this, we can also add another discrepancy between the two constructions regarding the syntactic context in which they can appear. Collins and Postal (2012: 50) show that both imposters and appositives can appear in subject and object position in examples such as (38).

(38) a. Gwen wrote to me (, Nixon).
 b. Me (, Nixon), she will never write to.
 c. You (, Gladys), and I (, Nixon), should see more of each other.

However, when we extend the scope to include possessors, we find that while imposters are fully acceptable in this position, appositives are not, as seen by the ungrammatical (39b).

(39) a. Nixon[1]'s autobiography did not sell as hoped.
 b. *My, Nixon's, autobiography did not sell as hoped.

Incorporation provides a second environment which appears to allow imposters while excluding appositives. The context for (40a) is one in which a father speaks to his child, asking her whether or not "Mommy" can participate in the game of "daddy-hunting."

(40) a. Can Mommy go Daddy[1]-hunting too?
 b. *Can Mommy go, me, Daddy[1]-hunting too?

Here, "Daddy" cannot refer to the generic act of hunting one's father, as it would then only obtain the sloppy reading in which permission is being asked for "Mommy" to hunt her own father. The perfect acceptability of the strict reading thus appears to necessitate an imposter construction, but crucially, the incorporated object cannot be replaced by an appositive, as shown in (40b).

Both (40) and (39) suggest that there exist environments which are perhaps in some sense too small to accommodate appositives but which gladly host imposters. While I do not aim here to offer a solution to these English facts, I would like to avoid a similar difficulty with the Indonesian data, which we turn to now.

3.2 THE SIZE PROBLEM

As discussed above, one consequence of Collins and Postal (2012) is that imposters have a larger structure than ordinary DPs. This appears problematic from the perspective of Indonesian because for some speakers, what can appear in the proclitic position appears to be less than even a single DP.[14] For these speakers, determiners, adjectival modification, and relatives (although perhaps not NP possessors) are blocked in proclitic position. Furthermore, no speakers allow a full overt appositive in the proclitic position.

Compare the acceptable actor voice clause in (41a) with the rejected procliticized version in (41b). In the former, an imposter modified by a relative clause appears in subject position. In the latter, the modified imposter is blocked from appearing in proclitic position.

(41) a. [Bapak yang terhormat][2] sudah memilih itu
father RELT respected already AV:choose that
"Respectable sir already chose that one."
b. *Mana yang [bapak yang terhormat][2]=pilih?
which RELT father RELT respected=choose
(For, "Which one does respected sir (you) choose?")

Nishiyama (2003) claims that only X^0 elements can undergo proclisis, citing the example in (42) where bare pronominals appear in proclitic position but the DP headed by a determiner cannot.

(42) a. Buku ini akan saya/kamu/dia/mereka=beli
book this FUTURE 1SG/2SG/3SG/3PL=buy
"This book will be bought by me/you/him."
b. *Buku itu akan mereka itu beli
book that FUTURE 3PL that buy
(For, "This book will be bought by them.")
c. *Buku ini akan orang itu beli
book this FUT person that buy
(For, "This book will be bought by that man.") (Nishiyama 2003: 111)

In these cases, complex imposters surface post-verbally, in the position of regular third-person patient voice agents, as shown in (43).

(43) a. Mana yang di-pilih [bapak yang terhormat][2]?
which RELT PV-choose father RELT respected
"Which one did father choose?"

[14] This was rather clearly the case in Classical Malay to a large extent and is still reflected in formal Indonesian. See footnotes 2 and 8 regarding variation in the current language and historical varieties, and see below for the inclusion of possessor NPs.

b. Buku itu akan di-beli oleh mereka itu
book that FUTURE PV-buy by 3PL that
"The book will be bought by those people." (Nishiyama 2003: 111)

Note, however, that the evidence is not entirely unequivocal on this point. Sentences like (44) were judged by native speakers as acceptable, although naturally occurring instances were not found.

(44) Koran ini sudah [mama dan papa][1/2]=baca
paper this already mama and papa=read
"Mommy and Daddy already read this paper."

Mahdi (2001) furthermore cites examples such as (45) and (46), for which he suggests that the complex PV-agent is still pronounced with the prosody characteristic of shorter clitics.

(45) Katakan=lah, gambar mana=kah yang paling
tell=EMPH picture which=QM RELT most
[tamu-tamu=ku=yang=terhormat][2]=senang-i
guest-PL=1S.GEN=RELT=respected=like
"Do tell me, which of the pictures you [my respected guests] like the most." (Mahdi 2001: 189)

(46) Anak-anak, kalau anak-anak rajin, anak-anak nanti
child-PL if child-PL diligent child-PL later
[pak=guru=mu=ini][1]=berikan angka baik
sir=teacher=2S.GEN=this=give grade good
"Children, if you [children] are diligent, I [this teacher of yours] will give you [children] good marks." (Mahdi 2001: 189)

While these were not judged unacceptable, I show in section 4.1 that they represent an innovative structure which is significantly different from the proclitic construction we are concerned with here. More universally rejected are examples such as (47b), which directly reflect the appositive structure thought to underlie imposters in English. Note that appositives do exist more generally in Indonesian, as exemplified by (47a).

(47) a. Aku, bapak-mu, memilih itu
1SG father-2SG.GEN AV.choose that
"I, your father, choose that one."
b. Mana yang bisa (*aku,) bapak=pilih?
which RELT FUTURE 1SG father=choose
"Which one will father (I) choose?"

The fact that an imposter reading is fully acceptable with arguments in proclitic position more generally seems to suggest that there is no larger covert structure for the majority of speakers, who reject examples like (41b) and (47).

Honing in on the size of minimal imposter expressions, we find that certain elements thought to be present in simple DPs cannot be included in procliticized imposters either. Pronominals in argument position can be followed by modifying demonstratives in Indonesian, as in (48).[15] Pronouns modified by demonstratives cannot, however, appear in proclitic position, as shown in (49) (ignoring for the moment the example in (46) to which we return in section 5.4.1).

(48) Saya ini sudah mem-baca koran itu
1SG this already AV-read newspaper that
"I already read that newspaper."

(49) a. Koran itu sudah saya=baca
paper that already 1SG=read
"This paper was already read by me"

b. *Koran itu sudah [saya ini]=baca
paper that already 1SG this=read

For the speakers whose judgments are reported here, it would appear from the above that the proclitic position should be restricted to being occupied by an NP constituent.[16] Note, however, that examples such as (14) and (16), repeated here as (50), show an imposter NP containing a possessor (which in the case of (50) is also an imposter). Recall that this example is from the earliest text in the Malay Concordance, and thus the proclitic domain must have already included possessors at this early stage.

(50) Hamba[1]=lah bayan yang **tuan hamba**[2]=pelihara-kan dahulu itu
slave=EMPH parrot RELT master slave=care.for-APPL earlier that
"It was slave (I) who was the parrot slave's master (you) cared for at the time." (Bayan Budiman 14: 26)

There is no paradox here, as demonstratives are external to possessors in Indonesian, as seen in (51).

(51) rumah (*itu) Ali (itu)
house that Ali that
"That house of Ali's"

[15] Although unusual, we find a potential structural cognate in Hebrew *ha-hu*, *ha-hi* (DEF-3SG.MSC) and (DEF-3SG.FEM), respectively. The demonstrative modification of pronominals strongly supports the [local] feature. First and second person pronouns can only be modified by *ini* PROXIMATE/LOCAL, while only third person pronouns can be modified by *itu* DISTAL/NON-LOCAL. Compare to the English imposter "this reporter," where the proximate demonstrative refers to the first person.

[16] Note, though, that all speakers accept complex names in proclitic position, e.g., *yang [Ibu Husna]=beli* (RELT mother Husna=buy) "what Mrs. Husna bought." This can be accounted for plausibly by reanalysis of complex names as simple NPs.

The size of the imposter can thus be described as a subtree along the DP projection which contains possessors but excludes demonstratives and relatives.

As suggested earlier, the position of the PV-agent proclitic in Indonesian has been steadily increasing in featural and syntactic scope over time. Whereas this position originally disallowed third person pronouns, it now accepts them. Similarly, while the position appears to have originally excluded complex imposters (i.e., larger than NP + possessor), certain types of complex imposters are acceptable to a large number of speakers. However, the fact that there exist varieties which disallow complex constituents in this position is taken to be central in the following.

4. A Morphological Theory of Imposters

The Indonesian facts reviewed above appear to demand a theory that countenances "small imposters," that is, imposters that are no larger than medium-size noun phrases. Evidence for this came from the fact that complex imposters (containing demonstratives, relative modification, and appositives) are unacceptable to many speakers, suggesting that only smaller phrases can procliticize to the patient voice verb.

In this section, I will sketch out a rather different approach to imposters that does not treat the indexical pronoun associated with imposters as a covert noun phrase. Rather, the indexical nature of imposters will stem from morphological features that are merged to a lexical noun phrase. The syntactic representation of an imposter is thus no different from its corresponding plain NP, the only difference being that the imposter carries with it local person features, for example, as suggested by the notation in *Mommy*[1], *Daddy*[2].[17] Thus, while the input for an ordinary noun phrase *father* could be trivially represented as {father}, the same expression as a second person imposter would have the input {father, [+2]}. This can be viewed as a compromise that allows for a real morphosyntactic difference between imposter and non-imposter noun phrases while at the same time avoiding some of the thorny size issues reviewed above. In the following, I examine one approach to local person proclisis in Indonesian and its extension to imposters.

4.1 DERIVING PROCLISIS

The facts to be accounted for here can be divided into those that are common to all varieties, given in (52), and the additional conservative features enumerated in (53).

[17] I argue in Kaufman (2010) on the basis of the syntax of second-position clitics that certain differences between clitic and free pronominals are best modeled by allowing features to be merged directly to terminal nodes as well as phrase edges. If there exists such a degree of freedom in the merging of functional features, we can easily conceive of imposters as ordinary noun phrases to which person features have been added.

(52) Features of All Varieties
  a. Proclitics do not double NPs in argument position
  b. Proclisis only occurs in the PATIENT VOICE and not in the ACTIVE VOICE
  c. Indonesian languages show an implicational hierarchy for proclisis: third person if second person and second person if first person

(53) Distinctive Features of Conservative Dialect
  a. Proclisis is restricted to local [+1/+2] persons
  b. Local persons are highly marked as post-verbal agents
  c. Only X^0 elements can procliticize

Although the proposal put forth here relies more on morphological features than covert functional phrases, a purely morphological solution is clearly impossible. Such an approach would treat local person proclitics as the spell-out of a patient voice head merged with [+1]/[+2] features in AgrS or some such similar projection, as in (54). The default spell-out of the patient voice head would be the prefix *di-* (54-a), which, following the Elsewhere Condition (Kiparsky 1973), would surface only in the absence of more specified inputs, such as in (54-b) and (c).

(54) a. Voice[Pat] → *di-*
  b. Voice[Pat] + AgrS[1sg] → *ku-*
  c. Voice[Pat] + AgrS[2sg] → *kau-*

While this treatment could handle the verb morphology, by treating the proclitics as agreement, we wrongly predict clitic doubling, as in (55). Furthermore, a purely morphological account would have no way to insert imposters in the place of the local person proclitics.[18]

(55) a. Ini yang ku=beli (*aku)
  this RELT 1SG=buy 1SG
  "This is the one I bought."

[18] Legate (2012: 516–517) makes precisely the same argument against treating a similar phenomenon in the related Achenese language as agreement. Acehnese, like Indonesian, also allows for the use of imposters as verbal proclitics, as shown in (i-b) (in comparison with (i-a) with second person morphology). Unlike Indonesian, the proclitics in Acehnese double the agent argument rather than being in complementary distribution with it. Nonetheless, Legate argues that the use of imposters in this position, as well as the lack of a regular syntactic position for the trigger, still militates against a canonical agreement analysis.

(i) *Acehnese*
  a. Teungku neu-piyôh u dalam
  religious.scholar 2.POL-rest to inside
  "You teungku, please rest inside here." (Legate 2012: 516)
  b. Teungku teungku=piyôh u dalam
  religious.scholar religious.scholar=rest to inside
  "You 'teungku,' please rest inside here." (Asyik 1987: 274)

b. Mana yang kau=beli (*kamu)?
which RELT 2SG=buy 2SG
"Which one did you buy?"

Based on the preceding, we may assume that both pronominal clitics and imposters originate in the base position in the same way as their (third person) referential expression counterparts. If this can be agreed upon, then proclisis of local person arguments can be analyzed via movement of intervening material, phrasal movement of the agent, or verb movement. I review these different analyses in turn below.

Assuming the canonical base structure [Agt [V Pat]] across actor voice and patient voice, apparent proclisis can be derived by movement of the functional material between the ultimate position of the Agt and the V in the patient voice. Proclisis would thus be epiphenomenal, a possibly welcome result, as it would account for its application to full NPs as well as traditional clitics. However, such an approach would have to treat the actor voice and patient voice asymmetrically, as shown in (56), since evacuation of auxiliaries and adverbs from their base position could not occur in the actor voice. While the two voices are typically analyzed as corresponding to different movements of their arguments, such differences could not be extended to motivate movement of the functional complex between the subject and the verb. It is unclear if there exists any plausible motivation for the movement of modals, negation, and other functional heads in this case.

(56) a. Aku sudah tidak bisa mem-bantu
1SG already NEG can AV-help
"I can no longer help."
b. Sudah_i tidak_j bisa_k ku $t_i t_j t_k$ bantu
already NEG can 1SG help
"I can no longer help."

Voskuil (1996) considers and rejects this approach based on the fact that independent evidence for auxiliary movement in Indonesian shows that certain auxiliaries, for example, *telah* "already" in (57), cannot move but nonetheless appear to the left of local person proclitics in the patient voice. This, in addition to the unmotivated movement of intervening functional heads in one voice but not the other, is sufficient to remove the above analysis from serious consideration.

(57) a. Sudah=kah kamu mem-baca buku itu?
ALREADY=QM 2SG AV-read book that
"Have you read that book already?"
b. *Telah=kah kamu mem-baca buku itu?
ALREADY=QM 2SG AV-read book that
(For, "Have you read that book already?") (Voskuil 1996: 61)

The second approach treats the proclitic position as the base position of Agents. The difference between procliticized and post-verbal patient voice agents then boils down to verb movement. When the verb does not move, as in (58), the agent surfaces to its left. When the verb moves to the higher functional projection headed by *di-* (labeled by Voskuil (1996) FP), as in (59), then the agent surfaces post-verbally.

(58)

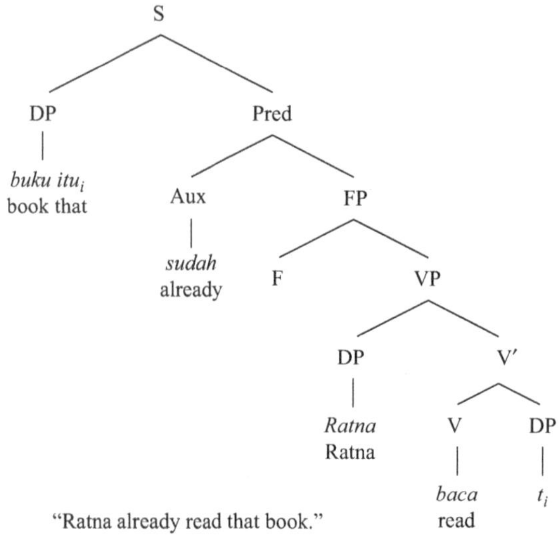

(59)

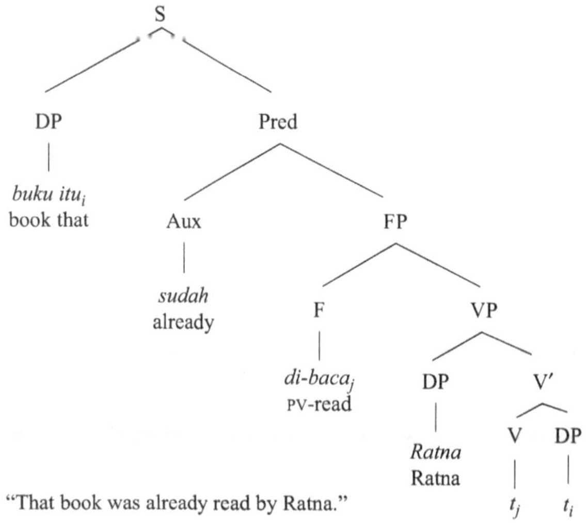

This derivation succeeds in obtaining the order of proclitics but over-generates for the conservative dialect of interest here in predicting that DPs of all sizes and person feature compositions will appear in proclitic position. While this may be true of innovative dialects, it is clearly incorrect for more conservative contemporary dialects. Nishiyama (2003) takes a similar approach while recognizing the differences between local and non-local agents. Agents which cannot be procliticized on his account must be "demoted" to post-verbal position. As this step requires lowering of a subject to a previously occupied object position, it is not a particularly attractive option.

Taking proclisis as both the result of movement of local person arguments to higher functional projections in addition to verb movement can avoid these problems as well as offer a unified account of the variation discussed here. We turn now to fleshing out such a proposal. Given the lack of clitic doubling, I assume movement from argument position to proclitic position. The fact that proclisis is restricted to local persons can be derived by positing articulated agreement projections corresponding to [+1] and [+2] person features. If pronouns and NPs must move around the verb from their base generated argument position to 1P and 2P when they possess the relevant person features, we can account for why only local persons cliticize to the left side of the verb. Pronouns and DPs which lack these features remain down below and surface to the right of the verb. We can further derive the implicational hierarchy in (52c) if 1P dominates 2P. In familiar fashion, the extent of verb movement in any given language will determine which persons procliticize and which encliticize. If the verb stays put, we expect all person markers to surface to the left of the verb, deriving either proclisis or prefixation. If the verb moves only to the first projection, it will have crossed the position of a non-local external argument but will remain below the positions of external arguments with [+1] or [+2] features, as in the conservative Indonesian variety. If the verb continues to move to the next projection, then only first person agents should surface to the verb's left, deriving the situation found in Gayo and Karo Batak, among others.[19] Finally, if the verb moves above the person projections entirely, then all persons will be encliticized, as in Old Malay. The typological possibilities with their attestations are given in (60), where the lower domain represents the base positions of arguments and the higher domain represents the functional field in which person features are checked. (See Bianchi (2006) and references therein for the basis of a person feature domain.)

(60) a. (Sbj)... $\mathbf{V}_i$ 1P 2P DP_{Ext} t_i — All enclisis (*Old Malay*)
b. (Sbj)... 1P $\mathbf{V}_i$ 2P DP_{Ext} t_i — Only 1st person proclisis (*Gayo/Karo Batak*)
c. (Sbj)... 1P 2P $\mathbf{V}_i$ DP_{Ext} t_i — Only 1st and 2nd person proclisis (*Conservative Indo.*)
d. (Sbj)... 1P 2P DP_{Ext} $\mathbf{V}$ — All proclisis (*Minangkabau*)

We now have to account for the fact that proclisis only occurs in the patient voice, feature (52b) above. There exist only two voices in Indonesian, Actor Voice ($Voice_{Act}$), which developed historically from a less transitive form (ANTIPASSIVE, on the ergative analysis), and Patient Voice ($Voice_{Pat}$), which developed from the canonical

[19] As seen in Table 5.3, Gayo requires proclisis of 1PL.EXCL forms where Karo Batak prohibits it. This distinction is perhaps more difficult to derive meaningfully in a syntactic fashion.

transitive form. I posit that Voice_{Pat} attracts the verb but that Voice_{Act} does not.[20] When the patient voice head attracts the verb, it also requires the external argument to check any local person features it may have in 1P or 2P. When the external argument is a pronoun, it is spelled out as one of the traditional proclitics given earlier in Table 5.1. However, when the external argument is a DP with local person features, that is, an imposter, this results in Indonesian's unique pattern of imposter clisis. A simplified derivation is shown below for a minimal pair of sentences in which the external argument of a patient voice clause is a DP with a local person feature (61), and without (62).[21]

(61) a. Itu sudah bapak[1] tulis
that already father write
"Father (I) already wrote that."

b.

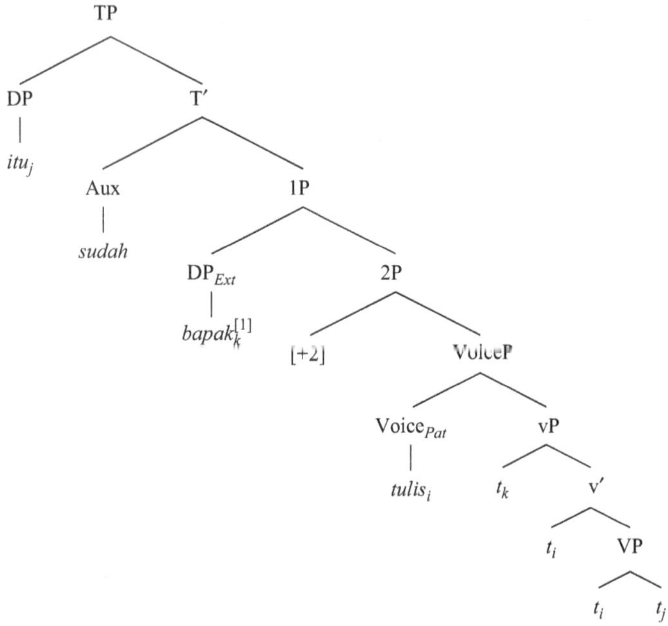

[20] This should also ultimately be able to account for the independent word order facts discussed extensively by Cumming (1991) whereby both arguments tend to follow a patient voice verb but where the external argument subject precedes an actor voice verb.

[21] Guilfoyle et al. (1992) also derive Indonesian word order via similar movement of the verb and external argument. However, they treat the default instantiation of patient voice as a third person proclitic and thus cannot account for enclisis of third person pronominals. See Musgrave (2001) for a more general critique of their account. Note also that earlier arguments against verb movement in Indonesian by Adisasmito-Smith (1998) do not hold if the verb is raising below the domain of auxiliaries and adverbs. There are several recent proposals for the derivation of Indonesian word order and extraction restrictions in a Minimalist framework (Cole et al. 2008; Aldridge 2008; Chung 2008; Nomoto 2006; Soh 1998; *inter alia*). Chung (2008) offers a good summary of the issues regarding V versus VP movement, arguing that both may be necessary to capture different varieties. As this chapter concentrates solely on the syntax of imposters, I leave it to further work to integrate this account with extraction restrictions and other aspects of the syntax.

(62) a. Itu sudah di-tulis bapak
that already PV-write father
"Father already wrote that."

b.

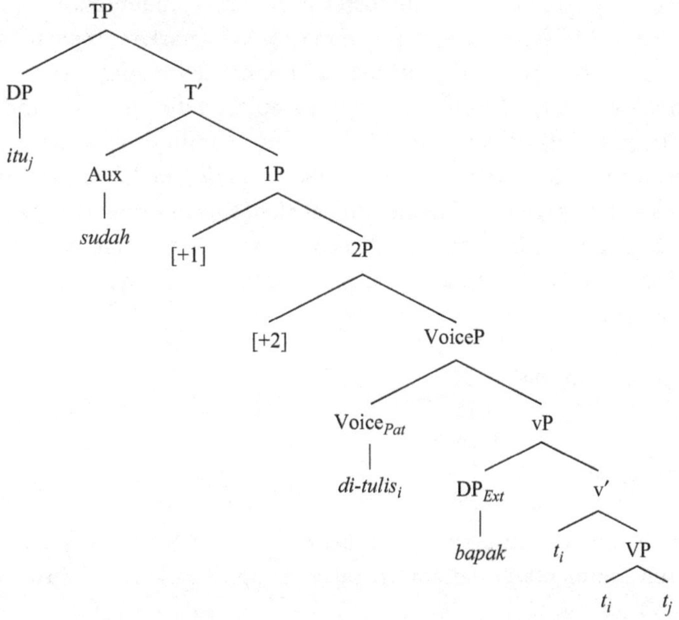

The X^0 or XP status of the proclitics is purposefully left vague. In the conservative and historical varieties, it tends strongly to be X^0, whereas in innovative varieties, it becomes increasingly larger, as seen clearly by the acceptability of sentences such as Mahdi's (2001) (46) above.[22] The innovative features which characterize colloquial Jakartan and other contemporary varieties are shown in (63). These have been discussed by Cole and Hermon (2005b) and Nomoto (2006), among others.

(63) Distinctive Features of Innovative Dialects
a. Proclisis applies to all persons
b. Proclisis applies to both XP and X categories[23]

Given the derivation sketched out above, we can easily derive the innovative dialects via the lack of verb movement in the patient voice and movement to the specifiers of the local feature phrases rather than their heads.

[22] Recall, though, that even in its largest instantiations, this position does not allow appositives of the type required by Collins and Postal (2012), as seen earlier.

[23] As Chris Collins (p.c.) points out, the XP vs. X^0 distinction in proclisis can alternatively be cast as one between DPs and NPs, respectively. Unfortunately, I am unable here to explore ways of distinguishing these two possibilities.

4.2 PERSONAL *SI-*

There is one further distinction of considerable interest between otherwise homophonous imposter and non-imposter arguments. Indonesian *si-*, inherited from the Proto-Malayo-Polynesian nominative case marker for personal names, has lost its case function but continues to (optionally) mark personal names as arguments. Currently, *si-* precedes names employed diminutively and also has a derivational function, turning adjectives into nominals that denote persons characterized by those adjectives, for example, *kecil* "small," *si kecil* "small one, baby," *gemuk* "fat," *si gemuk* "fat one." In Tagalog, this morpheme appears obligatorily with names, as in (64), and also constitutes the initial part of the third person pronouns *siya* 3SG.NOM and *sila* 3PL.NOM, but does not appear on first or second person pronouns.

(64) Tagalog personal *si-*
Ito *(si) Juan
this PERS.NOM Juan
"This is Juan."

Crucially, the Indonesian personal marker of the same form, while optional with third person arguments, is ungrammatical with imposters, as shown in (65) and (66).

(65) Indonesian Personal *si-* with Proper Names
a. (Si) Lia sudah datang
PERS Lia already arrive
"Lia has already arrived."
b. (*Si) Lia[2] sudah datang
PERS Lia already arrive
"Lia (you) has already arrived."

(66) Indonesian Personal *si-* with Titles
a. (Si) ibu sudah datang
PERS mother already arrive
"Mother/Madame has already arrived."
b. (*Si) ibu[2] sudah datang
PERS mother already arrive
"Mother/Madame (you) has already arrived."

This behavior is expected if *si-* is a third person determiner and thus unable to agree with a complement containing first or second person features. On this analysis, the distribution of *si-* also appears to lend support to a morphologically oriented theory of imposters, as it is a direct reflection of the third person features of non-imposter DPs. On a notional theory of imposters, the ungrammaticality of (66b) and (65b) is unexpected, as there is no reason that arguments such as *si ibu* would be any more difficult to interpret semantically as addressees than those without the determiner *si-*.

5. Conclusion

I have aimed here to show the relevance of Indonesian proclisis to imposter phenomena more generally. Indonesian shows in spectacular clarity that a purely notional theory of imposters cannot derive the basic morphosyntactic facts discussed here. Specifically, on a notional theory, structures like (61) where the phrase *bapak* "father" indicates the speaker, and (62) where it does not, should be identical. On the other hand, the largely syntactic theory argued for by Collins and Postal (2012) was shown to also be problematic for deriving these facts. In particular, while imposters had a unique syntax, they behaved significantly differently from appositives. The theory briefly sketched out here takes imposters to be structurally identical to non-imposter DPs, only differing in containing local person features. In Indonesian, a DP with such features is attracted above the verb, resulting in proclisis. A DP without such features remains in a lower position. The two types of DPs are furthermore distinguished by agreement with *si-*, a third person determiner that attaches to personal names. It is predicted that other languages which show sensitivity to local person features (i.e., Algonquian-style inverse languages) should also treat imposters differently from ordinary DPs in the syntax.

References

Adisasmito-Smith, Niken. 1998. Sentence structure and adverbs in Indonesian. *Cornell Working Papers in Linguistics* 118(10): 1–33.

Aldridge, Edith. 2008. Phase-based account of extraction in Indonesian. *Lingua* 118: 1440–1469.

Arka, Wayan, and Christopher Manning. 1998. Voice and grammatical relations in Indonesian: A new perspective. In *LFG Proceedings*. http://csli-publications.stanford.edu/LFG/3/lfg98-toc.html

Asyik, Abdul-Gani. 1987. A contextual grammar of Acehnese sentences. Doctoral dissertation, University of Michigan, Ann Arbor.

Bianchi, Valentina. 2006. On the syntax of personal arguments. *Lingua* 116(12): 2023–2067.

Chung, Sandra. 1976. On the subject of two passives in Indonesian. In *Subject and Topic*, ed. Charles Li, 57–97. New York: Academic Press.

Chung, Sandra. 2008. Indonesian clause structure from an Austronesian perspective. *Lingua* 118(10): 1554–1582.

Cole, Peter, and Gabriella Hermon. 2005a. The typology of Malay reflexives. *Lingua* 115(5): 627–644.

Cole, Peter, and Gabriella Hermon. 2005b. Subject and non-subject relativization in Indonesian. *Journal of East Asian Linguistics* 14(1): 59–88.

Cole, Peter, Gabriella Hermon, and Yanti. 2008. Voice in Malay/Indonesian. *Lingua* 118(10): 1500–1553.

Collins, Chris, and Paul Postal. 2012. *Imposters: A Study of Pronominal Agreement*. Cambridge, MA: MIT Press.

Cumming, Susanna. 1991. *Functional Change: The Case of Malay Constituent Order*. Berlin: Walter de Gruyter.

Dardjowidjojo, Soenjono. 1976. *Sentence Patterns of Indonesian*. Honolulu: University of Hawaii Press.

Donohue, Mark, and John Charles Smith. 1998. What's happened to us? Developments in Malay pronouns. *Oceanic Linguistics* 37: 65–84.

Guilfoyle, Etienne, Henrietta Hung, and Lisa Travis. 1992. Spec of IP and Spec of VP: Two subjects in Austronesian languages. *Natural Language and Linguistic Theory* 10: 375–414.

Haaksma, Rémy. 1933. *Inleiding tot de studie der vervoegde vormen in de Indonesische talen*. Leiden: Boekhandel en Drukkerij voorheen E. J. Brill.

Kaufman, Daniel. 2010. The morphosyntax of Tagalog clitics: A typological approach. Doctoral dissertation, Cornell University, Ithaca, NY.

Kiparsky, Paul. 1973. "Elsewhere" in phonology. In *A festschrift for Morris Halle*, ed. Paul Kiparsky and Stephen Anderson, 93–106. New York: Holt, Rinehart and Winston.

Legate, Julie Anne. 2012. Subjects in Acehnese and the nature of the passive. *Language* 88: 495–525.

Mahdi, Waruno. 2001. Personal nominal words in Indonesian: An anomaly in morphological classification. In *Issues in Austronesian Morphology: A focusschrift for Byron W. Bender*, eds. Joel Bradshaw and Kenneth L. Rehg, Number 519, 163–193. Canberra: Pacific Linguistics, Research School of Pacific Asian Studies, ANU.

Marsden, William. 1812. *A Grammar of the Malayan Language: With an Introduction and Praxis*, Volume 1. London: Cox and Baylis.

Musgrave, Simon. 2001. Pronouns and morphology: Undergoer subject clauses in Indonesian. In *Yearbook of Morphology 2000*, ed. Geert Booij and Jaap van Marle, 155–186. Dordrecht: Kluwer.

Nishiyama, Kunio. 2003. Post-syntactic passivization and the abstract clitic position in Indonesian. In *Cornell Working Papers in Linguistics*, eds. Anastasia Riehl and Thess Savella, Volume 19, 107–121. Ithaca: Cornell University.

Nomoto, Hiroki. 2006. Voice in colloquial Malay relatives. *Gengojouhougaku Kenkyuuhoukoku* 12: 97–116 Tokyo, Japan: Tokyo University of Foreign Studies.

Sie, Ing Djiang. 1989. The syntactic passive in Bahasa Indonesia. Doctoral dissertation, University of Amsterdam.

Sneddon, Jim N. 1996. *Indonesian: A Comprehensive Grammar.* London: Routledge.

Sneddon, Jim N, Alexander Adelaaar, Dwi Noverini Djenar, and Michael C. Ewing. 2010. *Indonesian Reference Grammar*, 2nd edition. Allen & Unwin, St. Leonards: Sydney, NSW, Australia.

Soh, Hooi Ling. 1998. Certain restrictions on A-bar movement in Malay. In *Proceedings of the 3rd and 4th Meetings of the Austronesian Formal Linguistics Association (AFLA)*, ed. Matthew Pearson, Number 21 in *UCLA Occasional Papers in Linguistics*, 295–307. Los Angeles: University of California.

Tadmor, Uri. 2007. Grammatical borrowing in Indonesian. In *Grammatical Borrowing in Cross-linguistic Perspective* (Empirical Approaches to Language Typology), eds. Y. Matras and J. Sakel, Mouton de Berlin: Gruyter.

Thomason, Sarah Grey, and Daniel Everett. 2001. Pronoun borrowing. Unpublished manuscript, University of Michigan and University of Manchester.

Voskuil, Jan. 1996. *Comparative Morphology: Verb Taxonomy in Indonesian, Tagalog, and Dutch*. HIL Dissertations. The Hague: Holland Academic Graphics.

Wang, Arthur. 2009. Some notes on Chinese imposters. In *NYU Working Papers in Linguistics*, eds. Patricia Irwin and Violeta Vázquez Rojas Maldonado, Volume 2. http://linguistics.as.nyu.edu/object/linguistics.grad.nyuwpl#vol2

Wolff, John. 1996. The development of the passive verb with pronominal prefix in Western Austronesian langauges. In *Reconstruction, Classification, description: Festschrift in honor of Isidore Dyen*, ed. Bernd Nothofer, 15–40. Hamburg: Abera.

6

Imposters and Secondary Sources in Italian

EMILIO SERVIDIO

1. Introduction

Collins and Postal (2012) investigate a number of (mostly English) expressions that share the following property: they are nominal expressions (Determiner Phrases) that, despite appearing to be like regular non-pronominal DPs, are systematically used to refer either to the speaker or to the addressee. In other words, they can serve to some extent the function of first or second person pronouns. They dub such expressions "imposters" and "camouflage DPs," depending on some differences to be summarized below. Their critical target is what they call the Notional View, which they hold has been tacitly maintained by the few linguists who have discussed such phenomena. According to the Notional View, imposters and camouflage expressions are syntactically ordinary DPs that refer to the speaker or to the addressee through merely pragmatic means.

In contrast, Collins and Postal (2012) argue for a syntactic analysis of imposters and camouflage DPs that posits a complex inner structure. These expressions have a layered DP architecture which includes a pronominal core that consists of a first or second person pronoun, depending on whether the expressions are used to refer to the speaker or to the addressee, respectively. Possibly the strongest empirical evidence for such an analysis is the fact that most English imposters and camouflage DPs can optionally trigger first or second person pronominal agreement in addition to ordinary third person agreement. Further support comes from other phenomena of non-third person agreement in English (they introduce the technical notion of "secondary source" to cover all these diverse phenomena).

This chapter offers a survey of secondary source phenomena in Italian. Much like French, which Collins and Postal occasionally discuss in their book, Italian is an interesting testing ground because of its rich person and number inflectional morphology on finite verbs. This makes it possible to test Collins and Postal's theory by looking at person features on reflexives and other co-referential pronominal expressions, but also by taking into account verbal inflection. I show that Italian offers a set of counterexamples that make it necessary to devise a different parametric setting with respect to English or some language-specific constraints. I will divide Italian imposters in two classes, which I dub "deep imposters" and "ordinary imposters." I will argue that both classes of imposters have the kind of complex structure proposed by Collins and Postal, but that a further, language-specific constraint restricts the range of person agreement in the latter class.[1]

In sections 2 and 3, I discuss data concerning imposters and camouflage expressions. Section 4 attempts an analysis of the Italian imposter and camouflage data in the framework of Collins and Postal (2012), and proposes a language-specific constraint to account for the basic Italian findings. For completeness, section 5 deals with other types of secondary sources, subjects of predicate nominals, and the set DP of partitive constructions. Section 6 concludes.

2. Imposters

An imposter is a notionally *n* person DP that is grammatically *m* person, for *n* different from *m* (see Collins and Postal, Ch. 18). Many of the imposter expressions discussed by Collins and Postal (2012) translate literally into Italian. Many others have close equivalents, the most notable exceptions being the type *this reporter*, which is not productive in Italian[2] and two imposters originating from correspondence (*yours truly* and *your faithful correspondent*). Following Collins and Postal (2012), here is a list of Italian imposters:

[1] First person imposter phenomena have been discussed by Cattaneo (2009) for the Italian dialect Bellinzonese, spoken in Switzerland. Bellinzonese displays a set of clitic subjects, which are a further locus of person agreement. The reader should be warned, though, that an extension of Cattaneo's findings to Italian is not obvious. Like most so-called Italian dialects, Bellinzonese differs considerably from Italian and might more reasonably be considered a different language (see Maiden and Parry 1997, Poletto 2000 on Northern Italian Dialects). This chapter discusses data from colloquial Italian as spoken by a Roman speaker with university level education (namely, me). I informally consulted a few other speakers. In footnotes, I will report any interesting differences. Regional variation might also exist, and a fair amount of individual variation is more than likely. One cannot also exclude that especially for non-linguists some judgments might be obfuscated by prescriptive issues. It is noteworthy, though, that the main datum of Cattaneo's (the opposition between the equivalent of *the undersigned* and other imposters) is observed in my Italian variety as well.

[2] A candidate would be the type *questo povero NP* (*this poor NP*), used (most often jocularly) to refer to oneself. Nevertheless, the type is restricted to few instances (*questo povero vecchio*, "*this poor old man*") that rarely occur in spontaneous speech. No expression of this type sounds very natural to me.

(1) First person imposters

a. *l'autore* (the author), *gli autori* (the authors),[3] *il/la sottoscritto/a* (the undersigned), *il/la qui presente* (lit., the here present),[4] *la Corte* (the Court).

b. personal names: *Emilio*.

c. members of a set of (diminutive and nondiminutive) kinship terms:[5] *(il) papà* (daddy), *(la) mamma* (mommy), *(il) nonno* (grandfather), *(la) nonna* (grandmother), *(lo) zio* (uncle), *(la) zia* (aunt), and so on.

d. various nondiminutive kinship terms plus a personal name: *zio Emilio*, and so on.

(2) Second person imposters

a. *(la) signora*, *(il) signore*,[6] *il* + Common Noun denoting ranks in a military organization: *il colonnello*, *il mio tesoro* (my sweetheart), *il lettore* (the reader).

b. the elements of (1b), especially when talking to very small children and pets (*Emilio/Emilietto vuole un gelato?*, Would (little) Emilio like some ice-cream?).

c. the elements of (1c).

In section 2.1, I show that most Italian imposters do not admit a person agreement other than third person. This holds both for singular or plural imposters and for coordinations involving imposters (henceforth, conjoined imposters). In section 2.2, I briefly discuss what Collins and Postal call pronominal imposters, and I show that most English expressions have direct Italian counterparts with similar properties. In section 2.3, I isolate two imposters that stand out among the others in admitting first person plural agreement when conjoined, *il sottoscritto* (the undersigned) and *il qui presente* (lit., the here present). Lastly, I discuss social hierarchy camouflage expressions, and I show that they admit second person plural agreement when conjoined.

2.1 ORDINARY IMPOSTERS

English imposters admit non-third person agreement with elements like reflexives. In the dialect of English studied by Collins and Postal, this only happens with plural or conjoined imposters, never with singular imposters. A number

[3] These are the closest equivalents to English *the present author/authors*. As documented by Collins and Postal (2012: 13), *the author, the authors* are attested for English as well.

[4] For the latter imposters, I give both the masculine and feminine versions.

[5] Unlike Collins and Postal's English examples, my *zio, zia* and *nonno, nonna* are nondiminutive. Diminutives do exist (*zietto, zietta* and *nonnino, nonnina*), but they sound too affected to me. Their use as first person imposters is widespread and natural. Also notice the optionality of the definite article on all these kinship terms. Personally, I find the versions with no article more natural, but both are commonly heard.

[6] Here the presence vs. absence of the definite article does matter. *Signora, signore* are used in addressing somebody in a polite way (*Signora, ha bisogno di aiuto?*, Madam, do you need some help?). In this case, verbal agreement is third person singular, as expected whenever a *forma di cortesia* (polite form) is involved. This determiner-less form cannot be conjoined, though. Coordinations involving one of such imposters always display the article (*La signora e la sua amica hanno bisogno di aiuto?*, Do Madam and her friend need some help?).

constraint seems to be at work: only plural imposter expressions admit non-third person agreement. The examples in (3) show that in Italian singular imposters do not admit non-third person agreement, neither with verbs nor with reflexives:[7]

(3) First person singular imposters

a. *L'autore cercherà di difendere se stesso.*
the-author tryFUT3SG of defend him self
"The author will try to defend himself."

b. **L'autore cercherò di difendere me stesso.*
the-author tryFUT1SG of defend my self
"The author will try to defend myself."

c. **Il sottoscritto cercherò di difendere me stesso.*
"The undersigned will try to defend myself."

d. **Emilio cercherò di difendere me stesso.*
"Emilio will try to defend myself."

e. **Papà cercherò di difendere me stesso.*
"Daddy will try to defend myself."

f. **Zio Emilio cercherò di difendere me stesso.*
"Uncle Emilio will try to defend myself."

(4) Second person singular imposters

a. *La signora cercherà di difendere se stessa.*
the lady tryFUT3SG to defend you3SG self
"Madam will try to defend herself."

[7] Two provisos on the choice of examples. All the examples in what follows are modeled after sentences discussed in Collins and Postal, hence the choice of predicates translating *to defend oneself, to take care of oneself.* In object positions, the examples have free non-clitic reflexives of the series *me, te, se stesso* rather than clitic reflexives (*mi, ti, si*). As a result, the examples are better if thought of as answers to WH-questions on the object. In fact, non-clitic reflexives are typically focused in Italian. This also implies that I could not use inherently reflexive predicates like the equivalent of *to behave oneself.* Such predicates do not admit non-clitic reflexives, plausibly because they would have to be focused:

1) *Quel ragazzo si comporta bene.*
that boy himself behaves well
"That boy behaves himself."

2) **Quel ragazzo comporta se stesso bene.*
that boy behaves himself well

In the cases of *la signora* and *il colonnello,* two options are shown for each example. In addition to ordinary second person singular agreement, second person plural agreement is shown. Since expressions like *la signora* or *il colonnello* suggest a certain degree of formality, second person singular might be unacceptable for reasons independent of imposters. Second person plural can be argued to be correct for the formality factor, since it is an option for polite speech, even though stylistically and dialectally marked with respect to the widely used third person singular (which cannot be adopted for the present purposes, being indistinguishable from regular agreement with the grammatical surface of imposter expressions).

b. **La signora cercherai/cercherete di difendere te/voi stessa.*
the lady tryFUT2SG/tryFUT2PL to defend you2SG/2PL self
"Madam will try to defend yourself."

c. **Il colonnello cercherai/cercherete di difendere te/voi stesso.*
"The colonel will try to defend yourself."

d. **Il mio tesoro cercherai di difendere te stesso.*
"My sweetheart will try to defend yourself."

e. **Emilietto cercherai di difendere te stesso.*
"Little Emilio will try to defend yourself."

I have not shown any examples with mismatching person features on the finite verb and on the reflexive: **Papà cercherà di difendere me stesso*, **Papà cercherò di difendere se stesso*. The reason is that they are systematically unacceptable, and the same holds of imposters that do admit non-third person agreement in itself (see section 2.3 below). I will not discuss such examples in this chapter.[8]

Most Italian imposters do not admit non-third person agreement even when plural or pluralized via coordination:

(5) [*Gli autori*]

a. *Gli autori cercheranno di difendere loro/se stessi.*
the authors attemptFUT3PL of defend them selves

b. **Gli autori cercheremo di difendere noi stessi.*
the authors attemptFUT1PL of defend our selves

(6) [*l'autore* & DP]

a. *L'autore e il suo collaboratore cercheranno di difendere loro/se stessi.*
the-author and the his partner attemptFUT3PL of defend them selves

b. **L'autore e il suo collaboratore cercheremo di difendere noi stessi.*
the-author and the his partner attemptFUT1PL of defend our selves

(7) [Kinship term, conjoined]

a. *Papà e mamma si prenderanno cura di se stessi.*
daddy and mummy RefCl takeFUT3PL care of them selves

b. **Papà e mamma ci prenderemo cura di noi stessi.*
daddy and mummy RefCl takeFUT1PL care of our selves

(8) [Nondiminutive Kinship term, conjoined]

a. *Zio Emilio e zia Angela si prenderanno cura di se stessi.*
uncle Emilio and aunt Angela RefCl takeFUT3PL care of them selves

b. **Zio Emilio e zia Angela ci prenderemo cura di noi stessi.*
uncle Emilio and aunt Angela RefCl takeFUT1PL care of our selves

(9) [Proper name, conjoined]

a. *Emilio e Angela si prenderanno cura di se stessi.*
Emilio and Angela RefCl takeFUT3PL care of them selves

b. **Emilio e Angela ci prenderemo cura di noi stessi.*
Emilio and Angela RefCl takeFUT1PL care of our selves

[8] Collins and Postal (2012: 126–127) propose an extension of the notion of homogeneity in order to account for some matching effects in French. As far as I can see, a similar approach might do for Italian as well. I refer the reader to the book for details.

The same point can be made for the second person imposters listed in (4). For brevity, I will only show the relevant paradigm for *il colonnello*:

(10) a. *Il colonnello e gli altri ospiti si prenderanno cura di se stessi.*
the colonel and the other guests RefCl takeFUT3PL care of them selves
"The colonel and the other guests will take care of themselves."
b. **Il colonnello e gli altri ospiti vi prenderete cura di voi stessi.*
the colonel and the other guests RefCl takeFUT2PL care of your selves
"The colonel and the other guests will take care of yourselves."

Collins and Postal (2012) analyze imposters in terms of agreement with the abstract indexicals AUTHOR and ADDRESSEE, assumed to be syntactically present as arguments of a high performative verb that take root clauses as complements (see Chapter 1 of this volume for a summary). The general rule for pronominal agreement is that non-expletive pronominals must agree with a source. Sources include antecedents, antecedence being defined as a primitive asymmetric relation. Imposters are then analyzed as complex DP structures that have a visible third person shell and a non-third person core that is ultimately anteceded by AUTHOR or ADDRESSE. In virtue of a certain pattern of antecedence, an imposter is then predicted to allow both third person agreement (because of the shell DP) and non-third person agreement (because of the ultimate antecedent).

Unlike English imposters, Italian imposters force third person agreement on verbs and reflexives. This is true of singular, plural, and conjoined imposters (some notable exceptions are discussed in section 2.3). At first glance, this looks problematic for Collins and Postal's theory. In principle, this might be taken as evidence of the fact that the interpretation of imposters as referring to the speaker or to the addressee cannot be ascribed to the antecedence properties of a pronominal core. Less radically, one could preserve the analysis of imposter DPs as layered structures with a first or second person pronominal core, responsible for the interpretation, while revising or denying the status of sources for agreement with ultimate antecedents of imposters (that is, to AUTHOR and ADDRESSEE). I will choose the latter option. On the other hand, in section 2.3, I will introduce a class of Italian imposters that patterns with English imposters as far as non-third person agreement is concerned. A constraint on ordinary imposters in Italian will have to take this second class of imposters into account. See section 4.2 below for a constraint to this effect.

2.2 PRONOMINAL IMPOSTERS

In principle, nothing precludes an imposter DP from being pronominal. Collins and Postal (2012) actually discuss a number of plausible candidates for pronominal imposters, that is, pronouns whose interpretation differs systematically in reference from what would be expected from their grammatical person value. The so-called Nurse-*we* has a literal equivalent in Italian.[9] Because Italian is a null subject language, these pronominal imposters can be (and typically are) null. Under any other respect, Italian mirrors English quite closely, so one can easily import the analyses of Collins and Postal as they are. For completeness, Italian pronominal imposters are exemplified in this section:

(11) [Nurse-*noi*]

a. *Ci sentiamo un po' meglio oggi?*
RefCl feel1PL a bit better today
"Are we feeling a bit better today?"

b. *Siamo elegantissimi oggi!*
be1PL very-elegant today
"We are very elegant today."

As in English, a first person plural subject pronoun is used by the speaker to refer to the addressee. This use might be prototypically associated with certain communicative settings (hence the label "Nurse-*we*"), as suggested by example (11a). Example (11b), though, exemplifies the same use in a less specific setting (say, a friend commenting on one's new suit). A relevant factor might possibly be thought to be sympathy to the addressee. Collins and Postal (2012) analyze Nurse-*we* as an inherently plural pronoun with ADDRESSEE as ultimate antecedent. To account for the first person value, they postulate AUTHOR as a secondary source, hence the first person agreement.

A second type of pronominal imposters, also discussed by Collins and Postal, is attested in Italian: generic *you*. Again, the only obvious difference is that its Italian counterpart is mostly null:

(12) a. *Se (tu) fai del male agli altri, prima o poi qualcuno te la fa pagare.*
if (you) do2SG of harm at others sooner or later somebody youCl itCL makes pay
"If you are always hurting other people, sooner or later somebody makes you pay for it."

b. *Devi avere rispetto delle persone anziane.*
must2SG have respect of-the persons old
"You must respect the elderly."

In neither example is the second person singular subject meant to refer to the addressee specifically. They are a general statement and a general maxim of behavior, respectively. Collins and Postal propose to analyze generic *you* as having a generic quantifier as immediate antecedent and ADDRESSEE as a secondary source.

[9] By contrast, no equivalent of singular-*they* exists, as far as I know.

2.3 DEEP IMPOSTERS

As anticipated above, the pattern of agreement for Italian imposters has two notable exceptions. In section 2.1, I showed that ordinary imposters do not admit non-third person agreement, not even when plural or conjoined. This does not hold of *il sottoscritto* (the undersigned) and *il qui presente* (the here present).[10]

Both expressions disallow first person singular agreement, just like other Italian or English singular imposters:

(13) [*Il sottoscritto*]
a. *Il sottoscritto cercherà di difendere se stesso.*
the undersigned attemptFUT3SG of defend him self
b. **Il sottoscritto cercherò di difendere me stesso.*
the undersigned attemptFUT1SG of defend my self

(14) [*Il qui presente*]
a. *Il qui presente cercherà di difendere se stesso.*
the here present attemptFUT3SG of defend him self
b. **Il qui presente cercherò di difendere me stesso.*
the here present attemptFUT1SG of defend my self

Things change when it comes to plural examples. The grammatically plural equivalents, *i sottoscritti* and *i qui presenti*, do not sound natural.[11] However, one can obtain plural DPs by conjoining the imposters with other DPs. Unlike the imposters discussed in section 2.1, and like English imposters, the DPs thus obtained admit first person plural subject-verb agreement and pronominal agreement. The result is only slightly marginal (I give only the paradigm for *il sottoscritto*; the one for *il qui presente* is analogous):[12]

(15) a. *Maria e il sottoscritto cercheranno di difendere se stessi.*
Maria and the undersigned attemptFUT3PL of defend them selves
b. ?*Maria e il sottoscritto cercheremo di difendere noi stessi.*
Maria and the undersigned attemptFUT1PL of defend our selves
c. *Il sottoscritto e Maria cercheranno di difendere se stessi.*
the undersigned and Maria attemptFUT3PL of defend them selves

[10] Both expressions originated from bureaucratic writing. Nevertheless, they are now used in spoken Italian, with jocular connotations at times. Notice that only the imposter reading of *il qui presente* concerns us here. The expression also enters in constructions used to refer to a third person. This generally requires the expression to modify a nominal expression, e.g., *il professore qui presente, il qui presente professore*. As for whether the latter expressions can also be used as imposters, see section 4.2 below.

[11] Of course, these plural versions do exist in the original, bureaucratic written register, but I have never heard them spoken, and I have no intuitions about them.

[12] The contrast between the two imposters at hand and those listed in section 2.1 is shared among the speakers I have consulted. All of them accepted first person agreement with conjoined *il/la sottoscritto/a, il/la qui presente* to a good extent, and rejected non-third person agreement with other conjoined imposters in most, though not all, cases.

d. ?**Il sottoscritto e Maria cercheremo di difendere noi stessi.*
the undersigned and Maria attemptFUT1PL of defend our selves

Notice that order matters. Coordinations with the imposter as last member are systematically, even though not dramatically, better than the other case.[13]

The imposters at hand resemble English imposters in that they admit non-third person agreements, even though slightly marginally. Since according to Collins and Postal's theory these agreement values result from the properties of the inner pronominal core of the imposter expressions, I name these English-like imposters *deep* imposters, meaning that that they display agreement with the most deeply embedded layer of the structure.[14]

The following examples show that conjoined deep imposters can antecede embedded subjects and possessives respectively, even when subject-verb agreement is 1PL:

(16) [Bind embedded 1Pl Subj]
a. ?*Maria e il sottoscritto abbiamo deciso che non compreremo quest'auto.*
Maria and the undersigned have1PL decided that not buyFUT1PL this-car
b. ??*Il sottoscritto e Maria abbiamo deciso che non compreremo quest'auto.*
the undersigned and Maria have1PL decided that not buyFUT1PL this-car

(17) [Bind 1Pl Possessive]
a. *Maria e il sottoscritto cercheranno di difendere la loro proposta.*
Maria and the undersigned attemptFUT3PL of defend the their proposal
b. ?*Maria e il sottoscritto cercheremo di difendere la nostra proposta.*
Maria and the undersigned attemptFUT1PL of defend the our proposal
c. *Il sottoscritto e Maria cercheranno di difendere la loro proposta.*
the undersigned and Maria attemptFUT3PL of defend the their proposal
d. ??*Il sottoscritto e Maria cercheremo di difendere la nostra proposta.*
the undersigned and Maria attemptFUT1PL of defend the our proposal

One can reasonably wonder what *il/la sottoscritto/a* and *il/la qui presente* have in common. A possible answer suggests itself: both have participial morphology, something that singles them out among the ordinary imposters discussed in

[13] This also holds of coordination involving more than two conjuncts, but the effect is subtler:

1) *Maria, Luca e il sottoscritto cercheremo di difendere noi stessi.*
Maria Luca and the undersigned tryFUT1PL of defend our selves
"Maria, Luca and the undersigned will try to defend ourselves."
2) ??*Il sottoscritto, Maria e Luca cercheremo di difendere noi stessi.*
3) ??*Maria, il sottoscritto e Luca cercheremo di difendere noi stessi.*

Other speakers' judgments do not show the same order effects. Interestingly, though, Cattaneo (2009) reported analogous contrasts in his Bellinzonese variety.

[14] In making an analogous distinction between two classes of Bellinzonese imposters, Cattaneo (2009) uses the label *pseudo-imposters* vs. *true imposters*.

section 2.1. More specifically, *sottoscritto* looks like the past participle of the verb *sottoscrivere* (*to undersign*) and *presente* can be analyzed (at least etymologically) as a present participle related to the verb *essere* (*to be*).[15] Chris Collins (p.c.) suggests that this property could be responsible for the different agreement patterns. One could hypothesize that such pseudo-participial expressions structurally include a further null nominal element, which would make it somehow easier for the core phi-features to percolate up and override the third person features of the outer shell. This would obviously require a suitable implementation. Technicalities aside, however, the proposal is not without difficulties. The data presented in section 3 below suggest that this could not be the whole story about Italian. The agreement patterns on camouflage expressions also have to be accounted for.

Summing up, Italian (non-pronominal) imposters divide neatly into two classes. One was discussed in section 2.1 under the label "ordinary imposters," but one might as well call them *surface* imposters, as opposed to deep imposters. These DPs systematically refer to the speaker or to the addressee, but they only admit third person agreement, in either singular or plural. The second class, discussed here, consists of *il/la sottoscritto/a* and *il/la qui presente*. These imposters do admit first person agreement when conjoined. While the latter class of imposters can be thought of as directly analogous to English imposters, something must be said of the former class. I delay discussion of these problems until section 4.2.

3. Camouflage Expressions

Like imposters, camouflage expressions are grammatically third person DPs that are systematically used to refer to the speaker or the addressee. Like imposters, they admit non-third person agreement in some circumstances. Collins and Postal maintain that camouflage expressions, like imposters, have a layered syntactic structure involving a pronominal core, which accounts for their agreement properties. The fundamental difference would be that while in imposters such a core is always covert, in camouflage expressions it is overt and surfaces as a possessor, for instance, the expression *Your Majesty* is used to address a monarch,

[15] The claim that these two deep imposters are participial needs to be qualified. *Sottoscritto/a* surely looks like a participle, and some (but not all) dictionaries list it as the past participle of *sottoscrivere*. But *sottoscrivere* means "to sign and approve a document'" If so, *sottoscritto* should be thought of as derived from the (active) past participle rather than from the passive participle of *sottoscrivere*, which would be expected to denote the undersigned thing, rather than the undersigner. But that is not a productive derivational option in Italian: adjectives or nouns obtained from past participles are usually passive in meaning. As for *presente*, its present participle morphology is inherited from a remote Latin basis (PRAESENS, from PRAE-SUM, "to be present"; see *Oxford Latin Dictionary*, hereafter OLD), and it is in no way transparent to Italian speakers. Whatever role participial morphology is supposed to play here, it cannot possibly be a productive one. Nevertheless, the coincidence is striking.

and it features a second person possessive pronoun. Analogous expressions are available in Italian, and I now turn to discuss their agreement properties. To the best of my knowledge, no equivalent of the colloquial camouflage type *your ass* (first discussed in Collins et al. 2008) is available in Italian.

I illustrate Italian social hierarchy camouflage expressions (SHCs) with *Vostra Maestà* (Your Majesty). Others of the same type are *Vostra Altezza* (Your Highness), *Vostra Eccellenza* (Your Excellency), *Vostra Eminenza* (Your Eminence), *Vostra Grazia* (Your Grace). Notice that, like English SHCs, these expressions have counterparts with third person singular, rather than second person plural, possessives (see Collins and Postal (2012: 207ff) for analysis).[16]

Like singular imposters (both in Italian and in English), Italian singular SHCs do not admit second person (singular or plural) agreement on main verbs or with reflexives:

(18) a. *Vostra Maestà cercherà di difendere se stessa.*
Your Majesty tryFUT3SG of defend her self
"Your Majesty will try to defend herself."
b. **Vostra Maestà cercherai di difendere te stessa.*
Your Majesty tryFUT2SG of defend you-SG
c. **Vostra Maestà cercherete di difendere voi stessa.*
Your Majesty tryFUT2PL of defend you-PL self

This is unsurprising. The ban on non-third person agreement with non-plural antecedents, besides being shared with both classes of Italian imposters, is common to English imposters as well. The relevant examples are the plural ones. In principle, grammatically plural SHCs would be available, for example, *le Vostre Maestà*, to address two persons each being either a queen or a king. Since intuitions on these items are shaky, I resort to coordination again:

(19) a. *Vostra Maestà e il primo ministro cercheranno di difendere loro stessi.*
Your Majesty and the prime minister tryFUT3PL of defend them selves
"Your Majesty and the prime minister will try to defend themselves."
b. *Vostra Maestà e il primo ministro cercherete di difendere voi stessi.*
Your Majesty and the prime minister tryFUT2PL of defend your selves
"Your Majesty and the prime minister will try to defend yourselves."

This shows that, like deep imposters, Italian SHCs admit agreement with their pronominal core. For comparison, let us check a second person imposter (*il colonnello*) in coordination:

[16] A further example is *Santità* (Holiness). For some reason, the second person version *Vostra Santità* does not sound good to me, as opposed to the third person *Sua Santità*. This is likely to be nothing more than an idiolectal feature. Google hits for *Vostra Santità* are in the order of tens of thousands, the same order of size as other SHCs with second person possessives.

(20) a. *Il colonnello e il primo ministro cercheranno di difendere loro stessi.*
the colonel and the prime minister tryFUT3PL of defend them selves
"The colonel and the prime minister will try to defend themselves."
b. **Il colonnello e il primo ministro cercherete di difendere voi stessi.*
the colonel and the prime minister tryFUT2PL of defend your selves

These data strengthen the picture of the imposter and camouflage lexicon in Italian as divided into two classes, one that rigidly requires agreement with the third person outer layer (most imposters), the other that admits, at least to a good extent, agreement with the pronominal core of the structure (deep imposters, SHCs).

4. Discussion

4.1 IMPOSTERS AND CAMOUFLAGE DPs IN ITALIAN

Given the analysis in Collins and Postal (2012), it is easy to see that the theory accounts for the data on deep imposters (section 2.3 above) and SHCs. I abstract away from the ban on singular imposters: however it might be ultimately implemented, it is shared with Collins and Postal's dialect of English, so Italian and English are on a par as far as the treatment of that restriction is concerned.

For the reader unfamiliar with Collins and Postal (2012), I illustrate the analysis of a relevant example of first person agreement with a conjoined imposter, repeated from (15):[17]

(21) a. *Maria e il sottoscritto cercheranno di difendere se stessi.*
Maria and the undersigned tryFUT3PL of defend them selves
"Maria and the undersigned will try to defend themselves."
b. ?*Maria e il sottoscritto cercheremo di difendere noi stessi.*
Maria and the undersigned tryFUT1PL of defend our selves
"Maria and the undersigned will try to defend ourselves."

The reflexives are third and first person plural in (21a) and (21b), respectively. Then it follows from the Pronominal Agreement Condition that a suitable source must be available in both sentences (see Chapter 1 of to this volume). A candidate is the coordinate DP in subject position, which because of binding theory must antecede the reflexive. Two different person values for the DP *Maria e il sottoscritto* are available. A conjunctive coordinate DP agrees in person with its key conjuncts, that is, with the conjuncts with the highest ranking person

[17] A concise account of Collins and Postal's (2012) framework is presented in Chapter 1 of this volume.

features in the hierarchy 1>2>3 (Collins and Postal 2012, Chap. 9.). In (21), *il sottoscritto* is a key conjunct in virtue of its first person core. The whole coordinate DP can be first or third person, because it can agree with either of two antecedents: AUTHOR (the immediate antecedent of *il sottoscritto*, and by transitivity a source for the coordinate DP) or *il sottoscritto* itself. If the coordinate DP agrees with *il sottoscritto*, it will be third person, hence the grammaticality of (21a). If it agrees with AUTHOR, it will be first person, hence the grammaticality of (21b).

Except for the slight marginality of (21b), things go exactly as expected. Italian SHCs also behave like English ones in admitting second person agreement, the difference being that in my intuitions only conjoined examples are fine.[18]

What distinguishes Italian and English is the behavior of the other class of imposters (section 2.1). Ordinary imposters never admit non-third person agreement, independently of number and coordination.[19] The problem arises of how to model this contrast.

From a cross-linguistic point of view, the pattern is interesting but unexpected. If one abstracts away from deep imposters for a while, Italian appears to be a candidate for an (a) type language in Collins and Postal's cross-linguistic typology:[20]

(22) The Pronominal Agreement Parameter
If an imposter A immediately antecedes a pronominal P, then:
a. P agrees only with A.
b. P agrees only with A's ultimate antecedent.
c. P agrees with A or A's ultimate antecedent.

But the existence of deep imposters shows that things cannot be so easy. The availability of at least some imposters that allow agreements with ultimate antecedents makes Italian a (d) type language (like Bellinzonese; see note 1 above). But if so, why do most Italian imposters resist non-third person agreement? Let us turn to Collins' suggestion, mentioned in section 2.3, and elaborate on it some more.

4.2 ONE ADDITIONAL CONSTRAINT

Let us briefly review the structural analysis proposed for imposters by Collins and Postal. Imposters are thought to be derivationally related to the so-called precursor structures. Precursor structures are instances of appositive

[18] Notice, though, that one informant also accepted the following non-conjoined SHC:

1) *Vostra Maestà cercherete di difendere voi stessa.*
Your Majesty tryFUT2PL of defend your self
"Your Majesty will try to defend yourself."

[19] This is attested by me and most other informants. Only one informant accepted first person agreement with the conjoined DPs *Emilio e Angela* and *zio Emilio e zia Angela*.

[20] Collins and Postal (2012: 225). Cf. Chapter 1 of this volume.

modification: a pronominal DP is merged with a reduced clause constituent that non-restrictively modifies it (the dashed lines signal antecedence):

(25)
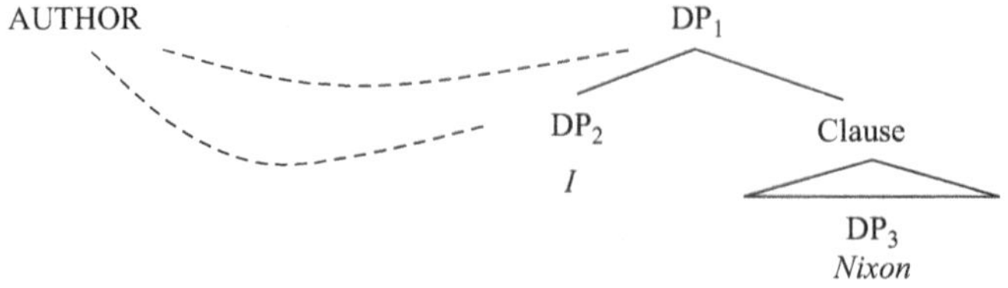

In imposters, the predicate nominal inside the appositive clause moves past the pronominal DP to the specifier of a high D projection in the layered DP structure:

(26)
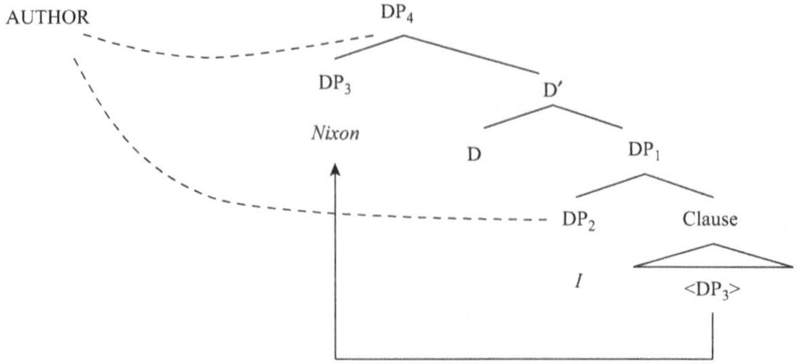

By hypothesis, the person value of the whole DP is determined by the DP sub-constituent highest in the structure. This is either because the latter DP enters into a Spec-Head relation with the highest D head, or because the search mechanism involved in subject-verb agreement looks no further than the highest phi-valued DP it can find (Collins and Postal 2012: 66). So in (25), DP_2 makes DP_1 first person, while in (26), DP_3 makes DP_4 third person. As far as agreement is concerned, the observed pattern is derived according to the definitions and constraints discussed in Chapter 1 of this volume. Due to the fact that AUTHOR antecedes the whole DP_4 structure, an element agreeing with an imposter may agree either with DP_4 (third person) or with the ultimate antecedent of DP_4, AUTHOR (first person).[21]

I argue that (i) Italian, like English, has imposters, and (ii) all imposter expressions have a pronominal core. The restrictive agreement properties of ordinary imposters in Italian can be reduced to a further, language-particular constraint. As mentioned in section 2.3, the two deep imposters share some form of participial morphology. I take this to hint at a structure different from other imposters. I take these expressions to be deverbal adjectives. The structure includes a null nominal element, which *sottoscritto* and *qui presente* modify:

[21] For a proof of the fact that AUTHOR antecedes not only *I* but also the whole structure, see Collins and Postal (2012), section 5.5.

(27)

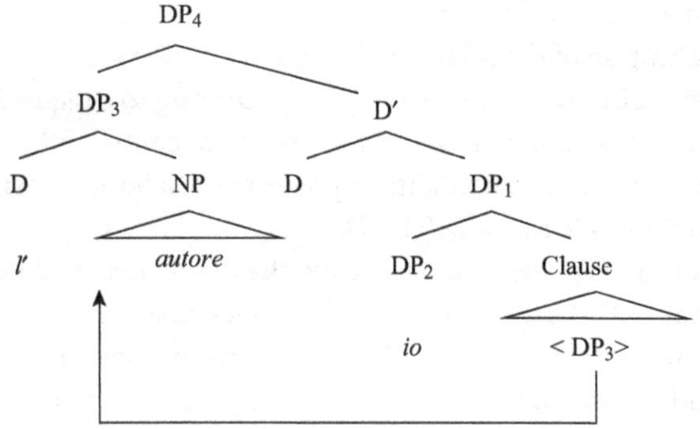

(28)

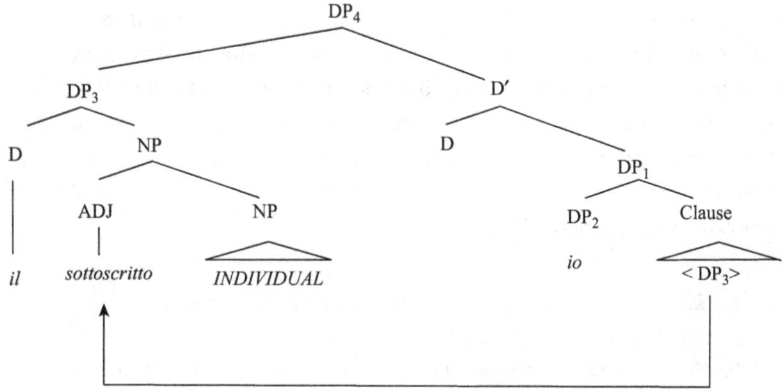

In (27), the predicative nominal *l'autore* is moved to a position in the DP structure higher than the pronominal core *io*. In (28), the same holds of *il sottoscritto*, except for the fact that, by hypothesis, *sottoscritto* is a participial adjective modifying a null nominal. One can stipulate that the null nominal modified by the participle is somewhat defective in its featural content. Whatever mechanism is responsible for the person features of DP_4, it can be sensitive to the realization of the lexical, nominal component of the highest DP in the structure. Notice that, according to the definition of lexical basis (Collins and Postal 2012: 59), DP_3 *l'autore* in (27) is lexically based on the noun *autore*, while DP_3 *il sottoscritto* in (28) is based on the postulated null noun. I suggest the following constraint:

(29) a. The Nominal Content Constraint
If the head of a DP A is in a Spec-Head configuration with a DP that is lexically based on a "contentful noun," then the ultimate antecedent of A is an inaccessible source.

b. Definition: Inaccessible source
A source *s* of A is inaccessible iff A cannot agree with *s*.

By "contentful noun" I mean a noun rich enough in phonetic, formal, and semantic features. A proper definition of the relevant class is needed. Crucially, though, the null nominal element (either an N head or an NP, according to Cinque 2010) modified by *sottoscritto* and *qui presente* would not count as "contentful." It can be thought of as a silent common noun, highly impoverished in both formal and semantic features, paraphrasable as "INDIVIDUAL."

Adding the constraint in (29) allows one to leave the definitions and principles of Collins and Postal (2012) unchanged. The difference between the classes of Italian imposters is ultimately reduced to lexical variation: some imposters, which share a certain adjectival quality, include a null nominal element. Other more run-of-the-mill imposters, like *l'autore* or *il colonnello*, have "contentful" nouns (*autore, colonnello*) instead. In the latter case, (29) dictates that no agreeing element can agree with the ultimate antecedent of the imposter, because the ultimate antecedent is an inaccessible source. The constraint overrides the alternatives made available by Collins and Postal's general theory (i.e., antecedents are expected to be sources for agreement). (29) correctly rules out both first person agreement with non-conjoined singular or plural ordinary imposters (30) and agreement with conjunctive coordinate DPs consisting of an ordinary imposter plus non-imposter DP(s) (31):

(30) a. *L'autore cercherò di difendere me stesso.
the-author tryFUT1SG of defend my self

b. *Gli autori cercheremo di difendere noi stessi.
the authors attemptFUT1PL of defend our selves

(31) *L'autore e il suo collaboratore cercheremo di difendere noi stessi.
the-author and the his partner attemptFUT1PL of defend our selves

According to the structure exemplified by (27), both imposters in (30) have DPs lexically based on "contentful" nouns (*autore, autori*) in the topmost specifier position. Hence, the ultimate antecedent of these imposters (AUTHOR) is inaccessible, and nothing for which AUTHOR is a source (e.g., the reflexive) can agree with it. In (31), the coordinate DP agrees with a source of one of its key conjuncts. Its only key conjunct is *l'autore*, so it must agree with a member of one of the sources of *l'autore*. The ultimate antecedent of *l'autore*, AUTHOR, is a source, but it is inaccessible because of (29), so the reflexive cannot agree with it.

Notice also that the constraint correctly rules in first person agreement in the following example, with a conjunctive coordinate DP including a deep imposter and a second person ordinary imposter (*il colonnello*):

(32) Il colonnello e il sottoscritto cercheremo di difendere noi stessi.
the colonel and the undersigned tryFUT1PL to defend our selves

The example is basically acceptable (the slight marginality mark ? is in line with other examples involving deep imposters in my judgment). The Nominal Content

Constraint prevents il *colonnello* from providing ADDRESSEE as an accessible source. If *il colonnello* were to determine the agreement on the coordinate DP, the coordinate DP would be forced to be third person, since the second person feature provided by ADDRESSEE would be unavailable. But the sources of *il sottoscritto* include the ultimate antecedent, AUTHOR, which is an accessible source because the highest DP in *il sottoscritto* is based on a null noun. Since *il sottoscritto* comes to be the key conjunct (in virtue of the first person of AUTHOR vs. the second person of ADDRESSEE), the coordinate DP will be able to agree with any source of *il sottoscritto*. Both third and first person agreement would then be available.

The formulation of (29) is general. It does not refer specifically to imposters, while not affecting constructions involving secondary sources like subjects of predicate nominals or set DPs of partitives (see section 5 below). More interestingly, (29) also accounts for the fact that SHCs do admit non-third person agreement (at least when conjoined). Let us look at the structure and antecedence properties of an SHC:

(33)

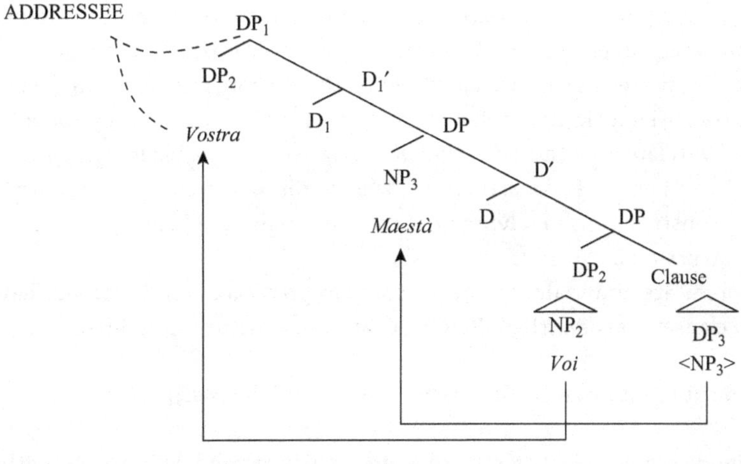

The structure of *Vostra Maestà* is modeled in (33) as identical to the structure proposed for *Your Majesty* in Collins and Postal (2012: 84). *Maestà* is originally merged as a predicate nominal. The possessive *Vostra*, which corresponds to the pronominal core of precursor structures (see above), moves to the topmost DP projection, DP_1. Both the whole DP_1 and *Vostra* have ADDRESSEE as their ultimate antecedent. Pending a proper definition of "contentful nominal," one should presumably admit that DP_1 includes such a nominal (*Maestà*). Notice, though, that *Maestà* is not the topmost DP in structure in (33). Instead, DP_1 has in its specifier position DP_2, which is based on the possessive determiner *Vostra*. If one can envisage a notion of contentfulness that does not include possessive determiners, SHCs like *Vostra Maestà* will not be affected by (29).

In search of independent evidence to posit (29), one could look at constructions that arguably involve the deep imposter expressions *sottoscritto* and *qui presente* together with a common noun like *professore*. *Professore* surely looks like a "contentful noun": it is phonetically realized, it has phi-features of its own, it has semantic, notional content. Then one would expect that DPs of the form *il professore qui presente, il professore sottoscritto* would be prevented by (29) from triggering first person agreement. Unfortunately, the speakers' intuitions about these forms are weak, since unlike the simpler imposters *il/la sottoscritto/a* and *il/la qui presente*, they do not belong to conversational Italian. On the contrary, they are largely confined to the bureaucratic register from which these imposters originated.

5. Other Secondary Sources

5.1 SUBJECTS OF PREDICATE NOMINALS

Imposters and camouflage expressions are two of a range of constructions with unexpected agreement properties discussed by Collins and Postal, as summarized in the introduction to this volume. The theory resorts to a general notion of source to account for the extra agreement options. In the case of imposters and camouflage expressions, the option of non-third person agreement is due to a peculiar pattern of antecedence, which the authors take to be an asymmetric and transitive primitive relation, and the assumption that antecedents are sources. Two clauses of the definition of source are responsible for the agreement properties of two other constructions, which I discuss in turn. In this section, I consider constructions involving predicate nominals, and I briefly discuss partitive constructions.

The predicate nominals at issue are complex predicate nominals modified by a relative clause. Consider the following example (structure simplified):

(34) I am [DP_1 a [$teacher_i$ [CP [DP_2 who t_i] takes care of himself]]].

In a sentence like (34), the reflexive *himself* is analyzed as agreeing with the whole predicate nominal DP_1 which contains it. This is obtained indirectly as follows. The reflexive is immediately anteceded by DP_2. In turn, the larger constituent DP_1 is a source for DP_2 because the two share a lexical basis. In virtue of the inductive clause of the definition of source, DP_1 is also a source for the reflexive, hence the reflexive can agree with DP_1. Since DP_1 is uncontroversially third person, the person feature on the reflexive must be third person as well.

Collins and Postal report that, in addition to the agreement pattern exemplified by (34), a further option is available in English:

(35) I am [DP_1 a [teacher [CP [DP_2 who] takes care of myself]]].

The analysis summarized above does not explain the first person feature on the reflexive. To account for such cases, Collins and Postal add a clause to the definition of source, stating that the subject of a predicate nominal is a source for everything the predicate nominal is a source for; this means that, in (35), *I* is a source for DP_2. Since DP_2 is a source for the reflexive in virtue of immediately anteceding it, the subject is also a source for the reflexive.

In this section, I present Italian data on the constructions in (34) and (35). In what follows, I give judgments for all the combinations of non-third person and number on the subject. In each case, I compare the regular third person agreement in (a) with the alternative one in (b):

(36)	a.	*Sono*	*una*	*persona*	*che*	*si*	*prende*	*cura*	*di se*	*stessa.*
		am	a	person	who	RefCl	take3SG	care	of him	self
	b.	??*Sono*	*una*	*persona*	*che*	*mi*	*prendo*	*cura*	*di me*	*stesso/a.*
		am	a	person	who	RefCl	take1SG	care	of my	self
(37)	a.	*Sei*	*una*	*persona*	*che*	*si*	*prende*	*cura*	*di se*	*stessa.*
		be2SG	a	person	who	RefCl	take3SG	care	of him	self
	b.	?**Sei*	*una*	*persona*	*che*	*ti*	*prendi*	*cura*	*di te*	*stesso/a.*
		be2SG	a	person	who	RefCl	take2SG	care	of your	self
(38)	a.	*Siamo*		*persone*	*che*	*si*	*prendono*	*cura*	*di se*	*stesse.*
		be1Pl		persons	who	RefCl	take3PL	care	of them	selves
	b.	?*Siamo*		*persone*	*che*	*ci*	*prendiamo*	*cura*	*di noi*	*stessi.*
		be1Pl		persons	who	RefCl	take1PL	care	of our	selves
(39)	a.	*Siete*		*persone*	*che*	*si*	*prendono*	*cura*	*di se*	*stesse.*
		be2Pl		persons	who	RefCl	take3PL	care	of them	selves
	b.	?*Siete*		*persone*	*che*	*vi*	*prendete*	*cura*	*di voi*	*stessi.*
		be2Pl		persons	who	RefCl	take2PL	care	of your	selves

Notice that some orthogonal issues enter into the paradigm, thus resulting in the fact that no pair is, strictly speaking, minimal. Singular examples have predicate nominals with indefinite articles; plural examples have bare plurals instead. This is the most natural form in the context (alternatively, the partitive article *delle persone* could be used). The grammatical gender of reflexives (*stessa* vs. *stesso* in the singular, *stesse* vs. *stessi* in the plural) has not been glossed for better readability. The differences are due to the fact that in third person examples the reflexives agree with the noun *persona/persone* in gender as well as in person and number, which is grammatically feminine. In the non-third person examples, the reflexives agree in gender with the subjects, hence in the singular they are either masculine or feminine depending on the (non-grammatical) gender of the subject, and in the plural they are masculine because of the grammatically masculine conventional gender of groups of people including both males and females.

Abstracting away from these details, the pattern in the examples (36) to (39) is less neat than one would hopefully expect. Agreement with plural subjects is only slightly marginal. Agreement with singular subjects, though not plainly ungrammatical, is more degraded. These judgments of mine, though, have proven to be idiolectal. Some speakers judged at least some of the (b) sentences in (36) to (39) to be fully acceptable. One speaker also accepted the mismatch pattern [Verb: 3PL; Refl: 2PL]: *Siete persone che si prendono cura di voi stessi*. The singular/plural divide, which is perceptible to me, was not replicated: those who accept to some extent the plural examples also accept the singular examples.[22]

In the lack of a plausible explanation for the graded nature of these judgments, I tentatively propose to simplify the pattern as follows. As for my own idiolect, one could take plural examples to be good, and account for them. Actually, they have the same ? acceptability mark observed in many examples with coordinate imposters illustrated above. Singular examples, being severely degraded, would be taken to be ungrammatical. If so, the idiolect at hand can be seen as extending the ban on singular secondary sources (attested in Italian and English for imposters) to subjects of predicate nominals. As for those who accept both the singular and the plural examples, they align neatly with the dialect of English described in Collins and Postal (2012).

5.2 PARTITIVES

According to the theory developed by Collins and Postal, a further type of secondary source for agreement is the set DP of a partitive construction (see also Chapter 1 of this volume). They offer the following schema of the construction at hand:

(40) [DP_1 Quantifier + [NP Noun (= one(s))] + (of) DP_2].

In (40), DP_2 is the set DP of the construction. A clause in the definition of source in Collins and Postal (2012: 156) states that set DPs are sources for agreement. This is illustrated by sentences like the following:

(41) a. Every one of us thinks she is talented.
b. Every one of us think we are talented.

In (41a), the subject pronoun in the embedded clause is interpreted as a variable bound by the quantifier *every one of us*. The sentence can be roughly paraphrased as "For every *x* such that *x* is one of us, *x* thinks that *x* is talented." Here the subject pronoun agrees with the complex DP *every one of us*. Crucially, (41b) is compatible with the very same bound variable reading, but now the embedded subject agrees in person with the set DP *us*: *us* must be the source of the first person feature on *we*.

[22] Corpora research is not revealing. The (b) patterns of agreement are extremely rare in the Italian Google corpus. Hits for strings of the form "BE *a person who* ReflCl TAKE" are on the order of a few units for first or second person forms of BE and TAKE.

In this section, I present some data on this construction, whose status in Italian is not easy to assess. Consider the following:

(42) a. ??*Ognuno di noi pensa che siamo in gamba.*
each of us think3SG that be1PL smart
"Every one of us thinks we are smart."
b. ??*Ognuno di voi pensa che siete in gamba.*
each of youPl think3SG that be2PL smart
"Every one of you thinks you are smart."
c. ??*Ognuno di loro pensa che sono in gamba.*
each of them think3SG that be3PL smart
"Every one of them thinks they are smart."

Under the relevant reading, all the sentences in (38) are degraded but not ungrammatical. The same sentences are totally acceptable under a collective reading ("For every *x* such that *x* is one of us, *x* thinks that we as a group are smart"). For the present concerns, this is irrelevant. My Italian grammar has at least two acceptable ways to express the relevant reading. The first involves an infinitive embedded clause (a control structure):

(43) *Ognuno di noi pensa di essere in gamba.*
each of us think3SG of be smart
"Every one of us thinks she is smart."

This is also likely to be the standard and prescriptively correct form. The following structure with an indicative finite embedded sentence is acceptable to me:

(44) *Ognuno di noi pensa che è in gamba.*
each of us think3SG that is smart

The judgments on such sentences will vary, depending on whether one accepts indicative embedded clauses selected by *pensare*, which always selects the subjunctive in the literary standard. By the way, a subjunctive verb in (44) is excluded for independent reasons. Subjects of subjunctive complement clauses display obviation effects in Italian: usually, they must be distinct (cannot co-refer with) from matrix subjects. The ban also applies to cases with quantificational matrix subjects.

Notice that one could force the distributive reading by using predicate nominals like the following:

(45) a. **Ognuno di noi pensa che siamo una persona unica.*
each of us think3SG that be1PL a person unique
"Every one of us thinks we are a unique person."

b. ??*Ognuno di noi pensa che siamo persone uniche.*
each of us think3SG that be1PL personPL uniquePL
"Every one of us thinks we are unique persons."

Interestingly, the sentence with the singular nominal predicate "a unique person" in (45a) is totally unacceptable.[23] The counterpart with the plural predicate is on a par with the previous examples.

As in section 5.1, one has to decide how to handle the marginality of the data sentences. If sentences like (42) are to be considered ungrammatical, one could conjecture that the clause on partitives in the definition of source should be dropped in Italian, or that set DPs of partitives are inaccessible sources as defined in section 4.2 above. That is, Italian parametrically differs from English in lacking that kind of secondary source. Alternatively, if one argues that the examples at hand are not degraded enough to be ungrammatical, one should admit that the partitive clause of the definition of source is active in Italian. The marginal status of the examples could be due to extraneous factors.[24] However, if sentences like (42) can be taken to be grammatical, in virtue of a certain degree of acceptability, the generalization proposed in section 5.1 vacuously extends to partitives: since all of the pronominal set DPs in (42) are plural, it is trivially true that all the secondary sources are plural in the dialect at hand.

6. Conclusion

This chapter has surveyed a range of secondary source phenomena in Italian. The analysis presented in Collins and Postal (2012) was applied to the Italian data. The main empirical finding is the existence of two classes of imposters with different agreement properties. The imposters I have dubbed ordinary are a large class of expressions used to refer either to the speaker or to the addressee. These imposters never admit non-third person agreement, neither singular, nor plural, nor conjoined. The second class consists of what I call deep imposters. They are two imposter expressions (*il/la sottoscritto/a, il/la qui presente*) that behave like English imposters in admitting first person agreement when conjoined.

Collins and Postal's theory accounts for the deep imposters with no further adjustment. The properties of ordinary imposters have been accounted for by

[23] In this respect, Italian differs from the dialect of English that accepts sentences like *Each one of us believes we are a unique individual*; see Collins and Postal (2012: 171).

[24] The ambiguity between the relevant reading and the (preferred) collective reading might be somehow involved as well. In the main text, I presented two other constructions that unambiguously express the relevant meaning. Strictly speaking, only the infinitive construction is really unambiguous. In the indicative finite construction, the embedded null subject can also be interpreted as referring to a salient individual. Nevertheless, neither construction has the further collective reading that is preferred for the construction exemplified in (42).

formulating a language-specific constraint, the Nominal Content Constraint, which entails that ordinary imposters do not have their ultimate antecedents as a source for agreement in Italian. Deep imposters differ from ordinary imposters in including null nouns, thus avoiding the constraint. By resorting to this constraint, I have retained both the general theoretical apparatus formulated by Collins and Postal and the analysis of ordinary imposters as involving a pronominal core.

As for other secondary source phenomena (agreement with the subject of a predicate nominal or with the set DP of a partitive construction), the analysis of Collins and Postal can be applied without any additions or changes. It must be kept in mind, though, that a fair amount of variation exists among Italian speakers.

Many thanks to Chris Collins and Paul Postal for extensive commentary and criticism on a previous draft of this contribution. I also thank Gabi Soare and all the participants in the Seminar in Syntax at New York University in the fall of 2010 for the useful discussion. The usual disclaimers apply.

References

Cattaneo, Andrea. 2009. Imposters and pseudo-imposters in Bellinzonese and English. Unpublished manuscript, New York University.

Cinque, Guglielmo. 2010. *The Syntax of Adjectives*. Cambridge, MA: MIT Press.

Collins, Chris, Simanique Moody, and Paul M. Postal. 2008. An AAE camouflage construction. *Language* 84: 29–68.

Collins, Chris, and Paul M. Postal. 2012. *Imposters*. Cambridge, MA: MIT Press.

Maiden, Martin, and Mair Parry, eds. 1997. *The Dialects of Italy*. London and New York: Routledge.

Oxford Latin Dictionary (OLD). 1968. Oxford: Clarendon Press.

Poletto, Cecilia. 2000. *The Higher Functional Field: Evidence from Northern Italian Dialects*. Oxford: Oxford University Press.

7

Person Imposters: The View from Two Romance Languages

GABRIELA SOARE

1. Introduction

Collins and Postal (2012) investigate a class of expressions they refer to as "person imposters," or simply "imposters." This is illustrated by the example below, in which a father is talking to his child, and refers to himself as *Daddy*:

(1) Daddy is going to buy you a new iPad tomorrow.

This is an example of a first person imposter. The DP *Daddy* is notionally first person, referring to the speaker, but grammatically third person. (2) is an example of a second person imposter, where the addressee is referred to by a third person DP *Madam*:

(2) Would Madam like to join us for a walk?

Such expressions that usually have the syntactic form of a standard third person DP while denoting either the speaker or the addressee are defined as in (3).

(3) An imposter is a notionally X person DP that is grammatically Y person, X ≠ Y.

Collins and Postal (2012) argue in favor of a syntactic analysis of imposter DPs and show that an imposter DP has a complex structure that involves another DP which is a covert first person or second person pronominal, which explains the first or the second person denotation. As opposed to ordinary third person DPs, imposters DPs have special antecedence possibilities in the sense that they give rise to first or second person pronominal agreement in addition to regular third person agreement. Thus, in (4), containing a first person imposter, the pronominal alternation is not accompanied by any difference in truth conditions:

(4) In this reply, the present authors$_1$ (= the writers of the reply) attempt to defend ourselves$_1$/themselves$_1$ against the scurrilous charges which have been made. (Collins and Postal 2012: 17 (6b))

The reflexive pronoun can either be third person, agreeing in phi-feature values with the antecedent *the present authors*, or first person plural. A similar pronominal alternation is manifested by a distinct class of expressions that are called camouflage DPs (Collins and Postal 2012; Collins, Moody, and Postal 2008). This is exemplified below:

(5) Your Majesty must protect *itself/yourself/himself/*herself (spoken to King). (Collins and Postal 2012: 181 (2a))

One major property that imposter and camouflage DPs share is that they contain a pronominal DP. However, in the camouflage cases, the pronominal is overt and appears as a possessor.

This kind of pronominal alternation also characterizes other structures, such as the copular sentence whose predicate is modified by a restrictive relative clause in (6) and the partitive structure in (7). These alternations in pronominal phi-features do not correlate with any truth conditional differences.

(6) I am a teacher who takes care of myself/himself.
(7) Every one of us thinks we/they/he are/is a genius.

Collins and Postal provide an extensive discussion of pronominal alternations of the sort seen in the examples above and argue in favor of a unified account of cases like (4–7). In each case, a pronominal (be it a reflexive or non-reflexive pronoun) can agree in phi-feature values with its immediate antecedent, or with some other DP that is syntactically related to its immediate antecedent.

This chapter offers a survey of imposters in Romanian and French, which due to the overt, morphologically rich verbal agreement, represent a good testing ground for some theoretical claims put forth by Collins and Postal. It provides a description of the effects of plural imposters and of coordinate structures with an imposter DP on verbal and pronominal agreement. In addition, it considers potential sources of phi-feature values for the verb in structures like (6) and (7). Therefore, the main aim of this chapter is to examine the behavior of imposter DPs with respect to verbal agreement. Regarding pronominal agreement, both languages are subject to a constraint that determines person and number feature sameness between verbal and pronominal agreement (the existence of this constraint, called *harmony*, has already been pointed out by Collins and Postal 2012: 126 for French).

This chapter is organized as follows: section 2 lays down the theoretical background and introduces the theoretical apparatus that will be used in the sections to follow. Sections 3 and 4 provide an inventory of imposters in Romanian and

French. Then section 5 discusses some cases of singular imposter DPs, which behave like English imposters in not permitting pronominal alternation. Cases of plural imposters are subsequently examined in section 6 with respect to both verbal and pronominal agreement. The two languages allow first person plural agreement on the condition that the imposter DP is modified by an indexical element, such as *here present*. In their turn, coordinate structures containing an imposter conjunct are also subject to one condition: first person plural verbal agreement is obtained as a result of the coordinate DP undergoing topicalization to the left periphery of the clause. This is related to the properties of clitic doubling of the two languages. It is argued that first person verbal agreement is a result of agreement with [1PL] *pro* in Romanian and covert *nous* in French. This is the focus of section 7. Section 8 deals with the status of predicate nominals modified by a restrictive relative clause, and the status of the subjects of those predicate nominals, both being able to function as a source of phi-feature values for verbal agreement. Another potential source of phi-feature values for the subject of an embedded clause that determines first person (or second person) agreement on the verb is presented by partitive cases like (7). Both Romanian and French are richer than English in allowing one extra option of agreement of the main clause verb. This is discussed in section 9. Section 10 tackles the issue of gender agreement with camouflage DPs in the two languages, and it will be seen that they differ from their English counterparts. Section 11 is the conclusion.

2. Theoretical Background

This section introduces a few background notions that are needed for the discussions below. First, as mentioned, Collins and Postal argue that imposter DPs are structurally complex in that they are made up of a dominating DP shell, which is third person, and an inner DP, the core, which contains a null pronoun. For instance, a first person imposter has a null first person pronoun, whereas a second person imposter has a null second person pronoun. This is illustrated below:

(8)
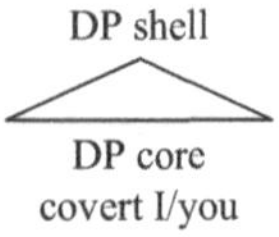

Under this view, imposter DPs are structurally similar to appositives, which involve two DPs in a predicative relation.

Second, the two authors argue in favor of a syntactic relation between a pronoun and its antecedent. Crucially, all phi-feature values of a pronoun are the result of agreement with an antecedent or with some source. Thus, in order to account for the pronominal alternation observed in the examples (4–7) above, Collins and Postal (2012) argue in favor of the condition in (9).

(9) Pronominal Agreement Condition:
If P is a non-expletive pronominal, then for all phi-features F of P for which P is not inherently valued, P agrees with some source.

Related to this condition, they assume that there are null DPs called AUTHOR and ADDRESSEE in the left periphery of the clause that expresses the relation between event participants and speech participants (see also Bianchi 2003, 2010; Sigurðsson 2004, 2011). AUTHOR and ADDRESSEE thus function as antecedents of pronouns and have inherent first and second person, singular or plural feature values. A pronoun may have several antecedents, called the immediate antecedent and the ultimate antecedent. For instance, in (4) above, the immediate antecedent of the reflexive is *the present authors*, which is third person plural, whereas the ultimate antecedent is AUTHOR, which is first person plural. The reflexive can thus agree with either. The immediate antecedent from which the reflexive gets its phi-feature values is in fact its primary source, in other words, a direct source of phi-feature values. Similarly, in (5) above, the immediate antecedent of the reflexive is *Your Majesty* and the ultimate antecedent is ADDRESSEE. Since both the immediate and the ultimate antecedent are sources, by condition (9), agreement with either is allowed. The definition of primary source is provided below:

(10) A is a primary source for B if and only if
a. A immediately antecedes B, or
b. A is a key conjunct of B, or
c. A shares a lexical basis with B.

(Collins and Postal 2012: 188)

As the notion of immediate antecedent is now quite straightforward, that of key conjunct needs some explanation: it is used in the calculation of the phi-feature values of the DP, part of a coordinate structure, which will determine the phi-feature values of a coordinate structure. This notion will be used in section 7, when discussing the behavior of coordinate structures containing an imposter DP in Romanian and French. The definition of primary source also relies on the notion of lexical basis that is defined below:

(11) A DP Q is lexically based on a noun V (V is a lexical basis for Q) if and only if Q dominates V and there exists a path of nodes Q . . . V where every node between Q and V is nominal, a non-conjunct, and a non-specifier.

(Collins and Postal 2012: 59)

In camouflage DPs like (5) above, the pronominal possessor DP and the shell DP share a lexical basis. In structures like (6), the DP *a professor* and the other DP *who* in the structure [*a professor who . . .*] also share a lexical basis, which is the noun *professor*. (10c) of the definition of primary sources will be used when discussing relative clauses inside copular sentences in section 8.

Third, besides primary sources of phi-feature values for a pronoun, which represent direct sources of phi-feature values, a pronoun can, under certain conditions, agree with other elements, which are called secondary sources. They are defined as follows:

(12) A is a secondary source for B if and only if A is a source for B and not a primary source for B. (Collins and Postal 2012: 156)

By and large, such secondary sources are indirect sources of phi-feature values of a pronoun. Without entering into a detailed discussion of pronominal/verbal agreement of cases like (6) and (7), it suffices to remark at this point that the very fact that the first person pronoun is allowed in both examples is illustrative of the presence of such secondary sources, which are the subject *I* in (6) and the DP part of the partitive structure, *us*, in (7), respectively. The sources in these structures will be presented and discussed in detail in section 8.

3. An Inventory of Imposters in Romanian

Romanian shares (as does French) many of the imposters and camouflage expressions that are discussed in Collins and Postal for English. However, Romanian does not have the counterpart of *yours truly*. The other imposter originating from correspondence, *your faithful correspondent*, has a counterpart, *al Dumneavoastră devotat correspondent (, Alexandru Ionescu)* which is not very productive. The class of Romanian imposters includes the following elements:

a. First person imposters
   (i) *autorul* "the author," *autorii* "the authors," *subsemnatul* "the undersigned. M.SG," *subsemnații* "the undersigned.M.PL," *juratul* "the juror," *jurații* "the jurors"
   (ii) personal names
   (iii) members of the set of diminutive kinship terms: *mămica/mami* "Mommy," *tăticul/tati* "Daddy," *mătuşa/tuşa* "auntie," *buni* "Grandma"
   (iv) various (non)diminutive kinship terms + a personal name: *unchiul Gigi* uncle Gigi," *mătuşa/tuşa Maria* "aunt/auntie Maria," *vărul Ion* "cousin Ion," *bunica Sofia* "grandma Sofia"
b. Second person imposters
   (i) *Doamna 'Madam,' Domnul 'Mister,' domunl 'Mister'* + common nouns denoting ranks in a military organization (*Domnul General* "Mister General,"

Domnul Colonel "Mister Colonel"), *domnul 'Mister'/doamna 'Mrs.'* + common nouns denoting high ranks (*Domnul Director* "Mister Director," *Doamna Directoare* "Mrs. Director"), *Tatăl nostru* "our Father," *domnul meu* "my lord," *doamna mea* "my lady," *copilaşul (meu)* "(my) baby," *bebe* "baby," *draga mea* "my darling.F," *dragul meu* "my darling.M," *iubirea mea* "my love"

(ii) the elements of (aii), especially when talking to small children and pets
(iii) the elements of (aiii)
(iv) the elements of (aiv)

Below are some examples of imposters in Romanian:

(13) a. *Autorul semnează/ *semnez articolul din Kabul.*
Author.the sign.3SG/ sign.1SG article.the from Kabul
"The author signs the article from Kabul."

b. *Doamna se simte /*vă simţiţi bine astăzi?*
Madam.the 3REFL feel.3SG /2REFL feel.2PL well today
"Does Madam feel good today?"

The form in (13a) is a first person imposter denoting the speaker, and that in (13b) is a second person imposter denoting the addressee. Singular imposters in Romanian, like in English, have the superficial morphology of standard third person DPs and invariably determine third person verbal agreement.

Some examples of camouflage DPs, which are expressions containing an overt possessor, are given below:

(14) a. *Domnia/Excelenţa/Maiestatea/Alteţea/Sfinţia/Eminenţa Voastră/Sa/Ei/Lui*[1]
Lordship/Excellency/Majesty/Highness/Holiness/Reverence Your/Her/His
"Your/His/Her Lordship/Excellency/Majesty/Highness/Holiness/Reverence"

b. *Domniile/Excelenţele/Maiestăţile/Alteţele/Sfinţiile/Eminenţele Voastre/Lor/Sale*
Lordships/Excellencies/Majesties/Highnesses/Holinesses/Reverences Your/Their
"Your/Their Lordships/Excellencies/Majesties/Highnesses/Holinesses/Reverences"

These forms, which Collins and Postal (2012) label the social hierarchy camouflage construction (SHCC), behave like imposters in that they also, in certain circumstances, display a phi-feature value mismatch between the pronominal core and the shell. With respect to verbal agreement, (15) shows that the third person camouflage DP can determine only third person singular on the verb.

[1] The third person possessor forms in the feminine *ei* "her" and in the masculine *lui* "his" are less reverent. For a brief discussion of these forms, see section 10. Romanian also has a third person agreeing possessor form, *său*, which is used as an equivalent of the genitive forms *lui* "his" and *ei* "her" (the form *sa* in (14a) is marked feminine, singular, and the form *sale* in (14b) is marked feminine, plural).

(15) *Maiestatea Voastră ar trebuie să meargă/*mergeți la palat acum.*[2]
Majesty Your should SUBJ go.3SG/ go.2PL to palace now
"Your Majesty should go to the palace now."

Collins and Postal (2012) also discuss another type of camouflage structure, called the ass-Camouflage Construction (ACC) of the type below (see also Collins, Moody, and Postal 2008):

(16) a. His ass ain' going nowhere.
He is not going anywhere.
b. Your ass in trouble.
You are in trouble.
(Collins and Postal 2012: 1 (123))

Romanian does not have equivalent forms of ACC. The closest it can get is an interjection phrase like (17) with the DP *fundul tău* "your ass."

(17) *Vai de fundul tău! Acum chiar ai dat de bucluc.*
"Poor your ass! Now you really are in big trouble!"

The next section contains an inventory of imposters in French.

4. An Inventory of Imposters in French

The class of imposters in French contains the following elements:

a. First person imposters
  (i) *l'auteur* "the author," *les auteurs* "the authors," *le sous-signé* "the undersigned.M.SG, *les sous-signés* "the undersigned.M.PL," *le juré* "the juror.M.SG"
  (ii) personal names
  (iii) members of the set of diminutive kinship terms: *maman* "Mommy," *papa* "Daddy," *tata* "auntie," *tonton* "uncle," *grand-maman/mami* "Grandma," *grand-papa/papi* "Grandpa"
  (iv) various (non)diminutive kinship terms + a personal name: *tonton* Eric "uncle Eric," *tata Marie* "auntie Marie," *grand-maman Sophie* "grandma Sophie"

[2] The second person plural verbal form, the politeness form, is grammatical under the vocative interpretation of the camouflage DP.

b. Second person imposters
   (i) *Madame* "Madam," *Monsieur* "Mister," *Monsieur* "Mister" + common nouns denoting ranks in a military organization (*Monsieur le Général* "Mister General"), *Monsieur* "Mister"/*Madame* "Mrs." + common nouns denoting high ranks (*Monsieur le Directeur* "Mister Director," *Madame la Directrice* "Mrs. Director"), *Monseigneur (l'Evêque)* [approximately] "Your Grace," *Notre Père* "Our Father," *Mon Dieu* "my lord," *mon enfant* "my child," *mon bébé* "my baby," *mon amour* "my love," *ma puce* "my sweatheart," *ma choupette* "my sweetie"
   (ii) the elements of (aii), especially when talking to small children and pets
   (iii) the elements of (aiii)
   (iv) the elements of (aiv)

Like Romanian and English, and many other languages (see typology in Chapter 1 of this volume), French singular imposters determine only third person verbal agreement. This is shown in (18).

(18) a. *Papa va /*vais t'acheter une glace si tu es sage.*
Daddy is.going.to /am.going.to you buy an icecream if you are good
"Daddy is going to buy you an icecream if you behave yourself."
b. *Tata Carol reviendra /*reviendrai te voir demain.*
Auntie Carol come.back.FUT.3SG/*come.back.FUT.3SG you see tomorrow
"Auntie Carol will come back to see you tomorrow."
c. *Madame voudrait-elle /*voudrez-vous encore quelque chose?*[3]
Madam would.like.3SG-she/would.like. 2PL-you anything else
"Would Madam like anything else?"
d. *Comment va /*vais ma puce/ma choupette ce soir?*
How goes. 3SG /go. 2SG my sweetheart/my sweetie tonight
"How is my sweetheart/my sweetie doing tonight?"

Some examples of SHCC DPs are provided in (19). These DPs have a possessor part that determines the denotational properties of the whole DP, and an outer shell part that determines the form of the subject-verb agreement, which is third person in (20). Since the third person camouflage DP is the (immediate) antecedent of the reflexive, the latter is third person.

(19) a. *Son Excellence/Sa Majesté/Son Altesse/Sa Sanctеté/Son Eminence*[4]
"His Excellence/Her Majesty/His Highness/Her Holiness/His Reverence"

[3] The second person plural verbal form, which is the politeness form, is accepted only on the vocative interpretation of the DP *Madame*, and in this case an intonational break cuts off the DP from the rest of the clause.

[4] The glosses for *Son Excellence*, *Son Altesse* and *Son Eminence*, all feminine nouns in French, contain the English "his," as these nouns begin with a vowel, which makes the use of the masculine possessor form *son* "his" obligatory (for a brief discussion of similar forms, see section 10).

b. *Votre Excellence/Majesté/Altesse/Sancteté/Eminence*
"Your Excellence/Majesty/Highness/Holiness/Reverence"

c. *Ses/Vos Excellences/Majestés/Altesses/Sanctetés/Eminences*
"Their/Your Excellences/Majesties/Highnesses/Holinesses/Reverences"

(20) *Sa Majesté devrait se reposer maintenant.*
His Majesty should 3REFL rest now
"His Majesty should rest now."

To the best of my knowledge, French does not have the equivalent of the English ACC (16).

5. Singular Imposter DPs

As mentioned above, English allows non-third person pronominal agreement with plural imposters and with coordinate structures containing an imposter. With singular imposters, only third person pronominal agreement is permitted, as in (21) below:

(21) a. Daddy is enjoying himself/*myself.
b. The General should speak his/*your mind.

Considering verbal agreement, Romanian and French pattern with English in determining only third person agreement with singular imposters. This is illustrated in (22) and (23).

(22) a. *Mami o să îți cumpere/*cumpăr o păpușă.*
Mommy AUX.FUT you buy.3SG/buy.1SG a doll
"Mommy is going to buy you a doll."

b. *Iepurașul ne va /*vei spune ce s- a întâmplat?*
Sweetie.the us will.3SG/will.2SG tell what 3REFL-has happened
"Will sweetie tell us what has happened?"

(23) a. *Maman va t'acheter /*vais t'acheter une poupée.*
Mommy is.going you buy / am.going you buy a doll
"Mommy is going to buy you a doll."

b. *La choupette nous dira -t-elle/*diras-tu ce qui s'est passé?*
The sweetie us tell.FUT.3SG-t-she/tell.FUT.2SG-you what 3REFL has happened
"Will sweetie tell us what has happened?"

I leave the question open as to why singular imposters are unable to determine first person agreement on the verb and cannot antecede a non-third person pronominal in (21). It should be pointed out that the only exception is the imposter *subsemnatul* "the undersigned" in Romanian, which can, under certain circumstances, trigger first person verbal (and pronominal agreement), and this may be due to its participial nature (see Servidio, this volume, and Wood, this volume).[5]

6. Plural Structures: Verbal and Pronominal Agreement

Because English has impoverished subject-verb agreement morphology, the two Romance languages represent a good testing ground for (some of) the theoretical assumptions in Collins and Postal (2012). The goal of this section is to provide a description of the effects of plural imposters on pronominal and especially on verbal agreement in the two languages, which exhibit rich subject-verb agreement morphology, Romanian being a *pro*-drop language. It will be seen that plural imposters in both Romanian and French trigger the same type of verbal agreement. These patterns are compared to English.

6.1 PLURAL IMPOSTER DPs IN ROMANIAN

Let us first consider the behavior of the first person plural imposter *autorii* "authors" with respect to verbal and pronominal agreement, exemplified below, and compare it to the English case in (26):

(24) a. *Autorii vor aduce alte argumente.*
Authors.the will.3PL bring other arguments
"The authors will bring other arguments."
b. **Autorii vom aduce alte argumente.*
Authors.the will.1PL bring other arguments
"The authors will bring other arguments."

[5] The form *subsemnatul* "the undersigned," which is masculine singular, and its agreeing forms, are specific to the written style. The singular DP can determine first person verbal agreement only in an appositive configuration of the form in (i). As expected, regular third person verbal agreement is also instantiated.

(i) *Subsemnatul, Alexandru Popescu, vă rog/ vă roagă a aproba*
Undersigned.the Alexandru Popescu you ask.1SG/ you ask.3SG a.INF approve
cererea de schimbare de domiciliu.
demand.the of change of address
"The undersigned, Alexandru Popescu, kindly asks you to approve of the demand of the address change."

In the absence of the appositive structure, first person verbal agreement is no longer possible, as shown in (ii).

(ii) **Subsemnatul vă rog a aproba cererea de schimbare de domiciliu.*
Undersigned.the you ask.1SG a.INF approve demand.the of change of address

I will not discuss this imposter here.

(25) a. *Autorii sunt mândri de ei înşişi.*
Authors.the are.3PL proud.MPL of them selves
"The authors are proud of themselves."
b. **Autorii suntem mândri de noi înşine.*
Authors.the are.1PL proud.MPL of us selves
"The authors are proud of ourselves."
(26) The authors are proud of ourselves/themselves.

These examples show that the same first person imposter behaves differently in the two languages: while English allows both a third and first person reflexive, Romanian permits only the third person pronoun. Regarding verbal agreement, the ungrammaticality of (24b) and (25b) indicates that the imposter cannot trigger first plural agreement on the verb, the only option being third person plural on the auxiliary *vor* in (24a) and on the copula *sunt* in (25a). On the assumption that subject-verb agreement and pronominal agreement must match (see discussion in section 6.2), an explanation must be given for the behavior of plural imposters in Romanian. It has to do with secondary sources as potential sources of phi-features for the pronoun. The pronominal in the English case (26) agrees with the immediate antecedent, *the authors*, and, by condition (9), can also agree with its ultimate antecedent, AUTHOR, the secondary source. This accounts for the observed alternations in pronominal phi-features. In Romanian, the pronoun gets its phi-feature values from the immediate antecedent (the primary source), *autorii* "the authors," which is third person plural, but, as opposed to English, the phi-features of the ultimate antecedent of the plural imposter are unavailable for pronominal (or verbal) agreement.

However, if the plural imposter *autorii* is modified by the deictic adjective *aici prezenţi* "here present," there is an ameliorating effect of the structure, as in (27).

(27) a. ?*Autorii aici prezenţi am găsit cele mai bune soluţii.*
Authors.the here present.MPL have.3PL found the best solutions
"The authors here present found the best solutions."
b. ?*Autorii aici prezenţi suntem mândri de noi înşine.*
Authors.the here present.M.PL are.1PL proud.MPL of us ourselves
"The authors here present are proud of ourselves."

Though there is speaker variability as to the acceptability of (27), there are speakers, including this author, who find that the presence of the deictic adjective *aici prezenţi* "here present (M.PL)" within the structure of the imposter induces an ameliorating effect on the first plural subject-verb agreement. Consequently, due to matching between verbal and pronominal agreement (see the Matching Condition in (35) below), the anaphor is also first person plural in (27b). I assume that the ameliorating effect is due to the more complex structure of the imposter *autorii aici prezenţi* "the authors here present." In particular, it contains a predicative small clause (or Relator Phrase in the sense of den Dikken 2006) that contains the covert subject *noi* "we" in Spec R(elator)P and the adjectival predicate *aici prezenți* "here present." This is schematically represented in (28c). It is at this level that subject-verb agreement in person, number, and gender is realized. Thus, starting from the appositive structure in (28a), the imposter comes to be of the form in (28b) after movement operations have taken place. In (28b), the portion of the relative clause including the relative pronoun and the verb (and copies of moved elements) is covert.

(28) a. *Noi, autorii aici prezenți . . .*
We, authors.the here present.MPL
"We, the authors here present . . ."

b. *Autorii < care suntem > aici prezenți . . .*
Authors who are.1PL here present.MPL
"The authors < who are.1PL > here present . . ."

The derivation of (28b) is given in (28c) below (it also contains its French counterpart):

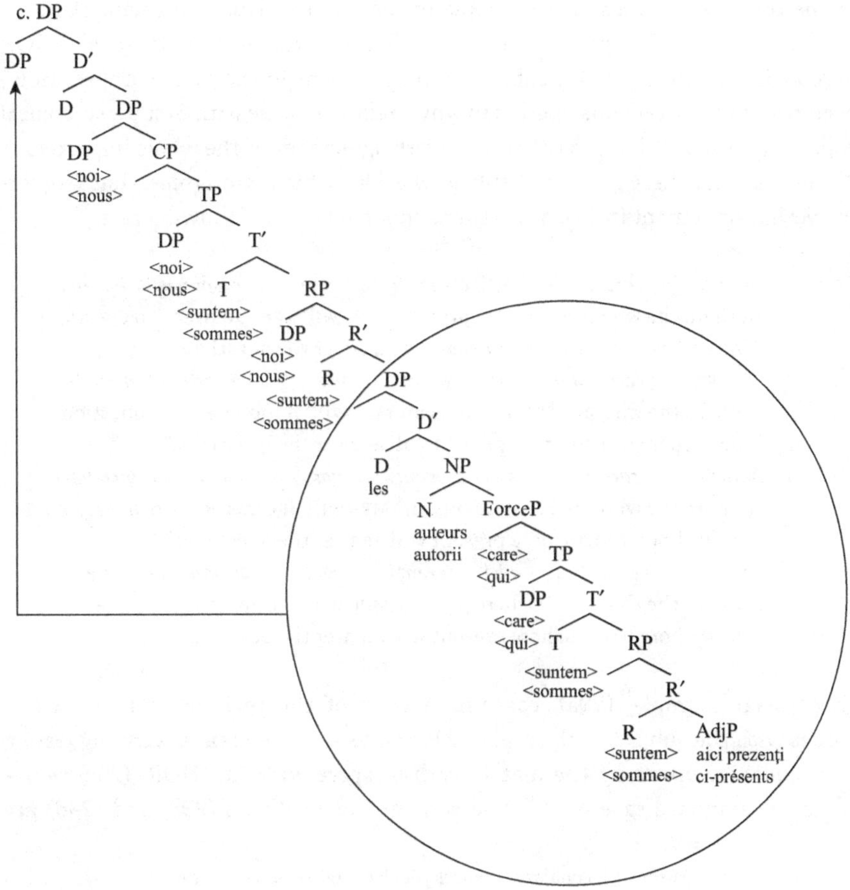

After the T head probes and agrees with the R(elator) head, the latter raises to T presumably due to the presence of an EPP feature on T. Subsequently, a relative clause, ForceP, is merged into the structure. The head of the relative clause is *autorii* "the authors," and the relative pronoun *care* "who" fills a left peripheral position (in cartographic terms, this position would correspond to RelP, but this is irrelevant here). Other details omitted, the covert pronoun *noi* "we" in Spec RP moves to Spec TP and subsequently to the specifier position of the DP dominating the CP. The structure thus obtained corresponds to the appositive clause *noi, autorii aici prezenți* "we, the authors here present." In order to get the imposter reading, the larger DP, which is the complement of the higher R head, moves to the highest Spec DP.

One possible way to understand why the verb *suntem* "are.1PL" is allowed in the relative clause is to consider the nature of the relative pronoun *care*. It is inherently marked for the features [Nominal] and [wh] (it is the *which*-pronoun), but it is not marked for [Animacy] and [Person]. Since it is not specified for the feature [Person], it can agree either with the subject of the higher RP, the covert *noi*, or with the third person DP *autorii*, which thus accounts for the first person or the third person form of the copula in the relative clause.[6] It seems that, for some reason, once first person agreement obtains in the relative clause, AUTHOR becomes more accessible for subject-verb agreement in the matrix clause. However, the question remains open as to why a relative clause with first person plural copular agreement changes the subject-verb agreement of the whole imposter.

The fact that there is a covert subject *noi* with which *care* agrees, thus triggering verbal agreement in 1PL, is further supported by the following facts.

(29) a. *Autorii care suntem aici prezenți vom răspunde la întrebări.*
Authors.the who are.1PL here present.M.PL will.1PL answer to questions
"The authors who are here present will answer the questions."

b. **Autorii care suntem aici prezenți vor răspunde la întrebări.*
Authors.the who are.1PL here present.MPL will.3PL answer to questions
"The authors who are here present will answer the questions."

c. *Autorii care sunt aici prezenți vor răspunde la întrebări.*
Authors.the who are.3PL here present.MPL will.3PL answer to questions
"The authors who are here present will answer the questions."

d. **Autorii care sunt aici prezenți vom răspunde la întrebări.*
Authors.the who are.3PL here present.MPL will.1PL answer to questions
"The authors who are here present will answer the questions."

The crucial example, (29a), contains a copy of the relative pronoun which agrees with the subject of the higher RP, *noi*. As has been tentatively suggested, this somehow opens up the matrix verb to agree with AUTHOR. (29c) represents the standard case of third person agreement. Cases (29b) and (29d) are

[6] For other structures with copular sentences which contain *care*, see section 8.

ungrammatical due to the clash in person features between the whole DP containing the relative clause and the main verb.

6.2 PLURAL IMPOSTERS IN FRENCH

Let us now turn to French. Consider the cases of verbal agreement in (30), and of both pronominal and verbal agreement in (31) below.

(30) a. *Les auteurs vont amener d'autres arguments.*
The authors will.3PL bring other arguments
"The authors will bring other arguments."
b. **Les auteurs allons amener d'autres arguments.*
The authors will.1PL bring other arguments
"The authors will bring other arguments."

(31) a. *Les auteurs sont contents d'eux-mêmes.*
The authors are.3PL happy-M.PL of them selves
"The authors are happy with themselves."
b. **Les auteurs sommes contents de nous-mêmes.*
The authors are.1PL happy-M.PL of our selves
"The authors are happy with ourselves."

Verbal agreement with a first person plural imposter in French, like in Romanian, is only third person plural and, similarly, the third person reflexive agrees only with its immediate antecedent, *les auteurs* "the authors," and not with the ultimate antecedent, AUTHOR. The question is whether there is any ameliorating effect induced by the counterpart of *here present*. As illustrated in (32) and (33), though there is speaker variability, there are speakers for whom the presence of the indexical adjectival predicate considerably improves the first person plural subject-verb agreement. As a result, the first person reflexive form becomes possible in (33).

(32) ?*Les auteurs ci-présents allons amener d'autres arguments.*
The authors here present.MPL are.going.to.1PL bring other arguments
"The authors are going to bring other arguments."

(33) ?*Les auteurs ci-présents sommes fiers de nous-mêmes.*
The authors here present.MPL are.1PL proud.MPL of our selves
"The authors here present are happy with ourselves."

The plural imposter has the same structure as its Romanian counterpart in (28) above. On the assumption that the relative pronoun *qui* is not specified for person, it can agree with the first person plural subject of the higher RP, hence the first person plural form of the copula in the relative clause. In this case, AUTHOR becomes available for subject-verb agreement in the matrix clause. I leave this aspect of the analysis open.

As was the case in (29) in Romanian, French also displays the patterns in (34), which contain an overt relative pronoun and two verbal agreement possibilities.

(34) a. *Les auteurs qui sommes ci-présents allons répondre aux*
The authors who are.1PL here present.MPL are.going.to.1PL answer to
questions
questions.
"The authors who are here present are going to answer the questions."

b. **Les auteurs qui sommes ci-présents vont répondre aux*
The authors who are.1PL here present.MPL are.going.to.3PL answer to
questions
questions.
"The authors who are here present are going to answer the questions."

c. *Les auteurs qui sont ci-présents vont répondre aux* .
The authors who are.3PL here present.MPL are.going.to.3PL answer to
questions
questions
"The authors who are here present are going to answer the questions."

d. **Les auteurs qui sont ci-présents allons répondre aux*
The authors who are.3PL here present.MPL are.going.to.1PL answer to
questions.
questions
"The authors who are here present are going to answer the questions."

Crucially, in (34a), the subject DP, the copy of *qui*, agrees with the covert *nous* and thus determines first person agreement on the copula *sommes* "are." Since AUTHOR seems to be available, the matrix verb is first person plural. When the subject DP containing the relative clause is third person, as in (34c), the form of the matrix verb is also third person. Person mismatch between the two verbs leads to ungrammaticality, as in (34b) and (34d).

Regarding pronominal agreement, as already noted, both French and Romanian exhibit sameness of person and number features between subject-verb agreement and pronominal agreement (this corresponds to Collins and Postal's (2012: 126) notion of harmony). In other words, both languages are subject to (35) below:

(35) Matching Effect
If the subject is the antecedent of a pronoun, then the subject verb agreement and pronominal agreement must match.

This is illustrated in (36) for French.

(36) a. ?*Les auteurs ci-présents sommes contents de nous-mêmes.*
The authors here present.MPL are.1PL happy.MPL of our selves
"The authors are happy with themselves."

b. **Le auteurs ci-présents sommes contents d'eux-mêmes.*
The authors here present.MPL are.1PL happy.MPL of them selves

c.	*Les*	*auteurs*	*ci-présents*	*sont*	*contents*	*d'eux-mêmes.*
	The	authors	here present.MPL	are.3PL	happy.MPL	of them selves
d.	**Les*	*auteurs*	*ci-présents*	*sont*	*contents*	*de nous-mêmes.*
	The	authors	here present.MPL	are.3PL	happy.MPL	of our selves

The first person plural subject imposter in (36a) determines verbal agreement in first person (plural), and pronominal agreement is also first person (plural). The same imposter is third person plural in (36c) and agrees with the verb in third person (and number), and the pronoun is also third person (plural). (36b) and (36d) indicate that mixed cases are ungrammatical due to a violation of the Matching Effect.

It has been seen in this section that a plural imposter can determine first person plural agreement on the verb (and, by the Matching effect, on the pronominal) on the condition that it gets modified by an indexical element. It should be noted, however, that no such effect obtains in the case of singular imposters, as the ungrammaticality of (37) in both Romanian and French shows.

(37)	a.	*Autorul*	*aici prezent*	*va*	/**voi*	*răspunde*	*la*	*întrebări.*
		Author.the	here present	will.3SG	/will.1SG	answer	to	questions
		"The author here present will answer the questions."						
	b.	*L'auteur*	*ci-présent*	*répondra*	/**répondrai*	*aux*	*questions.*	
		The author	here present	answer.3SG	/answer.1SG	to	questions	
		"The author here present will answer the questions."						

Neither in Romanian nor in French can the auxiliary or the verb be first person singular. I leave this issue open.

7. Coordinate Structures

Since, in the system employed here, a pronominal can agree either with its immediate antecedent or with a secondary source, it appears interesting to study pronominal and verbal agreement in coordination cases, where one of the conjuncts is precisely an imposter DP. It should be said from the beginning that both Romanian and French are well behaved with respect to the calculus of person (and plural) feature in conjunctive coordination with regular non-imposter DPs in the sense that verb agreement distinguishes differing persons in plural cases:[7] if coordination of DPs contains a DP which is [first person], then the conjoined node is [first person]; if coordination contains a DP which is [second person] (and no first person conjunct), then the conjoined node is [second person]; if

[7] It is well known that there are languages that exhibit differing number agreement patterns with coordinate phrases depending on position, for instance, of the pre-verbal or post-verbal position of the conjoined subject (e.g., Kiss 2012 on Hungarian; Citko 2004 on Polish; Benmamoun 1992, Aoun et al. 1999 on Arabic, etc.).

coordination contains DPs which are [-first person, -second person], then the dominant node is [-first person, -second person], that is, third person.

7.1 COORDINATE STRUCTURES IN ROMANIAN

Consider first the coordination of the first person imposter *mami* "mommy" in (38) and *autorul* "the author" in (39) with an ordinary third person DP.

(The mother addressing her child)

(38)	a.	*Mami*	*și*	*bunica*	*Sofia*	*ți-au*	*cumpărat*	*un*	*iPad.*
		Mommy	and	grand-mother	Sofia	you-have.3PL	bought	an	iPad.
		"Mommy and Grandmother Sofia bought you an iPad."							
	b.	??*Mami*	*și*	*bunica*	*Sofia*	*ți-am*	*cumpărat*	*un*	*iPad.*
		Mommy	and	grand-mother	Sofia	you-have.1PL	bought	an	iPad.
		"Mommy and Grandmother Sofia bought you an iPad."							

(The author addressing the audience)

(39)	a.	*Autorul*	*și*	*coautorul*	*o să*	*răspundă*	*la*	*întrebări.*
		Author.the	and	coauthor.the	AUX.FUT	answer.3PL	to	questions
		"The author and the coauthor will answer the questions."						
	b.	??*Autorul*	*și*	*coautorul*	*o să*	*răspundem*	*la*	*întrebări.*
		Author.the	and	coauthor.the	AUX.FUT	answer.1PL	to	questions
		"The author and the coauthor will answer the questions."						

All the speakers consulted find third person verbal agreement grammatical and only some marginally accept first person verbal agreement. In Collins and Postal (2012: 112), the Key Conjunct is defined as the conjunct that determines the phi-features of the whole coordinate structure. In (38), the key conjunct of the coordinate subject is the imposter *mami* "mommy," and since it is third person, the coordinate DP is third person. This accounts for the third person verb form. In other words, the phi-feature values of the ultimate antecedent are unavailable in Romanian. Similarly, in (39), the key conjunct is the imposter DP *autorul* "the author," which contains only the third person imposter itself, but not its first person ultimate antecedent AUTHOR. Thus, the coordinate node can only be third person, and, consequently, verbal agreement is in third person plural.

However, if some material intervenes between the subject coordinate DP and the verb, there is a considerable amelioration of the sentence. This is illustrated below:

(40)	a.	(?)*Mami*	*și*	*bunica*	*Sofia, uite,*	*ți-am*	*cumpărat*	*un*
		Mommy	and	grand-mother	Sofia look.IMP.2SG	you-have.1PL	bought	an

iPad.
iPad.
"Look, Mommy and Grandmother Sofia have bought an iPad."

b. (?)*Mami şi bunica Sofia, foarte curând, o să îţi cumpăram un*
Mommy and grand-mother Sofia very soon AUX.FUT you buy.1PL an
iPad.
iPad
"Very soon Mommy and grandmother Sofia are going to buy you an iPad."

c. (?)*Mami si bunica Sofia, un iPad, o să îţi cumpăram foarte*
Mommy and grandmother Sofia, an iPad AUX.FUT you buy.1PL very
curând.
soon
"An iPad, Mommy and grandmother Sofia are going to buy you very soon."

(41) a. (?)*Autorul şi coautorul, uitaţi, o să răspundem la întrebări.*
Author.the and coauthor.the look.IMP2PL AUX.FUT answer.1PL to questions
"Look, the author and the coauthor will answer the questions."

b. (?)*Autorul şi coautorul, foarte curând, o să răspundem la întrebări.*
Author.the and coauthor.the very soon AUX.FUT answer.1PL to questions
"Very soon the author and the coauthor will answer the questions."

c. (?)*Autorul şi coautorul, la întrebările d.voastră, o să răspundem*
Author.the and coauthor.the to your questions AUX.FUT answer.1PL
imediat.
presently
"The author and the coauthor are going to presently answer your questions."

On the assumption that the imperative verb *uite* "look" in (40) and (41) fills a left-peripheral position (see Cardinaletti 1997 on parentheticals), the subject coordinate structure moves to its left, to Spec TopP. Similarly, in (40b) and (41b), the adverb plausibly fills a high position, Spec ModP in the IP-field, and the subject coordinate DP moves to a higher position, which is Spec TopP. Likewise, (40c) and (41c) are instances of topicalization of the DP across another topic, the DP *un iPad* "an iPad" and the PP *la întrebările d.voastră* "to your questions." I suggest an analysis of these cases along the lines of the "big DP" hypothesis that has been proposed for clitic doubling structures, where both the clitic pronoun and the doubled lexical argument originate within the same DP (Uriagereka 1995; Cecchetto 2000; Cornilescu 2006; a.o.). I suggest that *pro* and the lexical part start out in the same DP. Although more complex configurations may be resorted to, I will adopt the following minimal one that is compatible with the data:

(42)
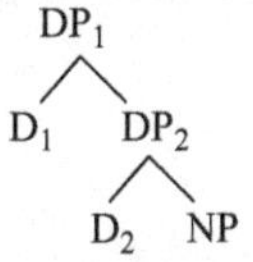

D_1 corresponds to *pro*, whereas DP_2 corresponds to the lexical part. *Pro* can agree with the DP_2, the coordinate DP, which is a regular third person DP, and this gives rise to the standard third person verbal agreement. Crucially, *pro* can also agree with the secondary source, AUTHOR (first person plural), and verbal agreement is with [+1, +PL] *pro*. In the course of the derivation, DP_2 moves to the left-peripheral position, whereas *pro* moves to Spec IP. In discussing Spanish plural imposters and their capacity for determining first person verbal agreement quite freely, Dudley (this volume) also links this to clitic doubling.[8]

In sum, what appears to be first person plural verbal agreement with a left-peripheral coordinate structure containing an imposter conjunct is in fact agreement with a *pro* anteceded by the secondary source.[9]

7.2 COORDINATE STRUCTURES IN FRENCH

This section deals with the behavior of coordinate DPs with an imposter conjunct in French, more precisely with the kind of agreement the phi-features of the coordinate structure determine on the verb. Consider the coordination of the first person imposter *maman* "Mommy" in (43) and *l'auteur* "the author" in (44) with a regular third person DP.

(The mother addressing her child)

(43) a. *Maman et grand-maman t'ont acheté un iPad.*
Mommy and grand-mother you have.3PL bought an iPad
"Mommy and Grandmother Sofia bought you an iPad."
b. ?*Maman et grand-maman t'avons acheté un iPad.*
Mommy and grand-mother you have.1PL bought an iPad
"Mommy and Grandmother Sofia bought you an iPad."

(The author addressing the audience)

(44) a. *L'auteur et le co-auteur vont répondre aux questions.*
The author and the coauthor are.going.to.3PL answer to questions
"The author and the coauthor are going to answer the questions."

[8] Note also that in other languages coordinate subjects in the left periphery behave differently from their IP-internal position. For instance, in Hungarian (Kiss 2012), only a topicalized (or a focalized) singular coordinate subject can trigger plural agreement on the verb, otherwise the verb is singular.

[9] It should be stressed that the clitic doubling property of Romanian is also involved in cases of topicalized plural imposters, such as (i) below:

(i) ?*Autorii, foarte curănd, o să răspundem la întrebări.*
Authors.the very soon AUX.FUT answer.1PL to questions
"Very soon the author will answer the questions."

Under topicalization, plural imposters behave like coordinate DPs with an imposter conjunct. In both cases, the double moves to Spec TopP, and the verb agrees with the first person plural *pro*. In this respect, Romanian patterns with Spanish.

b. ?*L'auteur et le co-auteur allons répondre aux questions.*
The author and the coauthor are.going.to.1PL answer to questions
"The author and the coauthor are going to answer the questions."

There is a divide among French speakers as to the degree of acceptability of a coordinate subject containing an imposter DP: in an informal survey on six native speakers, four found (43b) and (44b) mildly acceptable, such judgments being represented above, and two found them ungrammatical. However, these four speakers and one of the two others judged them as being perfect if a temporal adverb intervenes between the coordinate subject and the verb and only slightly marginal if there is an intervening topic DP. This is shown in (45) and (46) below:

(45) a. *Maman et grand-maman, très bientôt, allons t'acheter un iPad.*
Mommy and grandma very soon are.going.to.1PL you buy an iPad
"Very soon Mommy and grandma are going to buy you an iPad."

b. ?*Maman et grand-maman, un iPad, allons te l'acheter très bientôt.*
Mommy and grandma, an iPad are.going.to.1PL you it buy very soon
"An iPad, Mommy and grandma are going to buy you very soon."

(46) a. *L'auteur et le co-auteur, très bientôt, allons répondre aux questions.*
The author and the coauthor very soon are.going.to.1PL answer to questions.
"Very soon the author and the coauthor are going to answer the questions."

b. ?*L'auteur et le co-auteur, à vos questions, allons y répondre dans un moment.*
The author and the coauthor, to your questions, are.going.to.1PL them answer in a moment
"Your questions, the author and the coauthor are going to answer in a moment."

The dominating coordinate node containing the first person imposter *maman* "Mommy" in (43a) and *l'auteur* "the author" in (44a) is third person because the DP conjuncts are third person, and thus the auxiliary is third person. The imposters in the two cases also have AUTHOR as their ultimate antecedent and thus form the keys of the respective coordinate subjects. In this case, the coordinate node can be first person, and this is verified by the auxiliaries *avons* in (43b) and *allons* in (44b).

The amelioration effect observed in (45a) and (46a) is due to movement of the coordinate subject DP across the adverb that fills ModP (Cinque 1999). As discussed by Rizzi and Shlonsky (2008) (see also Cardinaletti 2004), the higher part of the IP-field in French contains (at least) two subject positions, one above ModP, hosting non-pronominal DPs, and the other below, hosting subject clitics (and other kinds of weak pronouns). In (45a) and (46a), the coordinate DP moves to the higher position, plausibly the criterial subject position at the boundary between the CP-field and the IP-field. (45b) and (46b) are clear instances of topicalization to the left periphery. I propose to analyze (45) and (46) in terms of pronoun-drop, in a vein somewhat similar to Romanian. The pronoun and the lexical part represented by the coordinate DP start out in the same "big DP," and the latter moves to the left periphery, whereas the pronoun presumably stops in Spec IP. These are cases of *nous*-drop. This claim is supported by the parallelism in (47), in which the first person pronoun *nous* "we" may be overt.

(47) *Maman et grand-maman, un iPad, (nous) allons te l'acheter très bientôt.*
Mommy and grandma an iPad are.going.to.1PL you it buy very soon
"An iPad, Mommy and grandma are going to buy you very soon."

Indirect support for *nous*-drop comes from the cases of subject omission in French diary styles and in note style writing reported and discussed by Haegeman (2007).

Thus, in (45) and (46), it is the pronoun *nous* anteceded by AUTHOR that agrees with the verb.[10]

8. Predicate Nominals and Subjects of Predicate Nominals in Romanian and French

With plural imposters that are not modified by an indexical element, verbal agreement does not match the phi-feature values of the secondary sources of those imposters, only third person plural agreement being allowed. Conversely, the coordination cases in the previous section have shown the role played by the secondary source AUTHOR (or ADDRESSEE) in French verbal agreement. Besides the ultimate antecedent, AUTHOR (or ADDRESSEE), as one type of secondary source, Collins and Postal (2012) discuss other types of sources in English. These are illustrated by the cases below:

(48) a. I am a teacher who takes care of himself/myself.
b. Every one of us thinks he is/we are intelligent.

Recall the definition of secondary source in (12) repeated below as (49).

[10] Subject plural imposters in French pattern with coordinate DPs which contain an imposter in that they allow first person verbal agreement quite freely:

(i) (?)*Les auteurs, très bientôt, (nous) allons répondre aux questions.*
The authors very soon we are.going.to.1PL answer to questions.
"Very soon the authors are going to answer the questions."

This option is related to the *nous*-drop mechanism. The covert pronoun doubling the imposter agrees with the secondary source.

(49) A is a secondary source for B if and only if A is a source for B and not a primary source for B.

(Collins and Postal 2012: 156)

(49) involves the notion of primary source, which is part of the general definition of source:

(50) A is a *source* for B if and only if
a. A is a primary source for B, or
b. There is a C that is a source for B, and
i. A is a primary source for C, or
ii. C is a predicate nominal and A is C's subject, or
iii. C is a partitive DP and A is C's set DP.

(Collins and Postal 2012: 156)

The definition of primary source includes the notions of immediate antecedent and key conjunct that have been discussed in relation to plural imposters and coordination structures. It also includes the notion of lexical basis, which plays a crucial role in the analysis of the data below and which is schematized in (51).

(51)
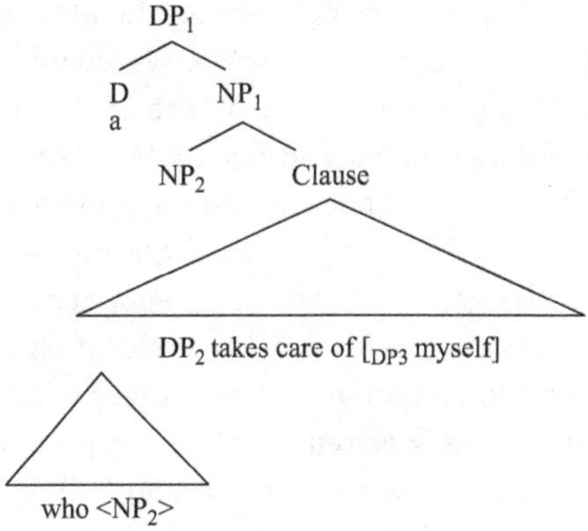

(Collins and Postal 2012: 160)

The lexical basis that DP_1 and DP_2 share is NP_2, and, via (10c) of the definition of primary source, DP_1 constitutes a primary source of DP_2.

The counterparts of (48a,b) in Romanian and French involve specifications (50bii) and (50biii) of the notion of source. In other words, both languages provide support for the idea that the subject DPs of predicate nominals can function as secondary sources for verbal agreement and consequently for pronominal agreement.

Consider the following paradigm in Romanian.

(52) a. *Sânt un profesor care a avut mereu grijă de el (însuşi).*
Am a professor who has.3SG had always care of him self
"I am a professor who has always taken care of himself."
b. **Sânt un profesor care a avut mereu grijă de mine (însumi).*
Am a professor who has.3SG had always care of me self
"I am a professor who has always taken care of myself."

Such cases show third person verbal agreement, and, by the Matching Effect, only a third person reflexive is allowed. Mismatching leads to ungrammaticality, as in (52b). DP_2 is the immediate antecedent and hence a (primary) source for the pronominal DP_3 via (50a). DP_1 and DP_2 share a lexical basis, the noun *profesor.* Since DP_1 is a (primary) source for DP_2, DP_1 is, via (50bi), a source for DP_3. In addition to the verbal and pronominal agreement possibilities in the copular sentences in (52), Romanian also allows the cases below, which show agreement in first person.

(53) a. *Sânt un professor care am avut mereu grijă de mine (însumi).*
Am a professor who have.1SG had always care of me self
"I am a professor who has always taken care of myself."
b. **Sânt un professor care am avut mereu grijă de el (însuşi).*
Am a professor who have.1SG had always care of him self
"I am a professor who has always taken care of himself."

In (53a), the auxiliary in the relative clause shows first person singular feature values agreeing with the subject *pro* in the copular sentence. We would like to suggest that this kind of agreement may be due to the nature of the relative pronoun *care* in the sense that it is inherently marked for the features [Nominal] and [wh] (it is the *which*-pronoun), but it is not marked for [Animacy] and [Person]. Therefore, the relative pronoun can get the [Person]-feature either from the DP *profesor,* with which it shares a lexical basis, or from the subject *pro* of the copular sentence. Cases like (53a) show that at least in certain contexts, such as copular sentences, verbal agreement in Romanian can be realized with a secondary source. Following Collins and Postal's system, first person pronominal agreement is accounted for in terms of the definitions (49) and (50bii): since the predicate nominal is a source for the relative pronoun, the subject of the predicate nominal, *pro,* is also a source—a secondary source—for the relative pronoun.

Below are provided further examples that show the two patterns of verbal agreement. As explained above, the DP *profesor/profesori* is a primary source of the relative *care.* Since *pro* is the subject of the predicate nominal, it is the source for anything that *profesor/profesori* is a source for. Thus, *pro* is a source of the relative DP, and the latter agrees with *pro* in first person singular/plural in (54a)/(56a), and second person singular/plural in (55a) and (57a). Alternatively, the relative pronoun agrees with the predicate nominal, hence third person agreement on the verb in (54b) to (57b).

(54) a. *Sânt un profesor care am mult succes (la studenți).*
Am a professor who have.1SG much success (to students)
"I am a professor who has much success with students."
b. *Sânt un profesor care are mult succes (la studenți).*
Am a professor who has.3SG much success (to students)
"I am a professor who has much success with students."

(55) a. *Eşti un profesor care ai mult succes (la studenți).*
Are.2SG a professor who have.2SG much success (to students)
"You are a professor who has much success with students."
b. *Eşti un profesor care are mult succes (la studenți).*
Are.2SG a professor who has.3SG much success (to students)
"You are a professor who has much success with students."

(56) a. *Suntem nişte profesori care avem mult succes (la studenți).*
Are.1PL some professors who have.1PL much success (to students)
"We are some professors who have much success with students."
b. ?*Suntem nişte profesori care au mult succes (la studenți).*
Are.1PL some professors who have.3PL much success (to students)
"We are some professors who have much success with students."

(57) a. Sunteți nişte profesori care aveți mult succes (la studenți).
Are.2PL some professors who have.2PL much success (to students)
"You are some professors who have much success with students."
b. ?*Sunteți niste profesori care au mult succes (la studenți).*
Are.2PL some professors who have.3PL much success (to students)
"You are some professors who have much success with students."

Next consider the case of French.

(58) a. *Je suis un prof qui a toujours bien pris soin de lui- même.*
I am a professor who has always well taken care of him self
"I am a professor who has always taken good care of himself."
b. ?(?)*Je suis un prof qui a toujours bien pris soin de moi-même.*
I am a professor who has always well taken care of my self
"I am a professor who has always taken good care of myself."

(59) a. *Je suis un prof qui ai toujours bien pris soin de moi-même.*
I am a professor who have.1SG always well taken care of my self
b. ?(?)*Je suis un prof qui ai toujours bien pris soin de lui-même.*
I am a professor who have.1SG always well taken care of him self
"I am a professor who has always taken good care of himself."

Although there is some speaker variability with respect to the examples (58b) and (59b), French patterns with Romanian. We would like to suggest that *qui*, the agreeing variant of *que* (Rizzi 1990), or analyzed more recently as *que* + *-i* (Taraldsen 2001; Rizzi and Shlonsky 2007), is not marked for the feature [Person]. On the assumption that DP_2 [*que* <*professeur*>] and DP_1 *un professeur* share a lexical basis, represented by the noun *professeur*, DP_1 is a primary source for the DP *que* (and the copy or copies it may contain), and this way the latter can get its third person feature value. This explains the third person agreement on the verb and, following the Matching Effect, the third person form of the reflexive. Since the subject of the predicate nominal, the DP *je*, is a source for DP_2, the latter gets first person, which then determines the first person (singular) form on the verb. In other words, in both French and Romanian, secondary source verbal agreement is needed in the context of equative sentences. It will be seen in the following section that there is another context that shows this kind of verbal agreement. This is represented by partitive structures.

9. Partitive Structures

Besides the subject of a predicate nominal in examples like the ones considered above, the partitive structure in (48b) above is argued by Collins and Postal (2012) to be relevant for secondary sources. In their analysis, a partitive phrase is of the form in (60), which contains a set DP, DP_2, and which represents the secondary source for phi-feature values of the pronoun *we*.

(60) [DP_1 Quantifier + [NP Noun (=one(s)) + (of) DP_2]

9.1 PARTITIVE STRUCTURES IN ROMANIAN

Below, the notion of a set DP as a secondary source is evaluated with respect to Romanian. Consider the following cases in Romanian.

(61) a.

Fiecare	*dintre*	*noi*	*crede*	*că*	*suntem*	*inteligenți.*
Everyone	among	us	believe.3SG	that	are.1PL	intelligent.MPL

"Every one of us thinks we are intelligent."

b.

Fiecare	*dintre*	*noi*	*crede*	*că*	*este*	*inteligent.*
Everyone	among	us	believe.3SG	that	is	intelligent

"Every one of us believes he is intelligent."

In (61a), *pro* in the embedded clause gets its phi-feature values from the set DP of the partitive DP, *noi* "us," and thus the verb in the embedded clause is first person plural. In (61b), the third person singular feature of *pro* matches the phi-feature value of its immediate antecedent, which is the whole DP *fiecare dintre noi* "every one of us," and hence the verb in the embedded clause is third person singular. In both examples, the verb in the main clause is singular, agreeing with the quantifier part of the partitive structure. However, Romanian also allows the agreement pattern in (62a) below, although with some degree of marginality:

(62) a. ?(?)*Fiecare dintre noi credem că suntem inteligenți.*
Everyone among us believe.1PL that are.1PL intelligent.MPL
"Every one of us believes we are intelligent."
b. **Fiecare dintre noi credem că este inteligent.*
Everyone among us believe.1PL that is intelligent
"Every one of us believes he is intelligent."

In cases like (62a), more characteristic of colloquial Romanian, *pro* gets its first person plural phi-feature values from the set DP of its immediate antecedent, and the copula is thus first person plural. But the first person plural form of the main verb indicates that agreement is equally realized with the set DP. In (62b), where the set DP agrees with the verb in first person plural, there is person feature mismatch between *pro* in the embedded clause and its antecedent, the set DP, which is specified [+Plural], and hence the bound variable reading is lost.

9.2 PARTITIVE STRUCTURES IN FRENCH

The role of the set DP as a potential secondary source is tested in French. Consider the data below:

(63) a. ?*Chacun de nous pense que nous sommes intelligents.*
Everyone of us believe.3SG that we are.1PL intelligent.MPL
"Every one of us thinks we are intelligent."
b. *Chacun de nous pense qu'il est intelligent.*
Everyone of us believe.3SG that he is intelligent
"Every one of us believes he is intelligent."

These cases show that French has the same pattern as Romanian. In (63a), the subject pronoun *nous* "we" gets its phi-feature values from the set DP of its immediate antecedent DP, whereas in (63b), the immediate antecedent of the subject pronoun *il* "he" is the entire DP *chacun de nous* "every one of us," and in both cases the verb agrees with the entire partitive DP.

As seen in Romanian above, French also has one further option, illustrated below:

(64) a. ?*Chacun de nous pensons que nous sommes intelligents.*
Everyone of us believe.1PL that we are.1PL intelligent.MPL
"Every one of us believes we are intelligent."
b. ??*Chacun de nous pensons qu'il est intelligent.*
Everyone of us believe.1PL that he is intelligent
"Every one of us believes he is intelligent."

The verb in the main clause can also agree with the set DP of the subject, being first person plural, and *pro* also gets its phi-feature values from the same source, the set DP. However, a bound variable configuration cannot be obtained if agreement on the verb in the main clause is with the set DP and the pronoun is singular.

To sum up, the set DP agreement facts show that in both Romanian and French, secondary source verb agreement is needed.

10. A Note on Gender Agreement

This section very briefly tackles the issue of gender agreement in Romanian and French. Consider first the camouflage DP below.

(65) a. ?*Maiestatea Voastră artrebui să participe ea însăşi la dezbateri.*
Majesty your should SUBJ participate.3SG her self.F.SG at debates
"Your Majesty should participate in the debates herself."
(spoken to King/Queen)
b. ?**Maiestatea Voastră artrebui să participe el însuşi la dezbateri.*
Majesty yours should SUBJ participate.3SG him self.M.SG at debates
"Your Majesty should participate in the debates himself."
(spoken to King)

The contrast shows that the source of the third person feature value of *ea însăşi* "she herself" is the immediate antecedent *maiestatea voastră* "your majesty." The immediate antecedent is also the source for gender agreement, as the noun *maiestate* is feminine. Therefore, with an SHC camouflage DP, Romanian does not show split agreement. Split agreement refers to cases where a pronominal matches one source on one phi-feature value and another source on another phi-feature value.

Though more investigation needs to be made, French seems to also pattern with Romanian. Consider example (66).

(66) a. *Votre Majesté participera elle-même aux débats.*
Your Majesty partipate.FUT.3SG her self to debates
"Your Majesty will participate herself in the debates."
(spoken to King/Queen)
b. ?**Votre Majesté participera lui-même aux débats.*
Your Majesty partipate.FUT.3SG himself to debates
"Your Majesty will participate himself in the debates."
(spoken to King)

The camouflage DP containing the feminine noun *majesté* "majesty" can only be the immediate antecedent of the third person pronominal form in the feminine. If further data support these preliminary observations, then the following condition seems to hold in the two languages:

(67) The SHC Gender Agreement Condition
If the immediate antecedent of a pronominal P is an SHC DP, P agrees in gender with it.

11. Conclusions

This chapter has offered a description of the behavior of Romanian and French imposter DPs with respect to verbal and pronominal agreement, and it has only briefly dealt with the behavior of camouflage DPs. Imposters in the two languages seem to be more constrained in that they are subject to some further conditions than English imposters are.

Plural imposters in French and Romanian determine first person agreement on the verb on the condition that they get modified by the indexical *here present*. However, under topicalization, plural imposters and coordinate DPs with imposter conjuncts pattern alike in allowing first person (plural) agreement more easily. This has been related to the properties of clitic doubling in Romanian and French. *Pro*-drop has been suggested for Romanian and *nous*-drop for French. Ultimately, the generalization is that agreement with a secondary source is not an instance of subject-verb agreement but of pronominal agreement. *Pro/nous* can agree with the secondary source.

Copular structures with a restrictive relative clause and partitive constructions show that secondary source verbal agreement is needed in both languages, and, by the Matching Effect, identity of person value is required on the anteceded pronominal.

This chapter constitutes preliminary work on what elements function as secondary sources for verbal (and pronominal) agreement in Romanian and French, and further research is needed in order to pin down the limits on secondary source agreement in either language.

I would like to express special thanks to Chris Collins for encouraging me to write this chapter and for his providing comments on earlier versions, and, more generally, for his continuous support. I also thank two anonymous reviewers for their comments and suggestions. I am grateful to Christopher Laenzlinger, Luigi Rizzi, and Ur Shlonsky for discussions of various aspects of the chapter. Special thanks also go to Paul Postal for his comments on an earlier draft. Needless to say, all remaining errors are mine.

References

Aoun, Joseph, Elabbas Benmamoun, and Dominique Sportiche. 1999. Further remarks on first conjunct agreement. *Linguistic Inquiry* 30: 669–681.

Benmamoun, Elabbas. 1992. Functional and inflectional morphology: Problems of projection, representation, and derivation. Doctoral dissertation, University of Southern California, Los Angeles.

Bianchi, Valentina. 2003. On finiteness as logophoric anchoring. In *Temps et Point de Vue/Tense and Point of View*, eds. Jacqueline Guéron and Liliane Tasmovski, 213–246. Paris: Université Paris X Nanterre.

Bianchi, Valentina. 2010. The person feature and the "cartographic" representation of the context. Manuscript, University of Siena. http://www.ciscl.unisi.it/persone/bianchi.htm

Cardinaletti, Anna. 1997. "Subjects and clause structure." In *The New Comparative Syntax*, ed. Liliane Haegeman, 33–63. New York: Longman.

Cardinaletti, Anna. 2004. Toward a cartography of subject positions. In *The cartography of Syntactic Structures*. Volume 2, *The Structure of CP and IP*, ed. Luigi Rizzi, 115–165. Oxford: Oxford University Press.

Cecchetto, Carlo. 2000. Doubling structures and reconstruction. *Probus* 12(1): 1–34.

Cinque, Guglielmo. 1999. *Adverbs and Functional Heads: A Cross-Linguistic Perspective*. New York: Oxford University Press.

Citko, Barbara. 2004. Agreement asymmetries in coordinate structures. In *Formal Approaches to Slavic linguistics: The Ottawa Meeting 2003*, eds. Olga Arnaudova, Wayles Browne, Maria Luisa Rivero, and Danijela Stojanović, 91–108. Ann Arbor: Michigan Slavic Publications.

Collins, Chris, Simanique Moody, and Paul M. Postal. 2008. An AAE camouflage construction. *Language* 84: 29–68.

Collins, Chris, and Paul M. Postal. 2012. *Imposters: A Study of Pronominal Agreement*. Cambridge, MA: MIT Press.

Cornilescu, Alexandra. 2006. On clitic doubling and parasitic gaps in Romanian. *Revue roumaine de linguistique* 1: 23–42.

Dikken, Marcel den. 2006. *Relators and Linkers. The Syntax of Predication, Predicate Inversion, and Copulas*. Cambridge, MA: MIT Press.

Haegeman, Liliane. 2007. Subject omission in present-day written English. *Rivista di Grammatica Generativa* 3: 91–124

Kiss, Katalin E. 2012. Patterns of agreement with coordinate noun phrases in Hungarian. *Natural Language and Linguistic Theory* 30: 1027–1060.

Rizzi, Luigi. 1990. *Relativized Minimality*. Cambridge, MA: MIT Press.

Rizzi, Luigi, and Ur Shlonsky. 2007. Strategies of subject extraction. In *Interfaces + Recursion = Language?*, eds. Hans-Martin Gärtner and Uli Sauerland, 115–160. Berlin: Mouton de Gruyter.

Sigurðsson, Halldór Ármann. 2004. The syntax of Person, Tense, and speech features. *Italian Journal of Linguistics* 16: 219–251. [Special issue, edited by Valentina Bianchi and Ken Safir.]

Sigurðsson, Halldór Ármann. 2011. Conditions on argument drop. *Linguistic Inquiry* 42: 267–304.

Taraldsen, Knut T. 2001. Subject extraction, the distribution of expletives and stylistic inversion. In *Subject Inversion in Romance and the Theory Of Universal Grammar*, eds. Aafke Hulk and Jean-Yves Pollock, 163–182. New York: Oxford University Press.

Uriagereka, Juan. 1995. Aspects of the syntax of clitic placement in Western Romance. *Linguistic Inquiry* 26: 79–123.

8

Mandarin Pseudo-Imposters

CHYAN-AN ARTHUR WANG

1. Introduction

In Collins and Postal (2012), an imposter refers to a particular kind of nominal expression that denotes the speaker(s) or the addressee(s) but does not have the usual first or second person pronominal form. They provide a formal definition of an imposter as in (1):

(1) An imposter is a notionally *n* person DP which is grammatically *m* person, $n \neq m$.

Some typical examples are given in (2) and (3):

(2) {*Yours truly/Daddy/Nixon/This report*} is going to resign. (Collins and Postal 2012: 3)
(3) Is {*Madam/the general*} not feeling well?

In (2) and (3), the italicized DPs are what they call imposters. Each appears to be a third person nominal expression since none of them is grammatically different from other regular instances of third person DPs. However, they denote the first person speaker in (2) and the second person addressee in (3), respectively. As also exemplified by the verbal agreement, the subject DPs in both cases are indeed grammatically third person (cf. (2) and (3)):

(4) *{*Yours truly/Daddy/Nixon/This report*} am going to resign.
(5) *Are {*Madam/the general*} not feeling well?

This is the reason that they are imposters; namely, they are grammatically third person DPs with non-third person denotations. Unsurprisingly, Mandarin Chinese (henceforth Mandarin) also seems to have imposter DPs that behave similarly, and, as a matter of fact, they are quite productive.

(6) *Laoshi* *zhende* *hen* *bu* *xihuan* *ma* *ren.*[1]
teacher really very NEG like scold person
"Teacher (= I) really doesn't like to scold anyone."

As one can imagine, the sentence (6) can be uttered by a teacher in a classroom. In other words, the subject *laoshi* "teacher" can certainly refer to the speaker himself or herself. The reason that this appears to be a parallel counterpart of English imposters is that the same DP can otherwise serve as a regular third person DP that refers to neither first person (the speaker) nor second person (the addressee).[2]

(7) *Laoshi* *zuotian* *ma* *le* *wo* *liang* *xiaoshi.*
teacher yesterday scold ASP me two hour
"The teacher scolded me for two hours yesterday."

In this chapter, I propose that Mandarin imposters like (6) are structurally different from their English counterparts. Factual observations clearly reveal that imposter DPs from the two languages are fundamentally different in their ambivalent person denotations. As a result, a more precise term for Mandarin imposter DPs should be pseudo-imposters.[3] Moreover, the structure of Mandarin pseudo-imposters is not different from other non-imposter DPs. No distinct derivation is required, as opposed to the one proposed for English imposters by Collins and Postal (2012). In particular, Mandarin pseudo-imposters are on a par with a kind of nominal expression in which a pronoun follows a regular third person DP, and, as I will show, the pronoun in question plays the main role in determining the ϕ-feature values. This particular characteristic is the underlying reason that the two languages exhibit differences with respect to grammatical person denotations in (pseudo) imposters.

This chapter is organized as follows. In section 2, I will provide a comprehensive comparison of (pseudo) imposter DPs from the two languages. The syntactic proposal will be laid out in section 3. Some particular characteristics of the co-occurring pronouns, which can serve as evidence for the proposal, will be covered in section 4. Section 5 concerns some potential alternatives, and the last section, section 6, concludes this chapter.

[1] Abbreviations: ASP = Aspect Marker, CL = Classifier, NEG = Negation, PL = Plural, POSS = Possessive, Q = Question Marker, VOC = Vocative.

[2] In Mandarin, a bare noun can be definite or have a denotation similar to definiteness in other languages.

[3] Since this chapter does not discuss any imposter cases of the English sort (i.e., "genuine" imposters) in Mandarin, I will occasionally use "pseudo-imposters" and "imposters" in an interchangeable fashion for the Mandarin data.

2. Mandarin Pseudo-Imposters

As in the discussion of (2) to (5), the verbal agreement pattern clearly suggests that the aforementioned imposter DPs in English are grammatically third person (singular) because they uniformly take the third person (singular) subject-verb agreement (i.e., *is* instead of *am* or *are*). Together with the non-third person denotation, the ambivalent behavior indicates that they are genuine imposters, as the grammatical person is different from the notional one, as per the definition in (1).

However, as is widely known, there is no overt verbal agreement in Mandarin, which means there is no simple way to examine whether or not the subject imposter DPs like *laoshi* "teacher" in (6) are really grammatically third person merely by verbal agreement. Therefore, in dealing with Mandarin (pseudo) imposters, I will rely on pronominal agreement between imposter DPs and bound pronouns/reflexives. In the following, I will provide representative data to show that Mandarin imposter DPs can only agree with pronouns/reflexives of the same notional person. In other words, there is no sign to show that the grammatical person and the notional person in Mandarin (pseudo) imposter DPs can be different. The discussion in this section includes systematic comparison with respect to bound pronouns, local and long-distance reflexives, controlled elements of control clauses, plurality, and coordination.

2.1 BOUND PRONOUNS

When an imposter DP that notionally denotes first person binds a possessive pronoun in English, the pronoun in question can be one of the third person variants (i.e., *his* or *her* and *he* or *she*), as exemplified in (8) and (9):

Imposters and bound pronouns in English

(8) *This reporter*$_1$ thinks that he$_1$ deserves credit. (Collins and Postal 2012: 95)
(9) Is *the general*$_1$ going to dine in his$_1$ suite? (Collins and Postal 2012: 3)

This is in sharp contrast to the Mandarin parallel examples provided in (10)–(13), where the third person pronoun *ta* "he/she"[4] is never possible[5] and only the notional person pronoun (i.e., the first person *wo* "I'" or the second person *ni* "you") is allowed.
First person imposters and bound pronouns in Mandarin

(10) *Laoshi*$_1$ *kuai yao shiqu {*ta*$_1$*/wo*$_1$*} de naixing le.*
teacher almost going.to lose he I POSS patience ASP
"Teacher$_1$ (= I) is going to lose {*his$_1$/ *her$_1$/my$_1$} patience."

[4] There is no gender distinction with respect to pronouns in Mandarin.

[5] Note that the third person pronoun is allowed when the subject DP *laoshi* "teacher" is in its usual third person usage.

(11) *Benren*$_1$ *yijing jueding {*ta*$_1$*/wo*$_1$*} zhe ge yue bu chu guo le.*
this.person already decide he I this CL month NEG exit country ASP
"This person$_1$ (= I) decided that {*he$_1$/I$_1$} would not go abroad this month."

Second person imposters and bound pronouns in Mandarin

(12) *Furen*$_1$ *juede {*ta*$_1$*/ni*$_1$*} de yifu tai da ma?*
Madam feel she you POSS dress too big Q
"Does Madam$_1$ (= you) feel that {*her$_1$/your$_1$} dress is too big?"

(13) *Laoban*$_1$ *yijing jueding {*ta*$_1$*/ni*$_1$*} zhe ge yue bu chu guo le ma?*
boss already decide he you this CL month NEG exit country ASP Q
"Has the boss$_1$ (= you) decided that {*he$_1$/*she$_1$/you$_1$} will not go abroad this month?"

2.2 LOCAL AND LONG-DISTANCE REFLEXIVES

Similar to the case of bound pronouns, the data on reflexive binding suggest exactly the same contrast between the two languages. In (14) and (15), the reflexive *himself* can be bound by first person imposter DPs like *yours truly* and *Daddy*.

Local and long-distance reflexives in English

(14) *Yours truly*$_1$ will only vote for {himself$_1$/*myself$_1$}. (Collins and Postal 2012: 20)

(15) *Daddy*$_1$ doesn't consider Captain Marvel to be much different than {himself$_1$/?myself$_1$}. (Collins and Postal 2012: 22)

On the contrary, the Mandarin examples in (16)–(18) evidently show that the third person *ta-ziji* "him/her-self" is never allowed to be bound by a first or a second person imposter DP. In other words, only the first person *wo-ziji* "myself" and the second person *ni-ziji* "yourself" are attested, respectively.[6]

Local and long-distance reflexives in Mandarin

(16) *A-Bian*$_1$ *zhi hui tou gei {*ta-ziji*$_1$ */ wo-ziji*$_1$*}.*[7]
A-Bian only will vote to he-self / I-self
"A-Bian$_1$ (= I) will only vote for {*himself$_1$/myself$_1$}"

(17) *Baba*$_1$ *bu renwei chaoren bi {*ta-ziji*$_1$ */ wo-ziji*$_1$*} hai yonggan.*
Daddy NEG think Superman than he-self I-self more brave
"Daddy$_1$ (= I) doesn't think that Superman is braver than {*himself$_1$/ myself$_1$}."

(18) *Jiangjun*$_1$ *bu renwei na ge ren bi {*ta-ziji*$_1$ */ ni-ziji*$_1$*} hai congming ma?*
general NEG think that CL person than he-self you-self more smart Q
"Doesn't General$_1$ (= you) think that that guy is smarter than {*himself$_1$/yourself$_1$}?"

[6] Note that it is also possible to use the person-neutral reflexive *ziji* "self" in this sentence.

[7] *A-Bian* is the nickname of a former President of Taiwan. In fact, many politicians in Taiwan tend to call themselves by their own (nick)names so as to make the audience feel more intimate.

2.3 CONTROL CLAUSES

An interesting situation is observed in control clauses in English. When the word order of the binding imposters and the bound reflexives is reversed in purpose clause examples, the first person (singular) reflexive, in addition to the usual third person (singular) one, is actually attested.[8]

Control clauses and imposters in English

(19) PRO$_1$ to keep {?myself$_1$/himself$_1$} from getting sunburned, *Daddy*$_1$ will put on suntan lotion. (Collins and Postal 2012: 96)

However, Mandarin invariably exhibits only non-third person agreement between an imposter and its bound reflexive, as shown in (20) and (21):

Control clauses and imposters in Mandarin

(20) PRO$_1$ *yao rang {*ta-ziji$_1$/wo-ziji$_1$} gen jiankang, laoshi$_1$ jueding tiantian.*
want.to make he-self I-self more healthy teacher decide everyday
yundong
exercise
"To make {*himself$_1$/myself$_1$} healthier, teacher$_1$ (= I) decided to exercise everyday."

(21) PRO$_1$ *yao rang {*ta-ziji$_1$/ni-ziji$_1$} gen chuming, jiangjun yinggai duo shang*
want.to make he-self you-self more famous general should more show.up
dianshi.
TV
"To make {*himself$_1$/yourself$_1$} more famous, General$_1$ (= you) should show up more on TV."

2.4 PLURAL IMPOSTERS

Similar to the case of control clauses, plural imposters in English, in addition to the third person plural reflexive, are also allowed to bind the first person plural one, as exemplified in (22):

Plural imposters in English

(22) In this reply, the present authors$_1$ (= the writers of the reply) attempt to defend {ourselves$_1$/themselves$_1$} against the scurrilous charges which have been made. (Collins and Postal 2012: 17)

Once again, Mandarin rigidly chooses non-third person (i.e., notional) agreement, and in this case, the first and second person plural pronouns *women* "we" and *nimen* "you" are used, as shown in (23) and (24), respectively.

[8] See Collins and Postal (2012, Chapter 7) for an account of this ambivalent behavior.

Plural imposters in Mandarin

(23) *Jizhe-men*$_1$ *faxian* {**tamen*$_1$/*women*$_1$} *zuixian laidao chushi xianchang.*
reporter-PL found they we earliest arrive accident scene
"Reporters$_1$ (= we) found that {*they$_1$/we$_1$} are those who arrived at the accident scene the earliest."

(24) *Furen-men*$_1$ *shi-bu-shi yijing xiang hui* {**tamen*$_1$/*nimen*$_1$} *de jia le?*[9]
Madam-PL be-NEG-be already want return they you POSS home ASP
"Do Madams$_1$ (= you) already want to return to {*their$_1$/your$_1$} home?"

2.5 COORDINATION

Finally, the same contrast between the two languages is also found in coordination. In particular, English allows both notional and third person agreement, just like the case of plural imposters discussed in the last section.
Imposters in coordination in English

(25) *Yours truly* and Jerome will devote {ourselves/themselves} to music.

(Collins and Postal 2012: 108)

Mandarin, on the other hand, resists the third person agreement in this context:

Imposters in coordination in Mandarin

(26) [*Bizhe han tongshi*]$_1$ *xiwang* {**tamen-ziji*$_1$ / *women-ziji*$_1$} *keyi hen kuai you xin faxian.*
author and colleague expect they-self we-self can very soon have new finding
"[The present author (=I) and colleague(s)]$_1$ expect {*themselves$_1$/ourselves$_1$} to have new findings very soon."

(27) [*Jiangjun han zhangguan-men*]$_1$ *shi-bu-shi juede* {**tamen*$_1$ / *nimen*$_1$} *gai xiuxi le?*
general and officer-PL be-NEG-be feel they you should rest ASP
"Do [General (=you) and officers]$_1$ feel that {*they$_1$/you$_1$} should take some rest?"

To sum up, the comprehensive comparison clearly reveals that Mandarin uniformly exhibits non-third person agreement between pseudo-imposter DPs and bound pronouns/reflexives in various contexts. So the binding is always with

[9] Mandarin has a special kind of question, the so-called A-*not*-A question, in which a negative element (e.g., *bu* or *mei*) occurs between two modals or two verbs to express something similar to a *yes-no* question in other languages.

the notional person (i.e., first or second person), and there is no case where third person agreement is attested, which is in sharp contrast to English imposters.

3. Mandarin Pseudo-Imposters as Complex DPs

3.1 THE STRUCTURE OF MANDARIN PSEUDO-IMPOSTERS

The fact that Mandarin exhibits systematic differences from English with respect to person agreement in binding leads to a suggestion that imposter DPs in the two languages arguably have very different structures.[10] To recap, Mandarin imposter DPs always agree notionally in binding. In other words, even if the imposter DP in Mandarin looks like a regular instance of a third person expression, the person agreement is never based on third person. This suggests that the entire imposter DP in Mandarin bears the notional (i.e., first or second) person value. As such, I propose that Mandarin imposter DPs are complex in that a notional pronoun occupies the D^0 position (cf. Postal 1966; Longobardi 1994; Kayne 2005) from which it projects the whole complex DP. The third person part (e.g., *laoshi* "teacher" and *furen* "Madam"), in the form of a DP, is merged in the specifier position of the aforementioned DP. The schematic structure that integrates these ideas is provided in (29), and, for convenience, I repeat two examples in (28):

(28) a. *Laoshi*$_1$ *kuai almost yao shiqu wo*$_1$ *de naixing le.*
teacher almost going.to lose I POSS patience ASP
"Teacher$_1$ (= I) is going to lose my$_1$ patience."

b. *Furen*$_1$ *juede ni*$_1$ *de yifu tai da ma?*
Madam feel you POSS dress too big Q
"Does Madam$_1$ (= you) feel that your$_1$ dress is too big?"

(29) The Structure of Mandarin Pseudo-Imposters:

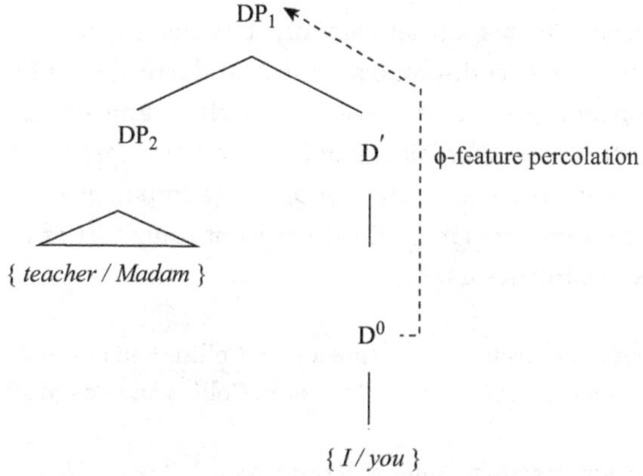

[10] This actually conforms to what Collins and Postal (2012) call the syntactic view of imposters. See section 3.3 for further discussion.

By assuming that the head of the complex DP (i.e., DP_1) is a notional pronoun, the behavior of Mandarin imposter DPs follows naturally. That is, as demonstrated in (29), the whole complex DP bears the ϕ-feature value percolated from the head (i.e., a pronoun denoting the notional person), resulting in the uniform non-third person agreement in binding as evidenced in the previous discussion. To put it differently, the rigid non-third person agreement found in Mandarin pseudo-imposters is fully expected since it is simply what one would expect for a DP whose head is a non-third person pronoun.

Since it is argued that all imposter DPs in Mandarin involve a notional pronoun in the head position, there are two issues that have to be addressed. First, it has to be shown that the notional pronoun in question does really exist so as to project the entire DP. Second, given the data previously noted, it is also necessary to account for why the notional pronoun under consideration can be covert, leading to the apparent similarity with English imposter DPs.

Note also that the proposed analysis actually suggests that Mandarin imposter DPs should by no means be regarded as imposters of the English sort. Recall the definition of imposters in Collins and Postal (2012), repeated here as (30):

(30) An imposter is a notionally *n* person DP which is grammatically *m* person, $n \neq m$.

It seems clear that, if the proposed analysis is on the right track, imposter DPs in Mandarin have the same person both notionally and grammatically because the ϕ-feature value is determined by the notional pronoun in the head position. It amounts to saying that they are not imposters, despite the apparent similarity of relevant cases between the two languages. That is also why they are called pseudo-imposters in this chapter.

3.2 THE STRUCTURE OF ENGLISH IMPOSTERS

Given the sharp differences in person agreement, it is not surprising to see that the proposed structure of pseudo-imposters in Mandarin should be different from that of English imposters to some extent. Collins and Postal (2012) propose that the (imposter) precursor, as exemplified in (31a), provides all the syntactic and semantic elements needed to compose the imposter in (31b). In particular, they argue that imposters in English represent some sort of syntactic deformations of (imposter) precursors.

(31) a. I, *Nixon*, am going to get even. (precursor; Collins and Postal 2012: 48)
b. *Nixon* is going to get even. (imposter; Collins and Postal 2012: 48)

The (imposter) precursor, as they suggest, contains a DP (e.g., *Nixon*) which they take to be a predicate nominal. This gives rise to a structure as shown in the following (Collins and Postal 2012: 49):

(32) I, *Nixon*, am going to get even. (precursor)

The Structure of English (Imposter) Precursors:

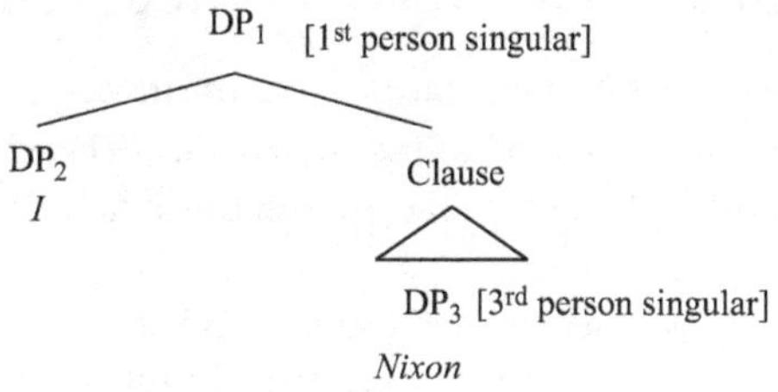

The complex precursor structure is further embedded in yet another DP (i.e., DP_4), which is merged above DP_1, as in (33) (Collins and Postal 2012: 66). DP_3, being a predicate nominal, undergoes predicate inversion in the sense of den Dikken (2006) to the specifier position of DP_4.

(33) *Nixon* is going to get even. (imposter)

The Structure of English Imposters:

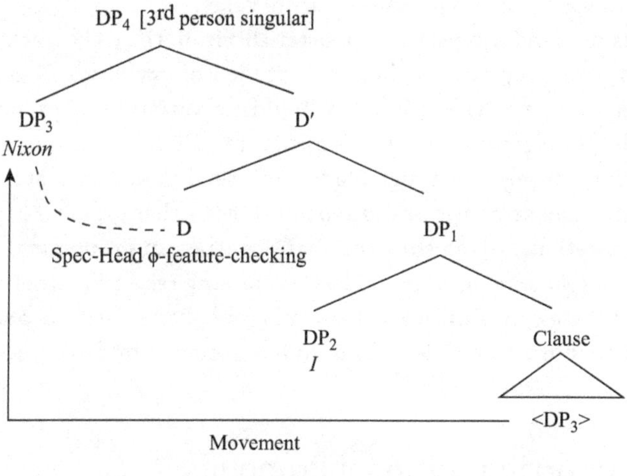

The reason that the whole complex DP_4 bears the third person ϕ-feature value is because the displaced DP_3, *Nixon*, agrees with the head of DP_4 via the usual Spec-Head feature-checking (cf. Chomsky 1995). Accordingly, the head percolates its third person ϕ-feature value obtained from the displaced DP_3 (i.e., *Nixon*) up to the entire DP_4.

As we can see, the structure is different from the one proposed for Mandarin pseudo-imposters. The most notable difference is that the third person part (e.g., *laoshi* "teacher" or *furen* "Madam") in Mandarin plays absolutely no role in determining the ϕ-feature values; rather, it is the notional pronoun in the head position that does the job.

3.3 NOTIONAL VERSUS SYNTACTIC VIEWS OF IMPOSTERS

In this section, I briefly discuss an important implication from the investigation of pseudo-imposters in Mandarin. As discussed in Collins and Postal (2012: 9), there are two competing views of imposters: the notional view and the syntactic view:

(34) *The Notional View*: Imposters are just instances of regular third person DPs with the semantic or discourse property that they denote either the speaker(s) or the addressee(s). The specific syntactic properties distinguishing imposters from other DPs are nonexistent.

(35) *The Syntactic View*: Imposters are a particular kind of DP with non-third person denotations. The availability of such denotations is due to some specific syntactic properties distinguishing imposters from other DPs.

The analysis of imposters in Collins and Postal (2012) clearly conforms to the syntactic view[11] since an imposter DP in English is considered to be a special kind of complex DP that involves some DP-internal syntactic operation (i.e., predicate inversion), resulting in having third person (verbal) agreement while notionally denoting a non-third person ϕ-feature value.

If the analysis of Mandarin pseudo-imposter DPs is on the right track, it undoubtedly offers strong support for the syntactic view of imposters. That is, the proposed analysis suggests that the cross-linguistic variation of pronominal agreement results from different syntactic structures. Under the notional view, however, both English imposters and Mandarin pseudo-imposters are simply regular DPs with some semantic or discourse property that gives rise to non-third person denotations. Given this, the sharp contrast in pronominal agreement between the two languages would be a surprising result. In other words, under the notional view, it is unclear what could straightforwardly account for the cross-linguistic difference unless some ad hoc semantic or discourse condition is stipulated.

4. The Co-occurring Notional Pronouns

In this section, I approach the two issues mentioned in the last section; namely, the existence and the optionally (c)overt nature of the proposed notional pronoun that heads a complex (pseudo-imposter) DP in Mandarin.

[11] See Collins and Postal (2012: 12) for a few more pieces of evidence in favor of the syntactic view.

4.1 THE CO-OCCURRENCE OF NOTIONAL PRONOUNS

It has been proposed in section 3 that Mandarin pseudo-imposter DPs involve a covert notional pronoun occupying the D^0 position. This is the underlying reason that the person agreement in binding is so different from English imposters. In fact, Mandarin pseudo-imposters can generally be followed by an overt pronoun that denotes the notional person. This argues for the existence of the proposed pronoun, even though it can be covert.[12]

As shown in (36) and (37), the first person singular pronoun *wo* "I" can felicitously occur after the pseudo-imposters *laoshi* "teacher" and *benren* "this person" when these two (seemingly regular third person) DPs notionally denote the speaker.

(36) *Laoshi*$_1$ *wo*$_1$ *kuai yao shiqu wo*$_1$ *de naixing le.*
teacher I almost going.to lose I POSS patience ASP
"Teacher$_1$ I$_1$ is going to lose my$_1$ patience."

(37) *Benren*$_1$ *wo*$_1$ *yijing jueding wo*$_1$ *bu chu guo le.*
this.person I already decide I NEG exit country ASP
"This person$_1$ I$_1$ decided that I$_1$ would not go abroad."

Similarly, the second person singular pronoun *ni* "you" can as well freely occur after the imposters *furen* "Madam" and *laoban* "boss" when they are used to denote the addressee. This observation is exemplified in (38) and (39):

(38) *Furen*$_1$ *ni*$_1$ *juede ni*$_1$ *de yifu tai da ma?*
Madam you feel you POSS dress too big Q
"Does Madam$_1$ you$_1$ feel that your$_1$ dress is too big?"

(39) *Laoban*$_1$ *ni*$_1$ *yijing jueding ni*$_1$ *zhe ge yue bu chu guo le ma?*
boss you already decide you this CL month NEG exit country ASP Q
"Has the boss$_1$ you$_1$ decided that you$_1$ will not go abroad this month?"

For plural and coordinate imposters, they can also be followed by a pronoun with the corresponding person and number:[13]

(40) *Jizhe*$_1$ *women*$_1$ *faxian women*$_1$ *zuixian laidao chushi xianchang.*
reporter we found we earliest arrive accident scene
"Reporters$_1$ we$_1$ found that we$_1$ are those who arrived at the accident scene the earliest."

[12] The optionally null behavior of the pronoun in question will be discussed in section 4.2.

[13] Note that, in the plural imposter cases like (23), the pseudo-imposters are marked by the suffix *-men* which is commonly assumed to denote some sort of plurality for Mandarin animate nouns. However, for some unknown reason, when a plural pseudo-imposter is followed by the first person plural pronoun *women* "we" which already contains the suffix *-men,* it does not sound okay, though not totally bad, if the pseudo-imposter *jizhe* "reporter," for example, is also marked by *-men.* I tentatively suggest that the oddness may be due to some phonological reason, since the occurrence of two instances of *-men* clearly leads to repetitiveness and redundancy.

(41) [*Bizhe han tongshi*]$_1$ *women*$_1$ *xiwang women-ziji*$_1$ *keyi hen kuai you xin*
author and colleague we expect we-self can very soon have new
faxian.
finding
"[The present author and colleague(s)]$_1$ we$_1$ expect ourselves$_1$ to have new findings very soon."

On the contrary, as exemplified in (42), this particular property is not shared by English imposters, since the co-occurrence of a pronoun degrades the sentence.

(42) **This reporter*$_1$ {he/she/I} lost {his$_1$/her$_1$} cool.

One thing to note is that the co-occurring pronouns in Mandarin could potentially be considered to be DP-external (e.g., emphatic adverbs or the like). If this were really the case, the proposal that the notional pronouns reside in the D^0 position would be untenable. Therefore, it is necessary to show that the pronouns in question are really DP-internal. As evidenced in (43) and (44), the fact that the notional pronoun *wo* "I," together with a pseudo-imposter, can appear as either one of the conjuncts with the connective word *han* "and" argues for the DP-internal status of the pronouns under investigation.

(43) [*Furen*$_1$ *ni*$_1$ *han Xiaomei*] *shi-bu-shi yao yiqi qu meiguo?*
Madam you and Xiaomei be-NEG-be want together go U.S.
"Do [Madam$_1$ you$_1$ and Xiaomei] want to go to the U.S. together?"

(44) [*Xiaomei han Furen*$_1$ *ni*$_1$] *shi-bu-shi yao yiqi qu meiguo?*
Xiaomei and Madam you be-NEG-be want together go U.S.
"Do [Xiaomei and Madam$_1$ you$_1$] want to go to the U.S. together?"

In addition, such a combination (i.e., a third person part plus a notional pronoun) can occur in the complement position of a preposition as well as in the object position. This suggests that the pronouns in question are very likely to be DP-internal.

(45) *Xiaozhang xiang laoshi*$_1$ *wo*$_1$ *baozheng jiaoshi yiding hui zhengxiu.*
principal to teacher I promise classroom definitely will renovate
"The principal promised teacher$_1$ I$_1$ that the classroom will definitely be renovated."

(46) *Bu yao zai yi ci remao laoshi*$_1$ *wo*$_1$ *le!*
NEG want again one time annoy teacher I ASP
"Don't ever annoy teacher$_1$ I$_1$ again!"

To sum up, the first issue has been addressed: the existence of the proposed notional pronoun in Mandarin is warranted. The discussion not only shows that a pronoun that denotes the notional person can occur after a pseudo-imposter in Mandarin but also proves that the pronoun in question is DP-internal, forming a complex constituent with the pseudo-imposter.

4.2 THE OPTIONALLY OVERT NOTIONAL PRONOUNS

As briefly mentioned, the fact that the proposed notional pronoun in question can be null is the underlying reason that Mandarin has pseudo-imposter DPs that look quite similar to the English counterparts. Therefore, the second issue that needs to be explained is why the co-occurring notional pronouns can be optionally overt.

As is widely known, Mandarin is a *pro*-drop language, meaning that a pronoun, under certain appropriate contexts, can be left unpronounced. The interpretation can then be recovered and inferred from the licensing context. For example, a simple declarative sentence (47), with the subject position left blank, can have various interpretations (i.e., first, second, or third person), depending on the situation.

(47) [___] *lai* *le.*
come ASP
"I/You/He/She/We/They come."

I suggest that the *pro*-drop characteristic offers a clear window on the second issue. That is, the proposed notional pronoun that goes with a pseudo-imposter can be covert since the context provided by the sentences that involve a pseudo-imposter already supplies the identity of the notional person. For instance, the sentence in (36), repeated here as (48), can probably be heard in school or in a classroom. So when one knows that such a sentence is uttered by a teacher, the third person part *laoshi* "teacher" will certainly have the first person denotation even without the appearance of the notional pronoun. In other words, Mandarin independently allows the pronouns to be null under some appropriate context, and the omission of the notional pronoun is thus licensed.

(48) *Laoshi*$_1$ *(wo)* *kuai* *yao* *shiqu* *wo*$_1$ *de* *naixing* *le.*
teacher I almost going.to lose I POSS patience ASP
"Teacher$_1$ (I) is going to lose my$_1$ patience."

There is another way to show that the optionally overt nature of the notional pronouns in Mandarin pseudo-imposter DPs is correlated with the manifestation of some appropriate context. Notice that almost all sentences that involve a second person imposter (e.g., *furen* "Madam" and *jiangjun* "General") in the previous discussion are in the form of a polar (i.e., *yes-no*) question. The reason for that is to induce the imposter sort of reading. That is, it is much easier to imagine that pseudo-imposters like *furen* "Madam" or *jiangjun* "General" can denote the addressee in a polar question configuration.

(49) *Furen* *juede* *yifu* *tai* *da* *ma?*
Madam feel dress too big Q
"Does Madam (= you) feel that the dress is too big?"

In contrast, second person imposter DPs in Mandarin fail to have this advantage when they occur in a neutral declarative sentence. As such, sentences like (50) cannot be naturally understood as involving the imposter sort of reading (i.e., *furen* "Madam" to denote the addressee), and the dominant reading is that the subject *furen* "Madam" refers to some entity other than the addressee (i.e., third person).

(50) *(Wo tingshuo) furen jueding bu zai mai renhe yifu le.*
I hear Madam decide NEG again buy any dress ASP
"(I heard) Madam (?= you) decided not to buy any dress."

Nevertheless, when the second person pronoun *ni* "you" occurs after *furen* "Madam," the imposter reading can be re-obtained and is actually the only reading available, as shown in (51):

(51) *(Wo tingshuo) furen*$_1$ *ni*$_1$ *yijing jueding bu zai mai renhe yifu le.*
I hear Madam you already decide NEG again buy any dress ASP
"(I heard) Madam$_1$ you$_1$ already decided not to buy any dress."

The discussion in this section suggests that the notional pronouns in Mandarin pseudo-imposters are covert when the associated context provides enough information so as to license the omission. The result is thus the optional phonetic realization of the notional pronouns.

4.3 THE WIDE AVAILABILITY OF CO-OCCURRING PRONOUNS

In this section, I show that notional pronouns can generally co-occur with (almost)[14] all kinds of DPs in Mandarin. This indicates that no special structure is required to account for pseudo-imposters in Mandarin with first or second person denotations, and that all sorts of person denotations follow naturally from the proposed structure in (29).

Recall that a pronoun denoting the notional person can co-occur with a pseudo-imposter DP in Mandarin. This predicts that any regular third person DP can as well be followed by the third person (singular or plural) pronoun since the proposed structure in (29) does not set any restriction in this respect. The prediction is borne out, as evidenced by the following examples.

(52) *Zhangsan*$_1$ *ta*$_1$ *hen congming.*
Zhangsan he very smart
"Zhangsan$_1$ he$_1$ is very smart."

[14] The only potential exception I can think of is the use of inanimate nouns. However, the exception can be independently accounted for, since it is quite rare for the third person pronoun (i.e., *ta*) to refer to inanimate entities in spoken Mandarin (cf. Li 1997).

(53) *Zhangsan$_1$ ta$_1$ han Xiaoming dou mai le xin shouji.*
Zhangsan he and Xiaoming all buy ASP new cell-phone
"Zhangsan$_1$ he$_1$ and Xiaoming both bought a new cell phone."

In (53), the possibility for the sequence *Zhangsan ta* 'Zhangsan he' to be in a coordinating structure further strengthens the idea that it is indeed a constituent and is on a par with those pseudo-imposter DPs that involve a co-occurring first or second person pronoun. In other words, the third person examples in (52) and (53) are structurally parallel to the pseudo-imposter DPs under investigation.

The fact that even the third person singular pronoun *ta* "he/she" can co-occur with a regular third person DP is reminiscent of a proposal in Kayne (2005). That is, (at least) some binding phenomena can be subsumed under movement.

(54) John thinks he is smart. (Kayne 2005: 77)
a. John thinks [PRO-he] is smart. (without co-reference)
b. John$_1$ thinks [t$_1$-he] is smart. (with co-reference)

As in (54b), the traditional antecedence relation regulated by Binding Principle B can be recaptured by the idea that the antecedent (i.e., *John*) undergoes raising to some higher position from its launching site where it forms a constituent with the bound pronoun (i.e., *he*). On the other hand, when there is no antecedence relation, as in (54a), the complex unit, in addition to the pronoun *he*, contains a null pronominal expression (i.e., *PRO*) whose referent is contextually determined. In relation to pronoun doubling and the fact that pronouns can be null in Mandarin, there are two logically possible ways to reconsider the nature of Mandarin DPs. First, somewhat more radically, all DPs, including regular third person ones, accompany a (mostly) null pronoun that corresponds to its notional person (e.g., *Zhangsan (ta)* "Zhangsan (he)" and *zhe ge ren (ta)* "this person (he)"). Second, only a subset of DPs co-occur with a (null) notional pronoun, among which the most notable examples, in particular, are those that involve the imposter sort of interpretation, that is, pseudo-imposter DPs. In other words, the possibility that all DPs can be followed by a notional pronoun does not mean that they have to be. I leave this question open for further research.

4.4 THE SOURCE OF Φ-FEATURES

In section 4.3, it has been shown that pseudo-imposter DPs in Mandarin are not so different from other regular instances of DPs since they all can be followed by a pronoun that denotes the notional person. In this section, I further show that what looks like an imposter DP (i.e., pseudo-imposter) in Mandarin can actually denote any of the three grammatical persons with the help of a co-occurring pronoun. This indicates that the third person part (e.g., *laoshi* "teacher") plays absolutely no role in determining the ϕ-feature values. In contrast, as previously discussed in

(33), an imposter DP in English undergoes the usual Spec-Head feature-checking so that the entire imposter DP inherits the ϕ-feature values from its head.

As can be seen from (55) and (56) in the following, Mandarin pseudo-imposters like *laoshi* "teacher" and *furen* "Madam" can optionally be followed by any of the three singular pronouns. Among them, the first and second person readings are what are being regarded as the imposter sort of interpretation.[15]

(55) *Laoshi$_1$ {wo$_1$/ni$_1$ /ta$_1$} hen congming.*
teacher I you he very smart
"Laoshi$_1$ {I$_1$/you$_1$/he$_1$} is very smart."

(56) *Furen$_1$ {wo$_1$/ni$_1$ /ta$_1$} hen piaoliang.*
Madam I you she very beautiful
"Madam$_1$ {I$_1$/you$_1$/she$_1$} is very beautiful."

Granted that, since the pronouns, overt or covert,[16] are supposed to be responsible for determining the ϕ-feature value of the entire DP, this leads to a conclusion that the third person part itself has nothing to do with the person agreement, and accordingly plays no role in ϕ-feature value checking or percolation. In other words, the current analysis of Mandarin pseudo-imposters is supported.

4.5 ADDITIONAL COMPARISONS

In this section, I provide a few more cases to reinforce the proposal that imposter DPs in English and pseudo-imposter DPs in Mandarin are essentially different so as to further validate their structural differences as suggested in section 3.1.

The first case has something to do with a singular pronoun being bound by an imposter DP that denotes the same notional person. Collins and Postal (2012: 95) provide the following examples in English.

(57) a. ??*Your faithful correspondent$_1$* thinks that I$_1$ should write more often.
b. ??Does *Madam$_1$* think you$_1$ will be able to contact the doctor?

As already discussed in section 2, pseudo-imposter DPs in Mandarin can only bind a pronoun of the same notional person, meaning that the restriction in

[15] The distribution of a notional pronoun with a co-referring DP seems to be quite widespread. For example, the so-called antilogophor *renjia* discussed in Liu (2001, 2004) can co-occur with the first and third person (singular) pronouns (but not with the second person singular pronoun), and notionally refers to the speaker and some third person referent, respectively.

(i) *Renjia {wo/ *ni/ ta} bu renshi shizhang de nuer.*
RENJIA I you he NEG know mayor POSS daughter
"{I/*you/he} do/esn't know the mayor's daughter."

[16] Note that, as mentioned in section 4.2, when the first and second person pronouns are covert in these examples, the imposter sort of interpretation (i.e. non-third person) requires licensing from contextual information.

English, as exemplified in (57), is not attested. Two relevant examples are provided below.

(58) *Laoshi*$_1$ *zi ren wo*$_1$ *yizhi hen chengshi, danshi mei ren xiangxin wo*$_1$.
teacher self think I always very honest but NEG person believe me
"Teacher$_1$ (= I) think(s) that I$_1$ am very honest, but no one believes in me$_1$."

(59) *Furen*$_1$ *shi-bu-shi renwei ni*$_1$ *hui zhong tou jiang?*
Madam be-NEG-be think you will win head prize
"Does Madam$_1$ (= you) think that you$_1$ will win the grand prize?"

The grammaticality contrast again supports the argument that (pseudo) imposters are different between the two languages. Moreover, with the appearance of a co-occurring pronoun, the grammaticality of the two sentences is fully expected. That is, the two sentences are parallel to the case where a matrix pronoun binds an embedded pronoun of the same person (e.g., *I*$_1$ *think that I*$_1$. . .).[17]

(60) *Laoshi*$_1$ *wo*$_1$ *zi ren wo*$_1$ *yizhi hen chengshi, danshi mei ren xiangxin wo*$_1$.
teacher I self think I always very honest but NEG person believe me
"Teacher$_1$ I$_1$ think(s) that I$_1$ am very honest, but no one believes in me$_1$."

(61) *Furen*$_1$ *ni*$_1$ *shi-bu-shi renwei ni*$_1$ *hui zhong tou jiang?*
Madam you be-NEG-be think you will win head prize
"Do(es) Madam$_1$ you$_1$ think that you$_1$ will win the grand prize?"

Another related observation that can be used to show that the two languages differ with respect to (pseudo) imposters concerns what Collins and Postal (2012: 217) call pronominal imposters. An example is given below.

(62) *Daddy*$_1$ said that he$_1$ needs to leave early.

The pronoun *he* in the embedded clause is a pronominal imposter[18] (bound by an imposter) because it is notionally first person though it has the usual third

[17] Here I set aside the possibility that the first person pronoun is anteceded by an ultimate antecedent which is called S in Baker (2008: 126) or AUTHOR in Collins and Postal (2012).

[18] Note that the pronoun *he* is an instance of an imposter because it conforms to the definition given in (1). In addition, Collins and Postal (2012) discuss some other cases of pronominal imposters such as Nurse-*we*. In fact, Mandarin also has something similar to an example cited in Collins and Postal (2012: 218).

(ii) Now students, last time we all filled out questionnaires.

(iii) *tongxue, shang ci women dou tian guo wenjuan le, . . .*
students last time we all fill ASP questionnaires ASP
"Students, last time we all filled out questionnaires, . . ."

The pronoun *we* in both languages is considered to be a pronominal imposter because the statement can be true even when the teacher has not filled out any questionnaire, meaning that the pronoun *we*, being a first person pronoun, does not have a denotation that includes the first person speaker.

person singular form *he*. As one may expect, there is no way to construct a parallel example of this sort since pseudo-imposter DPs in Mandarin always bind a pronoun of the same notional person.

In addition to the case where an imposter binds a pronoun, the reverse situation where an imposter is bound by a pronoun further shows the difference between the two languages. As observed in Collins and Postal (2012), the contrast between (63) and (64) in the following indicates that there is some sort of discrepancy between imposters bound by a third and a non-third person pronoun, respectively. As such, the question is whether or not an imposter DP is like an *R*-expression that must not be bound (according to Binding Principle C). However, the contrast in question results in an obvious dilemma. Simply saying that imposters can or cannot be bound does not account for the contrast, since either one of the two sides will still be left unexplained.

(63) *He$_1$ thinks that *yours truly*$_1$ was treated rather well. (Collins and Postal 2012: 131)
(64) I$_1$ think that *yours truly*$_1$ was treated rather well.

To deal with this problem, Collins and Postal (2012) propose the following principle.

(65) Principle C (Collins and Postal 2012: 131)

If a DP Q is an antecedent of a pronominal DP P, then P does not c-command Q.

They argue that the third person pronoun in (63) agrees with the imposter *yours truly* (in terms of the value of the shell), leading to the conclusion that *yours truly* is an immediate antecedent of the pronoun. According to the antecedence-based version of Principle C stated in (65), the sentence is ruled out because the pronoun in question mistakenly c-commands *yours truly*. On the other hand, the first person matrix subject pronoun in (64) is anteceded by an ultimate antecedent in the left periphery which they call AUTHOR, so the embedded subject imposter *yours truly* is not the immediate antecedent of the matrix pronoun. Granted that, no violation of the principle in (65) is triggered; hence the grammaticality.

The parallel sentences in Mandarin, as exemplified in (66) and (67), do not show any contrast from the English counterparts. That is, the same pattern is observed: the pseudo-imposter *laoshi* "teacher" can only be bound by the first person singular *wo* "I," but not by the third person singular *ta* "he."

(66) **Ta*$_1$ *zi ren [laoshi (wo)]*$_1$ *yizhi hen chengshi, danshi mei ren xiangxin wo*$_1$.
he self think teacher I always very honest but NEG person believe me
"He$_1$ thinks that teacher$_1$ (I)$_1$ am/is very honest, but no one believes in me$_1$."
(67) *Wo*$_1$ *zi ren [laoshi (wo)]*$_1$ *yizhi hen chengshi, danshi mei ren xiangxin wo*$_1$.
I self think teacher I always very honest but NEG person believe me
"I$_1$ think that teacher$_1$ (I)$_1$ am/is very honest, but no one believes in me$_1$."

However, the similarity does not mean that they have to be analyzed in the same fashion. In fact, the reason that the two Mandarin examples differ with respect to grammaticality can be reduced to one simple restriction; namely, person (mis)match[19] in binding. That is, the sentence (66) is ill-formed simply because the third person pronoun (i.e., the matrix subject) incorrectly antecedes the first person pronoun in the embedded clause (i.e., the co-occurring notional pronoun with the pseudo-imposter *laoshi* "teacher"). As a result, the sentence is ruled out for the same reason that a sentence that involves two co-indexed pronouns of different persons is ill-formed. By the same token, the sentence (67) is well-formed because it has two co-indexed pronouns of the same person: one is the first person subject pronoun in the matrix clause and the other, which likewise co-occurs with the pseudo-imposter *laoshi* "teacher," is in the embedded clause.

To sum up this section, the differences with regard to binding and person agreement further strengthen the idea that Mandarin pseudo-imposters are not on a par with English imposters, and confirm the proposed structural differences.

5. Some Alternatives

5.1 PSEUDO-IMPOSTERS ≠ TOPICS

As is well known, Mandarin is a *pro*-drop (as previously discussed in section 4.2) and topic-prominent (Li and Thompson 1981) language. In addition, it has no overt case marking on nominal expressions. These characteristics, together with the fact that the notional pronoun in Mandarin pseudo-imposters can be covert,[20] might lead to a suggestion that a subject pseudo-imposter could be considered to be a topic in the left periphery, and the co-occurring pronoun would be the subject of the sentence. Such an alternative would give rise to a structure like the following.

(68) *Laoshi*$_{topic,}$ *wo*$_{subject}$ *xia xueqi yao shoujia.*
teacher I next semester going.to recess
"(As for) Teacher$_1$, I$_1$ will be on leave next semester."

However, the alternative can easily be proven to be wrong. Note first that it is possible to have the (optional) element *a* that usually signals the existence of a topic to its left, as exemplified in (69):[21]

[19] This actually follows from what Collins and Postal (2012) call the Homogeneity Principle.

[20] And possibly all DPs in Mandarin (cf. section 4.3).

[21] The element *a* can also mark a DP to its left as a vocative expression. Therefore, (69) has a grammatical variant in which *Lisi* is used as a vocative expression. In this sense, it does not refer to the same entity as the subject.

(iv) *Lisi* ***a****, ta mai le yi liang chezi*
Lisi VOC he buy ASP one CL car
"(Hey) Lisi! He bought a car." (He ≠ Lisi)

(69) *Lisi*$_1$ *a,* *ta*$_1$ *mai le yi liang chezi.*
Lisi TOP, he buy ASP one CL car
"(As for) Lisi$_1$, he$_1$ bought a car."

Crucially, this option is never attested for cases that involve a pseudo-imposter DP. With that being said, the sentence (68) should be ruled out if the element *a* occurs after the pseudo-imposter *laoshi* "teacher." The prediction is met, as shown in (70):[22]

(70) **Laoshi*$_1$ *a,* *wo*$_1$ *xia xueqi yao shoujia.*
teacher TOP I next semester going.to recess
Int. "(As for) Teacher$_1$, I$_1$ will be on leave next semester."

In conclusion, the evidence presented in this section refutes the conjecture that pseudo-imposter DPs in Mandarin are topics.

5.2 PSEUDO-IMPOSTERS VERSUS *ASS*-CAMOUFLAGE CONSTRUCTIONS

Another alternative is to draw an analogy between Mandarin pseudo-imposters and English *ass*-camouflage constructions (henceforth ACC; Collins, Moody, and Postal 2008: Collins and Postal 2012). Some typical examples are provided below.

(71) a. *His ass* ain' going nowhere. (Collins and Postal 2012: 71)
"He is not going anywhere."
b. *Your ass* in trouble.
"You are in trouble."

As can be seen from (71), these nominal expressions, like imposters, also display a ϕ-feature value mismatch between a core pronominal (i.e., the genitive pronouns *his* and *your*) and a shell (i.e., the entire DP). Importantly, as also discussed in Collins and Postal (2012: 227), the pronominal agreement in ACC is similar to that of Mandarin pseudo-imposters. That is, ACC DPs exhibit notional person agreement, instead of the third person one with the shell.

(72) a. *Your ass* making a fool of {yourself/*itself/*hisself}. (Collins and Postal 2008: 39)
b. *Your ass* was late, wasn't {you/*he/*she/*it}?

The similarity leads to the possibility that Mandarin pseudo-imposters are parallel to English ACC DPs. The only difference is that Mandarin pseudo-imposter

[22] The sentence is ill-formed for not having the reading that the indices indicate.

DPs have an optionally null core pronoun, whereas English ACC DPs have an overt one realized in the genitive form. However, the parallelism seems to be just apparent because further factual observations about the two constructions suggest that they should be different to a certain extent. First, it is possible to have a genitive pronoun that serves as the possessor of a pseudo-imposter, and, importantly, the genitive pronoun in question never determines the notional person.

(73) *Ni de laoshi*$_1$ *(wo)*$_1$ *kuai yao shiqu wo*$_1$ *de naixing le.*
you POSS teacher I almost going.to lose I POSS patience ASP
"Your teacher$_1$ (I)$_1$ is going to lose my$_1$ patience."

As exemplified in (73), the appearance of a genitive pronoun does not result in any change of the person denotation. So the instance of a pseudo-imposter in (73) still denotes first person since, as previously mentioned, only the co-occurring pronoun can determine the ϕ-feature value. Crucially, when a first person genitive pronoun appears as the possessor, it is impossible to have a co-occurring first person pronoun after a pseudo-imposter DP.

(74) *Wo de laoshi*$_1$ *{ta*$_1$*/*wo*$_1$*} kuai yao shiqu {ta*$_1$*/*wo*$_1$*} de naixing le.*
I POSS teacher he I almost going.to lose he I POSS patience ASP
"My teacher$_1$ {he$_1$/*I$_1$} is going to lose {his$_1$/*my$_1$} patience."

In this case, the sentence can only have the usual third person denotation,[23] which means that the genitive pronoun preceding the pseudo-imposter DP plays absolutely no role in determining the ϕ-feature value. In other words, unlike English ACC DPs, such a genitive pronoun is not the pronominal core.

Second, pseudo-imposter DPs in Mandarin can felicitously serve as a possessor in the vanilla possessive construction. In (75), for example, the possessor *laoshi* "teacher" is a pseudo-imposter under investigation, and it can be a possessor while retaining its imposter sort of reading.

(75) *Laoshi de xiaohai jin nian yao qu meiguo nianshu.*
teacher POSS child this year going.to go U.S. study
"Teacher (=I)'s child is going to the U.S. to study this year."

On the contrary, an ACC DP in English, as Collins, Moody, and Postal (2008) note, cannot itself be a possessor.[24]

[23] In (74), when the constituent *wo de laoshi* "my teacher" co-occurs with the second person pronoun *ni* "you," the whole can actually denote the second person addressee.

[24] The restriction is not attested in another kind of camouflage construction that Collins and Postal (2012: 72) refer to as the *social hierarchy camouflage construction* (SHCC). Examples include *Her Majesty* and *Your Excellency.*

(76) a. I'm gonna fire his ass. (Collins, Moody, and Postal 2008: 36)
b. *I'm gonna fire his ass('s) friend.
c. His ass is ugly.
d. *His ass('s) car is ugly.

The divergence again undermines the idea that Mandarin pseudo-imposter DPs are on a par with English ACC DPs.

In conclusion, I presented two potential alternatives, and it has been shown that neither of them can account for Mandarin pseudo-imposter DPs or the differences between the two languages.

6. Conclusion

In this chapter, I have shown that Mandarin pseudo-imposters are structurally different from English imposters. In particular, Mandarin pseudo-imposters are parallel to the kind of nominal expression that has a co-occurring pronoun following a regular third person DP, and such a pronoun can generally occur in Mandarin DPs. This suggests that the structure of Mandarin pseudo-imposters is not so special from other instances of DPs, so no distinct sort of derivation is required. As I have argued, the pronoun in question occupies the head position and plays a crucial role in determining the ϕ-feature value of person denotation for the entire DP. In addition, the proposed analysis clearly supports the syntactic view of imposters. That is, (pseudo) imposter DPs from the two languages look quite similar, and yet their differences with regard to grammatical person denotations cannot be straightforwardly accounted for without resorting to their syntactic differences.

References

Baker, Mark. 2008. *The Syntax of Agreement and Concord*. Cambridge, UK: Cambridge University Press.

Cattaneo, Andrea. 2009. Imposters and pseudo-imposters in Bellinzonese and English. Manuscript, New York University.

Chomsky, Noam. 1995. *The Minimalist Program*. Cambridge, MA: MIT Press.

Collins, Chris, Stephanie Guitard, and Jim Wood. 2009. Imposters: An online survey of grammaticality judgments. In *NYU Working Papers in Linguistics* eds. Patricia Irwin and Violeta Vázquez Rojas Maldonado, Volume 2. New York: New York University Press.

Collins, Chris, Simanique Moody, and Paul Postal. 2008. An AAE camouflage construction. *Language* 84.1: 29–68.

Collins, Chris, and Paul M. Postal. 2012. *Imposters: A Study of Pronominal Agreement*. Cambridge, MA: MIT Press.

Dikken, Marcel den. 2006. *Relators and Linkers*. Cambridge, MA: MIT Press.

Dubinsky, Stanley, and Robert Hamilton. 1998. Epithets as Antilogophoric Pronouns. *Linguistic Inquiry* 29: 685–693.

Harley, Heidi, and Elizabeth Ritter. 2002. Person and number in pronouns: A feature-geometric analysis. *Language* 78(3): 482–526.

Huang, C.-T. James, Audrey Y.-H. Li, and Yafei Li. 2008. *The Syntax of Chinese*. Cambridge, UK: Cambridge University Press.

Kayne, Richard S. 2005. *Movement and Silence*. Oxford: Oxford University Press.

Kaufman, Daniel. 2009. Indonesian imposters. Handout for talk at New York University, October 6, 2009.

Li, Charles N. 1997. On zero anaphora. In *Essays on Language Function and Language Type. Dedicated to T. Givón*, eds. Joan Bybee, John Haiman, and Sandra A. Thompson, 275–300. Amsterdam: John Benjamins.

Li, Charles N., and Sandra A. Thompson. 1981. *Mandarin Chinese: A Functional Reference Grammar*. Berkeley: University of California Press.

Liu, C.-S. Luther. 2001. Antilogophoricity, sympathy and the sympathetic antilogophor *Renjia*. *Journal of East Asian Linguistics* 10: 307–336.

Liu, C.-S. Luther. 2004. Antilogophoricity, epithets and the empty antilogophor in Chinese. *Journal of East Asian Linguistics* 13: 257–287.

Longobardi, Giuseppe. 1994. Reference and Proper Names. *Linguistic Inquiry* 25: 609–666.

Postal, Paul M. 1966. On so-called pronouns in English. In *Report of the 17th Annual Round Table Meeting onLinguistics and Language Studies*, ed. Francis P. Dinneen, S.J., 177–206. Washington, DC: Georgetown University Press.

Stirling, Lesley, and Rodney Huddleston. 2002. Deixis and anaphora. In *The Cambridge Grammar of the English Language*, eds. Rodney Huddlestonand and Geoffrey K. Pullum, 1449–1564. Cambridge, UK: Cambridge University Press.

Wood, Jim. 2009. Icelandic imposters and the proprial article. In *NYU Working Papers in Linguistics* eds. Patricia Irwin and Violeta Vázquez Rojas Maldonado, Volume 2. New York: New York University Press.

9

Icelandic Verbal Agreement and Pronoun-Antecedent Relations

JIM WOOD AND EINAR FREYR SIGURÐSSON

1. Introduction

Collins and Postal (2012), building on work originating in Collins et al. (2008), study DPs that they refer to as "person imposters," or simply "imposters," which are defined as in (1):

(1) An imposter is a notionally X person DP that is grammatically Y person, X ≠ Y.

This is illustrated with the Icelandic example in which a father is talking to his son or daughter and refers to himself as *pabbi* "Daddy."[1]

(2) Svona svona, elskan, pabbi er hér.
there there dear Daddy is.1/3SG here
"There there, dear, Daddy is here."

This is an example of a first person imposter. The DP *pabbi* "Daddy" is notionally first person (referring to the speaker), but grammatically third person. (3) is an example of a second person imposter which has come into use in the colloquial language. Here, the speaker is referring to his addressee using a third person DP *kallinn* "the guy" instead of the second person pronoun *þú* "you."[2]

[1] The following abbreviations are used in this chapter: ACC = "accusative," DAT = "dative," F = "feminine," GEN = "genitive," IND = "indicative," INF = "infinitive," M = "masculine," NUM = "number," PL = "plural," PN = "person," REFL = "reflexive," SBJV = "subjunctive," SG = "singular," 1 = "first person," 2 = "second person," 3 = "third person." When a verb form is syncretic for person, we reflect this with a slash, so that 1/3SG in a verb's gloss means "syncretic for first and third person singular."

[2] For some imposters, we simply use the personal pronoun in the English translation line, for lack of a clear equivalent imposter in English.

(3) Hvað segir kallinn?
what says.2/3SG guy.the
"How are you?"

As we will show below, *kallinn* "the guy" can also be a first person imposter. In this chapter, we will mostly focus on first person imposters.[3]

Collins and Postal (2012) show that the syntactic behavior of imposters presents some interesting puzzles for our understanding of personhood and pronoun-antecedent relations. As discussed further below, phenomena involving imposters suggest that there is a syntactic relation between a pronoun and its antecedent, rather than a relation governed by reference (or even intended reference). In this chapter, we will address a number of issues relating to Icelandic imposters, with a focus on the effect of finite verb agreement on pronoun-antecedent relations.

Before continuing, some terminological discussion is in order. Collins and Postal (2012) argue that imposter DPs are structurally complex, and contain a null pronoun corresponding to the intended referent. For example, a first person imposter would have a null first person pronoun. The visible DP is referred to as the "secondary DP," and the null pronoun is referred to as the "notional core." These two DPs are argued to be embedded within a third DP, which is called the "shell DP." This is illustrated below.

(4)

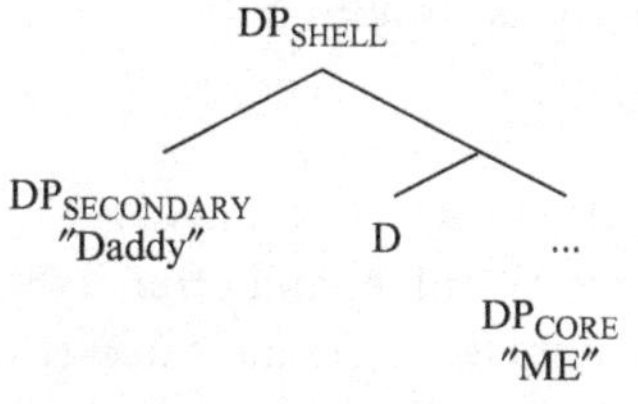

The idea of the shell DP is that imposters are similar in structure to appositives, which involve two DPs, in a predicative relation, that distribute like one DP. We will assume in what follows that imposters do have complex structure, but will remain uncommitted as to the exact nature of that structure; see Vázquez Rojas (this volume) for further discussion of the internal structure of imposter DPs.

[3] The impersonal pronoun *maður* "man, one" can also be used to refer to the speaker, and raises similar issues as imposters do, but is also different in a number of ways that go beyond the scope of this chapter (such as being formally indefinite); see Jónsson (1992) for some discussion of the antecedence properties of *maður* across clauses; see also H. Á. Sigurðsson and Egerland (2009) and E. F. Sigurðsson (2012: 94ff.) for further discussion of *maður*, and Collins and Postal (2012: 52–53) and Vázquez Rojas (this volume) for discussion of formally indefinite imposters.

2. Some Imposters in Icelandic

There are numerous examples of and types of imposters in modern Icelandic. In this study, we will for the most part limit ourselves to only a few. However, before turning to a more detailed look at agreement and pronominal/reflexive antecedence, we first give a cursory overview of a variety of imposters in the language.

One type of first person imposter involves a proper name or kinship relation, such as *mamma* "Mommy," *pabbi* "Daddy," *Jón* "John," or *Jón frændi* "Uncle John."[4]

(5) En pabbi er löngu búinn að segja þér það.
but Daddy is.1/3SG long finished to tell you that
"But Daddy already told you that a long time ago."

In this chapter, we will discuss the imposter *pabbi* "Daddy" in some detail, since its equivalent across languages has been studied in the past few years possibly more than any other type of imposter; this makes it useful for cross-linguistic comparison.

Another type of imposter, which we will also focus on here, is *undirritaður* "(the) undersigned (sg)."[5]

(6) Undirritaður hafði ætlað að hætta í stjórnmálum.
undersigned.M.SG had.1/3SG intended to stop in politics
"The undersigned had planned to quit politics."

An analogous expression has been described in a number of languages, such as English, Bellinzonese, Italian, Romanian, and Albanian, and often exhibits properties which distinguish it from other imposters (see references in section 3 below). In Icelandic, this turns out to be the case as well. First, it has the form of an adjectival participle. Second, unlike English, Romance, and Albanian, it is morphologically indefinite. Third, it can also be marked for number, and some differences between the behavior of *undirritaður* "undersigned (sg)" and *undirritaðir* "undersigned (pl)" will be discussed below.

[4] For imposter interpretations of *pabbi* "Daddy," Gunnar Hrafn Hrafnbjargarson (p.c.) prefers an extra pronoun, known as a 'proprial article', as in (i). See Wood (2009) for further discussion.

(i) En hann pabbi er löngu búinn að segja þér það.
but he Daddy is.1/3SG long finished to tell you that
"But Daddy already told you that a long time ago."

[5] As discussed below, this imposter inflects for gender and number depending on the person it refers to. When discussing the form in general, we will use the masculine singular form and in general, we will write '(sg)' or '(pl)' depending on whether it is singular or plural. All citations in conjoined phrases (e.g., *undirritaður og Jón*) are singular.

Another type of imposter is compositional and complex, and turns out to be rather common in parliament speeches. Icelandic has a kind of demonstrative, *sá* "the one," which does not necessarily require a head noun, but does require either a relative clause or some other kind of modifier. In the present case, we find a relative clause which refers to the speaker, such as *sá sem hér talar* "the one who is talking here" or *sá sem hér stendur* "the one who is standing here." The following is an attested example from a parliament discussion.[6]

(7) Þrír þingmenn úr þingflokki Vinstri hreyfingarinnar – græns framboðs,
three MPs from party Left movement – green candidate,
hv. þm.
honorable MP
Kolbrún Halldórsdóttir, hv. þm. Þuríður Backman og [**sá sem hér**
Kolbrún Halldórsdóttir, honorable MP Þuríður Backman and the.one who here
stendur],
stands.3SG
höfum lagt fram þáltill. sem hljómar á þessa lund, með leyfi
have.1PL laid forth resolution which sounds on this way, with permission
forseta.
president
"Three MPs from the Left-Green Movement, the honorable MP Kolbrún Halldórsdóttir, the honorable MP Þuríður Backman, and the one who stands here, have submitted a parliamentary resolution which sounds like this—with the permission of the president."[7]

This example is an imposter *par excellence*. Notice that the verb inside the relative clause is third person singular, showing that the relative head has the features or properties of a third person DP. However, the overall DP refers to the speaker, and despite being third singular, it is conjoined with another third person DP and controls first person agreement on the main clause verb.

Some imposters appear to have arisen rather recently, and are common in very informal speech among certain speakers, especially younger ones. The first is *kallinn*, sometimes spelled *kjellinn* (reflecting pronunciation; IPA = [kʰatl̥ɪn] and [kʰjɛtl̥ɪn], respectively). It is formally a noun with a definite suffix.[8] The second is *gamli* "old," also spelled *gjemli*. It is formally a "weak" adjective, marked as

[6] English examples similar to this are also discussed by Collins and Postal (2012: 178). The brackets in (7) are intended to help the reader parse *sá sem hér stendur* "the one who stands here" as a constituent.

[7] http://www.althingi.is/altext/125/12/r15213123.sgml

[8] The standard way of writing this is *karlinn*, though this is not how it is usually written. *Karlinn* means "the man / the old man," which is pronounced either [kʰartl̥ɪn], or the same way as *kallinn* (IPA = [kʰatl̥ɪn]). To our knowledge, *karlinn*, when written this way or pronounced [kʰartl̥ɪn], never has the imposter reading.

though it were modifying a definite noun. The examples below come from Google searches and Icelandic television.[9]

(8) a. en kjellinn ætlar samt að passa sig
but guy.the intends.2/3SG still to look.after REFL
að vera ekkert of mikið í þessu
to be not too much in this
"But I am still going to be careful not to be too involved in this."[10]

b. Fullt af monní á leiðinni. Og allir í vasann hjá **kjellinum**.
full of money on way.the and all in pocket.the by guy.the.DAT
"Lots of money on the way. And all of it into my pocket."(Næturvaktin, Ep. 10, 1: 03)

c. Nóg að gera hjá **gjémla**.
enough to do by old.DAT
"I've got plenty to do."[11]

Yet another type of imposter, *yðar einlægur*, is analogous to English *yours truly*, in form and meaning. It is similar in that like *yours truly*, it can be used to end a letter, or as an argument. The following example of it being used as an argument comes from a Google search.

(9) **Yðar einlægur** hefur undanfarnar vikur verið að velta fyrir sér . . .
yours truly has.2/3SG past.few weeks been to roll before REFL.3
"Yours truly has for the past few weeks been wondering . . ."[12]

It is different from English in that the form of the possessive pronoun, *yðar*, is an archaic honorific form (similar to German *Sie* "you") and not normally used in colloquial speech except in certain fixed expressions. Note that this form also occurs in certain fixed camouflage forms, such as *yðar hágöfgi* "your majesty" and *yðar hátign* "your highness."[13] Another camouflage construction, *þinn (lata) rass* "your (lazy) ass," uses the modern pronoun *þinn* "your."

(10) Mættu klukkan 9, ef þú getur dregið **þinn lata rass** fram úr rúminu.
meet clock 9, if you can drag your lazy ass out of bed.the
"Meet at 9 o'clock, if you can drag your lazy ass out of bed." (Wood 2009: 28)

[9] The example in (8c) is spelled with <jé> rather than <je>. This diacritic is basically redundant, since in Icelandic <é> and <je> both correspond to IPA [jɛ].

[10] http://bjorngayr.blogcentral.is/blog/2005/8/22/nau-nau-menningarnott-og-allur-pakkinn/

[11] http://www.facebook.com/permalink.php?story_fbid=104379866273338&id=113710038650861

[12] http://blogg.smugan.is/dofri/2009/12/17/ithrottaskoli-fyrir-6-8-ara-2/

[13] A camouflage construction is distinct from an imposter in that a DP determining the denotation of the whole camouflage DP is overt, in contrast to the situation with imposters. For example, *yðar hágöfgi* "your majesty" is used to refer to the addressee (i.e., it is second person), and *yðar* is a second person pronoun. In contrast, *yðar einlægur* "yours truly" is used to refer to the speaker, so the second person pronoun *yðar* is not the referent of the whole DP.

Certain relational expressions such as *þinn auðmjúki þjónn* "your humble servant" also have (first person, non-camouflage) imposter uses.

(11) **Þinn auðmjúki þjónn** bíður tilskipanar þinnar.
your humble servant awaits.2/3SG command your
"Your humble servant awaits your command." (Wood 2009: 27)

Imposters can also be formed with demonstratives such as *þessi* "this" plus a noun naming some kind of role or job title, as in *þessi fréttamaður* "this reporter." The following is an example taken from Google of an imposter use of *þessi bloggari* "this blogger."[14]

(12) Hann fer tvímælalaust á lista yfir bestu tónleika
it.M goes undoubtedly on list over best concerts
sem **þessi bloggari** hefur farið á.
that this blogger has.2/3SG gone to
"It undoubtedly goes on the list of the best concerts that this blogger has ever gone to."[15]

It is unclear whether plural imposters with demonstratives of this sort can be formed. Speakers seem to vary in whether they accept imposter uses of *þessir fréttamenn* "these reporters," in English as well as in Icelandic. A further, similar case involves nouns like "author." Translations for "the present authors" (*núverandi/viðstaddir höfundar*) do not have imposter readings in Icelandic. Imposters of the sort *höfundar þessarar greinar* "(the) authors of this article" (with genitive case on "this article") are possible. An example from the web is presented in (13).

(13) Í rúm tvö ár hafa **höfundar þessarar greinar**
for around two years have.3PL authors this.GEN article.GEN
verið í hópi þeirra fjölmörgu sem nota samskiptavefinn Facebook.
been in group those many who use networking.site.the Facebook
"For a little more than two years, the authors of this article have been among the many who use the networking site Facebook."[16]

[14] Strikingly, a singular demonstrative can occur without a noun and form an imposter. In the following example in (i), reportedly heard by Júlía Hermannsdóttir (p.c.), a father is speaking to his infant child:

(i) Kannski að **þessi** geti hjálpað þér.
maybe that this can.1/3.SG.SBJV help you
"Maybe this one (=I) can help you."

[15] http://www.raudhausar.com/jonknutur/?p=1466

[16] http://skemman.is/stream/get/1946/6833/18602/3/70-79_HilmarThorBjarnason_GudbjorgHKolbeins_FELMANbok.pdf

Unfortunately, we are not able to address plural definite imposters in Icelandic in this chapter. Such a study would be an important next step in understanding plural imposters such as *undirritaðir* "undersigned (pl)," but at a first pass, the relevant judgments are unclear, so it must unfortunately be set aside.

Before concluding this section, it seems appropriate to mention the existence of a construction which seems to be a type of camouflage construction, characteristic of children's speech. This form is illustrated below in (14) with an example from an online discussion of it.

(14)	Þinns	má	vera	Barbie	ef	minns	má	vera	Action Man.
	ÞINNS	may.1/3SG	be	Barbie	if	MINNS	may.1/3SG	be	Action Man.

"You can be Barbie if I can be Action Man."[17]

Here, we have the expressions *minns* and *þinns*, apparently constructed from masculine, singular, nominative possessive pronouns in the first and second person (*minn/þinn*) respectively, and an *-s* that resembles the genitive *-s*. Outside this usage, however, *minns* and *þinns* are not well-formed expressions in Icelandic.[18] This seems to be related to imposters and/or camouflage constructions in the sense that it is equally possible to use the ordinary first and second person pronouns in these cases.[19] This expression has the flavor of child language which is used in informal speech. It is not used exclusively by children, but when a speaker uses it, s/he relies on the other speaker knowing that it comes from child language.

Þinns and *minns* often control third person agreement and apparantly only occur in the first and second person. However, when conjoined with another third person DP, they can control first person agreement, as in the following example found on Google:

(15)	Minns	og	lögfræðingurinn	tilvonandi	**erum**	**búnir**	
	MINNS	and	lawyer.the	future	are.1PL	finished.M.PL	

	að	vera	húkkt	á	á	[*sic*]	þessum	geggjaða	leik.
	to	be	hooked	on	on		this	crazy	game

"Me and the future lawyer have been hooked on this awesome game."[20]

[17] http://www.visindavefur.is/svar.php?id=6411

[18] Hlíf Árnadóttir points out to us that the feminine form *míns* seems to exist in this use as well. Unlike *minns*, this morphological form does exist independently as the genitive forms of the masculine and neuter possessive pronouns. Presumably, in this use, it is structurally parallel to *minns*, being built on the nominative feminine form *mín* (*mín*+-s), its morphological relation to the masculine and neuter genitive forms being somewhat coincidental. Note also that *minns*, *þinns*, etc., apparently do not inflect for case.

[19] The imposter-like use of this construction can be illustrated also from a blog post titled *Minns á Google* "Minns on Google." The first line of the post says *Það að gúggla sjálfan sig er göfug íþrótt og góð skemmtan* "To google oneself is a noble activity and good fun." It is thus clear that the author is using *minns* to refer to himself. http://www.thorarinn.com/dagbok/20110701google

[20] http://leikari.blogspot.com/2004/05/keiluleikur-o.html

(16) Minns og Búbbó **erum komnar** í hóp sorglegra bloggara,
MINNS and Búbbó are.1PL come.F.PL in group sad bloggers.GEN
höngum hér heima, **rífumst** í druslum og **bloggum** um þá!
hang.1PL here at.home fight.1PL in sluts and blog.1PL about them
"Me and Búbbó have joined the group of sad bloggers, hanging around here at home, picking on sluts and blogging about them!"[21]

Note, moreover, that *minns* can control number and gender agreement on verbal participles, as shown in (15) with *búnir* "finished" and (16) with *komnar* "come." This happens even in the singular, where finite verb agreement is third person. We have also found an example of second person *þinns* anteceding what appears to be a third person reflexive possessive pronoun with the same -*s*, as shown in (18).

(17) En vildi bara láta vita að minns er **komin** heim.
but wanted just let know that MINNS is.1/3SG come.F.SG home
"But just wanted to let it be known that I have come home."[22]

(18) hvernær [*sic*] vill **þinns** fá fötin **sinn-s**??
when wants.3SG ÞINNS get clothes.the REFL.POSS-S
"When do you want to get your clothes?"[23]

There also seem to exist first and second person plural forms, *okka(r)s* and *ykka(r) s*, respectively, apparently built on the stem of the genitive/possessive forms of the pronouns (*okka-r*/*ykka-r*) plus -*s*. (The -*r*- appears variably.) These forms are less common, however, and not all speakers have heard of them. Examples of *okka(r)s* "we" can be found with third person agreement in the singular and plural, as well as first person plural agreement. We have not conducted a full study of the agreement possibilities with these forms, but such a study would seem to be a worthwhile topic for future research.

In the following section, we discuss previous work on imposters, in Icelandic and other languages. Then, we focus on the agreement and pronominal/reflexive antecedence properties of the following imposters: *undirritaður* "undersigned (sg)," *undirritaðir* "undersigned (pl)," *undirritaður og X* "the undersigned and X," *pabbi* "Daddy," and *mamma og pabbi* "Mommy and Daddy." We will discuss some other imposters along the way, and then turn to a closer look at some specific properties of *undirritaður* "undersigned (sg)."

3. Previous Work

Previous work on imposters has addressed a number of issues cross-linguistically, including some preliminary work on verbal agreement. Wood (2009)

[21] http://bibbobubbo.blogspot.com/2003_02_16_archive.html#89268523
[22] http://harpaskarpa.123.is/blog/2008/10/11/302894/
[23] http://telmag.blogcentral.is/blog/2005/10/5/helgin-byrjar-a-thridjudegi/

studies the interaction of Icelandic imposters with an optional pronoun (known as the "proprial article") that occurs with certain DPs in the language (see H. Á. Sigurðsson 2006). That study also includes a first probe into Icelandic verbal agreement with imposters, which is pursued in more detail here. Das (2011) discusses imposters in Bengali, a language which is apparently quite strict in that first and second person pronouns generally cannot take imposter antecedents. She proposes that this is related to the rich verbal agreement exhibited by Bengali, and provides some preliminary comparison with English, Italian, and Albanian. While we will show that the strictest form of Das's proposal cannot be maintained, we think that her intuition is on the right track and is worth refining. We will show that verbal agreement does indeed play a surprisingly important role in pronoun-antecedent relations in Icelandic. However, we will also show that the relevant facts are more complicated than Das's proposal would suggest. First, different imposters behave differently with respect to verbal agreement in Icelandic. Second, agreement effects can be shown, on the basis of syncretism and ECM contexts, to be only partially morphological. Third, in addition to agreement, a number of other properties are involved, including whether the pronoun is subject or object and whether the mood of the clause is subjunctive or indicative. For reflexives, the type of reflexive (inherent, natural, or disjoint) is apparently relevant in some cases as well. Fourth, and most importantly certain mismatches between agreement and antecedence are possible: an imposter that triggers third person agreement may antecede a first person pronoun, but an imposter that triggers first person agreement may not antecede a third person pronoun.

Our primary goal in this chapter is to refine our understanding of the role of verbal agreement in pronoun/reflexive-antecedent relations. Icelandic verbal agreement is quite "rich." Many verbal paradigms have a distinct form for each person/number slot. Others have syncretism in the singular between second and third person or first and third person.[24]

(19) *sjá* "see" (present ind.) *hafa* "have" (present ind.) *vera* "be" (present ind.)

	SG	PL		SG	PL		SG	PL
1st	sé	sjáum	1st	hef	höfum	1st	er	erum
2nd	sérð	sjáið	2nd	hefur	hafið	2nd	ert	eruð
3rd	sér	sjá	3rd	hefur	hafa	3rd	er	eru

Despite having rich agreement morphology, Icelandic is not a referential *pro*-drop language (see H. Á. Sigurðsson and Egerland 2009 and H. Á. Sigurðsson 2010 for recent discussion). The combination of rich agreement morphology and

[24] First and third person are syncretic in the past tense and subjunctive.

the absence of referential *pro* constrains the space of plausible analyses for the effects seen in this chapter.[25]

However, in order to study the effect of imposters on verbal agreement, a number of other issues must be addressed along the way. Work on imposters in the past few years has revealed several cross-linguistic tendencies, despite (often very fine-grained) differences among individual languages, dialects, and idiolects. Many of these tendencies are also evident in Icelandic. First, an imposter coordinated with a third person DP is more likely to show first person effects than a non-coordinate plural imposter, which in turn is more likely to show first person effects than a singular imposter. By "more likely" here, we are referring both to intraspeaker comparative judgments across constructions, as well as to variation across languages. Second, imposters corresponding to participial forms such as "the undersigned" tend to be more likely to show first person effects than imposters like "Daddy." This has been shown most clearly in Cattaneo (2007, 2009) for Bellinzonese (*al sotuscrit*), a northern Italian dialect, and similar facts have been presented in Servidio (this volume) for Italian (*il sottoscritto*), in Soare (2010) for Romanian (*subsemnatul*), and will be evident below in the Icelandic data on *undirritaður* as well.[26]

4. Verbal Agreement

In general, we will see that verbal agreement with imposters in Icelandic exhibits the following tendency: plural and coordinate imposters are more likely to control first person agreement than singular imposters, and among singular imposters, "the undersigned" is more likely to control first person agreement than "Daddy" or "this reporter." To illustrate these points, consider first that singular imposters basically do not allow first person agreement, as shown in (20a–b). By comparison, first person agreement on the plural *undirritaðir* "the undersigned (pl)," while not perfect, is much better than on the singular *undirritaður* "the undersigned (sg)," as shown in (20c).

(20) a. (Hann) pabbi {hefur / *hef} sagt þér það.
(he) Daddy {has.3SG / *1SG} told you that
"Daddy has told you that."
b. Undirritaður {hefur / *hef} ákveðið að hætta.
undersigned.M.SG {has.3SG / *1SG} decided to quit
"The undersigned (sg) has decided to quit."

[25] Rögnvaldsson (1993) proposes that referential *pro* is possible in Icelandic sentence coordination structures, but that *pro* cannot be identified by verbal inflection in Icelandic, essentially because Icelandic has oblique subjects, which do not agree with the finite verb. The important point for the present analysis is that rich agreement cannot identify, and in effect cannot license *pro* in Icelandic. See also Dudley (this volume) for independent arguments against a *pro* analysis of imposter agreement in Spanish; it is noted there that a *pro* analysis cannot easily account for the fact that plural imposters trigger first person agreement much more easily than singular imposters.

[26] Note that while not always explicitly discussed as special, "undersigned" imposters play a role in most of the other contributions to this volume as well.

c. Undirritaðir {hafa / ?höfum} haldið þessu fram.
undersigned.M.PL {have.3PL / ?1PL} held this forth
"The undersigned (pl) have claimed this."

While the second author and several other speakers we have consulted find a difference between *undirritaður* "undersigned (sg)" and *undirritaðir* "undersigned (pl)," as indicated in (20) above, we should note that we do find attested examples of *undirritaður* "undersigned (sg)" with first person agreement on the web, such as the following:[27]

(21) a. Undirritaður **hef** kynnt **mér**
undersigned.M.SG have.1SG familiarized myself
skilmála fyrir Dælulykil Atlantsolíu.
conditions for discount.key Atlantsolía
"The undersigned (sg) has familiarized myself with the conditions for the Atlantsolía discount key."

b. Undirritaður **hef** verið ráðgjafi fjölda fyrirtækja og
undersigned.M.SG have.1SG been consultant many.GEN companies and
fjárfesta.
investors
"The undersigned (sg) has been a consultant of many companies and investors."

In (22), we provide some attested examples of *undirritaðir/undirritaðar* "undersigned (pl.m/f)" taking first person plural agreement.[28]

(22) a. Undirritaðir **erum** að vinna að lokaritgerð
undersigned.M.PL are.1PL to work to final.thesis
til B.S gráðu í íþróttafræðum.
for B.S. degree in athletic.studies
"The undersigned (pl) are working on their final thesis for a B.S. degree in athletic studies."

b. Undirritaðar **ætlum** að taka það að **okkur** að
undersigned.F.PL intend.1PL to take it to ourselves to
versla í sameiginlega
shop in joint
máltíð fyrir laugardagskvöldið og kaupa smá snakk og nammi.
meal for Saturday.evening and buy little snack and candy
"The undersigned (pl) plan on taking it upon ourselves to shop together for Saturday evening's meal and buy some snacks and candy."

[27] (21a) was retrieved from https://secure.fib.is/daelulykill.php on 9/21/2011. Notice the reflexive in (21a) first person, consistent with the generalizations discussed below. (21b) was retrieved from http://blog.eyjan.is/larahanna/2008/07/20/peningar-um-peninga-fra-peningum-til-hvers-2/#comment-15029 on 9/21/2011.

[28] (22a) was retrieved from http://skemman.is/stream/get/1946/745/1956/2/Fylgiskjal.pdf on 9/14/2011; (22b) from http://idjur.blogcentral.is/blog/2010/10/11/ferdin-2010/ on 9/21/2011.

Despite the fact that first person agreement is attested with both singular and plural uses of "undersigned," we will continue to take seriously the native speaker judgments indicating that there is a difference, leaving open the possibility that some speakers might freely accept both variants. Note that in addition to the native speaker judgments in (20a), we have found no attested (or accepted) examples of imposter *pabbi* "Daddy" with first person singular agreement, which further illustrates the point shown below that "undersigned" shows first person effects more commonly/easily than "Daddy."

When we turn to coordinate DPs (CoPs), we find that first person agreement is more acceptable with certain imposters than others. When *undirritaður* "undersigned (sg)" is coordinated, either first or third person agreement is possible. When *pabbi* "Daddy" is coordinated, first person agreement is much less acceptable.

(23) a. Undirritaður og Jón {hafa / höfum } haldið þessu fram.
undersigned.M.SG and John {have.3PL / 1PL } held this forth
"The undersigned and John have claimed this."

b. Mamma og pabbi {hafa / ??höfum } sagt þér þetta áður.
Mamma og pabbi {have.3PL / ??1PL } told you this before
"Mommy and Daddy told you this before."

Not all speakers would agree with these judgments exactly. However, in each case—for speakers who get a contrast at all—first person is clearly better in the coordinated case than in the singular case, which is completely out. As far as we know, no speakers have the opposite judgment, preferring agreement in the singular case over the coordinated case.

Agreement with CoPs containing a second person pronoun varies crosslinguistically. In Icelandic, as originally discussed in Wood (2009), such agreement is always either third person (for the majority of speakers) or first person (for fewer speakers), but never second person, as far as we know.[29]

(24) a. *Þú og pabbi **ætlið** að fara saman í vinnuna í dag.
you and Daddy intend.2PL to go together to work today

b. % Þú og pabbi **ætla** að fara saman í vinnuna í dag.
you and Daddy intend.3PL to go together to work today

c. % Þú og pabbi **ætlum** að fara saman í vinnuna í dag.
you and Daddy intend.1PL to go together to work today
"You and Daddy are going to work together today." (Wood 2009: 19)

[29] The "%" notation in (24) is meant to indicate that speakers vary in terms of whether they accept (24b) or (24c). As noted in the main text, (24b) is more frequently accepted among the speakers we have asked than (24c).

(24b) is of particular interest because it threatens the Illegal Coordinate Person Value Assignment Condition (ICPVAC) of Collins and Postal (2012: 117). The ICPVAC says, "If C is a conjunctive coordinate DP, then no conjunct of C outranks C." "Outrank" refers to a hierarchy of person features where first person outranks second person, and second person outranks third person (as also discussed by Friðjónsson 1990–1991). Thus, *you and I* is a first person DP, and *you and John* is a second person DP. In example (24b), however, the verb agreement is third person, but one of the conjuncts is second person.

This seems to be more general than imposters. Friðjónsson (1990–1991) reports that a coordinated subject containing a second person pronoun is not always completely ungrammatical with third person agreement.

(25)	a.	?Þú	og	konan	fóru	á bíó.
		you	and	woman.the	went.3PL	to movie
		"You and the woman went to a movie."				
	b.	Þú	og	konan	fóruð	á bíó.
		you	and	woman.the	went.2PL	to movie
		"You and the woman went to a movie."				(Friðjónsson 1990–1991: 81)

Relatedly, with a second person genitive partitive, third person agreement is actually preferable, though second person agreement is possible. This is dependent on the person features of the partitive, as shown in (26c)

(26)	a.	Mörg	ykkar	vita	. . .
		many. NOM	you.PL.GEN	know.3PL	. . .
		"Many of you know . . ."			
	b.	(?) Mörg	ykkar	vitið	. . .
		many.NOM	you.PL.GEN	know.2PL	. . .
		"Many of you know . . ."			(Friðjónsson 1990–1991: 81)
	c.	*Mörg	okkar	vitið	. . .
		many. NOM	us.PL.GEN	know.2PL	

Partitives play an important role in uncovering conditions on pronominal antecedence in Collins and Postal (2012) (see especially pp. 169–176), and the data in (26) show that they might play an important role in developing a better understanding of the triggers of verbal agreement (see also den Dikken 2001 on "pluringulars"). For now, we point this out because it is another example of a complex DP containing second person features which may or may not result in third person agreement. The main point is that given that verbal agreement is a syntactic process, the ungrammaticality of (24a) shows that the interpretation of a third person DP as first person has its roots in a syntactic process.

5. Reflexive Antecedence

As has long been known, Icelandic has a rather complicated reflexive system (Sigurjónsdóttir 1992). In the typology of Reuland's (2011) monograph, Icelandic is described as having the most complex system (a "four-way" system), and is arguably even more complex than Reuland (2011) indicates. We will see below that reflexive/antecedence forms are sometimes sensitive to the type of reflexive construction. We are not in a position to offer an account as to why this is, but include it for now as a control on the data. More research would be required to understand exactly what the facts are with respect to a more sophisticated set of properties of reflexive predicates. For now, we will focus our preliminary discussion on three types of reflexives: inherent reflexives, natural reflexives, and naturally disjoint reflexives (cf. Schäfer 2012 and references therein). Inherent reflexives include *skemmta sér* "enjoy oneself/have fun" and *skammast sín* "be/feel ashamed of oneself." They have the property that they can only take a reflexive object (not a non-reflexive object), and a simplex reflexive at that (i.e., without "self").[30] The simplex reflexive can be accusative (*sig*), dative (*sér*), or genitive (*sín*). Natural reflexives include *auglýsa* "advertise" and *raka* "shave"; these verbs ordinarily take a simplex reflexive, but can take a non-reflexive DP object, and do allow a complex "self" reflexive, if used with contrastive focus. Naturally disjoint reflexives such as *elska* "love" do not normally allow a simplex reflexive, but rather require a complex "self" reflexive. This is summarized in (27) below.

(27)

	Simplex	"Self"	Disjoint obj.	Examples
Naturally disjoint	No	Yes	Yes	*elska* "love"
Natural reflexives	Yes	Focus	Yes	*auglýsa* "advertise" *raka* "shave"
Inherent reflexives	Yes	No	No	*skemmta* "enjoy" *skammast* "ashame"

This does not do full justice to the complexity of the reflexive system in Icelandic and the areas of grammar where it is relevent, but it is sufficient for present purposes. See Reuland (2011) for recent theoretical discussion and Árnadóttir et al. (2011) for a number of further subtypes of reflexive constructions.

As discussed in Collins and Postal (2012: 125–128) with respect to French, verbal agreement plays a role in the acceptability of reflexive antecedence. We will show that the same holds for Icelandic. This is perhaps a welcome and unsurprising result, given that a number of theories in recent years have proposed that the dependency between a reflexive and its antecedent is mediated by an

[30] As discussed by Árnadóttir et al., (2011), *skemmta* also has a non-reflexive use meaning "entertain," but the readings are distinct enough for present purposes.

agreement (or Agree) relation involving the verb, directly or indirectly (Reuland 2006, 2011; Heim 2008; Hicks 2009; Kratzer 2009). To illustrate with a clear case, when *undirritaður* "undersigned (sg)" is conjoined and takes first person agreement, only a first person reflexive is possible. When the same CoP takes third person agreement, only a third person reflexive is possible.[31,32]

(28) a. Undirritaður og Jón$_j$ skammast {*okkar$_{i+j}$ / sín$_{i+j}$ } fyrir
undersigned.M.SG and John shame.3PL {*ourselves / themselves } for
ummælin.
comments.the
"The undersigned and John feel ashamed for their comments."

b. Undirritaður$_i$ og Jón$_j$ skömmumst {okkar$_{i+j}$ / *sín } fyrir
undersigned.M.SG and John shame.1PL {ourselves / *themselves } for
ummælin.
comments.the
"The undersigned and John feel ashamed for their comments."

When the coordinate imposter is in an ECM subject position, and thus triggers no agreement, either is possible, though the first person reflexive is a bit odd in some cases.

(29) a. Þeir töldu undirritaðan$_i$ og Jón$_j$
they believed undersigned.M.SG.ACC and John
skammast {?okkar$_{i+j}$ / sín$_{i+j}$ } fyrir ummælin.
shame.INF {?ourselves / themselves } for comments.the
"They believed the undersigned and John to feel ashamed for our comments."

b. Þeir sáu undirritaðan$_i$ og Jón$_j$
they saw undersigned.M.SG.ACC and John
auglýsa {(?)okkur$_{i+j}$ / sig$_{i+j}$ } í sjónvarpinu.
advertise.INF {(?)ourselves / themselves } in television.the
"They saw the undersigned and John advertise themselves on TV."

c. Þeir töldu undirritaðan$_i$ og Jón$_j$
they believed undersigned.M.SG.ACC and John
elska sjálfa {?okkur$_{i+j}$ / sig$_{i+j}$ } meira en allt annað.
love.INF self {?our / their } more than everything else
"They believed the undersigned and John to love themselves more than anything else."

[31] In this and the following sections, subscripts will be used to indicate intended reference, with no commitment to any theoretical status of indices in grammar. Note also that in all of the following examples, "undersigned" or "Daddy" will be understood to be the speaker.

[32] Different verbs may assign different morphological cases to their objects, but as far as we can tell, this makes no difference for any of the judgments below, so we avoid cluttering the glosses with detailed annotations for case marking. For the interested reader, the cases of reflexive pronouns used below are as follows: *sig* "accusative," *sér* "dative" and *sín* "genitive," for third person; *mig* "accusative," *mér* "dative," and *mín* "genitive," for first person singular; *okkur* "accusative/dative (syncretic)" and *okkar* "genitive" for first person plural.

Since singular imposters do not easily take first person agreement, it might be expected independently of anything else that first person anaphors are not possible in finite contexts. This is so, even when the verb in question is morphologically syncretic for first and third person, as in the examples below.[33]

(30) a. Undirritaður skammast {*mín$_i$ / sín$_i$ } fyrir ummælin.
undersigned.M.SG shame.1/2/3SG {*myself / himself } for comments.the
"The undersigned (sg) feels ashamed due to his comments."
b. Pabbi$_i$ skemmti {*mér$_i$ / sér$_i$ } vel í gær.
Daddy enjoyed.1/3SG {*myself / himself } well yesterday
"Daddy enjoyed himself yesterday."

However, the asymmetry between singular and plural imposters goes further than this. Recall that when agreement is controlled for with an ECM predicate, the plural cases allow both first and third person reflexives, though the latter are preferable. Even when agreement is controlled for with an ECM predicate, where there is never any overt agreement, there is a clear contrast between the plural cases in (29) and the singular ones shown in (31) and (32) below.

(31) a. Þeir töldu undirritaðan$_i$
they believed undersigned.M.SG.ACC
skammast {*mín$_i$ / sín$_i$ } fyrir ummælin.
shame.INF {*myself / himself } for comments.the
"They believed the undersigned (sg) to feel ashamed for his comments."
b. Þeir sáu undirritaðan$_i$
they saw undersigned.M.SG.ACC
auglýsa {??mig$_i$ / sig$_i$ } í sjónvarpinu.
advertise.INF {??myself / himself } in television.the
"They saw the undersigned (sg) advertise himself on TV."
c. Þeir töldu undirritaðan$_i$
they believed undersigned.M.SG.ACC
elska sjálfan {*mig$_i$ / sig$_i$ } meira en allt annað.
love.INF self {*my / his } more than everything else
"They believed the undersigned (sg) to love himself more than anything else."

(32) a. Þeir sáu pabba$_i$ skemmta {*mér$_i$ / sér$_i$ } vel í gær.
they saw Daddy enjoy.INF {*myself / himself } well yestarday
"They saw Daddy enjoying himself yesterday."
b. Þeir sáu pabba$_i$ raka {*mig$_i$ / sig$_i$ } í gær.
they saw Daddy shave.INF {*myself / himself } yesterday
"They saw Daddy shaving himself yesterday."

[33] As indicated, *skammast* "shame" is in fact syncretic for all persons in the singular, though it does make person distinctions in the plural.

c. Þeir töldu pabba$_i$
they believed Daddy
elska sjálfan {*mig$_i$ / sig$_i$ } meira en allt annað.
love.INF self {*my / his } more than eveything else
"They believed Daddy to love himself more than anything else."

Just as morphological syncretism on the finite verb does not help singular imposters antecede first person reflexives, putting a singular imposter in a non-agreeing ECM subject position does not help either. This singular/plural asymmetry cannot, then, be attributed directly to the independent asymmetry with morphological agreement. When imposter *pabbi* "Daddy" is coordinated, the effect is somewhere in between these two cases—while inherent reflexives exclude a first person anaphor, for natural reflexives and naturally disjoint predicates, first person is not as bad as the singular case, but worse than coordinated *undirritaður* "undersigned (sg)."

(33) a. Þeir sáu mömmu og pabba$_j$
they saw Mommy and Daddy
skemmta {*okkur$_{i+j}$ / sér$_{i+j}$ } vel í gær.
enjoy.INF {*ourselves / themselves } well yesterday
"They saw Mommy and Daddy enjoy themselves yesterday."

b. Lögreglan sá mömmu$_i$ og pabba$_j$
police.the saw Mommy and Daddy
raka {??okkur$_{i+j}$ / sig$_{i+j}$ } á ströndinni í gær.
shave.INF {??ourselves/ themselves } on beach.the yesterday
"The police saw Mommy and Daddy shaving themselves on the beach yesterday."

c. Þeir töldu mömmu$_i$ og pabba$_j$
they believed Mommy and Daddy
elska sjálf {??okkur$_{i+j}$ / sig$_{i+j}$ } meira en allt annað.
love.INF self {??our / their } more than everything else
"They believed Mommy and Daddy to love themselves more than anything else."

Again, the difference between (32b-c) on the one hand and (33b-c) on the other cannot be attributed to morphological subject-verb agreement.

Undirritaðir "the undersigned (pl)" is slightly worse with a first person reflexive than *undirritaður og Jón* "the undersigned and John," but not as bad as *mamma og pabbi* "Mommy and Daddy."

(34) a. Þeir töldu undirritaða$_{i+j}$
they believed undersigned.M.PL.ACC
skammast {?okkar$_{i+j}$ / sín$_{i+j}$ } fyrir ummælin.
shame.INF {?ourselves / themselves } for comments.the
"They believed the undersigned (pl) to feel ashamed of ourselves for our comments."

Table 9.1 **Reflexive Predicates in ECM Contexts**

	1st Inherent	*1st Natural*	*1st Disjoint*
Daddy	*	*	*
Undersigned	*	??	*
Mommy and Daddy	*	??	??
Undersigned (plural)	?	?	??
Undersigned and John	?	(?)	?

b. Þeir sáu undirritaða$_{i+j}$
they saw undersigned.M.PL.ACC
auglýsa {?okkur$_{i+j}$ / sig$_{i+j}$ } í sjónvarpinu.
advertize.INF {?ourselves / themselves } in television.the
"They saw the undersigned (pl) advertize ourselves on TV."

c. Þeir töldu undirritaða$_{i+j}$
they believed undersigned.M.PL.ACC
elska sjálfa {??okkur$_{i+j}$ / sig$_{i+j}$} meira en allt annað.
love.INF self {??our / their} more than everything else
"They believed the undersigned (pl) to love ourselves more than anything else."

The data discussed so far are summarized in Table 9.1.

Here, we see that plurals with first person reflexives are generally better than singulars with first person reflexives. We also see some effects of the type of reflexives. Natural reflexives are slightly better than the others in the first person, and inherent reflexives are slightly better in the first person than disjoint reflexives are.

Given the above, it doesn't seem obvious that *mamma og pabbi* "Mommy and Daddy" behaves differently from singular *pabbi* "Daddy" and *undirrtaður* "the undersigned (sg)," since the reported difference between them is so slight ('??' versus '*'). However, turning to more complex constructions reveals a much stronger difference between singular *pabbi* "Daddy" and coordinated *mamma og pabbi* "Mommy and Daddy." Like in English, a preposed purpose clause improves the first person reflexive in the plural even more, to the point where third person is actually quite odd, as illustrated in (35a).[34]

[34] Control into purpose clauses can in general improve the first person reflexive with a plural imposter, and is better than control into a complement clause.

(i) Þeir létu mömmu$_i$ og pabba$_j$ byggja sérstakt herbergi til að
they made Mommy and Daddy build.INF special room for to
raka {?okkur$_{i+j}$ / sig$_{i+j}$ } í.
shave {?ourselves / themselves } in
"They made Mommy and Daddy build a special room to shave in."

(ii) Þeir telja mömmu$_i$ og pabba$_j$ vonast til að raka
they believe Mommy and Daddy hope.INF for to shave
{*okkur$_{i+j}$ / sig$_{i+j}$ } einhvern tímann.
{*ourselves / themselves } some time
"They believe Mommy and Daddy to hope to shave someday."

Note, however, that first person singular is still quite bad here, as illustrated in (35b).[35]

(35) a. Til þess að læra að raka {okkur$_{i+j}$ / *sig$_{i+j}$ } betur,
for it to learn to shave {ourselves / *themselves } better,
sagði Jón frændi mömmu$_i$ og pabba$_j$ að fara á námskeið.
told John Uncle Mommy and Daddy to go to class
"In order to learn to shave better, Uncle John told Mommy and Daddy to take a class."

b. Til þess að læra að raka {??mig$_i$ / sig$_j$ } betur,
for it to learn to shave {??myself / himself } better,
sagði mamma pabba$_i$ að fara á námskeið.
told Mommy Daddy to go to class
"In order to learn to shave better, Mommy told Daddy to take a class."

Thus, even with the imposter use of *pabbi* "Daddy," an imposter which doesn't seem to trigger first person agreement on its own, we can find a strong difference in coordinated cases such as *mamma og pabbi* "Mommy and Daddy."

What we have shown in this section is that different imposters react differently to different reflexive types—even when overt morphology is controlled for by using non-finite contexts. We also saw a number of other constraints that cannot be attributed directly to verbal agreement, such as the difference between singulars and plurals in terms of the availability of an imposter anteceding a first person reflexive (as illustrated by the contrast between (31) and (32), on the one hand, versus (33) and (34), on the other). Still, overt agreement morphology does make a difference in constraining reflexive-antecedent relations. When agreement is unambiguously first person, the reflexive must be first person. When agreement is third person, the reflexive must be third person.[36]

[35] Note that we find homogeneity (mismatch) effects as well, so that there can be a first person reflexive in the preposed clause and a third person reflexive in the lower clause.

(i) Til þess að læra að raka {okkur$_{i+j}$ / *sig$_{i+j}$ } betur, sagði Jón
for it to learn to shave {ourselves / *themselves } better told John
frændi mömmu$_i$ og pabba$_j$ að hvíla sig áður en
Uncle Mommy and Daddy to relax themselves before
námskeiðið byrjar.
class.the begins
"In order to learn to shave better, Uncle John told Mommy and Daddy to relax before the class begins."

This effect seems to be the same as in English, discussed in detail in Collins and Postal (2012: 186–189), though we cannot discuss it further here.

[36] The effect is weaker when agreement is third person, however.

6. Pronominal Antecedence

6.1 DIRECT OBJECTS

Many theories of reflexive antecedence might welcome the result that verbal agreement can constrain the ability of a third person DP to antecede a first person reflexive, as in, for example (28a), and that this can be ameliorated to some extent when agreement is controlled for, as in ECM contexts such as (29a). Most of them would probably be hard pressed to find an explanation for the strong singular/plural asymmetry, let alone the differences between different imposters. What is even more surprising, however, is that just as verbal agreement seems to make a difference in the acceptability of first person reflexives with imposter antecedents, so too does it make a difference with first person pronouns with imposter antecedents. To start with a particularly clear case, we illustrate with the coordinated "undersigned."[37]

(36) a. Undirritaður$_i$ og Jón$_j$ **hafa** áður sagt
undersigned.M.SG and John have.3PL before said
að yfirvöld vilji bara móðga {**okkur**$_{i+j}$ / ?**þá**$_{i+j}$ }.
that authorities want.SBJV just insult {us / ?them }
"The undersigned and John have said before that the authorities just want to insult us."

b. Undirritaður$_i$ og Jón$_j$ **höfum** áður sagt
undersigned.M.SG and John have.1PL before said
að yfirvöld vilji bara móðga {**okkur**$_{i+j}$ / ***þá**$_{i+j}$ }.
that authorities want.SBJV just insult {us / *them }
"The undersigned and John have said before that the authorities just want to insult us."

Here, the third person pronoun is not perfect in either case. But whereas it is only slightly odd when the antecedent controls third person agreement, it is much worse or completely out when the antecedent controls first person agreement. Note that the mood of the complement clause makes no difference in this case, as shown in the following examples which are indicative rather than subjunctive.

(37) a. Undirritaður$_i$ og Jón$_j$ **uppgötvuðu** í fyrra
undersigned.M.SG and John discovered.3PL last year
að stjórnin vill reka {**okkur**$_{i+j}$ / ?**þá**$_{i+j}$ }.
that management wants.IND fire {us / ?them }
"The undersigned and John discovered last year that management wants to fire us."

[37] In the following examples, some verbs glossed as subjunctive are morphologically syncretic with indicative forms (e.g., first/second plural forms); the glosses are based on syntactic distribution, and are in many cases morphologically distinct.

b. Undirritaður$_i$ og Jón$_j$ **uppgötvuðum** í fyrra
undersigned.M.SG and John discovered.1PL last year
að stjórnin vill reka {**okkur**$_{i+j}$ / *****þá**$_{i+j}$ }.
that management wants.IND fire {us / *them}
"The undersigned and John discovered last year that management wants to fire us."

The same effect obtains when plural "undersigned" takes first person agreement and antecedes a pronoun in the complement clause; the pronoun must be first person, and third person is unacceptable. The mood of the complement clause makes no difference here either.

(38) a. Undirritaðir$_{i+j}$ **höfum** áður sagt
undersigned.M.PL have.1PL before said
að yfirvöld **vilji** bara móðga {**okkur**$_{i+j}$ / *****þá**$_{i+j}$ }.
that authorities want.SBJV just insult {us / *them}
"The undersigned (pl) have said before that the authorities just want to insult us."

b. Undirritaðir$_{i+j}$ **uppgötvuðum** í fyrra
undersigned.M.PL discovered.1PL last year}
að stjórnin **vill** reka {**okkur**$_{i+j}$ / *****þá**$_{i+j}$ }.
that management wants.IND fire {us / *them}
"The undersigned (pl) discovered last year that management wants to fire us."

When plural "undersigned" takes third person agreement and antecedes a pronoun in a complement clause, the first person pronoun is generally preferred and the third person pronoun is at least dispreferred, in some cases odd. The contrast is a bit stronger in the indicative than in the subjunctive.[38]

(39) a. Undirritaðir$_{i+j}$ **hafa** áður sagt
undersigned.M.PL have.3PL before said
að yfirvöld **vilji** bara móðga {**okkur**$_{i+j}$ / (?)**þá**$_{i+j}$ }.
that authorities want.SBJV just insult {us / (?)them}
"The undersigned (pl) have said before that the authorities just want to insult us."

b. Undirritaðir$_{i+j}$ **uppgötvuðu** í fyrra
undersigned.M.PL discovered.3PL last year
að stjórnin **vill** reka {**okkur**$_{i+j}$ / ?**þá**$_{i+j}$ }.
that management wants.IND fire {us / ?them}
"The undersigned (pl) discovered last year that management wants to fire us."

[38] Like the classes of reflexives discussed in the previous section, we will not attempt in this chapter an explanation of the effect of mood on antecedence relations, but rather include this data to control for a potentially relevant grammatical property of the sentences we are looking at. Note that the morphological expression of mood makes a difference in the acceptability of long-distance reflexives for many (but not all) speakers (H. Á. Sigurðsson 1986).

With the imposter *mamma og pabbi* "Mommy and Daddy," the same contrast is evident, but here in the subjunctive rather than the indicative. (Recall that first person subject-verb agreement is generally not acceptable with "Mommy and Daddy" as a subject.)

(40) a. Mamma$_i$ og pabbi$_j$ **hafa** aldrei sagt
Mommy and Daddy have.3PL never said
að þú **megir** trufla {**okkur**$_{i+j}$ / ?**þau**$_{i+j}$ }.
that you may.SBJV disturb {us / ?them }
"Mommy and Daddy never said that you were allowed to disturb us."

b. Mamma$_i$ og pabbi$_j$ **uppgötvuðu** í morgun
Mommy and Daddy discovered.3PL this morning
að skrímslið **ætlar** að borða {**okkur**$_{i+j}$ /**þau**$_{i+j}$ }.
that monster.the intends.IND to eat {us /them }
"Mommy and Daddy discovered this morning that the monster is planning to eat us."

The mood of the complement clause seems to make a difference in the singular as well. When the embedded clause is subjunctive, "the undersigned" preferably antecedes a first person object pronoun, more so than "Daddy."

(41) a. Undirritaður$_i$ **hefur** áður sagt
undersigned.M.SG has.2/3SG before said
að þeir **vilji** bara móðga { **mig**$_i$ / (?)**hann**$_i$ }.
that they want.SBJV just insult { me / (?)him }
"The undersigned (sg) has said before that they just want to insult me."

b. Pabbi$_i$ **hefur** aldrei sagt
Daddy has.2/3SG never said
að þú **megir** trufla { **mig**$_i$ / **hann**$_i$ }.
that you may.SBJV disturb { me / him }
"Daddy never said that you were allowed to disturb him."

When the embedded clause is indicative, third person is preferred for both.

(42) a. Undirritaður$_i$ **uppgötvaði** í fyrra
undersigned.M.SG discovered.1/3SG last year
að þeir **vilja** reka {?**mig**$_i$ / **hann**$_i$ }.
that they want.IND fire {?me / him }
"The undersigned discovered last year that they want to fire me."

b. Pabbi$_i$ **uppgötvaði** í morgun
Daddy discovered.1/3SG this morning
að skrímslið **ætlar** að borða { (?)**mig**$_i$ / **hann**$_i$ }.
that monster.the intends.IND to eat { (?)me / him }
"Daddy discovered this morning that the monster plans to eat me."

Table 9.2 **Subject-Verb Agreement and Object Pronouns**

	Indicative		*Subjunctive*	
	1st obj	***3rd obj***	***1st obj***	***3rd obj***
Daddy (3rd agr)	(?)	✓	✓	✓
Undersigned (3rd agr)	?	✓	✓	(?)
Mommy and Daddy (3rd agr)	✓	✓	✓	?
Undersigned (plural) (3rd agr)	✓	?	✓	(?)
Undersigned and John (3rd agr)	✓	?	✓	?
Undersigned (plural) (1st agr)	✓	*	✓	*
Undersigned and John (1st agr)	✓	*	✓	*

These results are summarized in Table 9.2.

What we see in Table 9.2 is that whenever the agreement triggered in the superordinate clause is first person, the DP triggering that agreement cannot antecede a third person object pronoun. We also see a difference between singular and plural. For example, while *undirritaður* "undersigned (sg)" makes a slightly odd antecedent of a first person pronoun, third person being preferred, plural and coordinated "undersigned," even with third person agreement, preferably antecede a first person pronoun. Since the difference in mood is subtle, it should be tested with more speakers before any conclusions are drawn from it.

6.2 SUBJECTS

Subject pronouns show a paradigm similar to object pronouns in some respects, but distinct in others. If the verbal agreement is third person, either a first or third person subject pronoun is possible with coordinate structures.

(43) a. Undirritaður$_i$ og Jón$_j$ **hafa** áður sagt
undersigned.M.SG and John have.3PL before said
að {**við**$_{i+j}$ munum / **þeir**$_{i+j}$ muni } ekki styðja skattahækkanir.
that {we will.SBJV / they will.SBJV} not support tax.hikes
"The undersigned and John have said before that we will not support tax hikes."

b. Undirritaður$_i$ og Jón$_j$ **uppgötvuðu** í fyrra
undersigned.M.SG and John discovered.3PL last year
að {**við**$_{i+j}$ erum / **þeir**$_{i+j}$ eru } með krabbamein.
that {we are.IND / they are.IND} with cancer
"The undersigned and John discovered last year that we have cancer."

If the verbal agreement is first person, however, the third person pronoun is unacceptable.

(44) a. Undirritaður$_i$ og Jón$_j$ **höfum** áður sagt
undersigned.M.SG and John have.1PL before said
að {**við**$_{i+j}$ munum /***þeir**$_{i+j}$ muni } ekki styðja skattahækkanir.
that {we will.SBJV /* they will.SBJV } not support tax.hikes
"The undersigned and John have said before that we will not support tax hikes."

b. Undirritaður$_i$ og Jón$_j$ **uppgötvuðum** í fyrra
undersigned.M.SG and John discovered.1PL last year
að {**við**$_{i+j}$ erum / * **þeir**$_{i+j}$ eru } með krabbamein.
that {we are.IND / *they are.IND } with cancer
"The undersigned and John discovered last year that we have cancer."

With *undirritaðir* "undersigned (pl)" and third person agreement, either a first or a third person pronoun is possible.

(45) a. Undirritaðir$_{i+j}$ **hafa** áður sagt
undersigned.M.PL have.3PL before said
að {**við**$_{i+j}$ munum / **þeir**$_{i+j}$ muni } ekki styðja skattahækkanir.
that {we will.SBJV / they will.SBJV } not support tax.hikes
"The undersigned have said before that we/they will not support tax hikes."

b. Undirritaðir$_{i+j}$ **uppgötvuðu** í fyrra
undersigned.M.PL discovered.3PL last year
að {**við**$_{i+j}$ erum / **þeir**$_{i+j}$ eru } með krabbamein.
that {we are.IND / they are.IND } with cancer
"The undersigned (pl) discovered last year that we have cancer."

When *undirritaðir* "undersigned (pl)" occurs with first person agreement, the third person pronoun is unacceptable, and only a first person pronoun can take *undirritaðir* as an antecedent.

(46) a. Undirritaðir$_{i+j}$ **höfum** áður sagt
undersigned.M.PL have.1PL before said
að {**við**$_{i+j}$ munum / * **þeir**$_{i+j}$ muni } ekki styðja skattahækkanir.
that {we will.SBJV / *they will.SBJV} not support tax.hikes
"The undersigned (pl) have said before that we/they will not support tax hikes."

b. Undirritaðir$_{i+j}$ **uppgötvuðum** í fyrra
undersigned.M.PL discovered.1PL last year
að {**við**$_{i+j}$ erum / ***þeir**$_{i+j}$ eru } með krabbamein.
that {we are.IND / *they are.IND } with cancer
"The undersigned (pl) discovered last year that we have cancer."

Coordinated *mamma og pabbi* "Mommy and Daddy" behaves differently. To the extent that there is a contrast, it is the first person pronoun that is a bit marked.

The third person pronoun is preferred. Notice that this cannot be tied to verbal agreement in these cases, since *undirritaðir* "the undersigned (pl)" in the example above and *mamma og pabbi* "Mommy and Daddy" in the example below are controlling third person plural agreement.

(47) a. Mamma$_i$ og pabbi$_j$ **hafa** aldrei sagt
Mommy and Daddy have.3PL never said
að {(?)**við**$_{i+j}$ ætlum / **þau**$_{i+j}$ ætli } að kaupa nammi handa þér.
that {(?)we intend.SBJV / they intend.SBJV} to buy candy for you
"Mommy and Daddy never said that we planned on buying candy for you."
b. Mamma$_i$ og pabbi$_j$ **uppgötvuðu** í morgun
Mommy and Daddy discovered.3PL this morning
að {(?)**við**$_{i+j}$ þurfum / **þau**$_{i+j}$ þurfa } ekki að vinna í dag.
that {(?)we need.IND / they need.IND} not to work today
"Mommy and Daddy discovered this morning that we don't have to work today."

Turning to singular imposters, there is again a contrast between "undersigned" and "Daddy." For embedded subject pronouns, both prefer third person. However, the first person pronoun is considerably better for "the undersigned" than for "Daddy."

(48) a. Undirritaður$_i$ **hefur** áður sagt
undersigned.M.SG has.2/3SG before said
að {?**ég**$_i$ / **hann**$_i$} muni ekki styðja skattahækkanir.
that {?I / he } will.SBJV not support tax.hikes
"The undersigned (sg) has said before that he will not support tax hikes."
b. Pabbi$_i$ **hefur** aldrei sagt
Daddy has.2/3SG never said
að {??**ég**$_i$ / **hann**$_i$ } ætli að kaupa nammi handa þér.
that {??I / he } intends.SBJV to buy candy for you
"Daddy never said that he was going to buy candy for you."

There is no apparent difference depending on the mood of the embedded clause.

(49) a. Undirritaður$_i$ uppgötvaði í fyrra
undersigned.M.SG discovered.1/3SG last year
að {?ég$_i$ / hann$_i$} er með krabbamein.
that {?I / he } be.1/3SG.IND with cancer
"The undersigned (sg) discovered last year that he has cancer."
b. Pabbi$_i$ uppgötvaði í morgun
Daddy discovered.1/3SG this morning
að {??ég$_i$ / hann$_i$} þarf ekki að vinna í dag.
that {??I / he } need.1/3SG.IND not to work today
"Daddy discovered this morning that he doesn't need to work today."

Table 9.3 **Subject Pronouns**

	Indicative		*Subjunctive*	
	1st sub	***3rd sub***	***1st sub***	***3rd sub***
Daddy (3rd agr)	??	✓	??	✓
Undersigned (3rd agr)	?	✓	?	✓
Mommy and Daddy (3rd agr)	(?)	✓	(?)	✓
Undersigned (plural) (3rd agr)	✓	✓	✓	✓
Undersigned and John (3rd agr)	✓	✓	✓	✓
Undersigned (plural) (1st agr)	✓	*	✓	*
Undersigned and John (1st agr)	✓	*	✓	*

We summarize the results in Table 9.3.[39]

Several tendencies can be gleaned from these results. We see that third person pronouns are bad with antecedents controlling first person agreement, irrespective of the subject/object distinction, and irrespective of mood. First person pronouns are better as objects than subjects, and better with plurals than with singulars. First person is (slightly) better in the subjunctive than in the indicative. Third person is a bit worse on objects than on subjects, and with plural "undersigned." Third person is a bit worse in the subjunctive than in the indicative. We are not in a position to account for all of these facts, and it is in fact not clear how robust they are. We state them here to facilitate cross-linguistic comparison and as a stepping-stone to future work. What we will discuss below is the relationship between pronouns and their antecedents more generally, the singular/plural asymmetry, and the behavior of "undersigned."

7. Pronoun-Antecedent Relations and Agreement

In the early stages of the minimalist program, there was an attempt to relegate phenomena associated with Binding Theory (BT) to the LF interface. The idea was that there are interpretive restrictions on different kinds of DPs. The binding conditions proposed in Chomsky (1995: 211), for example, were the following:

(50) (For a DP α in local domain D . . .)

A. If α is an anaphor, interpret it as coreferential with a c-commanding phrase in D.

[39] We omit first person singular verb agreement in these tables because, as discussed earlier, singular imposters are generally unacceptable with first person agreement, so its effect on antecedence cannot easily be tested.

B. If α is a pronominal, interpret it as disjoint from every c-commanding phrase in D.
C. If α is an r-expression, interpret it as disjoint from every c-commanding phrase.

Imposter phenomena pose very serious challenges to this kind of binding theory. For one thing, this Condition B will clearly not suffice to rule out a sentence such as (51).

(51) *Undirritaður$_i$ og Jón$_j$ höfum áður sagt
undersigned.M.SG and John have.1PL before said
[$_{CP}$að þeir$_{i+j}$ muni ekki styðja skattahækkanir].
that they will.SBJV not support tax.hikes
"The undersigned and John have said before that we will not support tax hikes."

Here the embedded third person pronoun *þeir* "they" could easily refer to the same individuals as those referred to by *undirritaður og Jón* "undersigned and John"; it need only be interpreted as disjoint from every c-commanding phrase in the local domain, which in this case is the embedded CP (bracketed above). Neither the interpretation of the matrix imposter nor the verbal agreement would be expected to have an effect.

There are many other problems with this kind of binding theory, as emphasized in Collins and Postal (2012). There have been, within the minimalist program, a number of other proposals attempting to derive BT phenomena from properties of the syntactic derivation (Kayne 2002; Zwart 2002; Reuland 2006, 2011; Boeckx et al., 2007; Hicks 2008, 2009). Among these (and other) theories, some assume a syntactic relation between a non-reflexive pronoun and its antecedent, and others do not. Collins and Postal (2012) argue that a primitive relation "antecede" encodes referential dependencies among linguistic objects, and that this relation will hold between a pronoun and its antecedent. Kayne (2002) has proposed that movement underlies this dependency, such that the antecedent will form a constituent with the pronoun and move subsequently out of that constituent. H. Á. Sigurðsson (2004, 2010, 2011) has argued that pronouns undergo matching relations with functional heads in the left-perpiphery, and that in subordinate cases, these functional heads relate to the antecedent. We will discuss this approach further below. Note that in all of these accounts, the "antecedent" of a pronoun is not always pronounced. At the very least, "context linkers" in the left periphery of an utterance (or alternatively, unpronounced antecedent DPs) will be present to antecede "discourse free" pronouns and pronouns used deictically.

Imposter phenomena strongly suggest that pronouns do enter into syntactic dependencies with antecedents, either directly or indirectly. This has been argued extensively in Collins and Postal (2012), so we will not repeat all the arguments here. We will, however, briefly present one argument in favor of this conclusion relating to verbal agreement, the phenomenon of interest here.[40] Consider the view that pronouns refer freely, perhaps constrained by ϕ-features which add presuppositions that the referent meets some criterion (such as being female/feminine, for a pronoun like *she*). Such a view would have to be constrained so as to keep an ordinary third person pronoun from including the speaker in situations such as the following.

(52) María: Hvað gerðist? "What happened?"
Bjartur$_i$: Jón sagði að þeir$_{\{*i+j\}/\{k+l\}}$ væru heimskir.
John said that they were stupid
"John said that they were stupid."

As indicated with the indices, the speaker, Bjartur, cannot in this dialogue be understood as a member of the set of individuals referred to by the pronoun *þeir* "they." With a minor modification to the matrix clause, however, this is possible:

(53) María: Hvað gerðist? "What happened?"
Bjartur$_i$: Jón sagði undirrituðum$_{\{i+j\}}$ að þeir$_{\{i+j\}/\{k+l\}}$ væru heimskir.
John said undersigned.PL.DAT that they were stupid
"John told the undersigned (pl) that they were stupid."

The presence of an imposter antecedent, then, makes it possible for a third person pronoun to include the speaker. If pronouns were interpreted basically freely, this dependency on an antecedent would be a mystery. For the sake of argument, we might constrain the denotation of pronouns by invoking "definite descriptions." We might say that a third person pronoun can include the speaker if it can independently refer to some description of an individual who happens to be the speaker. The appearance of *undirritaðir* "undersigned (pl)" might then make such a description salient enough that the pronoun can pick out the referent of this description, which happens to be the speaker.

However, recall the effect of agreement on the embedded pronoun. Simplifying greatly, we have the following schema:[41]

(54) a. Imposter$_i$ . . . Agr-3 [pronoun$_i$-1/3]
b. Imposter$_i$ . . . Agr-1 [pronoun$_i$-1/*3]

Concentrating on the third person pronoun, consider the contrast in (55), repeated from above.

[40] This is related to and partly adapted from an argument in Collins and Postal (2012), but with verbal agreement specifically in mind.

[41] See Kallulli (this volume) for the same generalization in Albanian.

(55) a. Undirritaðir$_{i+j}$ **hafa** áður sagt
undersigned.M.PL have.3PL before said
að **þeir**$_{i+j}$ muni ekki styðja skattahækkanir.
that they will.SBJV not support tax.hikes
"The undersigned (pl) have said before that they will not support tax hikes."

b. *Undirritaðir$_{i+j}$ **höfum** áður sagt
undersigned.M.PL have.1PL before said
að **þeir**$_{i+j}$ muni ekki styðja skattahækkanir.
that they will.SBJV not support tax.hikes
"The undersigned (pl) have said before that they will not support tax hikes."

According to the account under consideration, the pronoun in (55a) can include the speaker because the matrix clause makes available/salient a description of an entity that the pronoun can refer to, and that description happens to pick out the speaker. However, (55b) clearly makes such a description available as well. We would be forced to say that a third person pronoun can include the speaker iff the linguistic element making the appropriate description available is third person, has third person ϕ-features, shows third person behavior, and so on. But note that invoking person features is a linguistic notion, not a referential notion. That is, in saving the idea that pronouns have no linguistic relation with their antecedent, we are forced to invoke linguistic properties of that very antecedent. This moves away from the very intuition of the assumption that pronouns refer freely, modulo the presuppostions induced by the ϕ-features that they are composed of. It asserts a relation between a linguistic element, the pronoun, and another linguistic element, the antecedent, and constrains the former with reference to linguistic properties of the latter. It would be far beyond the scope of this chapter to argue against every imaginable form of the assumption that pronouns do not have a syntactic relation with their antecedent. However, the basic form of the argument should be clear—the linguistic properties of pronouns seem to depend on the linguistic properties of their antecedents, and this is expected if there is a syntactic relation between the two.

8. Toward an Account

We adopt the overall approach in H. Á. Sigurðsson (2004, 2011), which is similar to Collins and Postal (2012) in many respects. H. Á. Sigurðsson (2004, 2011) argues that all pronouns must match left-peripheral *context linkers*. A typical first person pronoun will match a "logophoric agent," which roughly refers to the speaker (or the source of the clause). The logophoric agent is notated as Λ_A. This is obviously quite similar to AUTHOR in Collins and Postal (2012), though is not assumed to be a DP, but rather a left-peripheral head. A typical second person pronoun will match the "logophoric patient" (Λ_P), which corresponds roughly to ADDRESSEE in Collins and Postal (2012). Third person DPs, on the other hand, will match other context linkers; H. Á. Sigurðsson (2011), drawing on Frascarelli (2007), proposes several such linkers, relating in particular to various kinds of topics, such as aboutness-shift topics, familiar topics, contrastive topics, and so on. The discourse properties of the context linkers will not concern us here, so we will refer to any non-Λ_A/Λ_P context linker as CL.

Typically, the context linkers of embedded finite clauses will be controlled by the matrix context linkers. This can be illustrated by comparing an embedded *that*-clause with embedded direct speech. In (56), *John* and *Mary* are both linked to CLs, and the matrix CLs, including Λ_A and Λ_P, all control their counterparts in the embedded clause. The "control" relation is indicated with dotted lines, while matching relations are indicated with solid lines. In the embedded clauses, the first and second person pronouns match their local Λ_A and Λ_P heads, respectively.

(56) a. John told Mary that I love you.

b.

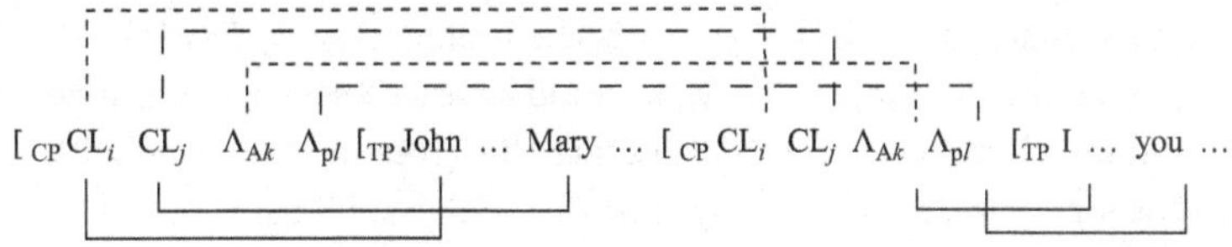

Here, the first and second person pronouns of the embedded clause have no overt antecedents in the matrix clause, but are rather linked to local Λ_A and Λ_P heads, which are in turn controlled by the Λ_A and Λ_P head in the matrix clause. In (57), on the other hand, it is the matrix arguments that control the embedded Λ_A and Λ_P heads. Thus, the first and second person pronoun in the embedded clause do have overt antecedents in the matrix clause.

(57) a. John told Mary, "I love you."

b.

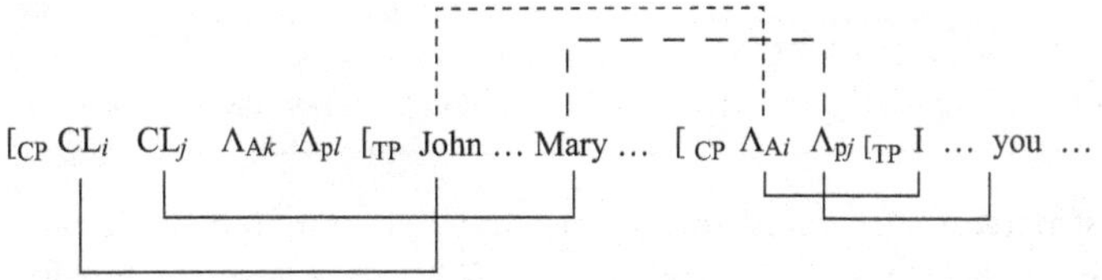

In what follows, we will only be concerned with cases like (56), where, all else being equal, the superordinate context linkers control the subordinate context linkers.

The left-peripheral context linkers mediate the relation between a pronoun and its antecedent. This is outlined schematically in (58), where again, the dotted line indicates the control relation between the higher and lower CL.

(58)

Consider now the effect of first person agreement on the pronoun-antecedent relation shown in (59), repeated from above.

(59) a. Undirritaðir$_{i+j}$ **hafa** áður sagt
undersigned.M.PL have.3PL before said
að **þeir**$_{i+j}$ muni ekki styðja skattahækkanir.
that they will.SBJV not support tax.hikes
"The undersigned (pl) have said before that they will not support tax hikes."

b. *Undirritaðir$_{i+j}$ **höfum** áður sagt
undersigned.M.PL have.1PL before said
að **þeir**$_{i+j}$ muni ekki styðja skattahækkanir.
that they will.SBJV not support tax.hikes
"The undersigned (pl) have said before that they will not support tax hikes."

In order for the pronoun *þeir* "they" to take the imposter as an antecedent, the imposter must match the CL that controls the CL matched by *þeir* "they." That is, for the imposter to antecede *þeir* "they," it would have to both trigger first person agreement and match a non-Λ_A CL.[42] We notate the agreement relation with a solid bar above the structure, and matching relations with a solid bar below the structure.

(60) $* \text{CL}_i \ \dots \ \Lambda_{Aj} \ \dots \ \text{T}^0{}_{1pl} \ \dots \ \text{DP} \ \dots \ [_{CP} \ \text{CL}_i \ \dots \ \Lambda_{Aj} \ \dots$ *þeir* 'they'

This configuration is evidently ill-formed. We can rule it out by assuming a DP triggering first person agreement must match Λ_A and no other CL. Given this much, we generate the following paradigm.

(61) a. $\# \text{CL}_i \ \dots \ \Lambda_{Aj} \dots \text{T}^0{}_{1pl} \dots \text{DP} \dots [_{CP} \ \text{CL}_i \ \dots \ \Lambda_{Aj} \dots$ *þeir* 'they'

b. $\text{CL}_i \ \dots \ \Lambda_{Aj} \dots \text{T}^0{}_{3pl} \dots \text{DP} \dots [_{CP} \ \text{CL}_i \ \dots \ \Lambda_{Aj} \dots$ *þeir* 'they'

Since first person agreement forces the imposter to match Λ_A, it cannot be the antecedent of *þeir* "they." The structure in (61a) is acceptable, but it is only acceptable on the reading where *þeir* "they" is distinct from the imposter.[43] In (61b), the imposter triggers third person agreement, so nothing stops it from matching the CL that controls the CL matched by *þeir* "they."[44]

Turning to *við* "we," the question is how we allow *við* "we" to take an imposter antecedent that triggers third person agreement.

[42] If a plural pronoun matches Λ_A, it would be pronounced as *við* "we."

[43] The "#" notation indicates that the configuration is fine, but does not generate the intended reading.

[44] We still assume here that the notional core matches Λ_A; the issue is what the DP as a whole matches and how that interacts with agreement.

(62) a. Undirritaðir$_{i+j}$ hafa áður sagt
undersigned.M.PL have.3PL before said
að við$_{i+j}$ munum ekki styðja skattahækkanir.
that we will.SBJV not support tax.hikes
"The undersigned have said before that we/they will not support tax hikes."

b. Undirritaðir$_{i+j}$ höfum áður sagt
undersigned.M.PL have.1PL before said
að við$_{i+j}$ munum ekki styðja skattahækkanir.
that we will.SBJV not support tax.hikes
"The undersigned (pl) have said before that we/they will not support tax hikes."

If *við* "we" matched only Λ_A, and third person agreement matched only a non-Λ_A CL, we would incorrectly generate the same "distinctness." However, notice that *við* "we" should not simply refer to the speaker, or even a plural speaker. It refers to the speaker plus some other entity, which must be available in the discourse. Suppose John is alone in a room, and someone walks in and asks, "What were you doing?"' If John were to answer, "We were reading," the response would sound as unusual as a third person pronoun with no referent. John's interlocuter would either think that John was talking about him/her, or else s/he would lack the appopriate referent for the other person John was talking about. Given this, suppose that við "we" matches both Λ_A and another CL.[45]

(63) a. $CL_i \ldots \Lambda_{Aj} \ldots T^0_{3pl} \ldots DP \ldots [_{CP}\ CL_i \ldots \Lambda_{Aj} \ldots$ we

b. $CL_i \ldots \Lambda_{Aj} \ldots T^0_{1pl} \ldots DP \ldots [_{CP}\ CL_i \ldots \Lambda_{Aj} \ldots$ we

When verbal agreement is first person, the imposter DP matches only Λ_A, which is fine because *við* "we" matches the lower Λ_A (which is controlled by the higher one). When verbal agreement is third person, the DP matches the other CL, which is also fine as long as it matches the CL that controls the CL matched by *við* "we."

Recall that a first person singular pronoun is less acceptable when anteceded by an imposter.[46] The examples in (64a–b) are adapted from (48a) and (45a) above (respectively).

(64) a. ?Undirritaðuri hefur áður sagt
undersigned.M.SG has.2/3SG before said
að ég$_i$ muni ekki styðja skattahækkanir.
that I will.SBJV not support tax.hikes
"The undersigned (sg) has said before that he will not support tax hikes."

[45] See H. Á. Sigurðsson (submitted) for a related and relevant discussion of "we" in a context-linking system.

[46] As mentioned earlier, this is stronger for subjects than objects. We have no explanation for this fact.

b. Undirritaðir$_{i+j}$ hafa áður sagt
undersigned.M.PL have.3PL before said
að$_{i+j}$ við munum ekki styðja skattahækkanir.
that we will.SBJV not support tax.hikes
"The undersigned have said before that we/they will not support tax hikes."

A singular first person pronoun would not have to match any CL other than Λ_A.

(65)
$CL_i \ldots \Lambda_{Aj} \ldots T^0_{3sg} \ldots DP \ldots [_{CP}\ CL_i \ldots \Lambda_{Aj} \ldots I$

This is probably stranger because the DP antecedent is matching a CL which is not controlling the Λ_A which the pronoun is matching. However, we do assume that the notional core of the matrix DP is matching Λ_A (not shown above), so it is not completely unacceptable. That is, singular *I* can be understood as linked to the imposter core, since the imposter core matches the Λ_A which controls the embedded Λ_A. However, in the case of plurals, the antecedent and the pronoun may match parallel context linkers. Since the imposter core matching involves matching of a null element, we indicate this relation with a dashed line (with no theoretical importance attached to this notational choice).

(66)
$CL_i \ldots \Lambda_{Aj} \ldots T^0_{3sg} \ldots [DP_{SHELL} \ldots DP_{CORE} \ldots] \ldots [_{CP}\ CL_i \ldots \Lambda_{Aj} \ldots I$

(67)
$CL_i \ldots \Lambda_{Aj} \ldots T^0_{3pl} \ldots [DP_{SHELL} \ldots DP_{CORE} \ldots] \ldots [_{CP}\ CL_i \ldots \Lambda_{Aj} \ldots we$

Note that this reasoning would not undermine our account of the cases we wanted to rule out above. In (61a), the imposter core and shell DP would both match Λ_A. Thus, the case in (68) simply does not generate a coreferential interpretation between "they" and the antecedent.

(68)
$\#CL_i \ldots \Lambda_{Aj} \ldots T^0_{1pl} \ldots [DP_{SHELL} \ldots DP_{CORE} \ldots] \ldots [_{CP}\ CL_i \ldots \Lambda_{Aj} \ldots they$

(69)
$CL_i \ldots \Lambda_{Aj} \ldots T^0_{1pl} \ldots [DP_{SHELL} \ldots DP_{CORE} \ldots] \ldots [_{CP}\ CL_i \ldots \Lambda_{Aj} \ldots we$

It is only with third person agreement that the imposter core and shell DP match different context linkers. The present account thus generates exactly the schematic paradigm in (58).

While we successfully generate cases where the antecedent of a first person pronoun triggers third person agreement, and we correctly do not generate cases where the antecedent of a third person pronoun triggers first person agreement, there is at least one potential problem with the proposed account, as Chris Collins (p.c.) points out to us. While "we" plausibly does link to two context linkers in many cases (Λ_A and CL), as outlined above, that does not seem to correspond to our intuitions regarding "we" when anteceded by imposters such as the "undersigned." The intuition is that the set denoted by "we" is co-extensive with the set denoted by the "the undersigned." This does not seem to raise a problem for the configuration in (67), with third person plural agreement, since the linkers matched by the pronoun are all controlled by the linkers matched by (subparts of) the antecedent. With first person plural agreement, however, as in (69), the embedded pronoun matches a context linker that is not controlled by anything matched by its antecedent. We can think of at least two solutions to this. The first is to allow "we" to optionally match only the Λ_A linker; this would still get the contrast between (66) and (67) as long as "I" is unable to match an additional context linker. The second option is to assume that "we" always matches an additional context linker, but the additional context linker need not always add anything to the reference set. That is, "we" still expresses the relation with a single Λ_A plus another entity, but the control relation with the matrix Λ_A allows for the understanding that this other entity is a part of the same reference set (i.e., "I+other" = "the undersigned"). This second option might be supported by the existence of seemingly singular uses of first person plural pronouns, such as the so-called "royal we" (though see (Collins and Postal 2012) for a view compatible with the first option; see also H. Á. Sigurðsson (submitted) on "context scanning".

In sum, the context linkers constrain pronoun-antecedent relations by enforcing certain syntactic conditions on the interpretation of pronouns. The link between a pronoun and its antecedent is syntactic, though indirect. The antecedent matches context linkers in the left periphery, and those context linkers control the context linkers of the embedded clause; the pronoun matches these context linkers. The effect of verbal agreement arises because in order for a DP to trigger first person agreement, it must match Λ_A. While we have simply stated this condition brute force, it could actually be made to follow from independent properties of the system. H. Á. Sigurðsson (2010) proposes that the matching of DPs to context linkers is mediated by a head Pn (person) in the inflectional complex. So for a first person pronoun, Pn first matches the DP, and then that DP and Pn together match Λ_A. Since this is how first person agreement arises, it would be impossible to trigger first person agreement without matching Λ_A.

9. Verbal Agreement with Different Imposters

While the analysis above is able to account for the effect of first person agreement on pronominal antecedence, it so far says nothing about why some imposters are able to trigger first person agreement while others are not. Recall the contrast between *undirritaður* "undersigned (sg)" and *undirritaðir* "undersigned (pl)" with first person agreement, repeated in (70) from (20b–c) above.

(70)	a.	Undirritaður	{ hefur / *hef }	ákveðið	að	hætta.	
		undersigned.M.SG	{ has.3SG / *1SG }	decided	to	quit	
		"The undersigned (sg) has decided to quit."					
	b.	Undirritaðir	{hafa / ?höfum }	haldið	þessu	fram.	
		undersigned.M.PL	{have.3PL / ?1PL }	held	this	forth	
		'The undersigned (pl) have claimed this."					

Contrasts like these are not easy to derive on any simple approach to agreement. We can move closer toward an explanatory account of this data, however, with three further assumptions, all of which have been independently proposed (though not necessarily together). The first is to assume with Béjar (2008) and H. Á. Sigurðsson and Holmberg (2008) that individual ϕ-features can probe separately. The second is to assume that number agreement only involves an Agree relation in the plural; from this perspective, singular agreement is a kind of "default" agreement. In fact, there are a number of phenomena cross-linguistically that suggest that plural features control agreement in a much more aggressive way than singular features do (den Dikken 2001; Nevins 2011; Myler submitted). Nevins (2011) has recently proposed that "singular" is actually the absence of a privative [PLURAL] feature rather than the presence of a [SG] feature or a [-PLURAL] feature (though see Harbour (2011a, b) for a different theory based on other facts). What is important here is that regardless of the correct theory of number features themselves, number agreement seems to involve plurals only, or at least in a much more robust way. The third assumption is that when a probe enters into an Agree relation with a goal, the entire ϕ-bundle of the probe is replaced by that of the goal, not just the probing feature. This has been made in different forms by Béjar (2003), Pesetsky and Torrego (2007), Harbour (2007, 2011b), Kratzer (2009), Béjar and Rezac (2009), and Myler (submitted).

Now, suppose that in the complex DP leading to *undirritaðir* "undersigned (m.pl)," the gender and number features are only active on the notional core, not on the secondary DP. This is independently plausible since the number and gender of *undirritaðir* "undersigned (m.pl)" are determined by the notional core, so that if it refers to a female, it would take the feminine form *undirritaðar* (see example (22b)). The forms of *undirritaður* "undersigned (sg)" are shown in Table 9.4.

In contrast, an imposter like *pabbi* "Daddy" is inherently masculine, as is an imposter like *þinn auðmjúki þjónn* "your humble servant," along with many other imposters which have inherently specified features. If *undirritaður* "undersigned (sg)" gets its number and gender features through valuation, then those features would be inactive upon valuation. (Inactive features are crossed out below.) If this and the assumptions outlined above are correct, then the different options

Table 9.4 **Forms of *undirritaður***

	Singular			*Plural*		
	Masc	*Fem*	*Neut*	*Masc*	*Fem*	*Neut*
NOM	undirritaður	undirrituð	undirritað	undirritaðir	undirritaðar	undirrituð
ACC	undirritaðan	undirritaða	undirritað	undirritaða	undirritaðar	undirrituð
DAT	undirrituðum	undirritaðri	undirrituðu	undirrituðum	undirrituðum	undirrituðum
GEN	undirritaðs	undirritaðrar	undirritaðs	undirritaðra	undirritaðra	undirritaðra

in (70) reflect which feature probes first. If number probes first, it will skip the secondary DP and Agree with the notional core. Once the probe's ϕ-bundle has been replaced with the goal's ϕ-bundle, it will no longer be a probe because all of its features will be valued. If the person feature probes, it will Agree with the secondary DP, resulting in third person plural agreement.

(71) Number probes first

a. $T^0_{\{PN:\,,\,NUM:\,\}}$ … [$_{DP}$ *undirritaðir*$_{\{3,\cancel{PL,M}\}}$ [*við*$_{\{1,PL,M\}}$]]

b. $T^0_{\{1,PL,M\}}$ … [$_{DP}$ *undirritaðir*$_{\{3,\cancel{PL,M}\}}$ [*við*$_{\{1,PL,M\}}$]]

Number Agree

(72) Person probes first

a. $T^0_{\{PN:\,,\,NUM:\,\}}$ … [$_{DP}$ *undirritaðir*$_{\{3,\cancel{PL,M}\}}$ [*við*$_{\{1,PL,M\}}$]]

b. $T^0_{\{3,PL,M\}}$ … [$_{DP}$ *undirritaðir*$_{\{3,\cancel{PL,M}\}}$ [*við*$_{\{1,PL,M\}}$]]

Person Agree

Thus, in the plural cases, either person or number may probe first, and the result is that either first or third person agreement on the verb is possible. In the singular cases, if number probes first, it will not find any goal, assuming that singular number agreement is a lack of number agreement. Then, when person probes, it will agree with the secondary DP. If person probes first, it will agree with the secondary DP right away. In this way, the singular/plural asymmetry follows from assuming that person and number probe separately, and that only plural agreement reflects the syntactic operation Agree.

Paul Postal (p.c.) raises the question of whether there is any independent evidence that verbs can agree with a subpart of a DP (a secondary source, in the terms of Collins and Postal 2012). In fact, the idea that first and second person agreement may involve agreement with a subpart of a complex DP (specifically, a silent pronoun embedded within it) is supported by the partitive genitive data cited above in (26a–b) repeated here in (73).

(73) a. Mörg ykkar vita …
Many.NOM you.PL.GEN know.3PL
"Many of you know …"

Table 9.5 **Forms of *margur***

	Singular			Plural		
	Masc	*Fem*	*Neut*	*Masc*	*Fem*	*Neut*
NOM	margur	mörg	margt	margir	margar	mörg
ACC	margan	marga	margt	marga	margar	mörg
DAT	mörgum	margri	mörgu	mörgum	mörgum	mörgum
GEN	margs	margrar	margs	margra	margra	margra

b. (?) Mörg ykkar vitið ...
Many.NOM you.PL.GEN know.2PL
"Many of you know . . ." (Friðjónsson 1990–1991: 81)

The quantifier *mörg* "many," like the participle *undirritaður* "undersigned," is not inherently specified for number, case or gender. Rather, it agrees with the head noun in number and gender, as illustrated in Table 9.5.

The derivation of the variation in (73) proceeds exactly as with plural "undersigned": if number probes first, it agrees with the partitive pronoun, like in (71), resulting in second person agreement; if person probes first, it agrees with the quantifier, like in (72), resulting in third person agreement.

10. Why Is "Undersigned" Special?

Before closing this chapter, we would like to briefly ask whether our analysis offers a way to understand why "undersigned" behaves differently from other imposters. It is possible, but there are several other reasonable hypotheses, which we will outline presently. We suggested that for elements like *undirritaður* "undersigned (sg)," the feature valuation assigning gender and number to the secondary DP makes those features inactive, allowing outside probes to Agree with the notional core past the secondary DP. The analysis extended directly to partitives with quantifiers, such as in (73). The logic of this analysis leads us to offer the following tentative hypothesis:

(74) The more features of a secondary DP that are not inherently specified, the more likely the person features of the notional core are to be visible to outside probes.

If true, (74) would follow nicely from our approach; but whether it actually holds in general is a matter for future research.

We should point out, however, that there is another difference between *undirritaður* "undersigned (sg)" and imposters like *pabbi* "Daddy": *undirritaður* "undersigned (sg)" is formally indefinite. Icelandic has no indefinite article, but for *undirritaður* "undersigned (sg)," there are actually two morphological paradigms: a "strong" paradigm which is used in indefinite contexts, and a "weak" paradigm which is used in definite contexts. Thus, in a non-imposter context, there is a formal distinction between ***undirritaði*** *höfundurinn* "the undersigned author" and ***undirritaður*** *höfundur* "an undersigned author." The imposter form is the strong, or "indefinite," form. Despite this, *undirritaður* "undersigned (sg)" (in its imposter use) can be shown to distribute like a definite DP.[47] In Icelandic, indefinite participles are allowed in a low position in various expletive constructions, as exemplified in (75a). *Undirritaður* "undersigned (sg)" is not possible in this position with the imposter reading, as shown in (75b).

(75) a. Það hafði víst verið vopnaður lögreglumaður í húsinu.
EXPL had apparently been armed.M.SG policeman in house.the
"There had apparently been an armed policeman in the house."
b. *Það hafði verið undirritaður í húsinu.
EXPL had been undersigned.M.SG in house.the

This is a clear case where the structural position of a DP is different depending on whether it is used as an imposter or not (see Kaufman (this volume) for another, particularly striking instance from Indonesian, where imposters distribute like clitic pronouns).

It is possible, however, that the indefinite form of *undirritaður* is misleading. It does strongly suggest that there is not an understood definite head noun such as *maðurinn* "the man.DEF," as was suggested for Italian by Servidio (this volume). If so, we would expect the weak form, *undirritaði*, rather than *undirritaður*, as in *undirritaði ~~maðurinn~~* "the undersigned man."[48] However, given the rarity of indefinite imposters cross-linguistically, and the definite behavior of *undirritaður* "undersigned (sg)," it would be odd to suppose that the head noun is indefinite, as in *undirritaður ~~maður~~* "an undersigned man";[49] this would also be at odds with the fact that definite morphology shows up with "undersigned" in many other languages.

[47] See Vázquez Rojas (this volume) for a similar demonstration with respect to a formally indefinite imposter in Mexican Spanish.

[48] For example, this seems to be exactly what is going on with the imposter *gamli/gjemli* "the old (guy)" cited in (8c), which is an adjective in the weak form, as though it were definite or modifying a definite head noun. For *gamli/gjemli*, an analysis in terms of a null definite head noun is morphologically plausible (perhaps *gamli ~~kallinn~~* "the old guy," since *gamli/gjemli* and *kallinn/kjellinn* seem to occupy the same register). The existence of *gamli/gjemli* shows that there is nothing about imposter DPs that intrinsically prevents them from taking the weak adjectival form or modifying a definite unpronounced noun—but that is not what is going on with *undirritaður* "undersigned (sg)."

[49] It is also worth pointing out that overt *maður* "man," as in *undirritaður maður* "an undersigned man" or *undirritaði maðurinn*, is quite odd, perhaps unacceptable; *undirritaður höfundur* "an undersigned author" and *undirritaður starfsmaður* "an undersigned employee" are acceptable, though the definite forms, *undirritaði höfundurinn/starfsmaðurinn* "the undersigned author/employee" are not very natural.

But another possibility exists. In Icelandic, the strong form of participles shows up not only in the attributive position of indefinite nouns, but also in the predicative position, as illustrated for *undirritaður* "undersigned (sg)" in the following example:

(76) Afhverju hringiði ekki, eða sendið bréf þar sem að
why call.you.PL not, or send letter there as that
þið allar eruð undirritaðar, til forlagsins og kvartið.
you.PL all.F.PL are.2PL undersigned.F.PL to publishing.house and complain
"Why don't you call, or send a letter to the publishing house where you will all be undersigned, and complain?"[50]

Thus, one possibility is that *undirritaður* "undersigned (sg)" in its imposter use is a reduced relative clause.[51] Then, it can be collapsed with the complex imposters seen earlier in (7), partially repeated here.

(77) ... Þuríður Backman og [**sá sem hér stendur**], **höfum** lagt fram ...
... Þuríður Backman and [the.one who here stands.3SG] have.1PL put forth ...
"... Þuríður Backman and the one who stands here have submitted ..."

In Icelandic, unlike languages like German or Russian, predicate adjectives and participles must agree in number, gender, and case with their subject, so this possibility is compatible with (74).

In sum, the present approach has the potential to understand the different behavior of different imposters on the basis of their grammatical properties. We have several working hypotheses. One possibility is that imposters with gender, number, or other features controlled by the notional core rather than by inherent specification are more likely to show first person effects. Another possibility is that formally indefinite, or perhaps predicative, imposters are more likely to show first person effects.[52] A third possibility is that imposters built on relative clauses are more likely to show first person effects than imposters built on other structures (such as appositives, as proposed in Collins and Postal 2012). The present approach would make sense of the first possibility more straightforwardly than the other two, but more cross-linguistic and analytical work needs to be done before it can be determined whether this is on the right track.

[50] https://bland.is/messageboard/messageboard.aspx?type=59&advid=22375790

[51] It is important to note, though, that it is not clear that *undirritaður* can refer to the speaker when used in the predicative position. This recalls the indefinite imposters disccused in Collins and Postal (2012: 53).

[52] One might object that, crosslinguistically, "undersigned" actually is definite, accompanied by the definite article. However, if "undersigned" really is the predicate of a reduced relative clause, the article would plausibly be related to the relative clause rather than "undersigned" itself. There are many cases like this; consider English *He made (*the) headway* versus *the headway he made*. Note that Icelandic uses a special demonstrative *sá* for these kinds of functions.

11. Conclusion

In this chapter, we have shown that verbal agreement can have a constraining effect on pronoun-antecedent relations. This is unexpected from the perspective of theories that take pronouns to be basically freely interpreted (modulo Condition B, however formulated), but is understandable if there is a syntactic relation between a pronoun and its antecedent. However, we have also shown, in at least two ways, that agreement is not the only constraining factor. First, while first person agreement controlled by a DP prevents that DP from anteceding a third person pronoun, third person agreement controlled by a DP does not necessarily prevent that DP from anteceding a first person pronoun. The ability to antecede a first person pronoun, then, cannot be *contingent* on agreement. Second, when agreement is controlled for with contexts where the antecedent DP is not in a position that controls agreement, such as in the embedded subject position of ECM constructions, there are still constraints on antecedence. So while agreement is a factor in pronoun-antecedent relations, it is not the only factor.

We have proposed that this can be understood if pronoun-antecedent relations are mediated by one or more silent functional heads, such as the context linkers of H. Á. Sigurðsson (2004, 2010, 2011). The relation between a pronoun and its antecedent is syntactic, but indirect. That is, it does not involve a direct Agree or movement dependency, but rather involves intermediate functional heads. Verbal agreement has an effect on pronoun-antecedent relations because verbal agreement in part reflects the relationship between a DP and the context linker it matches. We have also offered a tentative hypothesis as to why certain imposters trigger agreement more easily than others. The idea is that agreement with a subpart of a complex DP is more likely if that subpart controls features of a structurally higher subpart, such as the head of a partitive genitive construction or the secondary DP of an imposter. This provides a way of proceeding at least, so that in future work we can understand better how verbal agreement is triggered and what the effects of verbal agreement are. For now, we conclude that the fact that verbal agreement can have a constraining effect on pronoun-antecedent relations supports the claim that the relationship between a pronoun and its antecedent involves a syntactic relation.

We would like to thank Chris Collins for encouraging us to write this paper and commenting on several drafts along the way; Christer Platzack for his comments on a previous version of this work (Wood and E.F. Sigurðsson, 2011); and Halldór Ármann Sigurðsson, Jeroen van Craenenbroeck, Marcel Den Dikken, Inna Livitz, Paul Postal, Arhonto Terzi for various discussions of related issues. We would also like to thank Hallvarður Ásgeirsson, Júlía Hermannsdóttir and especially Gunnar Hrafn Hrafnbjargarson for discussions of some of the data.

References

Árnadóttir, Hlíf, Thórhallur Eythórsson, and Einar Freyr Sigurðsson. 2011. The passive of reflexive verbs in Icelandic. *Nordlyd* 37: 39–97.

Béjar, Susana. 2003. Phi Syntax: A Theory of Agreement. Doctoral dissertation, University of Toronto.

Béjar, Susana. 2008. Conditions on Phi-Agree. In *Phi Theory: Phi-Features across Modules and Interfaces*, eds. Daniel Harbour, David Adger, and Susana Béjar, 130–154. Oxford: Oxford University Press.

Béjar, Susana, and Milan Rezac. 2009. Cyclic agree. *Linguistic Inquiry* 40: 35–73.

Boeckx, Cedric, Norbert Hornstein, and Jairo Nunes. 2007. Overt copies in reflexive and control structures. *University of Maryland Working Papers in Linguistics* 15: 1–46.

Cattaneo, Andrea. 2007. Impostors and subject clitics: Four different types of impostors in Bellinzonese. Manuscript, New York University.

Cattaneo, Andrea. 2009. Imposters and pseudo-imposters in Bellinzonese and English. Manuscript, New York University.

Chomsky, Noam. 1995. *The Minimalist Program*. Malden, MA: MIT Press.

Collins, Chris, Simanique Moody, and Paul Postal. 2008. An AAE Camouflage Construction. *Language* 84: 29–68.

Collins, Chris, and Paul M. Postal. 2012. *Imposters: A Study of Pronominal Agreement*. Cambridge, MA: MIT Press.

Das, Satarupa. 2011. Bengali imposters. In *NYU Working Papers in Linguistics*, eds. Jim Wood and Neil Myler, Volume 3, 28–46. New York: New York University Press.

Dikken, Marcel den. 2001. 'Pluringulars,' pronouns and quirky agreement. *Linguistic Review* 18: 19–41.

Frascarelli, Mara. 2007. Subjects, topics and the interpretation of referential *pro*: An interface approach to the linking of (null) pronouns. *Natural Language and Linguistic Theory* 25: 691–734.

Friðjónsson, Jón G. 1990–1991. Beygingarsamræmi með samsettu frumlagi [Agreement with coordinated subjects]. *Íslenskt mál og almenn málfræði* 12–13: 79–103.

Harbour, Daniel. 2007. *Morphosemantic Number: From Kiowa Noun Classes to UG Number Features*. Dordrecht: Springer.

Harbour, Daniel. 2011a. Paucity, abundance, and the theory of number. Manuscript, Queen Mary University.

Harbour, Daniel. 2011b. Valence and atomic number. *Linguistic Inquiry* 42: 561–594.

Heim, Irene. 2008. Features on bound pronouns. In *Phi Theory: Phi-Features across Modules and Interfaces*, eds. Daniel Harbour, David Adger, and Susana Béjar, 35–56. Oxford: Oxford University Press.

Hicks, Glyn. 2008. Why the Binding Theory doesn't apply at LF. *Syntax* 11: 255–280.

Hicks, Glyn. 2009. *The Derivation of Anaphoric Relations*. Philadelphia, PA: John Benjamins.

Jónsson, Jóhannes Gísli. 1992. The pronoun *maður* in Icelandic. Manuscript, University of Massachusetts, Amherst.

Kayne, Richard. 2002. Pronouns and their antecedents. In *Derivation and Explanation in the Minimalist Program*, eds. Samuel David Epstein and T. Daniel Seely, 133–166. Oxford: Blackwell.

Kratzer, Angelika. 2009. Making a pronoun: Fake indexicals as windows into the properties of pronouns. *Linguistic Inquiry* 40: 187–237.

Myler, Neil. Submitted. Cliticization feeds agreement: A view from Quechua.

Nevins, Andrew. 2011. Multiple agree with clitics: Person complementarity vs. omnivorous number. *Natural Language and Linguistic Theory* 29: 939–971.

Pesetsky, David, and Esther Torrego. 2007. The syntax of valuation and the interpretability of features. In *Phrasal and Clausal Architecture: Syntactic Derivation and Interpretation. In Honor of Joseph E. Emonds*, eds. Simin Karimi, Vida Samiian, and Wendy K. Wilkins, 262–294. Amsterdam: John Benjamins.

Reuland, Eric. 2006. Agreeing to bind. In *Organizing Grammar: Linguistic Studies in Honor of Henk van Riemsdijk*, eds. Hans Broekhuis, Norbert Corver, Riny Huybregts, Ursula Kleinhenz, and Jan Koster, 505–513. Berlin: Mouton de Gruyter.

Reuland, Eric. 2011. *Anaphora and Language Design*. Cambridge, MA: MIT Press.

Rögnvaldsson, Eiríkur. 1993. Coordination, ATB-extractions, and the identification of *pro*. *Harvard Working Papers in Linguistics* 3: 153–180.

Schäfer, Florian. 2012. The passive of reflexive verbs and its implications for theories of binding and case. *Journal of Comparative Germanic Linguistics* 15: 213–268.

Sigurðsson, Einar Freyr. 2012. Germynd en samt þolmynd: Um nýju þolmyndina í íslensku [Active but still passive: On the New Passive in Icelandic]. M.A. Thesis, University of Iceland.

Sigurðsson, Halldór Ármann. 1986. Moods and (long distance) reflexives in Icelandic. *Working Papers in Scandinavian Syntax* 25: 1–53.

Sigurðsson, Halldór Ármann. 2004. The syntax of Person, Tense, and speech features. *Italian Journal of Linguistics / Rivista di Linguistica* 16: 219–251.

Sigurðsson, Halldór Ármann. 2006. The Icelandic noun phrase: Central traits. *Arkiv för nordisk filologi* 121: 193–236.

Sigurðsson, Halldór Ármann. 2010. On EPP effects. *Studia Linguistica* 64: 159–189.

Sigurðsson, Halldór Ármann. 2011. Conditions on argument drop. *Linguistic Inquiry* 42: 267–304.

Sigurðsson, Halldór Ármann. Submitted. About pronouns.

Sigurðsson, Halldór Ármann, and Verner Egerland. 2009. Impersonal null-subjects in Icelandic and elsewhere. *Studia Linguistica* 63: 158–185.

Sigurðsson, Halldór Ármann, and Anders Holmberg. 2008. Icelandic dative intervention: Person and number are separate probes. In *Agreement Restrictions*, eds. Roberta D'Alessandro, Susann Fischer, and Gunnar Hrafn Hrafnbjargarson, 251–280. Berlin: Mouton de Gruyter.

Sigurjónsdóttir, Sigríður. 1992. Binding in Icelandic: Evidence from Language Acquisition. Doctoral dissertation, University of California, Los Angeles.

Soare, Gabi. 2010. Person imposters in Romanian. Manuscript, University of Geneva.

Wood, Jim. 2009. Icelandic imposters and the proprial article. In *NYU Working Papers in Linguistics*, eds. Patricia Irwin and Violeta Vázquez Rojas, Volume 2. New York: New York University Press.

Wood, Jim, and Einar Freyr Sigurðsson. 2011. Icelandic verbal agreement and pronoun-antecedent relations. *Working Papers in Scandinavian Syntax* 88: 81–130.

Zwart, Jan-Wouter. 2002. Issues relating to a derivational theory of binding. In *Derivation and Explanation in the Minimalist Program*, eds. Samuel David Epstein and T. Daniel Seely, 269–304. Oxford: Blackwell.

10

Indefinite Imposters

VIOLETA VÁZQUEZ ROJAS

1. Introduction

Across languages, reference to the participants of the speech act is usually made by pronouns, while full determiner phrases are used to refer to other entities in the world. However, there are cases in which a full DP can be used to refer to the speaker or to the addressee of the utterance itself. Take, for instance, sentence (1), uttered by a father threatening his child:

(1) Daddy is going to sing "Hey Jude" and "All you need is love" as loud as I can.[1]

The nature of this phenomenon could be considered exclusively pragmatic, in which case, we would say that reference to the first person is made at the level of the utterance and that this decision has no effect in the structure of the sentence. But a closer look suggests that reference to the speaker/hearer is actually embedded in the syntax of these structures and is not a stylistic decision made after the syntax and semantics of the sentence have been computed. For instance, in (2a), the conjoined noun phrase *your sister and Daddy* can be the antecedent of the first person anaphor *ourselves*, but only if *Daddy* refers to the speaker. In this respect, the noun phrase *Daddy* behaves exactly like its pronominal counterpart in (2b):

(2) a. Now your sister and Daddy are going to get some ice cream for ourselves/themselves.
b. Now your sister and I are going to get some ice cream for ourselves/*themselves
c. Now your sister and John are going to get some ice cream for *ourselves/themselves

The conjoined subject noun phrase in (2c) cannot antecede a first person anaphor because *John* and *your sister* have their usual third person reference. Under

[1] http://prairiehome.publicradio.org/programs/2011/06/25/scripts/fritz.shtml

a pragmatic approach, it would remain a mystery why a conjoined determiner phrase with no first person features, like the subject of (2a), could license a first person anaphor. Collins and Postal (2012: 14) call DPs like the subject of (1a) and the second conjunct of the subject in (2a) *imposters*, and define them as follows:

(3) An imposter is a notionally *n* person DP which is grammatically *m* person, $n \neq m$.

The fact that the notional person of a DP has effects on pronominal and subject-verb agreement (for a description of such facts cross-linguistically, see the rest of the chapters of this volume) suggests that the phenomenon is not purely pragmatic and that it must have some bearing at the grammatical level. In particular, Collins and Postal (2012: 56) claim that imposters are actually complex DPs that contain both a covert personal pronoun and a full DP. In accordance with the terminology adopted there, we will call the covert personal pronoun the *notional DP*, the lexical DP will be called just that, and the whole complex DP that comprises both the notional and the lexical DP will be called the *shell DP*. Later in this chapter I will discuss the structure that supports the relation between the notional and the lexical DPs, but for the time being I will lay out the relation between these DPs in the following structure for the mere purpose of illustration. The pronominal in italics signals that this element is not overt:[2]

(4) $[_{DP}^{shell}\ \varnothing\ [_{DP}^{notional}\ \textit{I}]\ [_{DP}^{lexical}\ \text{Daddy}]]$

At first sight, it looks like any determiner phrase could be used to refer to a speech act participant, and that therefore, there is not a closed class of imposters. Collins and Postal (2012: 16) claim that, as much as the imposter class is open, some sub-types can be recognized. The cross-linguistic survey of imposters conducted in this volume also shows that, although the use of DPs as imposters is quite productive, the choice of the lexical DP is circumscribed to a particular class of nouns and a closed list of possible determiners (see also Collins and Postal 2012: 93). Two generalizations that seem to hold are that the imposter shell must be definite, and that the lexical DP must have a noun that is [+human].

This chapter is concerned with a particular imposter widely used in Spanish: *un servidor* (lit., "a servant"), which is roughly equivalent to the English *yours truly*.[3] The fact that this imposter is headed by an indefinite article defies the

[2] The structure in (4) violates binary branching, but I will not stick to this structure: its only function is to show the reader that 'complex DP' really means that a DP structure contains both the lexical DP, the overt DP and the silent notional pronoun. Also, the surface order of the notional and lexical DPs does not strictly have to be the one illustrated here.

[3] Although its presence is attested in different dialects, the data upon which the present work is based come mainly from Mexican Spanish.

generalization that all imposters must be definite. Its distribution, however, is different from other indefinites in the language, thus bringing support to the idea that its structure is more complex than a simple indefinite noun phrase. I will propose that, although not all imposters need to be definite, there are some constraints that apply to the choice of their lexical DP. One of them is that the head noun must refer to a *capacity* (in the sense of de Swart et al. 2007). The other one is that the lexical DP must contain a covert deictic element, which in some cases can be made explicit. These constraints explain why not every DP (for instance, a quantified DP or a numeral DP) can constitute an imposter. An indefinite like *un servidor* gets to be an imposter because it complies with the requirement of having a capacity noun, but in the discussion of our proposal it will be clear why there are not many other imposters like this one.

In the following section, I will present the agreement data that support that *un servidor* is an imposter by the definition provided in (3). Next, I will show that its distribution in "indefiniteness effect" contexts (Wang and McCready 2007) and its scopally independent reference bring more evidence in support of the presence of a covert personal pronoun. The fourth section lays out the details of the precursor structures from which imposters are derived according to Collins and Postal (2012), and proposes an alternative analysis of these structures as *Relator Phrases* (den Dikken and Longenecker 2005). I will argue for a constraint on the lexical DP of imposters to denote a capacity that is deictically anchored to the speech act. Based on data from Dudley (this volume), section 5 closes this chapter with a brief discussion of a counterexample to my analysis and offers a possible solution to it.

2. *Un servidor* as an Imposter

In Mexican Spanish (but also in other dialects), the DP *un servidor* "a servant" is commonly used to refer to the speaker of an utterance:

(5) *¿Qué tal, amigos?* Les **saluda** **un servidor** *desde el sur del país.*
what such friend.PL 3PL.DAT greet.3SG a servant from the south of.the country
"What's up, friends? Yours truly greets you from the south of the country."

(6) ***Una servidora*** **tuvo** el honor de conocer a la Dra. McDougall
a servant.FEM had the honor of meet ACC the.FEM Dr. M.
en Nueva York.
in New York
"Yours truly (fem) had the honor of meeting Dr. McDougall in New York."[4]

Even though the person referred to by *un servidor* is the speaker, the main verb agrees with the third person singular feature of the subject DP, as seen in (5)

[4] http://boletinesapm.blogspot.mx/2012/09/joyce-mcdougall.html

and (6).[5] Given its characteristic of notionally referring to the speaker of the utterance, while formally adopting third person grammatical features, the DP *un servidor* is clearly an *imposter* by the definition in (3) (see Dudley, this volume, for a more detailed account of the agreement characteritics of this and other imposters in Spanish). *Un servidor* also antecedes the third person reflexive *se* and the third person anaphor *sí mismo*, as shown in (7):

(7) a. ***Un servidor*** *está intentando engañarse a sí mismo.*
a servant be.3SG trying fool.INF.3SG.REFL ACC 3.REFL self
"Yours truly is trying to fool himself."

b. **Un servidor* *estoy intentando engañarme a mí mismo.*
a servant be.1SG trying fool.INF.1SG.REFL ACC 1.REFL self
Intended: "Yours truly is trying to fool himself."

Unlike DPs that have their regular third person reference, *un servidor* can antecede a first person pronoun outside of its clause, as in (8). In (8), the anaphor is not c-commanded by *un servidor*, but is anteceded by *PRO*, which in turn has first person features. This effect cannot be obtained by a regular DP with third person reference:

(8) a. *Es la especialidad de* ***un servidor*** *testificar por* ***mí*** ***mismo***
be.3SG the.FEM specialty of a servant testify.INF by 1SG.REFL self
en qué condiciones están esos lugares.
in what conditions be.3PL those places
"It is the specialty of yours truly to ascertain for myself the conditions in which those places are."

b. **Es la especialidad de* ***Pedro,*** *testificar por* ***mí*** ***mismo***
be.3SG the.FEM specialty of P. testify.INF by 1SG.REFL self
en qué condiciones están esos lugares.
in what conditions are those places
*"It's Pedro's specialty to ascertain for myself the conditions in which those places are."

The conjunct un servidor(a) of a coordinate structure can antecede a first person possessor:

(9) ***Mi esposo*** *y* **una servidora** nos subimos a **mi** *coche para alcanzarlos*
my husband and a servant 1PL.REFL climb.PST.1PL to my car to get.them
"My husband and yours truly hopped in my car to get them."

[5] Although this seems to be the rule, I have run into some examples like the following, where the verb agrees with the first person:

(i) ***Una servidora*** *lo* ***viví*** *a mi ingreso como docente de primaria.*
a servant 3SG.ACC live.PST.1SG at my entrance as teacher of elementary.school
"Yours truly went through it in my beginnings as an elementary school teacher."

Source: http://aprenderycompartirbix.blogspot.mx/index.html#650451451407298982

In coordination with a third person, *un servidor* triggers first-person plural agreement, as exemplified in (10). This sentence also shows, along with (9), that the noun takes the gender inflection that matches the gender of the speaker. It is also possible, although clearly less common, for *un servidor* to take plural inflection, as in (11):

(10) *El miércoles, Fernando y* ***una servidora*** *acompañamos a mi padre al*
the Wednesday, F and a servant.FEM accompanied.1PL ACC my father to
hospital.
hospital
"On Wednesday, Fernando and yours truly accompanied my father to the hospital."

(11) ***Unos servidores*** *vamos a seguir intentando que esta página sea*
a.PL servant.PL go.1PL to continue trying that this page be.SBJVE
de tu interés.
of your interest
"Yours truly (pl) will continue trying to make this website catch your interest."

Lastly, *un servidor* is subject to a disjoint reference constraint when anteceding a first-person plural pronoun (12). In this respect, it behaves like a first-person singular pronoun (13) and not like a regular DP with third person reference (14):

(12) **Un servidor nos aceptará.*
a servant 1ST.PL.ACC accept.FUT.3SG
*"Yours truly will accept us."

(13) *Yo los aceptaré /*nos aceptaré*
I 3RD.PL.ACC accept.FUT.1SG /1ST.PL.ACC accept.FUT
"I will accept them"/*"I will accept us"

(14) *Un cura nos aceptará*
a priest 1ST.PL.ACC accept.FUT.3SG
"A priest will accept us."

We have thus shown that *un servidor* has the characteristics of third person DPs in requiring third person agreement on the verb and anteceding third person reflexives and anaphors. It also has first person grammatical characteristics in triggering first person plural agreement when it occurs in conjoined subject DPs. The main difference between *un servidor* and any other imposter described so far in Spanish—and possibly in this volume—is that the shell DP is indefinite, while this is generally not the case for imposters. Compare for instance, (15a) and (15b) from English, and (16a) and (16b) from Spanish:

(15) a. Barbara and **this reporter** described ourselves to the investigator
b. *Barbara and **a reporter** described ourselves to the investigator.

(16) a. *Manuel y* ***este reportero*** *nos presentamos en el Cuartel.*
M and this reporter 1PL.REFL present.PST.1PL in the quarters
"Manuel and this reporter presented ourselves at the headquarters."
b. **Manuel y* ***un reportero*** *nos presentamos en el Cuartel.*
M and a reporter 1PL.REFL present.PST.1PL in the quarters
Intended: "Manuel and this reporter presented ourselves at the headquarters."

Collins and Postal (2012: 56) claim that, although indefinites usually are not used as imposters, there might be a couple of instances that show an indefinite noun phrase as an imposter. I repeat one of their examples in (17a), and provide a similar one in (17b):

(17) a. A girl can dream, can't I?
b. A guy wants to have some soup and this is what happens to me.

Although the indefinite noun phrases *a guy* and *a girl* are used to make reference to the speaker, it is not clear that they pattern with other English imposters. To begin with, when they are conjoined with another DP, they cannot antecede a first-person plural anaphor, as shown in (18a).

(18) a. *A guy and Barbara are going to get some cold beers for ourselves now.
b. This reporter and Barbara are going to get some cold beers for ourselves now.

(19) *A guy will take a beer from your fridge, may I?

Without getting into a deeper analysis of this phenomenon, at first glance it looks like sentences (17a) and (17b) can have an imposter-like reading only by virtue of making a generic statement about a kind. The imposter-like reading of the indefinite is absent from the same indefinite phrases in episodic sentences like (18a) and (19). It seems that the appropriate way to understand the reference of *a guy* and *a girl* in (17) is as generics; the imposter-like reading arises from implying that the speaker is a member of the kind denoted by the generic indefinite.[6] In other words, the indefinite subjects in (17) do not refer to the speaker, but rather to a kind to which the speaker belongs. This phenomenon is very different from "true" imposters as defined in (3).

The generalization that seems to hold is that imposters in English are always definite. This comprises the possibilities listed in (20) (Collins and Postal 2012: 12):

[6] Another characteristic of these noun phrases is that, unlike true indefinite imposters like *un servidor*, they cannot occur in "indefiniteness effect" contexts (Wang and McCready 2007), even if they are intended to be interpreted with first person reference: (i) *What do you think about a guy?, (ii) *Do you know where a guy is? We will describe the distribution of *un servidor* in these contexts in section 3.

(20) (a) DPs headed by the definite article (*the present reviewer, the undersigned*)
(b) DPs headed by demonstratives (*this reporter*)
(c) Proper names (*Elmo wants a ball!*)
(d) DPs with possessors (*your mommy/your humble servant will to take care of this*)
(e) Kinship terms with no overt possessive (*Mommy will take care of this*)

Spanish has more or less the same classes of imposters. As Dudley remarks in this volume, class (e) is replaced by overtly possessed kinship terms, although bare kinship nouns like *Mamá te ayudará* "Mommy will help you" are becoming increasingly common. In sum, there is a definiteness restriction on imposter DPs in English, Spanish, and possibly cross-linguistically, but indefinite phrases like *un servidor* seem to be an exception to this pattern.

3. Indefinite Imposters in Definite Contexts

Just as existential sentences reject definite noun phrases as arguments (and by "definite noun phrase" in this context I mean, at least, any constituent from the list in (21)), Wang and McCready (2007) identify a handful of contexts that reject indefinite noun phrases. I will show that *un servidor* is allowed in contexts where indefinites are rejected, but first I will provide evidence that *un servidor* cannot have an imposter interpretation when it occurs in an existential sentence. Sentence (21) can only have a third-person reference reading. Since under the imposter reading (21) is ungrammatical, but under a non-imposter reading it is fine, I use "#" to signal that the sentence does not admit the relevant imposter interpretation:[7]

(21) #*Hay* ***una servidora*** *que te puede ayudar.*
there.is a servant that 2SG.ACC can.PRES.3SG help
"There is a servant that can help you."

When embedded under the scope of a quantifier or an intensional operator, an indefinite phrase in Spanish can always be interpreted as referentially dependent on that operator. This is not the case when *un servidor* refers to the speaker. For example, the request made by sentence (22) with *un servidor* would not be fulfilled if every person supported different people, but only if everybody supported the same person, namely, the speaker of the utterance:

[7] With first person reference, *un(a) servidor(a)* can only occur in existential sentences with an overt deictic locative: *Aquí hay una servidora que te puede ayudar* "Here's a servant who can help you." However, I don't consider this construction a true case of an existential sentence; instead, it is a locative construction that does not require its theme to be indefinite, just as in *Aquí está la persona/una persona que te puede ayudar* "Here's a person/the person who can help you."

(22) *Ojalá que el próximo año Hispania se lleve el galardón,*
hopefully that the next year Hispania 3SG.REFL take.3SG.SBJVE the award
pero con todos apoyando a ***un servidor.***[8]
but with all.PL supporting ACC a servant
"Hopefully next year Hispania will take the award, but with everybody supporting yours truly."

If sentence (23a) is continued as in (23c), it can only have the non-imposter reading, and it would be true in a scenario where the subject refuses to make friends with whomever happens to be a servant. But if *una servidora* has an imposter interpretation in (23a), the continuation in (23b) is natural. I mark (23c) with "#" to signal that it is an infelicitous continuation of (23a) under its imposter interpretation.

(23) a. *El señorito no quiere hacer migas con* ***una servidora.***[9]
the young.master not want.3SG make friends with a servant
"The young master does not want to make friends with yours truly/a servant."
b. . . . *por más que lo intento.*
by more that 3SG.ACC try.PRES.1SG
". . . no matter how much I try."
c. # . . . *sea quien sea.*
be.SUBJVE.3SG who be.SUBJVE.3SG
". . . no matter who it is."

"Indefiniteness effect" contexts (Wang and McCready 2007) reject indefinite phrases, whether they are interpreted as non-specific or specific.[10] Even overt partitives, which display an explicit definite restriction, are rejected from such contexts. *Un servidor* is perfectly grammatical in such a context, and it can only be interpreted with a first person reading:

(24) a. *¿Qué pasa con* ***Juan / este periodista / *un portero / *varios estudiantes****?*
what happens with Juan / this journalist / a doorman / several students
"What's wrong with John / this journalist / *a doorman / *several students?"
b. *¿Quieres saber qué pasa con* ***un servidor****?*
want.PRES.2SG know what happens with a servant
"Do you want to know what's wrong with yours truly?"

(25) a. *¿Qué opinas* ***de este actor/ *un actor / *uno de los actores*** */ de mí?*
what think.PRES.2SG of this actor / an actor / one of the.PL actors / of me
"What do you think about this actor / *an actor / *one of the actors / me?"

[8] http://forum.dofus.com/es/31-papelera-reciclaje/591596-bravo-miss-mr-mundo-doce&page=1

[9] http://saldorada.blogspot.mx/2013/03/hojaldre-relleno-de-manzana-y-foie.html

[10] To my judgment and that of the speakers I have consulted, indefinites do not occur in these contexts even if they are partitive-specific (Enç 1991) or epistemically specific.

b. *¿Qué opinas de* ***un servidor****?*
what think.PRES.2SG of a servant
"What do you think about yours truly?"

(26) a. *A que no sabes dónde está* ***mi hermano*** / *****un ingeniero****.*
at that not know.PRES.2SG where is my brother / *an engineer
"I bet you don't know where my brother / *an engineer is."

b. *¡No se imaginan dónde está* ***un servidor****!*
not 2PL.REFL imagine.PRES.2PL where is a servant
"You can't imagine where yours truly is!"

What the contrasts in (24)–(26) show is that *un servidor* is not a regular indefinite phrase because it is allowed in contexts where indefinite phrases, no matter how specific, are rejected. And in every context in which it is allowed (24b, 25b, and 26b), it can only refer to the speaker. While the contexts in (24)–(26) reject indefinites, they allow definite noun phrases and, therefore, pronouns. What licenses the occurrence of *un servidor* in such contexts must be a covert first person pronoun that has the distribution of the overt pronoun in (27):

(27) a. *¿Quieres saber qué pasa* ***conmigo****?*
want.PRES.2SG know what happens with.me
"Do you want to know what's going on with me?"

b. *¿Qué opinas de* ***mí****?*
what think.PRES.2SG of me
"What do you think about me?"

c. *¡No se imaginan dónde estoy* ***yo****!*
not REFL.2PL imagine.PRES.2PL where am I
"You can't imagine where I am!"

So far I have shown that *un servidor* is a notionally first person determiner phrase which has overt grammatical third person features. In addition, I have shown that, despite being formally indefinite, *un servidor* does not give rise to referential dependencies even when it is embedded under a scope-taking operator. The distribution of *un servidor* in "indefiniteness effect" contexts supports the claim, put forth by Collins and Postal (2012), that imposter DPs are complex structures comprising a covert pronominal DP and a lexical DP. The pronominal DP is what licenses the occurrence of an indefinite in contexts that reject any other indefinite noun phrase, whether specific or non-specific. Thus, it appears that indefinite noun phrases can occur as first person imposters. But it is also a fact that the set of indefinite imposters in Spanish is quite limited, if not restricted to *un servidor* "a servant" and, less frequently, *un amigo* "a friend." In the next section, I lay out a proposal about where this restriction might originate.

4. Imposter Precursors

4.1 APPOSITIVES AND NON-RESTRICTIVE RELATIVE CLAUSES

According to Collins and Postal (2012: 66), an imposter is a complex DP with the following underlying structure:

(28)

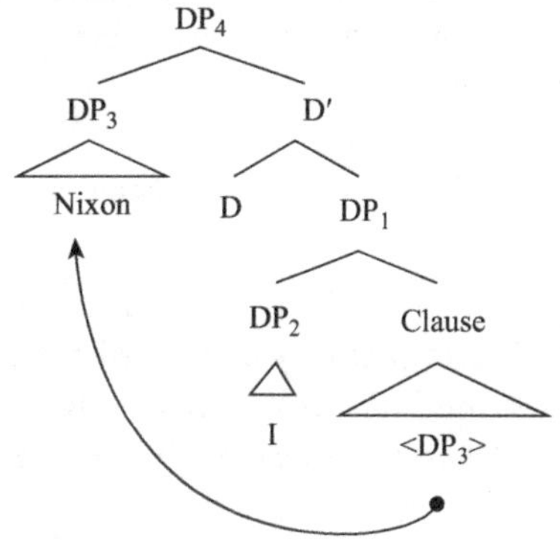

The notional DP (DP_2) is a silent pronoun—in the case at hand, a first person pronoun. DP_3 is a lexical DP embedded under some clausal structure, arguably an appositive relative. There is a predicative relation between the notional DP and the lexical DP. Crucial to their analysis, the predicative (lexical) DP rises to a higher position (Spec DP_4) from where it displays the phi-features that account for the whole imposter agreement facts.

The structure of imposters proposed in (28) derives from a structure similar to the ones in the subject phrases in (29), where the pronominal and the lexical DPs are expressed overtly and related either by a specifying apposition (as in Collins 2009) or by an non-restrictive relative clause (as proposed by Collins and Postal 2012: 66). These appositive structures are called the imposters' *precursors*.

(29) a. And I, Nixon, am here not for any romantic purpose.
b. I, who am your Daddy, am going to sing "Hey Jude" as loud as I can.

Independently of which particular structure we desire to maintain as the precursor for imposters, it is important that three facts obtain: (i) the notional DP must remain a silent pronoun, (ii) the lexical DP must rise from its predicate position to a position from where it can determine the phi-features of the whole imposter, and (iii) this movement must involve a whole DP and not just an NP (Collins and Postal 2012: 66).

Not just any noun phrase that appears in an appositive structure like (29a,b) can be the lexical DP in an imposter. For instance, determiner-less noun phrases can be appositives, but they cannot be used as imposters:

(30) a. I, owner of a gazillion lip balms, highly recommend this brand.[11]
b. *Owner of a gazillion lip balms highly recommends this brand.

A similar fact holds in Spanish, which rejects determiner-less common noun phrases as imposters, but accepts them as appositives:

(31) a. *Yo, (que soy) madre, me siento muy afortunada.*
I that am mother 1SG.REFL feel.PRES.1SG very fortunate
"I, (who am a) mother, feel very fortunate."
b. **Madre te va a ayudar con tu tarea.*
mother 2SG.ACC go.3SG to help with your homework
"Mother is going to help you with your homework."

Although the unacceptable cases in (30) and (31) may be filtered out by restriction (iii), indefinite DPs are perfectly common in non-restrictive clauses in English, as well as in non-clausal appositive structures. However, as previously stated, they cannot be used as imposters:

(32) a. I, who am a lady, have a slight Southern accent.
b. #A lady has a slight Southern accent.

The same is true for Spanish, which, apart from *un servidor* and *un amigo*, does not have a productive set of indefinite imposters. In (33b), "#" marks that the sentence, although grammatical, cannot have an imposter interpretation.

(33) a. *Yo, un alcohólico empedernido, no soltaba la botella.*
I an alcoholic stubborn not let.go.PST.1SG the bottle
"I, a stubborn alcoholic, did not let go of the bottle."
b. #*Un alcohólico empedernido no soltaba la botella.*
an alcoholic stubborn not let.go.PST.1SG the bottle
"A stubborn alcoholic did not let go of the bottle."

Likewise, not every DP that has an attested use as an imposter can easily enter into the appositive structures in (29). In particular, DPs headed by a demonstrative, which are a productive source for imposters, are not readily acceptable as appositives or as predicates in non-restrictive relatives:

(34) a. This reporter is following this breaking scandal closely.[12]
b. *I, (who am) this reporter, am following this breaking scandal closely.

[11] This is a slight adaptation of a naturally occuring example found at https://twitter.com/JanetWagner1/status/306551059034300416.

[12] http://kingdzbws.blogspot.mx/2009/12/shock-gravity-hoax.html

(35) a. *Este reportero está siguiendo de cerca el escándalo.*
this reporter be.3SG following of close the scandal.
"This reporter is following the scandal closely."

b. **Yo, este reportero, estoy siguiendo de cerca el escándalo.*
I this reporter be.1SG following of close the scandal
Lit. *"I, this reporter, am following the scandal closely."

Perhaps a more problematic case for the proposed precursor structure of imposters in Collins and Postal (2012) is that non-restrictive relative clauses cannot be "stacked" (de Vries 2006: 23). Imposters, on the other hand, can have their own non-restrictive relative. The following data could not be explained if imposters were derived from restrictive relatives:

(36) a. The editor in chief, who covered the case for the *Boston Globe*, has examined forty volumes of testimony.
b. *I, who am the editor in chief, who covered the case for the *Boston Globe*, have examined forty volumes of testimony.

Collins and Postal (2012: 16) claim that possibly any definite human DP can function as an imposter. This characterization is too general. Imposter DPs almost always contain a noun that denotes a *capacity* (in a sense that will be clarified below), which, in turn, is anchored to the speech situation by an overt or covert indexical.[13] I will not be able to offer a syntactic analysis of exactly where this deictic element is hosted, but I will present some data to support this generalization.

4.2 PREDICATIVE DPs AS *CAPACITIES*

Dudley (this volume) identifies the following list of possible imposters in Spanish:

(37) a. *los* "the" + common noun denoting sentient being
b. *este* "this" + common noun denoting sentient being
c. *el abajo firmante* "the undersigned"
d. *det* + servidor "servant"
e. *det* + menda "guy"
f. *tu* "your" + various non-diminutive kinship terms

Collins and Postal (2012: 7) also identify a possible class of imposters in English:

"It appears, then, that the class of English imposters will (properly) include the open sets *the* + Modifier + Human Proper Name and *this* +

[13] I will elaborate on this later. For the time being, "speech situation" refers to the situation that involves the speech act itself, with its participants (speaker, addressee) and the particular time and location where it takes place.

Common Noun denoting humans—more accurately, denoting sentient beings. Other imposters include the following:

(38) a. *first person imposters*
i. yours truly, your faithful correspondent, the (present) author(s), the present reviewer(s), the undersigned, the court, the (present) writer(s)
ii. personal names
iii. diminutive kinship terms: Daddy, Mommy, Auntie, Granny, Gramps
iv. non-diminutive kinship terms plus a personal name: Uncle + Name, Aunt + Name, Cousin + Name, Grampa + Name, Granma + Name"

First, note that kinship terms, whether in their diminutive or non-diminutive form, are a cross-linguistically stable source for imposters (see Collins and Postal 2012: 4 for examples in French, and throughout this volume for examples in other languages). Another safe source for imposters is the set of common nouns that denote roles directly related to the speech act: *the (present) authors, the (present) reviewers, the undersigned.* The common nouns in this kind of imposter refer to the role of author, reviewer or undersigned in the very speech act in which the noun phrase is embedded. Further, Dudley correctly points out (2013: 15, fn. 4) that imposters cross-linguistically can be "reinforced" by a deictic modifier, like *present, here,* or *under* in *undersigned.*

The deictic term employed in imposters always signals closest proximity to the speech situation or the speech participants. For instance, while a lot of imposters are formed by the proximal *this* (*this reporter, this dentist, this atheist*), none can be formed by the distal *that*, a fact also noted by Collins and Postal (2012). In Spanish, common deictic reinforcers for imposters are the proximal locatives *aquí/acá*, while the distal locatives *allí/allá* are disallowed from the same contexts. All the sentences in (39)–(41) can have an imposter reading, but only in the (a) sentences can the locative modify the imposter. In (39b), (40b), and (41b), the distal locatives *allí/allá* can only be interpreted as modifiers of the main predicate. I mark these sentences with "#" because they are unacceptable under the reading where the locative is a modifier of the subject noun phrase. Note that *un servidor* can also be modified by *aquí* "here" in (41a).

(39) a. ***Aquí tu mami*** *te va a ayudar con tu tarea.*
here your mom 2SG.ACC go.3SG to help with your homework
"Your mommy here is going to help you with your homework."

b. #***Allá tu mami*** *te va a ayudar con tu tarea.*
there your mom 2SG.ACC go.3SG to help with your homework
Lit. *"Your mommy there is going to help you with your homework."

(40) a. ***Aquí un amigo / este reportero*** *te va a donar algunas fotos.*
here a friend / this reporter 2SG.ACC go.fut.3SG to donate some pictures
"A friend / This reporter here will give you some pictures."

b. #***Allí un amigo / este reportero*** *te va a donar algunas fotos.*
there a friend / this reporter 2SG.ACC go.3SG to donate some pictures
Lit. * "There your friend / this reporter will give you some pictures."

(41) a. *Si desean más información,* ***aquí un servidor*** *les puede echar la mano.*
if wish.2PL more information here a servant 3PL.DAT can.3SG throw the hand
"If you want more information, yours truly here can give you a hand."

b. #*Si desean más información,* ***allá un servidor*** *les puede echar la mano.*
if wish.2PL more information there a servant 3PL.DAT can.3SG throw the hand
Lit. #"If you want more information, yours truly there can give you a hand."

So far we have encountered two regularities: (a) imposter nouns refer to capacities, which apply only to human referents and, to take a definition already available in the literature, "denote specific roles in society: professions, religions or nationalities" (de Swart et al. 2007). I would add to this definition the possibility of denoting a specific role in a speech act (*author, reviewer,* and *applicant* also denote capacities). Second, (b) imposters display or can be reinforced by overt deictic expressions that are always [+proximal].

These two facts can be captured by attributing to the lexical DP in an imposter the requirement that it denote a capacity that is deictically anchored to the speech situation. I use the term "situation" as in Elbourne (2005), following Barwise and Perry (1983), as referring to a part of a possible world that contains an individual or individuals and some of their properties or relations, along with a particular time and location, when relevant. In that vein, the *speech situation* is a specific situation that includes the utterance, the speaker, the addressee, and the time and location where the speech act takes place. I will also distinguish the speech situation from the *topic situation*, that is, the situation that a declarative speech act is about.

In sum, the lexical DP in an imposter denotes a capacity anchored to the speech situation, and this capacity, in turn, is ascribed to the speaker in a first person imposter, or to the hearer in second person imposters. We can relate the speaker or the addressee and the capacity ascribed to them in a precursor structure like the one put forth in Collins (2009), in which the notional DP and the lexical DP are linked to each other by a Relator Phrase. This kind of predicative structure does not display all the functional structure that a non-restrictive relative clause would require. I consider the head of this Relator Phrase to be the semantic equivalent of "as," so that the closest precursor structure to an imposter like (42a) is (42b):

(42) a. This reporter has examined forty volumes of testimony.
b. I, as a reporter in this situation, have examined forty volumes of testimony.
c. I, as a reporter (in $s_{[+proximal]}$), have examined forty volumes of testimony.

The relation between the predicate DP and the pronominal, mediated by "*as*," ensures that the predicate relates the subject of the predication to a certain role. In example (42), the subject of the predication would be the speaker, and the role that is predicated of him is the role of being a reporter in *s*.

Individuals fulfill social roles relative to specific situations. The same individual can have different capacities depending on the situation: suppose that Hugo Sánchez is a famous soccer player, but is also a dentist. If he advertises a certain brand of shoes in his role as a soccer player, I might want to buy that brand because it is advertised by a soccer player, but not because it is advertised by a dentist. In fact, there is a sense in which "*This brand is advertised by a dentist*" is not true in that scenario. Capacities are not interchangeable just because they happen to have the same extension in a particular world. For this reason, I propose that capacity predicates must always come with a situation argument, *s*.

In imposter structures, the situation in which the capacity described holds of a certain individual, call it *s*, must be close, spatio-temporally speaking, to the speech situation, s_{sp}. This includes the possibility for *s* to be contained within the speech situation itself. I signal this requirement by ascribing the feature [+proximal] to the situation argument *s* in the informal representation in (42c). This [+proximal] feature of the situation argument of the capacity noun is what is reinforced by locative adverbs like *here*, which in imposter structures do not refer to the spatial location of the event described by the sentence (i.e., the *topic situation*), but only have scope within the imposter DP, as we saw in (39)–(41) (cf. *Your mommy* ***here*** *is going to help you with your homework* ***over there***).

The predicative DP and the notional DP are related by the following minimal structure:

(43)

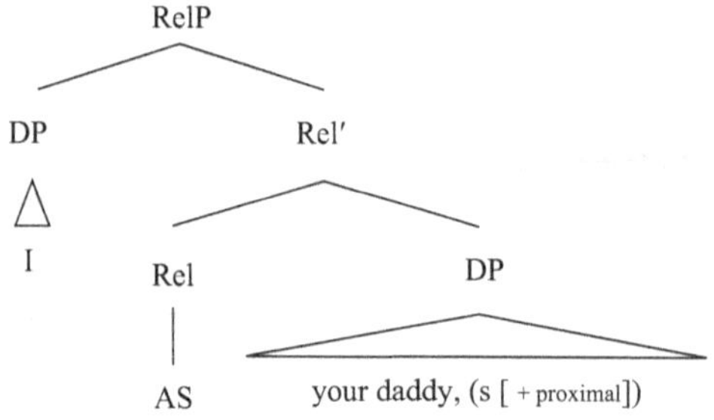

The last step required is that the lexical DP undergoes raising to the specifier of a higher DP in order to account for the agreement facts with the phi-features of the lexical DP. I propose that this raising is motivated by a higher D head marked as [+proximal], which attracts the [+proximal] predicative DP to its specifier:

(44)

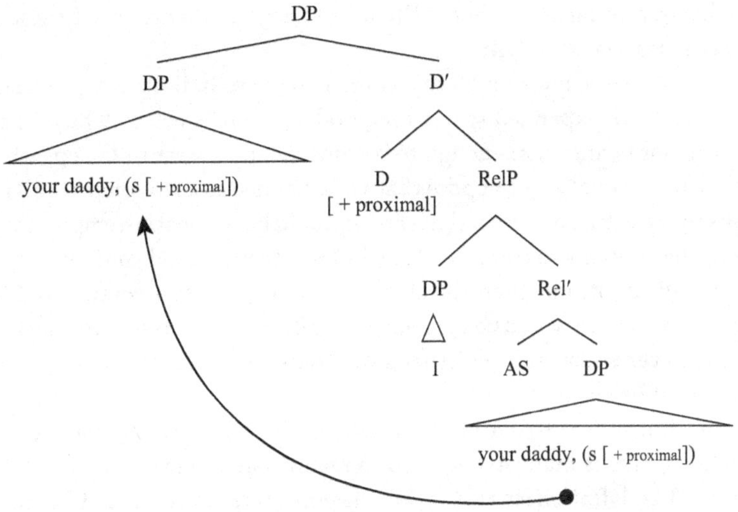

The present analysis does not predict that indefinite imposters would be ungrammatical, but that they would generally be dispreferred and highly marked. This is because, in order for the capacity situation argument to be [+proximal], it would also need to be *minimal*.[14]

I am taking here a rather informal and intuitive approach to *minimal situations*, without making any serious ontological commitments. For a formal approach to minimal situations, I refer the reader to Elbourne (2005) and Kratzer (1989). For the purposes of the present analysis, I consider a situation to be *minimal* if it is the smallest situation possible that contains an individual or individuals and a property or relation. A minimal situation might also contain a specific location and time, but that is not always necessary. Any such situation can be expanded to contain more properties, more individuals, expanded spatio-temporal locations, and so on. But if we reach a point where a situation cannot be "divided" into constituent sub-situations, then we have arrived at a minimal situation, and that is all we need to assume. For example, *s* can be a situation where Hugo is a dentist and nothing else that is not already entailed by him being a dentist. And *s* can be expanded to a more complex situation, call it *s*′, where Hugo is a dentist and a football player. Alternatively, *s* can be

[14] A fair question to ask at this point is why the fact that the [+proximal] situation is also minimal does not force the use of the definite article in examples like (42b), given that there must be only one individual satisfying the property "reporter." My answer to this problem is that, although minimal situations satisfy the uniqueness condition that definite articles presuppose, they do not automatically satisfy the existence presupposition triggered by the definite article. If this presupposition is satisfied—or if the speaker is willing to let the hearer accommodate this presupposition—then the definite article is legitimately used. If not, then we would expect an indefinite article, like in (42b).

expanded to a situation *s''*, where Hugo and Diego are dentists. Of these three, only *s* is a minimal situation.

If a situation *s* is big enough to comprise multiple individuals, properties, or relations, and an expanded spatio-temporal location, it will still be a situation, but it will not be minimal enough to be considered "closest to the speech situation" in a non-trivial way. Suppose that *s* is expanded so as to comprise all the situations in the actual world. In that case, it would have a spatio-temporal location close to the speech situation: so close, indeed, that *s* would contain the speech situation within it. But then the claim that *s* is spatio-temporally proximal to the speech situation would be true only trivially. For this reason, we must ensure that, whenever we evaluate whether a situation *s* is proximal to the speech situation, *s* must be *minimal*.

For each minimal situation, there should be the least number possible of individuals, just as many as required to instantiate the property or relation in question. The definiteness restriction on imposters comes from this minimality requirement. The feature [+proximal] applies to minimal situations, and the capacity predicate must be true of one individual per minimal situation at a time.[15] Minimality thus ensures uniqueness, and this in turn supports the use of a definite article when referring to an individual that instantiates a capacity at a particular situation.[16] For example, an appositive predication like "*I, a soccer player, will train your kids*" would mean "*I, a soccer player in a minimal situation s, will train your kids.*" Since there would be no more than one soccer player at *s*, we would interpret the predication as "*I, **the** soccer player in s, will train your kids.*"

The uniqueness of the individual that instantiates the capacity role at *s*, along with the temporal proximity/inclusiveness of *s* to the speech situation, triggers the use of demonstratives, possessors and definite determiners in the shell DP of an imposter.

We said that indefinite imposters should be marked, but not impossible to obtain. I attribute the existence of the Spanish indefinite imposter to a politeness effect. First, it does not require much analysis to acknowledge that by *un servidor* "a servant," the speaker means *un servidor de usted* "a servant of yours," that is, the capacity described is that of *servant of the addressee*. The construction allows for this role to be expressed by an indefinite: *Yo, un servidor de usted* "I, a servant of yours" or by a possessive: *Yo, su servidor* "I, your servant." In fact, this second form is also widely used as an imposter, although in this chapter I decided to concentrate only on its indefinite form. The overt

[15] I intend the restriction on minimality for [+proximal] situations to apply only to the situation argument of the capacity noun in an imposter DP. I have not analyzed the consequences of applying this restriction to any situation modified by a deictic proximal, because doing so is outside the scope of this chapter.

[16] Minimal situations have proven useful when dealing with the uniqueness interpretation of pronouns and definite descriptions in Donkey sentences (Elbourne 2005). However, I do not intend to give an explicit comparison of that proposal to the one advanced here, which is rather informal.

possessive carries the implication that the addressee has, even if only in that minimal situation, only one servant. The politeness effect consists in preventing this implication by selecting an indefinite rather than a definite or possessive determiner, therefore allowing the possibility[17] that the addressee might have multiple servants.

In a nutshell: indefinite imposters are in general disallowed because the role they denote must be tied to a minimal situation, and in that situation the role itself should be instantiated by the minimal number of individuals, namely, one. However, if the speaker decides to undermine this inference by implying that more than one entity can fulfill this role, the indefinite article can be used to obtain such an effect. As a consequence, an indefinite imposter is not outright impossible, but its motivation is ultimately pragmatic and marked.

It so happens that in Spanish this politeness trigger of the indefinite imposter *un servidor* has such an extended use that the imposter (and the noun itself) have been conventionalized, while in English this has not happened. But there is no principled syntactic reason, other than constraining the use of capacity nouns to minimal and most proximal situations, to ban indefinite imposters from the grammar.[12] http://kingdzbws.blogspot.mx/2009/12/shock-gravity-hoax.html

5. A Possible Counterexample

Dudley (this volume) analyzes examples like the following as an instance of imposters in Spanish:

(45)	*Los*	*mexicanos*	*comemos*	*mucho*	*chile.*
	the.PL	mexican PL.	eat.HAB.1PL	a.lot	chile
	"We Mexicans eat a lot of chile."				

The subject DP in (45) conforms to the imposter definition in (3) (see Dudley, this volume, for discussion). It also presents a counterexample to my claim that the lexical DP of imposters always denotes capacities with a [+proximal] situation argument. Since (45) is interpretable as a generic statement, there is no obvious way in which it can satisfy the [+proximal] requirement.

I do not have an explanation for this phenomenon, but I claim that, if cases like (45) are imposters, they constitute a class of their own. The main reason is that they allow first-person plural agreement even when they are quantified. This is true even if the restriction of the quantifier is not a definite DP, as in (46b):

[17] I will not commit to whether this inference is a presupposition or an implicature. I use the neutral term "implication" to cover both possibilities.

(46) a. *Todos los mexicanos comemos mucho chile.*
all the.PL mexican.PL eat.HAB.1PL a.lot chile
"All of us Mexicans eat a lot of chile.'"
b. *Algunos mexicanos comemos mucho chile.*
some.PL mexican.m.PL eat.HAB.1PL a.lot chile
"Some of us Mexicans eat a lot of chile."

The quantified subject DPs in (46) do not fit the precursor structure I have proposed here, nor any precursor structure proposed before in Collins (2009) or Collins and Postal (2012). The ungrammaticality of the corresponding appositive structures is shown in (47). Although they are ungrammatical, I offer a literal translation in English, which, not surprisingly, is ungrammatical as well.

(47) a. **Nosotros, todos los mexicanos, comemos mucho chile*
we all the.PL mexican.PL eat.HAB.1PL a.lot chile
Possible literal translation: "We, all the Mexicans, eat a lot of chile."
b. **Nosotros, algunos mexicanos, comemos mucho chile.*
we some.pl mexican.PL eat.HAB.1PL a.lot chile
Possible literal translation: "We, some Mexicans, eat a lot of chile."

In general, specifying appositives cannot be quantificational (Doron 1994), so if we wish to maintain the appositive precursor structure for imposters (in any of its versions), these examples must be treated separately.

One more reason that these DPs might not be imposters has been suggested to me by Aguilar-Guevara (p.c. 2013). Namely, if first person imposters refer to the speaker by a first person silent pronoun, it should be possible to use them in performative speech acts. This prediction is confirmed by (40) in English, and (41) in Spanish:

(48) Your daddy promises not to sing anymore.
(49) *Un/tu servidor te promete darle buen uso a esos mapas.*[18]
a/your servant 2SG.DAT promise.3SG give.3SG.DAT good use to those maps
"A/your servant promises to make good use of those maps."

In contrast, quantified noun phrases and plural generics, even if they trigger first person plural agreement in the verb, cannot be used in performative statements. I use "#" to signal that these sentences are infelicitous with the intended illocutionary force: (50a) and (50b) can only be interpreted as descriptive speech acts, but not as performatives. Conversely, sentences with an overt first person pronoun (50d) can be interpreted as performatives, and, interestingly,

[18] http://www.levelup.com/noticias/11415/El-primer-paquete-de-mapas-para-Black-Ops/

non-quantified definites (50c) fare a lot better with respect to this test than their quantified counterparts:

(50) a. *#Algunos mexicanos te prometemos cuidar el agua.*
some.PL mexican.PL 2SG.DAT promise.PRES.1PL take.care the water
Lit: "Some Mexicans promise you to save water."

b. *#Todos los mexicanos te prometemos cuidar el agua.*
all.PL the.PL mexican.PL 2SG.DAT promise.PRES.1PL take.care the water
Lit: "All Mexicans promise you to save water."

c. *# Los mexicanos te prometemos cuidar el agua.*
the.PL mexican.PL 2SG.DAT promise.PRES.1PL take.care the water
"The Mexicans promise you to save water."

d. *Nosotros los mexicanos te prometemos cuidar el agua.*
we the.PL mexican.PL 2SG.DAT promise.PRES.1PL take.care the water
"We the Mexicans promise you to save water."

In sum, my account of imposter lexical DPs finds a counterexample in imposters like the ones in (45). I do not have an explanation for these cases, but I think that any analysis we give to (45) should be equally applied to quantified cases like (46), which display the same agreement pattern. And since quantified DPs like those in (46) are not plausibly analyzed as "regular" imposters, it appears that the facts in (45) need a different analysis as well.

6. Conclusions

I have proposed in this chapter that the definiteness of imposter shells is determined by the following independent semantic and syntactic constraints:

(i) The notional DP and the lexical DP are related by a predicative structure (as in Collins 2009; Collins and Postal 2012).

(ii) The noun in the lexical DP must denote a *capacity* or social role. This captures the general fact that the noun denotes a sentient being (documented elsewhere).

(iii) The capacity noun has an argument *s*, for a minimal situation, that is specified as [+proximal], requiring that *s* take place at a spatio-temporal location closest to the speech situation, and possibly within the speech situation itself. The [+proximal] feature explains the natural occurrence of "deictic reinforcers" in imposters (Dudley, this volume), which have scope only within the DP, but which do not modify the event described by the main sentence.

(iv) The situation *s* is minimal. Otherwise, the feature [+proximal] would be trivial. It is thus required that the number of participants in *s* be kept at a minimum. The minimal number of individuals that fulfill the role denoted by the lexical noun is one. This enables the use of definite determiners (definite articles, demonstratives, and possessives), which trigger uniqueness presuppositions in imposter DPs.

(v) The uniqueness condition can be undermined for politeness reasons. The use of *un servidor* in Mexican Spanish has become the conventionalized way of implying that the addressee has multiple servants. The indefinite article prevents the presupposition that only one individual satisfies the descriptive content of the noun *servidor (de usted)* "servant (of yours)." Definite imposters are therefore not impossible, but it is predicted that their occurrence will be highly marked.

References

Barwise, Jon, and John Perry. 1983. *Situations and Attitudes*. Cambridge, MA: MIT Press.

Collins, Chris, and Paul Postal. 2012. *Imposters. A Study of Pronominal Agreement*. Cambridge, MA: MIT Press.

Collins, Chris. 2009. Imposters. Lecture notes from the Syntax Seminar. Manuscript, New York University.

Dikken, Marcel den, and Anna Longenecker. 2005. Relating the predicate to its subject. Paper presented at the 27th GLOW Colloquium in Thessaloniki, Greece.

Doron, Edit. 1994. The discourse function of appositives. In *IATL 1: Proceedings of the Ninth Annual Conference and the Workshop on Discourse of the Israel Association for Theoretical Linguistics*, eds. A. Mittwoch and M. Buchalla, 53–65. Academon: Jerusalem.

Dudley, Rachel. 2013. Spanish Imposters. In *Pronominal Agreement Cross-Linguistically: Case Studies on Imposters*. Oxford: Oxford University Press.

Elbourne, Paul. 2005. *Situations and Individuals*. Cambridge, MA: MIT Press.

Enç, Mürvet. 1991. The semantics of specificity. *Linguistic Inquiry* 22(1):1–25.

Kiparsky, Paul. 2002. Disjoint reference and the typology of pronouns. In *More Than Words. A Festschrift for Dieter Wunderlich*, eds. Ingrid Kaufmann and Barbara Stiebels, 179–226. Berlin: Akademie Verlag.

Kratzer, Angelika. 1989. An investigation of the lumps of thought. *Linguistics and Philosophy* 12: 607–653.

Swart, Henriëtte E. de, Yoad Winter, and Joost Zwarts. 2007. Bare nominals and reference to capacities. *Natural language and Linguistic Theory* 25(1): 195–222.

Vries, Mark de. 2006. The syntax of appositive relativization: On specifying coordination, false free relatives and promotion. *Linguistic Inquiry* 37: 229–270.

Wang, Linton, and Eric McCready. 2007. Aspects of the indefiniteness effect. In *New Frontiers in Artificial Intelligence JSAI 2006 Conference and Workshops*, eds. Takashi Washio, Ken Satoh, Hideaki Takeda, and Akihiro Inokuchi, Tokyo, Japan, June 5–9, 2006. Subseries of Lecture Notes in Computer Science (Revised Selected Papers. Lecture Notes in Artificial Intelligence 4384), eds. J. G. Carbonell and J. Siekmann. Berlin: Springer.

Language Index

Note: Letter 'n' followed by the locators refer to notes.

Author Index

Note: Letter 'n' followed by the locators refer to notes.

Subject Index

Note: Letter 'n' followed by the locators refer to notes.